She Devils at the Door

Additional work by Eliza Smith Brown

A Century of Heroes edited by Douglas R. Chambers (contributor)

Pittsburgh Legends and Visions: An Illustrated History

The Duquesne Club Cookbook: Four Seasons of Fine Dining edited by David G. Wilkins, with Ann Haigh and Eliza Smith Brown

A Legacy in Bricks and Mortar: African-American Landmarks in Allegheny County by Frank E. Bolden, Laurence A. Glasco, and Eliza Smith Brown

She Devils at the Door

ELIZA SMITH BROWN

Carnegie Mellon University Press
Pittsburgh 2023

Publications in which portions of *She Devils at the Door* have appeared:

Eliza Smith Brown. "The Day Women Took Over." *Pittsburgh Quarterly* (Fall 2020). A modified portion of Chapter 7. Winner of a 2021 Golden Quill Award from The Press Club of Western Pennsylvania.

Book design by Connie Amoroso

Library of Congress Control Number 2023943016
ISBN 978-0-88748-698-2

10   9   8   7   6   5   4   3   2

Inspired by the family chronicles of Templeton Smith

for
William Welsh Brown Jr.
Brendan Fergus Brown
Regina Devlin Kennedy Brown

in loving memory of their great-grandmother Eliza Kennedy Smith
and their great-great-aunt Lucy Kennedy Miller

"Freedom can be retained only through eternal vigilance which has always been its price."

—Elmer Davis, *But We Were Born Free*
1954

Contents

FOREWORD

Packrats only begins to describe my family's penchant for hanging on to things. For three generations now, it seems, family members on both my mother's and my father's side have kept archival records about themselves and each other with a staggering sense of stewardship. One has to wonder if they were just preserving their own memories—to be savored in their own lifetimes—or if they somehow believed that someone else, their descendants or unrelated scholars of Pittsburgh history, might someday pore over all of this material and find a story there of how two well-bred ladies came to be known as "She Devils."

To look at the elegant, well-ordered homes of my forebears, one would never know that below the surface they were jam-packed with the makings of a compelling story. This is not to say that the family papers were organized in the aggregate. Far from it. These archival materials have turned up in all sorts of places, some wrapped up in tidy labeled boxes, some thrown into catch-all boxes no doubt assembled in the haste to empty one house or another before selling it. As a collection, they were not ordered in any apparent way. In my parents' attic, I found every check my father's parents had written from the time they were married in 1915 until their deaths in the 1960s. My father used to say that the checks documented the life of a twentieth-century family by recording how they spent their money. Nearby was a not surprisingly enormous box labeled simply "Tax Returns," in which I found fifty years of federal income tax forms, beginning with the first return my great-grand-parents—parents of this story's protagonists—ever filed, in 1916, three years after the Sixteenth Amendment was ratified and the first year that the tax was actually collected.

In another corner of the attic, I found the letters that my grandmother and grandfather had exchanged during their courtship from 1913 to 1915. One photo album—capturing 1912 alone—revealed much about the final year of my grandmother's Vassar career, her graduation trip to the Panama Canal with her father to inspect his work as the consulting engineer for the Gatun Lock, and summer life at Muskoka in Canada, from the daily amusements to the interior décor of the house. In a box of letters to and from my great-aunt, I stumbled upon receipts from construction of the family home at 5400 Forbes Street in Pittsburgh. Speeches, memoirs, political cartoons by the famed *Pittsburgh Post-Gazette* cartoonist Cy Hungerford, and boxes and boxes of photos, some clearly labeled and some requiring the skills of a committed detective to identify the locations and the people, documented more than four decades of tireless work by the Allegheny County League of Women Voters on behalf of the voting public. All of these things sat for decades in the far reaches of my parents' house awaiting rediscovery and reexamination.

At the same time as I was assembling all these archival materials, my cousin Ted Smith and his wife Sally found more than twenty brittle, over-sized scrapbooks crumbling in the back of my aunt and uncle's old garage on Walnut Street in Pittsburgh. In them were decades' worth of daily news clippings chronicling the Pittsburgh of the 1920s, '30s, and '40s in which the She Devils lived and operated. In cleaning out my great-aunt's manor house on the Eastern Shore of Maryland, my second cousin Peter Shefler found the letters that she had sent home from Vassar between 1898 and 1902 and her correspondence with my great-uncle during their courtship and those rare times they were apart after marriage. My second cousin John Miller shared his vivid memories of vacations with them in a memoir entitled "A Bend in the Silver Spoon: Memories of Emerson Point Farm." From another, unknown source came selected League of Women Voters correspondence, including one series of exchanges with Helen Clay Frick, who supported the suffrage movement both philosophically and financially. Most recently, through the magic of ancestry.com, I have connected with second cousins I never knew I had, descended from Lucy and Eliza's brothers, Joe and Julian Jr., estranged for three generations. They, too, have added to the story.

Genetics tending as they do to impose the traits of one generation insistently on the next—no matter how much we may resist—I could not help but reserve a large, deep closet in my home to preserve these materials . . . at least until I could review everything. Assembled together at last, ordered into old-style letter boxes lined up like books on a shelf and neatly filed in stackable plastic boxes, all of it demanded to be sifted through, interpreted, and crafted into this story.

One more enormous body of source material came to me as an unexpected but serendipitous consequence of the 2020 COVID-19 pandemic. Quarantined for months at home, I discovered the joys of newspapers.com, through which I was able to follow—and corroborate—much of the story through not only the accounts of journalists but also the words of prominent figures who were copiously quoted in the days before radio or television would broadcast public speeches in their entirety.

For me as the unofficial family archivist and a writer at heart, then, it is not only my delight and privilege to tell this story. It is my obligation. It is as though my parents and grandparents sensed that someday someone would get around to making sense of it all. My father, Templeton Smith, certainly laid the groundwork with his biographies of Julian Kennedy, Eliza Kennedy Smith, and R. Templeton Smith, as well as his own autobiography, and for that I am most grateful. But an integrated story of the two Kennedy sisters, Lucy and Eliza—their lives inextricably intertwined and played out in the context of the Gilded Age and the subsequent Edwardian and Progressive eras—had yet to be written down with a general audience in mind. It had been preserved as an oral tradition, family lore that would inevitably fade with each successive generation's retelling of it.

I believe this story deserves a wider audience. It is my hope that it will not only entertain readers with the antics of Lucy and Eliza but will also serve as an instructive and inspiring recounting of the difference that two vigilant individuals can make in what sometimes seems like a hopelessly corrupt political and business environment. There's no telling how much long-term impact two formidable women, or any of us for that matter, might have.

Eliza Smith Brown
March 2022

INTRODUCTION

This is the story of two formidable women. Born as sisters a decade apart during the Gilded Age, Lucy and Eliza Kennedy shared similar, albeit sequential, childhoods and educations, an upbringing that was marked—but not defined—by privilege. As time led them to maturity, their paths increasingly intertwined around shared values and passions and a laser focus on the causes of voting rights and good government. Their unanimity earned them the moniker of "political twins." Their tenacity and tactics would eventually earn them the sobriquet of She Devils.

Sometimes troublemakers emerge from the most unlikely of places. The transformation of two Edwardian ingenues into a pair of She Devils might be surprising but for the values and life choices of their forebears and the progressive nature of a Vassar College education. These were two women driven by principle and a strong moral compass. They were hungry for truth and justice. Inspired and equipped by their upbringing and education, they pursued a lifelong quest that occupied their time and attention for more than half a century. It fueled their relentless work on behalf of women's suffrage. Ultimately it also drove their persistent vigilance in fighting another series of battles—those targeting corruption and advocating for efficiency and integrity in local government and the civic improvements that could only be realized when the gears of government were freed of major obstructions. Along the way, they exposed the underbelly of local government, subjected it to scrutiny, and at least in select moments, forced politicians into a new and unfamiliar posture of accountability.

Each of the sisters had a style that wielded impact. Lucy was outspoken, sometimes outrageous, and fearless against her political foes. In the course of one mayoral election, she went toe to toe with the bishop of the Episcopal

Diocese of Pittsburgh as he refused to retract his endorsement of a candidate with questionable morals, stridently calling him "a spineless jellyfish."

Eliza, on the other hand, had a reserve that made people listen when she chose to speak up. "I can remember how scared I was when I first started to speak," she wrote, "and how I had to bolster myself up and say, 'I can do it,' over and over again."[1] As she gained confidence and a reputation for getting things done, Eliza's voice spoke for many.

In their private lives, they were loved and loving, vulnerable and insecure, alternately frugal and extravagant, flawed and sometimes unforgiving. To the public, however, they were a strong, collective force to be reckoned with, unstoppable champions for justice, articulate go-to advocates for people without voice or power. If their story inspires just one like-minded soul to follow a similar path, it will have been worth the telling.

I Prologue

At the time of her death at age 75, Eliza Kennedy Smith still commanded public respect.

1 NO ONE WILL EVER KNOW

The last of the She Devils was gone. And the crowds were considerable. All day, they had streamed in and out of Samson's Funeral Home. A line formed out the double doors, down the stone steps, and onto the sidewalk outside the grand old mansion that served the elite of Pittsburgh's East End in their times of greatest sadness. It was October 1964. In anticipation of the large turnout, the family of Mrs. R. Templeton Smith had secured Samson's largest suite of reception rooms. The guest book filled rapidly with the names of prominent Pittsburgh business executives, attorneys, club people, family, and friends, along with politicians, Democrats and Republicans alike, and a long list of officers and leading members of the Allegheny County League of Women Voters. Amidst the din of animated conversation, the language of politics seemed to hang in the air. There were stories to tell, memories of skullduggery to share, and perhaps a bit of reckoning to be done.

Mrs. Smith's heartbroken husband Temp kept a constant vigil. Upon first viewing his beloved in her open casket, he retreated to a back room and wept freely. When he had married the beautiful young Eliza Kennedy half a century earlier, Temp had asked that the "obey" language be omitted from their wedding vows. He felt that the vows should be revised to say, "'Til death do us part . . . and beyond." Temp had spent fifty years adoring Eliza—and championing her causes—from the battle for women's suffrage to a relentless crusade for honesty and integrity in government.

Toward the end of the day, Temp had unsettled those gathered in the room by abruptly seizing the meticulously prepared corpse and embracing it with hugs and kisses. The family physician, standing nearby, advised the undertaker to leave him alone. Obligingly, the staff placed a few screens to shield Temp's private grief as the public crowd continued to flow through the building.

Finally, as the evening drew to a close, the Smith's oldest son, also Temp, was ready to terminate the viewing and go home. when one last visitor arrived. A small, middle-aged man in a worn, ill-fitting suit and scuffed shoes, with weathered face and hands, he asked to see Mrs. Smith. Thinking that this shabby-looking character surely was looking for some other Mrs. Smith, Temp hesitated. "Do you mean Mrs. *R. Templeton* Smith?" The man nodded.

He shuffled over to the open coffin and stood quietly looking down at the face of the corpse, its web of wrinkles frozen in a peaceful death mask beneath a perfect coif of wavy white hair. After a long time, he uttered in a husky stage whisper addressed to no one in particular, "No one will ever know how many people went straight for fear of her."

After pronouncing this epitaph, the stranger turned and departed without another word, shuffling back out into the dark night.

II The Making of Two She Devils

2 THE KENNEDY CLAN

It was an unremarkable day on an Ohio farmstead in the mid-1850s when a small, but robust boy—Julian Kennedy by name—crawled about unattended in the dirt of a bustling barnyard, chaotic but contained by a sturdy fence of stark white planks nailed in even rows to rugged log posts. He explored without hesitation as chickens strutted nervously and massive workhorses stood with their hooves firmly planted in place, swatting flies with their tails as they awaited the days' chores. Only when Julian wrapped himself around the hind leg of a large mare, and began to shimmy up past her shaggy fetlock, did the enormous animal take notice and flick the boy to the ground. Undaunted, the boy clambered off in search of other diversions.

There was plenty for a small boy to do and to learn on two hundred acres in mid-nineteenth-century rural Ohio, where traditional farming practices commingled with the dawn of new industrial technology. There were fertile fields to till, cows to milk and move from pasture to pasture, eggs to collect, hay to bale, bees to tend, chickens and cows and horses and family and farm-hands to feed. But a farmer had to master far more than a working knowledge of agriculture and animal husbandry. To run a fully integrated and self-suf-ficient operation, he also needed financial acuity as well as skills in building, engine mechanics, blacksmithing, and basic engineering. And he needed to be strong—strong enough to lift a bale of hay, wrestle a reluctant horse into compliance, or maneuver an awkwardly heavy steam engine into place on a wagon bed. This was a life best suited to the resilient and resourceful.

The Kennedy farm had been established in 1851 outside the small village of Poland, Ohio, the first chartered township in the Connecticut Western Reserve, seven miles southeast of Youngstown. The Kennedys were people of hardy stock who had emigrated four generations earlier from Ulster, one of Ireland's four provinces. And they were not alone in nineteenth-century rural

Ohio. Many of the farmers there, as well as in Pennsylvania and other parts of the original thirteen colonies, were also Scots-Irish Presbyterians from Ulster. Coming from England and Scotland, they had settled in Ulster during the seventeenth century in an effort to escape the oppressive rule of the Church of England. Ulster was almost entirely rural, and its small-scale farming relied heavily on the potato, a notoriously unreliable crop. When King Charles had attempted to force these Presbyterians into the Church of England beginning in the 1630s, many had chosen instead to seek the greater religious liberty promised in North America. Further attempts to force these dissidents into the Church of England, coupled with bad harvests, famine, and high rents, made life sufficiently difficult that hundreds of thousands more made the difficult and risky decision to leave Ulster and endure the treacherous sea passage to America. The migration continued throughout the eighteenth and nineteenth centuries. As early as 1776, Benjamin Franklin estimated that a third of Pennsylvania's 350,000 inhabitants were of this Scots-Irish stock. In Pennsylvania and Ohio, these industrious immigrants found not only religious freedom but also wide-open spaces, fertile land, ample timber and game, and seemingly limitless opportunity to engage as entrepreneurs. Fueled by the taste of freedom, many fought on behalf of their newly adopted country in the American War of Independence.

For the Kennedy family, the initial foray from Ulster to Pennsylvania had been made by Bailey Kennedy in 1752.[1] Born in 1730, Bailey had worked as a coachman on the estate of Samuel Stuart and his wife Mary, lesser members of Scotland's royal clan. The Stuarts' daughter, Moor Mary, caught Bailey's eye, or he caught hers. History does not record the details. But family lore preserves the story of how the two twenty-two-year-olds fell in love, a decidedly unfavorable match for the daughter of a noble family. Seeking to squelch the romance, the Stuarts put Moor "in confinement" and began packing up her wardrobe in preparation for sending her away, far from her unsuitable suitor. When Bailey learned of their plans, he secreted Moor away in the night and galloped with her on his horse to a nearby seaport, where his possessions were waiting in a large trunk, and they boarded a ship for America. By the time the family learned of the plan and rushed to the harbor the next morning, the ship was disappearing on the horizon. And by the time they landed in Philadelphia, the runaways were married.[2] Bailey went on to operate a tavern south of York, Pennsylvania, and served in a Revolutionary War militia.

Ultimately, Bailey and Moor settled on a 195-acre farm in Monaghan

Township, York County. The oldest of their four children was James, born in 1755. His only son, James II, was born in 1794 and would go on to have ten children. The fifth of those ten children, Bailey and Moor's great-grandson, was Thomas Walker Kennedy (1824–1896), part of the third generation of the Kennedy family to be born in America. Thomas would become the father of a remarkable man and the grandfather of two remarkable women.

Thomas had begun teaching at the age of seventeen and had used his first earnings to buy trees and create an orchard on a corner of his father's farm. But as a naturally gifted mechanic, he was also drawn to industry. He and his brothers had built a sawmill that provided the materials for the first frame houses, barns, and bridges in the area and sent the surplus lumber down the Ohio River. He had also started a blacksmith shop, ultimately producing equipment for the production of iron using ore mined from the rural landscape. In 1846, at the age of twenty-two, Thomas had dug deeper into the iron industry, assisting with the construction of the Philpot Furnace and later the first rolling mill at Youngstown, Ohio, later part of the Brown-Bonnell Iron Works.

Thomas was helping to build a gristmill on Big Run near New Castle, Pennsylvania, when he met Margaret Truesdale, who was visiting her sister from Ohio. Like the Kennedy family, the Truesdales had come to Pennsylvania from Ulster in the eighteenth century and had settled in Poland, Ohio, by the earliest years of the nineteenth. And like Thomas, Margaret was of practical, sturdy stock. Plain and austere looking, her straight black hair parted down the center and pulled tightly back above drooping, deep-set eyes, she was nonetheless strong, bright, and possessed of sufficient wit to attract Thomas into courtship.

Shortly before his marriage to Margaret on June 24, 1851, Thomas had acquired 200 acres of good farmland near Poland, Ohio, on which he built a large, comfortable farmhouse and two sizable barns. The twenty-seven-year-old groom brought his new bride, not quite twenty-six, to the pristine homestead, where they began building an agricultural operation, and a family. They would have seven sons and one daughter over the course of seventeen years. The oldest was Julian, born March 15, 1852.

Initially, Thomas taught school to supplement their farming income. At the same time, he was building his reputation as an engineer and traveling, extensively, to build and manage mills for the emerging steel industry in the Ohio Valley and environs, fueled by the wealth of natural resources in the

Julian (second from left) was the oldest of Thomas and Margaret Kennedy's eight children.

region—iron ore, coal, and timber. With Thomas often absent, Margaret took firm charge of the farm and their growing brood. She was a capable manager, commanding the whole operation with clear objectives to raise her eight children as educated and industrious citizens. She took them faithfully to the Struthers United Presbyterian Church, which she and Thomas had helped to found in the nearby town of Struthers, Ohio. The children attended Poland Union Seminary and were schooled at home in the Bible, in literature, and in music. Julian, in particular, developed an aptitude for mathematics and science but also an affinity for Shakespeare, Milton, and Kipling.

Julian was just twelve years old in 1864 when his father took charge of the construction of two large blast furnaces for James Wood & Sons of Pittsburgh. The relationship led to more work, as Wood also contracted Thomas to build the Clinton Furnace, the Briar Hill Furnace, which later became part of the Washed Steel Plant, and other furnaces in the Shenango Valley. Thomas became best known for his work at Struthers Furnace Company, where he became managing partner and chief engineer in 1869.[3] It was there that he engaged Julian, by then seventeen, in the design and construction of a new furnace, the Anna, which showcased an innovative new approach to managing the blast, a critical function of the operation that regulated the volume of air blown into the furnace. Julian took to the business of blast furnace design right away, studying the new technology and devising ways to make it even better. Ultimately, five of Julian's six brothers would go into the iron and steel industry. His brother James, the outlier, became an attorney and a US Congressman from Ohio.[4]

As the Kennedys were revolutionizing the burgeoning steel industry, the big players in steel—specifically the Carnegie syndicate—began to take notice. James Gayly, later vice president of the United States Steel Corporation, said it was the best work done between 1870 and 1880.[5] The *Encyclopedia of Pennsylvania Biography* described Thomas as "a constructive engineer of the very first rank." He went on to say, "He was the greatest designer and builder of blast furnaces of his day, and many of his inventions and improvements are now in general use and have been of incalculable benefit to the manufacturing world."[6] Thomas remained at Struthers for many years, continuing to design and implement improvements. He was the first to employ a chemist to analyze the furnace's raw materials of coke, limestone, and iron ore as well as its finished product of pig iron.

As the oldest child, Julian was the first to leave the nest. It was no surprise that he headed for engineering school, enrolling in the fall of 1872 in the Sheffield Scientific School of Yale College. There he studied civil engineering for two years before changing his focus to the chemistry of iron and steel, the newest technology of his day. He finished in three years, graduating in 1875, and then stayed on for two more years as an instructor in physics and a graduate student in the chemistry of iron and steel.

As valedictorian of his class, Julian read aloud his honors thesis on the mechanics of rowing. Rowing was the top sport

Julian and his boatmates won a rowing championship for Yale in 1873.

in collegiate athletics at that time, holding the status that would later be supplanted by football. The first intercollegiate athletic competition in America had been a six-oar crew race in 1852, seventeen years before the first intercollegiate football game that would pit Rutgers against Princeton. Large and powerful from his farmstead upbringing, Julian distinguished himself at crew, a worthy diversion from his demanding academic schedule. The Yale archives record his victories, which included setting two-mile records in both the pair and the single and culminated in stroking the Yale four to victory at the 1876 Centennial Regatta in Philadelphia.

Despite his technical bent, Julian was an avid proponent of a liberal arts education. Years later, after he was established as an internationally known engineer, he would speak at the 1909 graduation of his alma mater, advising those present to value a balanced education:

> It is much better for you to have a broad, liberal education and a little engineering knowledge when you leave here than to have a much greater amount of practical and technical knowledge without a liberal education.... At some stage of your career, ... you will find that the ability to write a contract from which not one word can be omitted and of which not one sentence can be construed in more than one way, will be of more value to you than even a knowledge of the method of least squares, which some of you may perchance have forgotten by that time.... In doing business you should remember that nine-tenths of the litigation in this world is caused by vague or incomplete understandings between buyer and seller ...[7]

Julian's first job was as a blower in a Youngstown steel plant, earning eight dollars a month. He was quickly promoted to superintendent and soon returned to Struthers Iron Company as blast furnace superintendent for construction and operation. In the first month alone, through his innovations in regulating the blast, he improved the furnace's output from fifty-three to sixty-eight tons per day.[8] A third job took him to the Morse Bridge Works near Youngstown as superintendent. Still a young man, he left an impression, as one industrial historian later recalled:

> ... Julian Kennedy, whose career as an engineer has benefitted the iron and steel industries in all parts of the world, came to the

Mahoning Valley as a young man just out of college, and, while we thought he was rather too fond of rowing a boat on the little river there, he was evidently not wasting his time in fishing while doing so.[9]

Somewhere between his second and third jobs, Julian struck up a relationship of sorts with Jennie Eliza Brenneman, an Ohio farm girl of German-Swiss and German extraction and his contemporary. Jennie was a tall young woman with intense eyes and coal black curly hair that was only partially tamed in a perpetually pulled-back style. Like Julian, she had graduated from Poland Union Seminary, and at sixteen she had begun teaching all twelve grades in a one-room schoolhouse near Lowellville, Ohio. Both Jennie and Julian valued their Christian faith and the advantages of a good education. Jennie had wanted to go to Vassar College, but the family could not afford it.

Jennie Eliza Brenneman caught Julian's eye, and they married in 1877.

Writing to her older brother Taylor during the summer of 1876, Jennie seemed interested in Julian but less than certain about her prospects. "I received a letter from our New Haven Friend stating that he was well and weighed 170 pounds without any clothing on and expected to race at the centennial," she wrote.[10] "[My friend] Ellen is looking at the glass sighing deeply for she does not know whether she is pretty enough for Hilary or not and I consoled her by saying that I would much rather be smart than good looking."[11] "... I have almost concluded to never teach again. I guess I will get married. What do you say? Can you not find me a man in all your travels? I presume you meet lots of amiable and rich young gentlemen. Please inquire if any of them wants a wife. Please then tell them what a good wise and gentle sister you have in the far away state of Ohio."[12]

Eventually the friendship between Jennie and Julian ripened into more, although not without its contentious moments. An apparent falling out along the way prompted her to write a withering invective to him, by then using her pet name for him:

Juke,

Yours of the 24th is at hand and in reply will say that you need give
yourself no nervousness concerning our holding your memory
sacred for such is not the case. We all consider you unworthy of
the slightest thought and you were so entirely blotted out from our
memories that we had almost forgotten your existence until your
letter brought back to us a recollection of your many virtues, but far
be it from me to censure you for anything you have done in the past,
but I trust in future you will cling as tenaciously to truth as you do
to revenge and then I will not only blot your name from my book of
remembrances but will also gladly and willingly say

God bless you and

Goodbye forever,

Jennie E. Brenneman[13]

As two strong-willed individuals, Julian and Jennie somehow weathered
that storm. They were not quite twenty-five when they married on November
14, 1877.

Drawn by the opportunity in and around Pittsburgh, the epicenter of iron
and steel production, Julian went to work in 1879 for Carnegie Brothers and
Company. He would stay for eleven years. At the Edgar Thomson Steel Works
in Braddock, Pennsylvania, he quickly rose to the rank of superintendent of
operation and construction. Dubbed "that furnace wizard" by Carnegie,
Julian dramatically increased production with considerably less fuel consumption. In the context of the larger Carnegie chronicle, "the iron making world
regarded the achievement with wonder."[14] Four years later, Carnegie moved
Julian to his Pittsburgh plant on the Allegheny River in the Lawrenceville
section of Pittsburgh, and two years after that to his Homestead plant on the
Monongahela River, where he installed the first basic open hearth shop in
the United States. In 1888, Julian was sent to Latrobe, Pennsylvania, as chief
engineer in charge of design and construction of an entirely new mill. On
each assignment, he achieved marked boosts in production through a series
of ingenious inventions, broadening his engineering prowess and building an
international reputation. As business historian Larry Schweikart contends,
"Carnegie's steel empire would not have been as dynamic without Julian Kennedy."[15] But Carnegie was a difficult taskmaster, and Julian couldn't seem to
break into the upper echelon of management in the booming business.

Finally, in 1890, at the age of thirty-eight, Julian took a leap of faith, left Carnegie, and opened a solo engineering practice. He rented two rooms of the Hamilton Building at 91 Fifth Avenue in the heart of downtown Pittsburgh, next to the Masonic Temple, across from the Pittsburgh Opera House, down the street from the Post Office, and around the corner from City Hall. Along the back alley were two Presbyterian churches—First and Third—as well as Trinity Episcopal Church. St. Paul's Cathedral was a block away.

Julian's printed announcement, dated February 11 of that year, outlined his areas of expertise:

> Dear Sir:
>
> The undersigned begs to announce that he has opened an office at the above address, and is prepared to act as Consulting Engineer to Iron and Steel Works, and to furnish drawings and specifications for the construction or remodeling of Blast Furnaces, Bessemer and Open Hearth Steel Works, Rolling Mills, Steam and Hydraulic Machinery, etc. or will contract to erect plants complete.
>
> Soliciting your favors, I am
Respectfully Yours,
Julian Kennedy

The business quickly took off, and Julian found himself in great demand. Carnegie continued to call upon his expertise, as did steel companies in Europe and beyond. He worked on the Dneiperpetrovsk Dam in Russia and provided some of the engineering of the Russian railway system. He consulted for the US government on the building of the Sault Ste. Marie Canal in 1895, the world's longest lock, the first to be operated with electricity, and the last link in the navigational chain from the Atlantic to Lake Superior. In the years that followed, he built

Julian's engineering business had him straddling the continents.

a major mill in Mariupol, Ukraine, and traveled to St. Petersburg, Russia, to consult for Company Stahl on the construction of a new steel plant there and what products offered the most promise.

At the age of sixteen, Eliza accompanied her father on a trip to the Panama Canal when he consulted on the engineering of the Gatun Locks.

When Carnegie and J. P. Morgan were joining forces to form the United States Steel Corporation in 1901 and needed to appraise production facilities, the two "tight-fisted moguls" agreed to have Julian walk through each plant and, without calculations on paper, assign a value to each one.[16] In 1905 he consulted on the Gatun Locks in the Panama Canal, with their enormous six-foot-diameter pipes. Arguably his most significant project was for Tata Iron & Steel Company (Tisco). Jamsetji Tata had appeared in Julian's Pittsburgh office in 1902 in his flowing robes and turban, declaring his intention to build the first blast furnace and first open hearth plant in India at Jamshedpur, west of Calcutta. Julian established a firm in Brussels, Belgium, to manage the project. Other contracts came to him from manufacturers in England, Germany, Italy, Sweden, Canada, and Wales. In the course of executing all these projects, Julian would patent some 160 inventions.

The Kennedy family had moved frequently in response to Julian's work opportunities, first to Lawrenceville, then to the bustling industrial towns of Munhall and Latrobe. In 1890, as he was establishing his consulting engineering business in downtown Pittsburgh, Julian and Jennie moved once again with their four children to the fashionable and rapidly developing East End of Pittsburgh, still a somewhat rural suburb.

Julian (far left) and Jennie (seated second from right) visited with the Tatas (second row, third from right and seated far right) while designing their new steel plant in India.

Lucy and Eliza grew up with three brothers, Joe, Julian Jr., and Tom.

They purchased a comfortable brick home on the northwest corner of Forbes Street and McKee Place, a neighborhood already developed with other comparable homes. From their central vantage point, with a generous front porch, the Kennedys could see a number of nearby estates with meandering drives and more imposing homes. The entire neighborhood commanded views of the Monongahela River, lined with industrial concerns like the Keystone Rolling Mill Company, the Pittsburgh Gas Company, and the Linden Steel Company.

As Julian's engineering business grew, so did the family and its fortunes. By the turn of the new century, the Kennedys would be a prosperous family of seven, ready to build their ultimate family home, one more befitting a captain of industry, and to leap headlong into the waning Gilded Age and the ensuing Edwardian era.

Sometime late in the 1890s the Kennedy clan gathered at the family homestead in Poland, Ohio. Julian (upper left, with straw boater), Jennie (lower right, with white hat), Eliza (front row, fourth from right), and Tom (front row, left) were all present. Lucy was likely off at Vassar.

3 GROWING UP GILDED

At age nine, Lucy could not have wished for a better Christmas present. Her little sister Eliza was born on Wednesday, December 11, 1889, in Latrobe, Pennsylvania. Lucy's younger brothers, Julian and Joe, were three and nearly five. Another brother, Hugh, had died in March that year at the age of one. Despite the span of nearly a decade between them, the two sisters shared a special bond from the very beginning. Eliza, a healthy ten-pound newborn, was not only the sister Lucy had longed for. She was also a bit of good news at the end of a year of tragedy.

The nearby city of Johnstown, Pennsylvania, still reeling and rebuilding from the catastrophic Memorial Day flood, had suffered another disaster the night before Eliza was born. The Parke Opera House, which had survived the flood despite its rickety condition, had been filled well beyond capacity that evening, with two hundred of the eight hundred people present crowded into the aisles and vacant spaces. It was a one-night stand of *Uncle Tom's Cabin*, C. W. Taylor's wildly popular dramatization of Harriet Beecher Stowe's anti-slavery novel of 1852. The action had reached the fifth and final act as the time approached ten thirty. All eyes were on the villainous Simon Legree onstage, as he threw his lash to the ground and ordered his slave Tom to beat another slave. It was then that a boy in the front row of the third gallery shouted "Fire!" As the panicked crowd thundered down the dingy stairway and stampeded for the exit, the pile of trampled humanity grew to eight people deep. In the end, at least thirteen people died of suffocation, and dozens more were injured. It was, as it turned out, a false alarm, but it was another horrifically sobering event for Western Pennsylvania.[1]

Meanwhile, the rest of the nation was celebrating the centennial of George Washington's inauguration. The country was expanding under President Harrison, with the Dakotas, Montana, and Washington state added to the union

Beginning in 1890, Julian Kennedy enjoyed a successful international practice as a consulting engineer.

and a 1.9-million-acre tract of Indian Territory opened for settlement. In the South, people were mourning the death of their confederate hero, Jefferson Davis. The Civil War was recent history, still fresh in many memories. Abroad, Americans joined the thirty-two million people who attended the World's Fair in Paris, where the newly opened Eiffel Tower was a chief attraction.

But for the Kennedy family, it was more a time of looking inward, focusing on their growing family and Julian's burgeoning career. It was not long after Eliza's birth that the family moved from Latrobe to Pittsburgh as Julian opened his new office as an independent consulting engineer.

The city Julian brought his family to was a bustling place, and as Lucy and Eliza were growing up, the city itself was growing up all around them. During the thirty years between 1870 and 1900, under the leadership of Andrew Carnegie, Henry Clay Frick, Henry Phipps, Benjamin Franklin Jones, James H. Laughlin, and others—and with Julian's engineering genius—steel production in the Pittsburgh region had increased sevenfold, from 3.2 million tons to 29.5 million tons. Additional developments in aluminum, glass, and other industries fueled the city's exponential growth.

During the second half of the century, the overall population had swelled from forty-nine thousand to 534,000. Within twenty years, between 1880 and 1900, Pittsburgh's foreign-born population had doubled. More than twenty-two thousand African Americans from the South arrived to join a thriving cultural and institutional community, although the Great Migration of Blacks would not come until World War I.

The Point—the triangle of land where the Allegheny and Monongahela Rivers joined to form the Ohio—was a cluttered mess of railroad and exposition buildings and warehouses. The wharf along the Monongahela was lined with rows of beached coal barges and steamships tied to floating docks. The Pennsylvania Railroad shared the main Liberty Avenue thoroughfare downtown with horse-drawn carriages and, by 1902, some five hundred of the new century's newest sensation, the automobile.

The impact of all this on the cityscape was both spectacular and devastating. Within walking distance of the industrial operations along and between the rivers were the tenements, where laborers and their families lived in densely packed blocks laced together by clotheslines draped above public privies, as clean laundry grew dirty again before it even dried. Children played among the dirt and rubble and rubbish in the shadowy spaces between the buildings as their parents hung over the rickety stoops above. The drain became "the resting place for innumerable empty tin cans, worn out brooms, old shoes, and other articles foreign to the lap of a respectable sewer,"[2] and it overflowed into cellar and basement kitchens. Inside, residents packed into rooms without cross ventilation, sometimes as many as twelve to a room, with some beds occupied by alternating shifts of day and night workers. Curtains, where they existed, billowed in and out, gathering and carrying the sooty air with them. Mill workers climbed up and down long, winding public steps to get to and from the waterfront mills.

These conditions were thoroughly documented between 1907 and 1914 by *The Pittsburgh Survey*, a pioneering response of Progressives and urban reformers that was intended to expose the ravaging effects of industrialization on life and labor for ordinary working people. Funded by the Russell Sage Foundation, it was the first comprehensive and critical study of urban conditions in the United States and would become a model for other cities. The survey involved some seventy investigators who generated detailed descriptions and countless photographs. Statisticians, social workers, engineers, lawyers, physicians, economists, labor investigators, and city planners examined such issues as housing, food, sanitation, play spaces, and healthcare. The Survey's findings were presented through *Collier's Magazine* and six bound volumes in hopes of effecting positive change through business and public policy. Pittsburgh's social conscience also manifested itself in philanthropic initiatives such as the creation of settlement houses and service agencies that sought to assimilate European immigrants and Black migrants into their new environment and alleviate some of the hardships of poverty and urban life. Growing up with these models of altruism before them, Lucy and Eliza would one day come to join in the efforts.

* * *

At the same time, many people of means sought to escape this scene of dirt and congestion by moving outward from downtown—including those who espoused Progressive policies and worked to alleviate some of the damage wrought by Pittsburgh's industrial success. Those who could had begun to settle in the new suburbs. Some moved across the Allegheny River to the west. Others headed two miles to the east into the surrounding farmland of Oakland and East Liberty. It was a sylvan tract of fields and pastures, defined by dramatic hills and deep, wooded ravines. Relatively few roads were paved, and major access routes to downtown had yet to be built.

By the time the Kennedys arrived in Pittsburgh in 1890, the pastoral landscape of the East End had been transformed into a thriving residential community. It had been annexed to the rapidly expanding City of Pittsburgh in 1867 and sparsely developed with farms and country estates centered on grand Classical, Italianate, and Second Empire villas with iron fences and manicured gardens. Schools had been established as early as 1840, and Pennsylvania Female College—later Pennsylvania College for Women, ultimately Chatham University—had opened its doors in 1869. The 196-acre Homewood Cemetery had opened in 1876.

In nearby Shadyside, a thriving residential suburb had grown up in response to the arrival of the Pennsylvania Railroad in 1852 and the extension of horsecar service from Oakland to East Liberty in 1872. Served by a new cable car system along Fifth Avenue in 1888, Shadyside's streets were lined with an eclectic mix of country and city houses.

Even as they were escaping, some of those in power dedicated themselves to recasting the city's built environment. Under the watchful eyes of a handful of patrons, a movement of civic improvement and cosmetic urbanism flourished, and the city underwent a commercial building boom. Downtown Pittsburgh was abuzz with construction as the fruits of industrialization began to manifest themselves in so-called "cathedrals of commerce" bankrolled by the leading patrons of the day: Andrew Carnegie, Henry Clay Frick, Andrew Mellon, Henry Phipps Jr., and others. In the thirteen years between 1893 and 1906 alone, some 350 new buildings were constructed downtown. They showcased the latest in style and construction techniques given life through the skills of both local architects and those of wider renown: H. H. Richardson, whose Romanesque courthouse was the centerpiece of downtown, along with Daniel Burnham of Chicago, George B. Post and Grosvenor Atterbury of New York, and others.

As this downtown building boom gathered momentum, what some would call the second founding of Pittsburgh was about to be launched. It would occur in Oakland, beginning the year the Kennedys moved in, and it was masterminded by Andrew Carnegie and Mary Schenley as philanthropists, Frank F. Nicola as speculator, and Edward Manning Bigelow as Pittsburgh's first director of public works. Bigelow's vision called for Mary Schenley—a wealthy daughter of Pittsburgh who had eloped at the age of fifteen with a forty-three-year-old British officer and moved to England in 1842—to donate some three hundred acres of farmland to the city for a park. In 1889, upon learning of her intention to sell the land to developers, Bigelow's agent raced to London, just ahead of a competing real estate agent who sought to buy the property. He returned with Schenley's commitment to donate the land.

The jewel of Schenley Park, Phipps Conservatory, was a gift to the city by industrialist and philanthropist Henry Phipps Jr. Under the direction of the prestigious New York firm of Lord and Burnham, the new $110,000 glass house took shape within one year. When it opened in 1893, it was the largest conservatory in the United States and boasted the finest collection of tropical plants, secured from the World's Columbian Exposition in Chicago that same year. The Exposition's monumental scale and strong classical aesthetic would wield considerable influence over the Pittsburgh built environment. That influence, coupled with the earlier development of the "park cemetery" in the mid-nineteenth century, led to the creation of "breathing" and outdoor recreation spaces. Bigelow hired William Falconer to act as superintendent of the park in 1896, and Falconer proceeded to introduce the most advanced standards of botany, horticulture, and landscape architecture.

Meanwhile, across the ravine, another monumental project was brewing. Grateful for the library made available to him as a youth, Andrew Carnegie sought to make books and culture available to the public through a single institution—Pittsburgh's "palace of culture"—incorporating a library and a music hall as well as museums of art and natural history. The founders chose to conduct an architectural competition, which attracted ninety-seven American architects and led to the selection of Longfellow, Alden & Harlow, a prominent practice with offices in Boston and Pittsburgh. Opening in 1895, the new Carnegie complex was unprecedented in its scale and grandeur. Yet Carnegie's vision was even larger. Between 1903 and 1907, he would quadruple the size of the building.

As his "palace of culture" was taking form, Carnegie began work on a

Elegantly dressed, Jennie Eliza Kennedy looked the part of the prosperous industrialist's wife.

"learning factory" next door. He established the Carnegie Technical School with a million-dollar endowment to the city in 1900. Henry Hornbostel, a partner in the New York practice of Palmer and Hornbostel, won the competition to master plan the new school in 1904. Construction of the original campus would take nineteen years, during which time the school was renamed Carnegie Institute of Technology in 1912. Meanwhile, the University of Pittsburgh relocated to the new Oakland civic center in 1908.

The resultant landscape in the Kennedys' new neighborhood was a peculiar juxtaposition of some remaining farmland with monumental buildings of brick and stone rising abruptly out of the open fields, looking impressive but a bit devoid of a proper surrounding cityscape.

Pittsburgh was booming and becoming beautiful, or at least as beautiful as a steaming, smoky, congested industrial city could be. The city's rising aristocracy was largely a new one, looked down upon by the upper crust of the East Coast and trying very hard to assume all the accoutrements of old money and established social stature. This was the setting in which Lucy and Eliza grew up.

Yet all the bold new additions to the cityscape—halls of government, commerce, and culture, City Beautiful parks, and grand homes, along with a host of new progressive social initiatives—did little to quell the oppressive cloud of dirty air that hung around them or the stench of dirty politics emanating from within. Those were problems awaiting a response.

* * *

In the midst of an urban scene that was characterized by extravagance, the Kennedys, too, began to embrace the lavish lifestyle made possible by Julian's successful international practice. For their part, Lucy and Eliza were not immediately comfortable with it all. They struggled at times to adapt to their rising social status and the expectations that accompanied it, rubbing elbows with the elite but not yet part of their inner circle. They were alternately awkward and boldly confident.

And they were, at least to a certain extent, casting about for role models. Lucy looked to her mother, whom she idolized and called by the pet name of "Spirit." Spirit stood a striking five-foot-seven, well above the era's average for women, with a regal bearing, a slender waist, and a crown of pure white hair that had changed abruptly from its original coal black when she was

Lucy would later dub herself an ugly duckling, but at the time she graduated from Thurston Preparatory School in 1898, she was a lovely ingenue.

only thirty. Lucy's admiration for Spirit bore an element of aspiration, and as the Kennedy family rose in social stature, she became increasingly aware of her mother's star power. At a towering, lanky five-foot-nine-and-a-half inches, with her long face and ruddy complexion, Lucy harbored no delusions about her own appearance. Comparing herself to her mother, she consistently came up short. "Everyone who sees that picture of you thinks I have a very handsome mother. Strange is it not??? —that she should have such a homely daughter." "This ugly duckling will most probably remain an ugly duckling until the last chapter." "The facility of looking well . . . was something left out of me at birth." "I won't be able to move in the same circles of society with you I fear . . . and Papa a guarantor of the Pittsburgh Orchestra. We will soon be in the ring at this rate." Lucy fantasized about being as beautiful, as graceful, and as revered as her mother, but had to be content with riding into society on the trains of her mother's dresses. Perhaps imagining that Spirit's regal grace and beauty might rub off, she preferred her mother's hand-me-down dresses to new dressmaker creations like the ones made for Eliza, who seemed to adapt to the limelight a bit more comfortably.

A beautiful child, Eliza was a popular partner at dancing class.

Hoping that her younger sister would be spared the social awkwardness that plagued her, Lucy begged her mother to enroll Eliza in dance class. "She positively must not grow up like her old sister without learning to dance." Lucy also chided Eliza to work on her social graces and to develop an appealing personality.

Eliza, it would seem, did not need much encouragement in social matters. "I had about six partners at dancing school," she wrote to Lucy in November 1900 at the age of eleven. "I refused the two small ones. I will always have partners enough. Everyone runs for me."

Lucy was not pleased. She let Eliza know exactly how she felt, pouring out a long and rambling admonition to check her conceit:

> . . . It is very nice to have lots of partners but it is not nice to think that we are a little better than everybody else or a little better looking. You are a very nice looking little girl but don't get conceited about it for good looking people are often not nearly so nice or nearly so well liked as very homely ones. Everyone hates a conceited girl and soon she won't have partners. . . . When the little boys ask you to dance you should always do it unless you have some very good excuse. . . . Never hurt people's feelings if you can avoid it either by anything you do or say. . . . If your face is proud and unkind looking it can never be beautiful and a beautiful face is the loveliest and kindest thing in the world. . . . Just about the time I was your age I thought that I was a little better and brighter than everybody else and it took a good many hard knocks to get that idea out of my head. . . . Cultivate every grace that you can for grace is a much greater power than beauty.
>
> With lots and lots of love and dozens of kisses,
>
> Lucy[3]

She then appealed to her mother: "I just finished a long moralizing letter to Eliza. I don't want her to grow up a conceited prig. You see too much of that . . . and everything ought to be done at home to eradicate such tendencies. . . . Her remarks . . . sound like those of a blasé society girl."[4]

* * *

Sometime around 1902, the Kennedys began construction of a new home at 5400 Forbes Street on a commanding four-acre hillside site at the entrance to Schenley Park, now transformed into a public green space of more than four hundred acres. By the time the Kennedys broke ground, the park had already been enhanced by a band shell, a carousel, and a 120-foot circular electric fountain on Flagstaff Hill that offered nighttime light shows. It had briefly been home to the Schenley Casino, with its indoor ice-skating rink, but that had been destroyed by fire after only a year. As the Kennedys' house was under construction and being completed, the park was being further improved with the addition of an eighteen-hole golf course, an oval horse-racing track, and Panther Hollow Lake with its picturesque boathouse, where patrons could hire rowboats and canoes in the summer and ice skate in the winter. It was a complete playground, right in the Kennedys' front yard.

The "Big House" or "5400," as the family alternately referred to it, was a massive stone block of the type that many successful Pittsburghers built to announce that they had "arrived" without succumbing to the excesses of exterior ostentation favored by their wealthy counterparts out east. It was the architectural embodiment of Scots-Irish character—sturdy, straightforward, built to last.

The Big House took nearly five years to build. As his architect, Julian Kennedy selected George S. Orth, who had begun his practice in the mid-1870s and been elected the first president of the newly formed Pittsburgh chapter of the American Institute of Architects in 1891. Orth had a considerable practice, exhibiting in five architectural exhibitions in Pittsburgh between 1898 and 1915. By the time he secured the Kennedy commission, Orth had completed the Spencer residence (1886) at Amberson Avenue in nearby Shadyside and the Western Pennsylvania School for Blind Children (1893–1894) in Oakland. He would go on to design a residence for industrialist William Penn Snyder on Ridge Avenue, the "millionaires' row" of old Allegheny City, which was annexed as Pittsburgh's North Side in 1907, as well as another home for

Architect George Orth designed the Kennedys' new home at 5400 Forbes Street, completed in 1907.

the Snyders in the countryside of Sewickley Heights. His designs were notably substantial, if architecturally undistinguished.

Orth gave the Kennedys a twenty-eight-room family home with understated exterior appointments. Viewed from Forbes Street up the hill and across the broad expanse of lawn, the only notable feature of the Kennedy house was its sheer size. Immediately upon completion, photos of the exterior and interior of the house were featured in the Pittsburgh Architectural Club Exhibition.[5] The main block of the structure featured three large, front-facing gables and four unusually tall chimneys. A porte-cochère and breezeway extended out to the left side to permit family and visitors to disembark from their carriages and automobiles and to enter the house under cover. A straightforward one-story portico sheltered the front door, which was likely seldom used, and an expansive open porch extended to the front. Behind the house, formal geometric gardens showcased Jennie's prize roses and peonies. A separate garage was built to accommodate five cars, which the family quickly acquired. The first was a Pope Toledo, the top of a short-lived line of motorcars manufactured in Toledo, Ohio, between 1903 and 1909. They retained a chauffeur to crank the cars, make minor repairs, change the unreliable tires, and keep the "machines" clean.

Inside, the centerpiece of the house was a two-story, oval music room with a Steinway parlor grand. Lucy played the piano, while Eliza instead took up watercolor painting. There was enough space for guest performers, flanked by the sweeping semicircular main stairway and the imposing entrance hall. Beyond the hall was the living room, twenty-five by forty feet in size and paneled in mahogany, with bookshelves full of leather-bound volumes of the English and American literary greats. The sulfur-heavy air of Pittsburgh would ultimately have devastating effects on the leather as it crumbled and spawled a colorful dust along the edges of the shelves. The dining room and billiard room were sized and outfitted with an eye toward entertaining, their heavy mahogany furniture newly purchased but evoking an impression of having been there for eons. On the second floor, the family quarters included four large bedrooms and three baths, while the third floor was reserved for servants. The house included a ten-by-six-foot closet just for Jennie's evening gowns. Fine rugs covered the floors throughout. The Kennedys had installed electricity in their old house in 1899, and the new house was both electrified and equipped with a telephone.

From the front windows and the front porch, the Big House offered a long vista down Forbes toward Andrew Carnegie's new Carnegie Technical School and, further down, his expanding Carnegie Institute. The Institute's Music Hall was home to the city's new orchestra, which had been founded in 1895 with a million-dollar gift from Carnegie. Under the direction of Victor Herbert between 1898 and 1904, the Pittsburgh Symphony had begun touring domestically and internationally in 1900 in addition to its regular concert season, which the Kennedys faithfully attended.

When 5400 was finally completed in 1907, Jennie outfitted it for a proper upper crust Edwardian lifestyle. The bills for the family's household linens, from Rosa Goldman's store on the North Side, were high—in excess of fourteen hundred dollars—more than seven times Joe's annual tuition and room and board at Yale. The tidy sum went far. Among the finery listed on Goldman's invoices were Irish lace, linen sheets, bedspreads, and dozens of tablecloths and napkins, many of them monogrammed, scalloped, and embroidered.

And there was the art. Henry Clay Frick, of course, outstripped his Pittsburgh peers in collecting. But others, guided largely by the local galleries of J. J. Gillespie, Wunderly Brothers, and M. Knoedler and Company, began to acquire paintings and sculpture by some of the up-and-coming artists of the day, with a particular penchant for the landscapes of the Barbizon School. One of the status symbols among the city's newly wealthy industrial giants was the commissioning of a portrait by Théobald Chartran or Raimundo de Madrazo y Garreta. Descended from the court painters of Spain, Madrazo was New York based, having snagged commissions for the likes of the Vanderbilts and

Whitneys. He then came to Pittsburgh to paint the up-and-comers who represented the city's new elite—anyone willing to pay his hefty five-thousand-dollar fee—among them the Byers, Porters, and Schoonmakers.[6] Arguably the most lavish of those were done for Alexander R. Peacock, a Carnegie Steel millionaire, his wife Irene, and their son Grant. The parents' portraits were unveiled in 1902 at a lavish party for eight hundred guests at the Peacocks' new home, Rowanlea, in the fashionable Highland Park neighborhood two miles north of the Kennedys' new home. Madrazo was there to meet the guests.[7] The Kennedys were likely there as well.

Perhaps in an effort to keep up with the Peacocks, the Kennedys commissioned Madrazo portraits of their own, not the grand, full-figure variety of the Peacocks but rather the more modest, bust-only compositions reserved for the more conservative or less pretentious or perhaps the less well-heeled. Julian's canvas portrayed him as a slightly less imposing figure than as he appeared in real life. In contrast with those of her peers, Jennie's portrait had a slightly more austere quality. Her wavy white hair was pulled back simply, with just a hint of a pompadour, framing a handsome face with a somewhat imperious expression, her piercing eyes staring firmly, immutably, from the canvas. Yet she wore just the hint of an almost-smile. Her dramatically elongated neck was unadorned with the pearls and other jewels that Mrs. Peacock flaunted. Her milky décolletage was framed by a broad lace collar that draped low but discreetly down to a pair of large blue flowers. There was none of the coquettish posing nor the costumes or props that so many of Madrazo's subjects favored. This was an elegant but no-nonsense woman, strong, imposing, not to be trifled with, the kind of woman who had become used to having her way.

Life inside the Big House was at once bustling and sedate. A flurry of activity behind the scenes made it possible for the family to entertain in what appeared to be effortless elegance. They had frequent dinner guests, before and after symphony concerts, sometimes staging musical performances of their own in the music room.

All of this relied wholly on the attentive care of a staff of six: a cook, who ably oversaw the whole operation, as well as a scullery maid, downstairs and upstairs maids who doubled as waitresses, a laundress, and a chauffeur who doubled as butler. The Kennedys reciprocated for the staff's diligent service with amenities that, for the day, were above normal expectations. All but the laundress and the chauffeur lived on the house's ample third floor, which was as well heated as the rest of the house, unlike the servants' quarters in many of the Fifth Avenue mansions of the city's tycoons. The staff also enjoyed their own parlor and dining room on the first floor where they could entertain their friends. Harkening back to his childhood on the Poland, Ohio, farm, where the hired hands ate with the family, Julian insisted that the menu for the staff be the same as that for the family.

If one had asked who wielded the power in a large, stratified household, different family and staff members might have given different answers. Julian was an undisputedly powerful man—physically, intellectually, and as a successful titan of industry—but it was Jennie who ruled the roost at home. During the day she often held court in her spacious blue bedroom at the back of the house, overlooking her cherished garden. In the evenings she presided over a formal and subdued dining table, where children were not encouraged to participate in the conversation. It was perhaps in response to that strictly enforced silence that Lucy and Eliza later formed their own ideas about what should go on at the family dinner table. Others might have said that it was the cook, who was at least in charge of her peers in the back of the house, who ran the show. She oversaw day-to-day operations that kept the house running, all while trying to keep the interpersonal drama under wraps. At times Lucy was put in charge of the house as her parents traveled abroad. It was a test of management skills, and Lucy excelled.

Next door to the Big House, at 5360 Forbes, stood the grander home of William Larimer Mellon, born into wealth as the eldest son of Judge Thomas Mellon and Rachel Larimer Mellon. W. L. had made his own mark when he founded the Gulf Oil Corporation in 1901. His thirty-eight-room stone home, Ben Elm, was completed in 1903 in a rambling vernacular Arts and Crafts style by the prestigious architectural firm of Alden & Harlow. Ben Elm's rolling landscape by the Olmsted firm of Boston, coupled with the sprawling terrain of Schenley Park to the west, enhanced the picturesque setting of the new Kennedy home.

Within view of the Mellon and Kennedy homes was the newly constructed Pittsburgh Golf Club, a grand Colonial Revival structure overlooking the golf course in Schenley Park. Although it was a new sport in America, "the game of the hour,"[8] golf had been enthusiastically received by upper crust Americans when it had been introduced from Scotland. Both Frick and Carnegie were avid golfers, and the Kennedys dabbled at it. With leisure time to spare, women of means took to the game and played in long skirts and understated hats. But country clubs, developed specifically to pursue what many viewed

as a quaint but peculiar pastime, were still a novelty. Founded in 1896, the
Shady Side Golf Club was renamed The Pittsburgh Golf Club a year later. It
was only the second country club in Western Pennsylvania. The club's membership—some six hundred as of 1906—was a virtual Who's Who of familiar
names of established businessmen and industrialists—among them the Fricks,
Mellons, Reeds, Speers, Laughlins, and Olivers, all of whom had business ties
with Julian. The first president was George Wilkins Guthrie, who would later
serve as the city's mayor and the US Ambassador to Japan under President
Wilson. Through a loose agreement with the city, notably negotiated by the
ladies of the club, the club enjoyed almost exclusive use of the Schenley Park
golf course for its first fifteen years or so, although by 1912 the course had been
made public and the club turned its attention to squash, tennis, bowling, and
billiards as well as fine dining in its well-appointed rooms. As in many clubs
of the day, women had their own separate rooms for dining, cards, sitting, and
lockers. To ensure that they stayed in their appointed areas, a house rule was
added in 1912 to make it explicitly clear that "Ladies are not permitted in the
downstairs café on any pretext, except on occasions when the Club House and
café have been rented for private use."[9] And even as the movement for women's
suffrage was gathering steam around it, the club seemed to achieve at least some
success in keeping women's ambitions in check. Many of the women associated
with the club lent their names to the movement against votes for women. The
"antis," as they were known, forwarded a host of arguments against suffrage,
which would only prove to focus the suffragist message in the years to come.

* * *

Not content with just the Big House in Pittsburgh, the Kennedys also
launched another ambitious building project, a sizable summer "cottage" in
Beaumaris, Ontario, 135 miles north of Toronto and east of Georgian Bay, on
Lake Muskoka. The Muskoka house was sited on a private oasis named Crusoe
Island, with a smaller rocky outcropping nearby that the Kennedys named
Friday Island. Beaumaris was the newest escape for wealthy Pittsburghers,
including the Kennedys' next-door neighbors on Forbes Street, the W. L.
Mellons. Some of the Beaumaris crowd had slipped away quietly from their
summer homes at the South Fork Fishing and Hunting Club, north of Johnstown, after the club's lake drained horrifically into the heart of Johnstown
on Memorial Day in 1889.

The Kennedy house at Beaumaris, perched atop Crusoe Island in Lake Muskoka, was accessible only by boat.

On Muskoka Lake, they found a new place to escape Pittsburgh's smoky atmosphere while taking its social scene with them intact. Their days, as Eliza described them, were "filled with the same kinds of frivolities."[10] There was sailing, rowing, fishing, and golf at the Royal Muskoka course. And there were parties, teas, dances, picnics, corn roasts, bridge and euchre games, and other wholesome pursuits. It was a magical place of endless visual delights, as Lucy described it. "Another day is clear as a crystal . . . to make your blood fairly gallop. Last night was the most beautiful I have almost ever seen. There were some great rocky looking clouds up in the sky which caught the afterglow and turned a dull angry purple red, while along the horizon it was all clear and a delicate saffron yellow so clear that every twig on [the] trees was silhouetted. In the east the sky was a turquoise shade that I have never seen at sunset before. Later the red clouds faded to a sooty black and the horizon looked as if the fire gods had kindled a circle of fire about the earth, and behold the crescent moon came out of the black cloud so dazzlingly clear . . . ."[11]

Much as they enjoyed the outdoors, the women were also careful to avoid excessive sun exposure. Hats were the norm, not just for fashion but to protect their lily-white skin. Too much of a tan would send a proper lady retreating into the shade, armed with lemon juice and other skin bleaches.

The house was a rambling three-story affair with gambrel roofs, large dormers, and a deep inset porch with views for miles down the lake to the south. From its raised rocky promontory, it looked down across a broad, sloping lawn and manicured flower beds to the boathouse and a sizeable dock with a tall flagpole. The Kennedys brought in oak trees to supplement the native plants on the island, and Jennie would sit out all day in their shade and boss the gardeners.[12]

Inside, the house affected a studied informality, a lodge-like ambiance with dark paneled walls and ceilings, and Mission-style tables and railings of heavy oak. The comfortable wicker furniture, arranged on dark oriental rugs, creaked with every movement while crackling log fires in the massive stone fireplace kept the house warm. All materials and laborers—as well as the daily mail—were transported to Crusoe Island by boat when the weather permitted, and the Kennedys ultimately maintained three mahogany launches with surrey-like striped awnings to ferry family and guests to and from the islands. "The piano came in tonight in the midst of a driving rain flanked by three dressers, a desk, and the lantern . . . ,"[13] Lucy wrote, as they raced to finish the house in time for their first house party in August 1909. "Three rooms are ready to receive guests and we are simply waiting for beds to fix the fourth."[14] "Fourteen extra is rather a big undertaking, and more fun for the guests than the hosts on the whole."[15] "Eliza and I have been toiling like mad."[16] At the end of the house party, the guests posed for a photo on the dock, surrounded by their trunks and leather valises, all smiles as they awaited the launches back to the mainland. And as Lucy reported afterward, "They have all had a splendiferous time."[17] The family's leather-bound guest book recorded a rich social life of daily "calls," parties, and sport. "Muskoka is a good place to spend a summer because there is no possible way of spending your money," Lucy wrote. "For the last two months I have spent absolutely nothing, but my shoes are all at rag tags from the rocks. It surely is a great life up here. . . ."[18]

* * *

Education was currency in the Kennedy household. It was expected that the children would pursue the kind of advanced education that Julian had secured and Jennie had craved. The boys were sent to Yale (Joseph W., Class of 1905, and Julian Jr., Class of 1908) and Cornell (Thomas, Class of 1919). The girls were sent to Vassar. And it was expected that they would apply their top-notch educations in ways that would make a difference—if not in business, then in civic improvement. They were, after all, living in the dawn of the Progressive Era. It was a time when those who were not hopelessly mired in the sea change

Eliza (white dress at center) helped to host the family's first house party at Lake Muskoka.

brought by industrialization, urbanization, and immigration—those who in fact benefitted from the boom times—could step back, examine the underbelly of the transformation, and try to mitigate its devastating effects. Widespread social activism and political reform occupied many of the privileged class. For the Kennedy family, the cause that would come to command the lion's share of their attention for the next decade was the Equal Franchise Federation.

By the end of 1908, both Kennedy houses were complete. Julian's business was prosperous. The family enjoyed a social standing that provided not only a steady stream of amusements, from dances to concerts to luncheon and tea parties, but also access to those who wielded power and influence in Pittsburgh. Lucy had graduated from Vassar, was adjusting to life as a new wife, and was coming into her own as a player on the Pittsburgh social and philanthropic stage. Eliza was headed to follow in Lucy's footsteps at Vassar. It was at Vassar that they encountered a world of progressive ideas that would change the course of their lives.

4 VASSAR COLLEGE

Vassar College was the obvious choice for the precocious first-born daughter of a loyal Yalie. The two schools had long been recognized as brother-sister institutions, with the requisite number of shared parties, dances, and inter-marriages. Jennie had wanted to attend the college herself as a young woman, but the option was not available to her. In Lucy's matriculation at Vassar, Jennie found vicarious enjoyment of an education she herself had long coveted.

So it was, on a gray late September morning in 1898, that Lucy came to settle into a private Pullman compartment, departing from Pittsburgh's East Liberty Station on an eastbound train for the twelve-hour ride to Poughkeepsie, New York. Dressed in a smartly tailored new traveling suit and firmly planted on the plush, tufted seat, she looked around to take in the rich aura of the private compartment: its dark paneled walls and polished brass appointments, its musty air redolent with a comforting, familiar aroma of Prince Albert pipe tobacco. Next to her in stately splendor sat her mother. Both of them were contemplating the adventure ahead as the car lurched into motion.

Lucy's gaze shifted to the window and remained fixed on the countryside rushing by outside, punctuated by the relentless rhythm of passing telegraph poles taking her further and further from home. Periodically, the train screeched into another station, diminutive rural whistlestops and larger towns—Harrisburg, Philadelphia, and New York, changing trains at Grand Central Station to take the New York Central & Hudson River Railroad another eighty miles north past Yonkers and Irvington—where more well-appointed young ladies boarded amidst the billowing smoke, each with a year's worth of steamer trunks, leather cases, and hat boxes, each headed in search of her future at Vassar.

A young lady's luggage typically consisted of steamer or "packer" trunks, constructed of wood, usually pine, and covered with leather, canvas, paper, or tin, finished with hardwood slats for added strength and stability. Custom boxes were constructed especially for the elaborate assortment of hats that well-heeled students might carry along to college. The luggage was often constructed by furniture companies. Since the advent of widespread travel was still a couple decades away, "suitcases" were not yet in wide use. The fledgling Hartmann Company, just twenty years old, was the American alternative to Louis Vuitton, which had been founded in Paris twenty years before that. Lucy may have had a smaller trunk in the compartment with her, but most of the luggage was stored in a separate train car for the journey. Arriving in Poughkeepsie, it would be transferred by porters onto the carriages that would carry the girls to the Vassar campus three miles up the road to the east.

Vassar in 1898 was a rigorous and rarified place, considerably more than a finishing school—yet still imbued with the accoutrements of grace and gentility expected by the affluent families who entrusted their daughters to the esteemed institution.

As the nation's second-oldest women's college and the first to receive a charter, Vassar was still only thirty-seven years old the year Lucy arrived. Only a few hundred women had received degrees in thirty-one graduating classes. And while Mount Holyoke had been founded sixty-one years earlier, Smith (1871), Wellesley (1875), Radcliffe (1879), Bryn Mawr (1885), and Barnard (1889) were still relative newcomers on the scene of elite women's colleges. The Seven Sisters—counterparts to the all-male Ivy League schools—would not be identified by that epithet until 1927.

Of the eight Ivies—Harvard, Yale, Princeton, Dartmouth, Columbia, Brown, Cornell, and the University of Pennsylvania—only Cornell admitted women when Lucy went to college. It had done so since 1870, but none of the other seven would follow suit until nearly a hundred years later, when Princeton and Yale went co-ed in 1969. Ivy League men consequently looked largely to the Seven Sisters for female companionship. Depending on who you asked, and when, the Ivies and Seven Sisters enjoyed unofficial pairings that became manifested in patterns of courtship and marriage among their graduates. Some were informally aligned by obvious geographic convenience—Harvard and Radcliffe in Cambridge, Columbia and Barnard in New York, Bryn Mawr and Penn in Philadelphia. Though geographically distant, Vassar and Yale were considered by some to be a pair—a link that would endure all the way until 1967, when Vassar trustees rejected a proposed merger with Yale before deciding to admit male students in 1969. Others considered Yale to be aligned with Smith and Princeton men to have a particular affinity for Bryn Mawr women. Brown had Pembroke College next door, its acknowledged sister but not considered part of the esteemed seven. And of course Mount Holyoke, Smith, and Wellesley enjoyed the added distractions of other men's colleges nearby in New England, such as Amherst, Williams, Trinity, and Wesleyan. The net effect of single-sex education in this era was a great deal of weekend train travel back and forth among the schools.

As a veteran member of the fledgling sisterhood of seven, Vassar attracted college-bound young women looking for a bit more than a strong liberal arts education and the credentials to teach. In his April 13, 1865, correspondence with the college's trustees, founder Matthew Vassar had noted, "It is my wish now . . . to build an institution for the culture of women in the highest character—an institution where women may be instructed in all the branches of literature and science suited to the sphere assigned them in social, moral, and religious life, and for preparation for the successful pursuit of every vocation wherein they can be made useful for their own maintenance, and for the good of society and the race—an institution, too, where, in due time, women shall be the teachers and educators of women."[1]

Proudly, he added, "I am pleased to observe that, since the inauguration of our enterprise in 1861, great changes have taken place in the public mind regarding what may be appropriately considered the sphere of woman."[2] So as Lucy approached her new base of operations, she surely sensed something promising in store, though perhaps not exactly just what.

The college's distinct educational philosophy had been launched with its first faculty hire, Maria Mitchell, a noted astronomer and the first woman to be elected a Fellow of the American Academy of Arts and Sciences in 1848 and of the American Association for the Advancement of Science in 1850. A hands-on educator, Mitchell traveled with her students to Iowa in 1869 and to Colorado in 1878 to witness a solar eclipse. She was famous for asking, "Did you observe that yourself, or did you read it in a book?" Likewise, Vassar's first history professor, Lucy Maynard Salmon, championed the study of social history and introduced everyday artifacts—laundry lists, advertisements, cookbooks, and diaries—to engage students in firsthand investigative learning. The Vassar philosophy urged students to "go to the source," to "dig, ferret out the truth," and never be satisfied with second-hand knowledge.[3]

Lucy took to it right away. She embraced English literature, Shakespeare in particular. Frequent guest speakers augmented the regular curriculum.

At Vassar, Lucy continued to blossom.

In February of 1902, the college hosted Richard Watson Gilder, editor of the *Century* magazine, who spoke on Abraham Lincoln's "power speeches" and told the girls that "they would stand on an equal [plane] with any of the great oratory of any country and that since his works have been collected he is getting to be considered even in England as one of the world's greatest statesmen."[4]

Inspired by the revered speakers who came to campus, the girls themselves learned oratory through debate. After one competition in the spring of 1901, Lucy proudly reported that the judges—a Professor Phelps from Yale, a professor of law from Columbia, and Miss Whitney of Vassar—said that "they had never heard as logical or finished a debate at any of the men's colleges. They also said that the leader on the winning side was the most eloquent woman speaker they had ever heard."[5]

Lucy welcomed the change that "Po'keep" provided from her "smoky, dingy, Pittsburgh days," and she quickly embraced Vassar life. "Everything is very regular here," she wrote to her mother. Breakfast was at half past seven, dinner at a quarter to one, and the girls were summoned to supper by a gong at six o'clock sharp. They dressed for dinner, slipping on a fresh shirtwaist.

The shirtwaist was simply a button-front blouse, modelled after menswear shirts, that was tucked into the waistband of a skirt. The standard model was advertised for one dollar apiece in magazines of the day, but by the time Lucy graduated from Vassar, the ubiquitous blouse was being embellished with colorful fabrics and trims, lace, fancy stitching, and frills and was being featured in *Vogue* magazine articles and advertisements. For winters in Poughkeepsie, Lucy favored the flannel ones. It was said that "a very fashionable woman with a half a hundred waists boasts that there are no two alike."[6] The iconic garment has been perhaps most vividly immortalized in the public's historical imagination by the infamous Triangle Shirtwaist Factory fire that would kill 146 immigrant garment workers locked in the top three floors of a ten-story

Greenwich Village building in 1911. But for the girls at Vassar, the shirtwaist was just part of standard daily wear, barely given a second thought, almost a uniform.

Classes consumed three hours per day. After dinner, nightly chapel ran from seven thirty to eight, with only three cuts permitted each semester, and the girls were in bed by ten. Evenings were often spent being read to as the girls sat, needles in hand, tending to their "fancy work." The dorm rooms also became the scenes of card parties and supper clubs.

Writing home about once a week, Lucy was candid yet gracious, confident yet self-deprecating. She was "ever so obliged" for the generous checks that arrived from home. She also welcomed boxes shipped by train, her name and "Vassar College, Poughkeepsie" painted on the outside, containing such forgotten essentials as a new golf cape, a silk kimono, cushions for her couch, a scrapbook for her pictures, curtains, rugs, and a skate key. Cakes and mince pies and plum pudding were always well received and quickly devoured by her friends with hot chocolate simmered in Lucy's chaffing dish. She gained fourteen pounds her freshman year.[7] Lucy insisted on reciprocity from her correspondents, and chided her mother and Eliza in particular to write back. "Eliza has never written to me. She is going to pay me in my own coin I guess."

Her senior year, Lucy and her two roommates set out to decorate their dorm room to be reminiscent of home. "We are going to have the room papered ... and are going to get bids from all the paper hangers in town. We hope to get it done for about 15 dollars. . . . It will make a perfectly stunning room if we get the right kind of paper and the furniture arranged all right. We are planning to have a Turkish corner if we can get one up for a comparatively small sum." Aspiring to emulate the Kennedy's Turkish corner back home, she asked, "Have you any idea how much yours cost? Of course we would not have nearly such expensive pillows but would use some kinds of silk or cotton covers which would give the general effect."[8]

The Vassar campus enjoyed "quite a nice lake," and Lucy rowed every day she could. She loved sharing her exploits:

> Yesterday we had a dandy row on the lake a regular handicap race and of course we won ... About two weeks ago Abby and I were out rowing. We rowed quite a long time, and then it began to rain. We hurried back to the landing. I was in such a rush to get out that I jumped before the boat had quite touched. Guess what happened.

My toe caught. Eclipse of Lucy in the muddy stream even up to her neck and, worst of all, her beautiful new back comb went floating down the tide, and now perchance some sea nymph is combing her long green locks with it. Well she pulled herself out of the icy water very quietly and once more stood on terra firma. She skipped home, changed her clothes, and never even got a cold. But now awful to say her classmates all ask her, "What are the properties of water? Why does water tend to attract towards the earth a golf skirt made bias in the back?" I took the skirt to the dressmaker and she fixed it all right, but I am still in mourning for my back comb. Now I get in and out of a boat with the greatest care, generally with two assistants, and everybody holds their breath until I am safely seated.

When the lake froze, they skated, their skirts billowing out from pinched waists and their hands elegantly warmed in fur muffs.

Vassar had birthed women's athletics, beginning with its revered baseball team, the Resolutes, in 1866, and would ultimately field teams in hockey, basketball, track, and tennis. Intent on strengthening and straightening her back, Lucy spent an hour and a half each day in the gym. "I am much stronger than I was and can now chin myself," she wrote. "I can also perform quite credibly on the punching bag. Just now I am learning to hang on the horizontal bar and swing violently backward and forward holding on entirely by my knees with my head hanging down."[9] A "Special Order of Exercises" recorded the apparatus, times, and weights for nearly thirty activities that included chest weights, flying rings, traveling rings, running, jumping, vaulting, parallel bars, and climbing. And she played basketball outside on the wet and "squishy" ground.

Vacations occurred two to three times a year. Coming home, Lucy preferred the overnight train, which left Poughkeepsie at eight thirty in the evening and arrived in Pittsburgh at eight thirty the next morning, just in time for breakfast at home. Thanksgiving found most of the girls staying on campus, where they were treated to an eleven-course meal, but Lucy preferred to spend Thanksgiving in New York with her parents when she could.

During Lucy's time at Vassar, the campus was enhanced by gifts from the industrial age's new millionaires. Writing in March 1901, she reported, "There is a new dormitory almost finished. . . . The other day John D. Rockefeller gave [$]110,000 to build another building just like it. The man who announced the glad tidings eulogized John D. at great length and gave out the hymn ten thousand times ten thousand. He then prayed for about half an hour that more millionaires' hearts would be softened to give us funds. The poor rich men are getting struck on all sides. We calculated that [$]110,000 would represent one minute of his income, therefore he was really not so generous."[10]

Established protocol for courting was embodied in the three large reception rooms on the ground floor of "Main," each with an unspoken purpose. The first, nearest the entrance, was for business purposes, admissions interviews, visiting parents, and the like. The second was for more intimate visits. The third was reserved exclusively for engaged couples. All three had glass walls looking out into the corridor, so one's status in the courting process was always on view.

Experiencing romance as an outside observer, Lucy was a bit perplexed by the wild imaginings, the abandonment of friends—and even oneself—that romance prompted among her peers. The self-proclaimed "ugly duckling" grew impatient with their swooning over West Point beaus. Writing about one friend, she declared, "She seems to be smitten with a certain Mr. Johnston and is in love with his divine eyes. When I get in love with anybody's divine eyes if I ever do I am not going to proclaim it from the housetops." She lamented that her dear friend Kit, living in New York, "could not come up as she had an invitation to a football game and of course trousers win over petticoats." "This continual marrying of our friends begins to be rather a drain."

Yet there was a longing there. Her sophomore year, Lucy had savored her first dance with a man, Harry McKinley, "an awfully nice fellow" with whom she shared the first, last, and supper dances in her "white point d'esprit trimmed with blue."[11] And she had to admit, as she got to know her dear friend Floss's beau, that "a man like that is worth having." As other girls returned from West Point aglow with their "conquests" and "expectations of getting another invitation," Lucy wondered to her mother, "Why weren't we born pretty instead of rich? Old maidenhood will be our fate I fear. Awful to contemplate is it not?" "Why wasn't I born with a beautiful voice? I would rather have that talent than any other." As senior year approached, she observed to her mother with just a hint of sarcasm, "It seems to me that all the girls I know are getting engaged. We will have to get a hurry on Mama darling."

While Vassar did its best to keep the girls occupied and content, it wasn't all to Lucy's liking. A few weeks into her first year, her restlessness was beginning to show: "We had a concert Friday evening, which was very long and stupid."

"Everything is as slow and stupid as possible and the Greek is atrocious." By her third year, she was beginning to have enough. ". . . we live here in one place all the time and see the same people all the time, so nothing new happens." Senior year, it would seem, was no better: "There is absolutely nothing doing in this dull old hole and I will be glad to get away from it for even one brief instant."

Boredom did not suit Lucy well, but she found ways to cope. Halfway through her Vassar career, she found herself embroiled in a mock election as President William McKinley and his Democratic challenger, William Jennings Bryan, faced a rematch of the 1896 election. "There is a good deal of excitement here over the elections," she wrote. "Everybody is prepared to have their allowances stopped and to go to the poor house if Bryan gets in."[12] But with the economy strong and the recent victory in the Spanish-American War, McKinley's slogan of "Four More Years of the Full Dinner Pail" resonated with voters. He and his running mate, Theodore Roosevelt, were elected handily. The girls' allowances were safe.

As graduation approached, Lucy became predictably nostalgic. "A few more short weeks and we will be going out of here forever," she wrote. "I really think that I will be quite sad to leave the dear old place and know I shall get homesick for the girls."

Far more exciting to Lucy than Vassar's offerings were the off-campus distractions. Just seventy-five miles and a short ride by boat down the Hudson River or by train along its shore, New York beckoned, and she seized every opportunity to venture to the city for shopping, fine dining, theater, and opera. Lucy loved New York. The city represented the pinnacle of sophistication and elegance that she craved, and it seductively drew her in.

By her second year at Vassar, Lucy had adopted New York as her own and had even identified her favorite haunts. She relished writing home on the Waldorf-Astoria's heavy, cream-colored hotel stationery with its raised gold Gothic lettering:

Dear Mama,

Your little daughter is dining at the Waldorf as you see. O to be a Vanderbilt and live in New York all the time. I never intend going to any other place when I come to New York. Just at the present moment the orchestra is playing the most beautiful piece and I feel as if I was in dreamland. Just think of settling down to humdrum life after this. Really life is worth living if you were only here. I am

writing this in the Turkish parlor and watching all the swell costumes and New York is the place to see them. . . . I am writing this
in time to the music and to catch my train. . . .

It was on one of her early forays into New York that Lucy began to realize
her fashion sense, such as it was. She discovered that "brown is a very swell
color this year" and reveled in the finery of French flannel and silk, the newest
silhouettes, and the latest millinery fashions. Toward the end of her first year
at Vassar, a letter home summed up the new trends in hats: "I was looking
at hats in New York. They [seem] to be wearing more black trimmed with
gold than anything else. Plumes are entirely out of date and hats are very low
and very plain. A great many wigs are worn too."[13] By 1900, she had decided
to simplify her style. She promised to "send home my plume. . . . If there is
anything I despise it's a heavy lid."

Indeed, hats occupied an inordinate amount of time and money among
young ladies of privilege, and for that matter among the American population
in general as well. The "heavy lid" that Lucy came to despise was the trademark
of the iconic Gibson Girl look, with its broad-brimmed and heavily decorated
hats, and her disdain was perhaps prophetic in foreshadowing its demise.
Illustrator Charles Dana Gibson's portrayal of a more traditional—and less
challenging—type of woman would begin to fade in popularity just as the
suffrage movement began to gain some momentum. In the meantime, it was
something to aspire to. Lucy's mother tried to encourage her to cultivate the
look, writing, "Mrs. Holden was telling me her daughter the artist thought
you looked like a Gibson Girl. Be sure to stand up straight."[14]

Under their hats, the girls sported any number of variations on the very
popular pompadour, that loosely swept-up heap of hair, curved away from the
face. To shape and support the hair, it was often drawn over a "rat" (a matted
pad or roll of hair) or a wire frame. Backcombing was also used to form a
matted foundation for the smooth outer layer of hair.

Lucy begged her mother to visit so that she could impress her friends. "I
want you to see everybody and be seen. The observed of all observers as it
were. Bring all your prettiest clothes but no low neck dresses . . . Simply a
swell bonnet, and pretty silk waists and your blue silk suit. I know I have the
handsomest mother and I want her to show off to the best advantage." While
still in her second year at Vassar, she asked for her graduation gift. A miniature
portrait of her mother, she explained in a letter, "by the best obtainable painter

would please me immensely." Spirit obliged with a diminutive full-length portrait by Pittsburgh painter Emil Hermann.

Arguably the most profound and lasting lesson Lucy learned at Vassar had to do with trust:

> My opinion is that trust and faith in people should be fostered just as long as possible for you have to learn distrust and the grim realities of life all too soon anyway. I often feel that I was born old before my time and lost much of the pleasure of childhood by becoming acquainted or aware of many of the evils and vices of age. Ingrained into my very soul is a deep distrust and suspicion of everybody's character and motives. In some ways it is a very useful thing but again it puts a sort of gloom over what might otherwise be very pleasant.[15]

How prophetic.

* * *

By the time Eliza entered Vassar in 1908, some two dozen girls from Pittsburgh were among the thousand students there.[16] It was still a rather provincial student body, with two-thirds coming from New York and the contiguous states. International students were still quite rare: four from Persia, two from Syria, one each from Canada, England, India, Italy, Japan, and the Philippine Islands.

Less flamboyant and rebellious than Lucy, Eliza kept her nose to the grindstone, focusing on academics. She chose to study economics, although she was also fascinated by biology and had great fun making displays in her dorm room of the entrails from various animals she had dissected, much to the horror of her squeamish roommate. Her serious passion for good and effective government was fueled by courses in History of Civil Service in the United States, Development of Municipal Government, Labor Problems and Socialism, Charities and Corrections, Public Finance, and Economic and Social Problems of City Life. A course in Contemporary History taught her about control of the press by political parties, legal regulation of the press, and freedom of the press.

Immersed as she was in academics, Eliza appeared not to take an active

part in extracurricular life, as if waiting
for a later time to come fully into her
own. She was not listed in the 1912
Vassarion yearbook in any leadership
capacity. She was not active in student
government or debate. She did not play
on any of the college's sports teams.
She did not sing in the Glee Club or
Choir or play in the Mandolin Club
or Orchestra. She was not a thespian
or an award-winning student. She was
not elected to Phi Beta Kappa. In fact,
the only listing of Eliza outside of her
senior portrait was as part of the Senior
Parlor Opening Committee. It would
seem that she played a rather quiet role
in college life.

Eliza followed in Lucy's footsteps, entering Vassar in fall 1908.

As would become evident in due time, however, she did soak up the college's intellectual offerings. Laura Johnson Wylie, herself a Vassar graduate
(Class of 1877) with a PhD from Yale, chaired the English Department and
filled four pages in the 1912 *Vassarion* with her own thoughts on the applica-
tion of education to life:

> The last year of college is peculiarly marked by the pervading sense
> of the issue of the morrow . . . This feeling of the difficulties and
> interests that are soon to engage us not only draws our thoughts
> and hopes beyond the boundaries of the present task, but enriches
> the present by making clear its relationship to the new order to
> which it is yielding. In the light of this sharpened perception of the
> day's significance, immediate problems take a new largeness and
> dignity, the wisdom of books comes home as never before to our
> business and bosoms, we feel ourselves to be passing into the main
> current of life. . . . Only in so far as we are intellectually upright,
> courageous and open minded in bringing thought to bear on prac-
> tice, can we work with those forces that today make for social and
> personal righteousness.

In addition to a reading list for life, Vassar exposed its fortunate students to a world of progressive thinking through the outside lecturers who regularly visited the campus. These speakers encouraged the students to think for themselves and to take their rightful place as leaders in a variety of venues. Eliza's senior year alone brought a list of at least twenty luminaries to speak on a variety of topics. Among them were Mrs. Florence Kelly of the National Consumer's League, railing against sweatshops, child labor, and poor working conditions for women; Miss Martha Berry, an educator and founder of Berry College who had founded schools to provide quality education for poor children in the rural mountains of Georgia; Mr. Robert E. Speer, a prolific author and Presbyterian leader who oversaw expansion of the church's foreign missions and wrote articles that addressed controversial social problems; and Mrs. Horace E. Deming, a leader in reform for good government in New York City.

Given her quiet embrace of all that Vassar had to offer, it is perhaps fitting that Eliza's photo in the *Vassarion* should be accompanied by a favorite line from *Othello* (act 2, scene 1, in which Iago describes Desdemona): "She that could think [and think] And ne'er disclose her mind." The full Iago monologue was an apt description of Eliza:

> She that was ever fair and never proud,
> Had tongue at will and yet was never loud,
> Never lacked gold and yet never went gay,
> Fled from her wish and yet said "Now I may,"
> She that being angered, her revenge being nigh,
> Bade her wrong stay and her displeasure fly,
> She that in wisdom never was so frail
> To change the cod's head for the salmon's tail,
> She that could think and ne'er disclose her mind,
> See suitors following and not look behind . . .

It would not be long, however, before Eliza would learn to disclose her mind and unleash the benefits of a Vassar education on an unsuspecting political scene.

In the meantime, she seemed to enjoy the quiet, sheltered life where the girls were cloistered away from men and the general public much of the time and where they dressed and coiffed themselves in a rather more informal manner. The silhouette for women's dresses had slimmed down from the Gibson Girl look of Lucy's era, with its pinched waist and pert bustle. Instead, the girls wore sailor suits by day and kimonos by night.

A prominent fellow student, a year ahead of Eliza, was Inez Milholland, the beautiful, wealthy, and radical New Yorker who reportedly once had held a suffrage meeting in a gloomy graveyard because of faculty objections to the use of the college chapel. While at Vassar, she set a world record for the eight-pound shot put, the college record for basketball throwing, and the college cup as best all-around athlete. The irrepressible Inez would go on to spurn convention by earning a law degree from New York University, proposing to her husband (three times), working as a wartime newspaper correspondent in Italy, and becoming one of the more fanatical suffragists in the country. It was she who would later cut a stunning figure parading on horseback with a large suffrage flag, earning her a reputation as "the most beautiful suffragist." Inez Milholland Boissevain campaigned with Emmeline Pankhurst in England, was thrown into jail for participating in a New York shirtwaist workers' strike, and refused to wear a wedding ring because she considered it "a badge of slavery." Many believed that it was overexertion, complicated by aplastic anemia, that would cause her collapse at a suffrage rally in 1916. Considered by many to be a martyr for the cause, Inez would pass away after a ten-week illness at the age of just thirty.

Eliza (holding the right corner of the banner) would remain close to her Vassar classmates for the rest of her life.

In an ironic turn of events, once the Kennedy sisters were out of school and in the midst of applying their Vassar educations to the fight for women's suffrage, the president of Vassar, Dr. James M. Taylor, announced his resignation in 1913. The reason, his friends believed, was the growing suffrage and socialist sentiment within the student body.[17]

All in all, Vassar equipped Lucy and Eliza well for what would become their life's work, all for just five hundred dollars per year for tuition and room and board.[18]

5 THE UGLY DUCKLING UNBOUND

Returning to Pittsburgh after her Vassar graduation in 1902, Lucy found herself in the midst of a whirl that was at once flattering and unfulfilling. She was becoming a player on the city's social stage. But like many of her college-educated peers, she hungered for more.

Lucy found some of the intellectual stimulation she craved in the Twentieth Century Club, a decidedly progressive name for a women's club that had been founded in 1894. She was elected a member in November 1902. The club carried the promise of new ideas and forward thinking to launch the city's leading women into the coming age prepared for the anticipated myriad of changes that the new century most certainly would bring—changes in social and political thought, in national economic policies, in international relations, in science and technology, in the built environment, and more. Clearly, the founders perceived themselves as poised on the cutting edge of modern life.

Indeed, the Club's charter set forth its intentions quite clearly, stating that it was to be dedicated to "the purpose of creating an organized center for women's work, thought, and action and the advancement of her interests and the promotion of science, literature, and art . . ." At a time when all good inspiration seemed to come from the East Coast, founder Julia Harding had drawn her inspiration for the new club from a visit in 1894 to the New Century Club in Philadelphia. She wasted no time in establishing a comparable institution in Pittsburgh. By the time Lucy joined the Club, a regular lecture series was bringing in notable speakers such as Julia Ward Howe, the prominent American abolitionist, social activist, poet, and the author of "The Battle Hymn of the Republic"; Booker T. Washington, the dominant leader of the African American community who served as an educator, author, orator, and advisor to presidents of the United States; and W. E. B. DuBois, a philosopher

By the time Lucy met John in 1905, she was growing in confidence.

and author of "The Individual and Social Conscience" (1905) as well as a founder of the National Association for the Advancement of Colored People (NAACP) in 1909. Yet despite the progressive nature of her lecture series for the club, it would be only a few years until Julia Harding would found and head the Pittsburgh Association Opposed to Woman Suffrage and would turn out to be something of a nemesis to Lucy.

Outside of the Twentieth Century Club, Lucy kept busy with less lofty pursuits and regularly found her way into the society pages. In August 1902, she hosted a house party at Beaumaris for a dozen Vassar friends.[1] That November, she was elected to the board of the Oakland Play Nursery. In July 1903, before a large crowd of invited guests, she christened the *Mongolia*, the second largest merchant vessel at the American Shipbuilding Company in Camden, New Jersey. Built for the Pacific Mail Steamship Company, the 615-foot ship was headed for trans-Pacific service to the Philippines and China. The *Mongolia*'s accommodations reflected its heavy use by Chinese emigrants: 350 first-class, 68 second-class, and 1,300 steerage.[2] In February 1904 she donned a pink Liberty silk dress with pink roses in her hair as a bridesmaid in Eliza Munhall's wedding to Arthur Braun, a large and "brilliant" affair with hundreds of guests, and the Kennedys gave a dinner dance at their home in honor of the couple.[3] In June she gave a card party for the newlywed Mrs. Braun, followed that evening by a dance for sixty hosted by Julian Jr. and Eliza.[4] In August she took a lake trip on a Carnegie ore boat.[5] Along the way, there were her piano recitals as "an advanced student" in the Pittsburg Conservatory of Music, along with frequent dinner parties and events to raise funds for the Vassar Students' Aid Society, including one play performed before an audience of a hundred at 5400 Forbes.[6] Lucy was living the life she was expected to live as a young woman of privilege.

Sometime that fall or winter, as 1904 slipped into 1905, Lucy met a handsome young banker named John Oliver Miller. Certain back in her college days that she would be "an ugly duckling to the end," Lucy, now at the

Lucy found her helpmate in a handsome young banker named John Oliver Miller.

advanced age of twenty-five, had finally found a beau. John had been born around 1875, one of the youngest of sixteen children, and had grown up on a farm in Somerset, Pennsylvania. A self-made man, he had started out in the coal industry before working his way to secure a law degree from the University of Michigan in 1899 and starting work as a cashier in the Homestead Bank, up the Monongahela River from Pittsburgh.

Just how Lucy and John first met remains a mystery, but they apparently connected early on over literature. On March 15, 1905, Lucy issued "My dear Mr. Miller" an invitation for a "little informal music and a general good time" on the coming Friday evening. By then John was employed at the First National Bank of McKeesport. In the written invitation, she also thanked him for sending her a copy of Joseph Conrad's latest novel, *Nostromo*, though noting that she did not expect to like it as much as her "beloved Stevenson."[7]

It was a riverboat trip in August 1905 that would prove to be the most memorable event for the twosome, who found themselves among a party of eight young guests aboard a passenger steamer on a Great Lakes tour, chaperoned by Mr. and Mrs. Reed Kennedy and including Lucy's brother Julian.[8] It was there that they fell in love, Lucy and John would later tell their children, and the riverboat trip must have been a particularly romantic setting for the new couple. Riverboats of the era were often elegantly appointed with grand staircases, mahogany paneling, plate glass mirrors, and ballrooms. Quietly powered by steam, they were also wrapped with layered decks of balconies that allowed for long, lingering promenades as the boats glided along the Detroit River and across the Great Lakes.

John captured Lucy's affections with his good looks, his sweet, gentle wisdom, and his love of books, although their literary tastes were three centuries apart. She quoted liberally from Shakespeare, he from the rising star of the time, Rudyard Kipling. His calm, uncomplicated manner was the perfect foil to Lucy's self-described "mercurial disposition" and her brash, impetuous antics.[9] Where Lucy was an anxious insomniac, John carried the discipline of having been raised on a farm, going early to bed and enjoying uninterrupted sleep until dawn. John was a frugal man with simple tastes, while Lucy was learning to enjoy the extravagances made possible by her father's success in business. Despite his modest demeanor, John was a natty dresser and fastidious in his habits, while Lucy could be a bit haphazard when it came to her personal appearance.[10]

Having little personal experience in the ways of romance, Lucy approached her new relationship with her characteristic candor, a bit clumsy at first, but without pretense or guile. John was charmed.

> Dearest John,
> . . . The love of a man and a woman plus such a friendship must be the great happiness. That is what I want. Don't adore me and worship me but just love me and understand. Let me come close all the time dear and I shall be happy. If I am to grow to love you more and more you must be willing to play father confessor. I should simply wither up and blow away if I were forced to spend a lifetime with a man that I couldn't tell my thoughts. To be afraid to tell the good and bad would be to me the heights of the most awful loneliness. . . . I know I am capable of loving you greatly and I do want to start right. . . .
> With all my love,
> Lucy[11]

Lucy and John were married on the evening of May 1, 1907, in a lavish ceremony at 5400 Forbes. The bride descended the sweeping stairway around the music room, and the ceremony took place in front of the library fireplace. The bridal party of eighteen dined in the drawing room, while the expansive porch was enclosed to serve as a dining room for guests.

Eliza, just eighteen, served as her sister's only attendant, while John had his brother as best man and six additional ushers.[12] The house was decorated with spring flowers and in particular yellow and white daisies, yellow iris, and white lilies. Accounts of the day did not suggest whether the yellow color choice was a subtle but intentional nod to the growing national women's suffrage movement, a choice that could be traced to an 1867 suffrage campaign in Kansas that featured the state's brilliantly yellow floral emblem, the sunflower.

Not long after they were married, in 1909, Lucy and John spent much of the year apart. Separation only intensified the love and the longing they shared. By this time, John was settled as Secretary and Treasurer of the Peoples Savings Bank in Pittsburgh, his name printed on the bank's letterhead along with five other officers. Lucy left in January to accompany her brother Julian on a trip to the West Coast in hopes that the climate there would improve their health. Once settled at the Miramar in Santa Barbara for the winter months, Lucy wrote nearly every day with expressions of undying love, interspersed with commentary on politics . . . and trees. Everywhere she went, Lucy noticed the trees.

John's letters back were longer, full of local political news but amorous as well. At the time, Julian was chairing the campaign of a Democratic candidate for mayor.

> Lucy, your father's speech was a peach. It was the best one delivered in the evening. He surprised me. I thought he might be nervous and timid but he . . . spoke in an easy, direct and conversational manner with perfect self possession, keeping the attention of 2,000 people all the time, and was heartily applauded when he made telling touches on the gang. He gave them lots of facts, a thing the rest of the speeches did not do, contenting themselves with generalities. He told several good stories right to the point, grew sarcastic at times, always emphatic and occasionally most eloquent. . . .[13]

And back and forth the letters went, sometimes two a day, pulsing with an intimacy and affection that the restrained banker and the outspoken troublemaker reserved only for each other.

> If I just had you in my arms a while I would feel like a different man. It is good to be in love, sweetheart, and your absence makes me realize how very dear and near you are to me. . . . I wish I were walking the beach with you tonight watching the sea and stars, both with glad hearts and feeling the joy of living and loving.[14]
>
> John

> I don't believe I realized before how absolutely essential you had become to my happiness. . . . Every once in a while I see some man that has a turn of the head or something that reminds me of you and gives me an awful twinge of John sickness . . . I just wish you could be here to walk along the beach with me.[15]
>
> Lucy

The worse the weather in Santa Barbara, the greater was their longing. And it was not a good year for weather in Santa Barbara.

> Dearest—
> I am so terribly homesick for you that I could weep if there were anybody to see me. I am just eaten up with the desire to be with you. A truly terrible feeling. The wind is blowing and blowing outside and I know that our cottage will be cold cold and I just want to curl up close to you and love you love you for ever and ever.[16]
>
> Lucy

> You dear old girl, . . . You are a mighty good girl and deserve the best love a man can give. . . . But that long distance between us—it makes me feel like a caged bird. When you come home you will remain here until I give you my consent, and I know from experience what that will cost. You are entirely too fine a prize to let go again. It makes me feel silly to think of having a sensation like this. Is it possible that in the brief span of two years I have grown so attached to a single human being that I can't dispense with her

anymore. . . that I find nothing in life that in any way would make it worthwhile without her?[17]

John

"When I get home I shall probably wear you out with caresses," Lucy promised.[18]

In the midst of their romantic exchanges, Lucy's passion for politics was already evident. "Please I want many political details—gossip, gossip, gossip," she would implore John.[19] And she had already established a keen sense of justice, which manifested itself in a loathing of dishonest dealings in business and politics. That loathing, which Eliza would come to share, would fuel their life's work.

Dearest—

The papers are most exciting but sometimes I wish I had never heard of a government. Everything is absolutely so rotten that it simply makes one lose all trust in human nature. I haven't a doubt that any one of those depositories named paid a big sum to council men. Again I say to you Mr. Miller that you can't keep your banker's sense of right and wrong too keen. I think all of them begin by little lapses. . . . If in the high circles of Pittsburgh finance there are more than twenty honest men, I will eat my hat. As I have argued with you before men who work with such a lenient and forgiving eye to the grosser failings of their fellow men are not apt to set a very smart pace of morality in any walk of life. Take that and smoke it if you will. . . .[20]

Lucy

The more attached she grew to John and her married life, the more detached Lucy became from her mother. Even spending time at her beloved Beaumaris was becoming a chore. "Life far from 5400 looks mighty good to me," she wrote. "What have you done about a house? Get busy. . . ."[21] At the same time as she was looking for a home in the city, Lucy dreamed of life in the country. "I wish dear we could live on a farm somewhere on the east coast where the weather was perpetually good. In that case I should never want to leave home at all."[22]

Lucy held onto that dream for a very long time. In the meantime, she was building a family that would ultimately expand to include three children: Julian (born 1910), Eliza (born 1915), and Barbara (born 1918). Even as she tended to her growing brood, Lucy launched into what would become her ten-year obsession.

III The Battle for Suffrage

6 RALLYING THE TROOPS

It was a spring afternoon in 1909 when Lucy, still a relative newlywed, hosted a lively band of eight "society girls" in the living room of her parents' home at 5400 Forbes Street. They were young, educated, and civic minded, and they were well versed in the news of the day. William Howard Taft had just been inaugurated as president, ushering in a period of unrest within the Republican Party that would lead to the spin-off of the Progressive Party under Theodore Roosevelt. With the Civil War forty years behind them, Taft was hopeful of knitting the still torn country back together. The National Association for the Advancement of Colored People was being founded in New York City by Black and white activists in response to rampant violence against African Americans across the nation. The Panama Canal was under construction, with Julian Kennedy making periodic visits to consult on the engineering of the Gatun Locks.

Eventually, the animated conversation in the Kennedys' living room that afternoon gravitated toward the topic of votes for women. They were inspired, perhaps, by a full-page piece in the *Sunday Post* headlined "Renaissance of Suffrage Movement in America." It featured ten women and accounts of how the movement had taken "a sudden and rapid stride forward" under the auspices of at least seventeen different organizations federated under the Interurban Woman Suffrage Council in New York. Members of those organizations had begun assembling every Monday night at Seventh Avenue and 125th Street.[1] The fact that it was emerging, initially at least, as a somewhat New-York-centric movement had to hold some extra appeal for Lucy. Beyond New York, suffragists were opening headquarters in various states, with Chicago, Sacramento, Washington, and Boston as particular hubs. And Mrs. Rachel Foster Avery had made a rousing suffrage speech to the Pittsburgh Chamber of Commerce in January. Or perhaps it was the notoriety of Emmeline

Pankhurst and her daughter Christabel, the militant English suffragettes who were making headlines and speaking tours in major US cities. Whatever the inspiration, the time was ripe as suffrage sentiment was growing across the nation.

Each of the young women in the group brought a different perspective and skill set to the mix. Mary Bakewell, the oldest of the group, was forty-one and would go on before the suffrage battle was even won to study theology at Hartford Theological Seminary in Connecticut and become an (unordained) Episcopal minister. Little did they know that she would also eventually defect from the mainstream suffrage movement and join the more militant movement. The others were in their twenties and early thirties. Mary Flinn, just twenty-two, was the daughter of State Senator William Flinn and had watched the workings of state government at close range. Having started her suffrage activities as a teenager, the winsome redhead would go on to marry John Lawrence and raise two sons while maintaining an active presence in political advocacy. Florence Harper was a hard worker with a comic streak who would later say that "no one devoid of a sense of humor need apply as a suffrage campaigner."[2] Hannah Patterson, thirty, was the daughter of a prominent banker and a graduate of Wilson College who studied finance at Columbia University and law at the University of Pennsylvania. With a no-nonsense demeanor, she had embarked on a career as an activist when she joined the Civic Club of Allegheny County and would become known for helping to establish a juvenile court. Jennie Bradley Roessing, twenty-eight, was the daughter of a tailor and had married a civil engineer, an unhappy marriage that would end in divorce. She would prove to be a master strategist in the campaign and ultimately go on to hold state and national leadership positions in the movement. Edna Schoyer, twenty-nine, was a gifted singer and self-avowed lesbian, the daughter of a Quaker mother and a Jewish father. Her upbringing in a family of attorneys no doubt fueled her keen sense of justice and advocacy. Penelope Whitehead, thirty-one, was the daughter of Bishop Cortlandt Whitehead, who had already headed the Episcopal Diocese for three decades. In due course, Lucy would have a run-in with the bishop, but for now his daughter represented access to an influential segment of the population. As a columnist at the time noted, "pioneers in social reforms are of a rugged type, insistent, persisting, and sometimes offensive. But the pioneer is ever fellowed by milder mannered, reasoning and calculating people."[3] Success in this endeavor would take all kinds.

* * *

Women's suffrage was certainly not a novel topic at the turn of the twentieth century. The whole issue of voting rights had been contested ever since the founding fathers had opted not to include any provisions for enfranchisement—for anyone—in the Constitution. The hardy band of eight in the Kennedys' living room stood on the shoulders of a host of women who had pursued the ballot for more than sixty years.

Even in the days of the Revolutionary War, First Lady Abigail Adams had lobbied her husband as he was off in Philadelphia at the Continental Congress helping to draft the laws of the new nation. "If particular care and attention are not paid to the ladies," she wrote, "we are determined to foment a rebellion and will not hold ourselves bound to obey any laws in which we have no voice or representation."[4]

Generally accepted as the dawn of the women's suffrage movement in the United States, the Seneca Falls Convention in July 1848 had a broader agenda. As they gathered for two days, the delegates adopted a list of eleven resolutions demanding equal rights for women. The ninth resolution, arguably the most controversial, was to secure the right to vote. They may have recognized that this was a watershed moment in the protracted saga of women's rights in America. They could not have anticipated, however, that the battle for women's suffrage would carry on for so many decades more.

It was not until after the Civil War, in 1866, that Elizabeth Cady Stanton and Susan B. Anthony formed the American Equal Rights Association, which sought to secure equality, particularly the right of suffrage, regardless of race, color, or sex. Two years later, the Fourteenth Amendment to the US Constitution was ratified, extending protection from unjust state laws to all citizens. But it defined "citizens" and "voters" as "male." Then, in 1870, the Fifteenth Amendment opened the door for Black men to vote. Still, the power to grant voting rights—or to deny them—remained with the states.

Finding themselves in disagreement over the issues of race and gender in the battle for enfranchisement, the national leaders of the women's rights movement were divided. Stanton and Anthony formed the National Woman Suffrage Association (NWSA) in New York, while in Boston, Lucy Stone, Henry Blackwell, and Julia Ward Howe established the more conservative American Woman Suffrage Association (AWSA), which favored a state-by-state approach. The NWSA argued for an alternative, a Sixteenth Amendment that would have provided universal suffrage. Finally, in 1878, a Woman Suffrage Amendment was introduced in the United States Congress. It failed, of course. But the wording of that amendment—"The right of citizens of the United States to vote shall not be denied or abridged by the United States or by any State on account of sex"—would remain intact until it finally became the law of the land.

Meanwhile, the movement had charted gains on the local level across the country. The right to vote had been granted to women sporadically even as the nation was in its infancy. In New Jersey, single women owning property "worth fifty pounds" were permitted to vote from 1776 until 1807, at which point the right was rolled back to white males only. And as early as 1838 in Kentucky and 1861 in Kansas, widows with school-age children were granted the right to vote in school elections.[5]

Statewide votes for women came later. By 1890, the NWSA and the AWSA were unified as the National American Woman Suffrage Association (NAWSA). The consolidated organization would both spearhead a national campaign and offer support to the grassroots efforts across the country as they garnered support one voter at a time. So it was that by the time Lucy and her hardy band of eight began rallying the troops in Western Pennsylvania in 1909, four states had already embraced the movement's rallying cry—Votes for Women!—and passed suffrage legislation within their own jurisdictions. Wyoming was the first when it joined the Union 1890 as its forty-fourth state, having first granted suffrage for women in 1869 when it was still just a territory. Colorado, Utah, and Idaho would follow to grant suffrage before the dawn of the new century.

The nascent suffrage movement had hit Western Pennsylvania early. Journalists like Bessie Bramble (aka Elizabeth A. Wade) and Jane Grey Swisshelm had advocated for it decades before. And Susan B. Anthony had visited Pittsburgh on multiple occasions, including most notably for a small gathering of men and women in 1880 at Lafayette Hall on Wood Street downtown. Gradually, small grassroots efforts began to emerge. The Wilkinsburg Women's Suffrage Club, based in a small municipality adjacent to Pittsburgh, held its first meeting in February 1889. So unpopular was the cause, according to one newspaper report, that the club soon chose to change its name to the Women's Civic Club of Wilkinsburg. But their focus remained on suffrage. In 1904, that club joined with several others to form the Allegheny County

Equal Rights Association, combining the energies of the Equal Rights Associations of Allegheny City, Bellevue, and Coraopolis and the Anthony Memorial Association of Homestead, whose name represented a nod to Susan B. Anthony. The new Allegheny County group had associated itself for a time with the NAWSA, but had lost momentum at some point before 1909.

* * *

Now reviving the moribund movement under the leadership of Mary Bakewell, the hardy group of eight organized what Lucy declared to be the county's first large-scale suffrage meeting in December 1909. Julian Kennedy presided, and Earl Barnes, a popular lecturer associated with The American Society for the Extension of University Teaching, was the featured speaker. Trained in child psychology, Barnes approached the topic of suffrage from the standpoint of giving women a voice in how schools were run. The organizers sold some twelve hundred tickets at twenty-five cents apiece. After all expenses were paid, they netted about four hundred dollars. With a success under their belts, they resolved to hold additional meetings.[6]

Lucy vividly recalled the second attempted gathering. "About a week before the day, the speaker telegraphed that she was unable to come. Being rather green, we naturally felt that we could not use any local speaker. Dr. Anna Howard Shaw, president of the American Women's Suffrage Association, was asked to come. Not only a leading suffragist but also a physician and one of the first ordained female Methodist ministers in the United States, Shaw was a busy woman. It was impossible for her to fill the engagement, and the meeting was called off. Many disgruntled people arrived at the church and found it closed."[7]

A month later, they tried again. Dr. Shaw arrived and was met at the train station by Lucy and her father. Tired and worn from her travel on behalf of the cause, Dr. Shaw was a short and stout woman whose first impression on the Kennedys was not altogether positive. She had a broad face with straight, heavy dark brows above her narrow piercing eyes. Her mouth was perpetually downturned in the manner of a seasoned skeptic, although when amused her somber face could dimple into a wry, closed-mouth hint of a smile. Her white hair was swept back in the most understated of pompadours, and she stood a full head shorter than Lucy. Julian looked over the top of Dr. Shaw's hat and shook his head at Lucy, silently suggesting that "it did not look very promising

Anna Howard Shaw, president of the American Woman Suffrage Association, would become Lucy's mentor.

for a good meeting." They took her back to 5400, where they had breakfast together. "I can well remember that my father was so fascinated with her that he stayed home all morning, and made no attempt to go to his office." And as it turned out, she was an outstanding orator, "a grand little person" who "preyed on the emotions of the audience as no one I have ever heard before, or since," Lucy recalled. "When she smiled and talked, she ceased to be a grand personality, and became one of the youngest and liveliest personalities I ever saw or heard."[8]

A dreary, rainy night diminished attendance at the second public meeting, but it was nonetheless deemed a success. Shaw stayed with the Kennedys for two or three days, during which they hosted a luncheon for a group of about twenty young women, who listened with rapt attention as she previewed her upcoming autobiography, *The Story of a Pioneer.*[9] Shaw became a mentor to Lucy, who described her as "one of the world's best speakers, with a fascinating and dynamic personality."[10]

It was on the heels of these gatherings that the Equal Franchise Federation of Allegheny County was formed in February 1910. Julian Kennedy agreed to head the organization if Mary Bakewell would assume all executive and administrative duties. As far as they knew, he was the first man in the country to head a woman's suffrage organization. At their organizational meeting, Julian encouraged those present to serve as ambassadors for the cause. "Circulate the idea of equal suffrage," he began. "Keep on talking about it and about the things that need reforming, and pretty soon the idea will become so popular that you may be able to keep the women from their bridge parties to hear about politics. . . . Within five years, I predict, women will vote in Pennsylvania, at least on city questions."[11]

The Black community also took up the gauntlet for women's suffrage, but the issue was understandably considered alongside the issue of racial inequality. As the Equal Franchise Federation was getting off the ground, the Loendi Club, a social and literary organization for the city's Black elite, hosted a Sunday afternoon symposium in which its president, W. H. Stanton introduced a general discussion on the topic, "Shall negro women take part as coequals or as auxiliaries in the Women's Suffrage movement?"[12] Given the nation's generally poor delivery on the Fourteenth and Fifteenth Amendments, which had promised reparations and prohibited voting discrimination on the basis of race, it was a bit more difficult for African Americans to wholeheartedly embrace women's suffrage.[13] Feeling betrayed by President Taft, many of them would look to Theodore Roosevelt's Progressive Party as

JULIAN KENNEDY.

IF but the brave deserve the fair,
  And we assume that this is true,
  What bounties rich of beauty rare
  To this bold knight are truly due.
With "Votes for Women" on his shield
  And Right and Justice for his cry,
He sweeps the broad forensic field
  Nor fears the stoutest foe to try.
And though hurled back in many a fray,
  His dauntless spirit battles still,
For though he may not win today,
  Win in the end, he must and will.

Julian Kennedy became an ardent suffragist and the first head of the Equal Franchise Federation.

the best option to forward the cause of justice in the 1912 presidential election. As they faced rampant disenfranchisement and violence, women's suffrage was not at the top of their priority list.

Nonetheless, there began a robust schedule of formal debates in Black churches and clubs on the topic of votes for women. Much of the subsequent activity to establish independent suffrage leagues for women of color was centered around Trinity Congregational Church, where the wife of the pastor, Mrs. I. S. Lee, would become a prominent figure. Lucy, Mary Bakewell, and others became frequent speakers at both the Lucy Stone Suffrage League and the Anna Howard Shaw Suffrage League, which served the Black community. And the *Pittsburgh Courier* launched a regular column inviting Black suffragists and anti-suffragists to submit opinion pieces.[14]

By the spring of 1911, the Equal Franchise Federation numbered almost five hundred members, both men and women. The group had set up headquarters on the seventh floor of the Jenkins Arcade, a new addition to the downtown skyline that featured a three-story open atrium lined with shops and offices. The office was to be open daily for use by the membership and included a stenographer ("in the faith that a typewriter will follow") and the beginnings of a suffrage library.[15]

At the final meeting before the summer break that May, Mary Bakewell presided and Miss May Allen gave a lengthy report of the suffrage parade in New York that spring. Mary had attended along with three others from the Pennsylvania delegation, marching the entire thirty-some blocks of the parade route in front of the state's float, ridden by Quakers in costume. Led by four "handsome" young society women, the New York parade had featured a few groupings of particular poignance. One was an entourage of mothers pushing baby carriages to signify that families would not be neglected as a result of suffrage and that the next generation stood to benefit from the cause. Another group of young women dressed in black and marching with black banners—survivors of the recent Triangle Shirtwaist Factory Fire—served as a sobering reminder of that horrific tragedy just weeks earlier. About a hundred members of the Men's League for Equal Suffrage also marched.[16] It was the Pittsburgh contingent's first parade, an inspiring spectacle and an instructive learning experience.

Jennie Roessing later recalled the first parade they staged back home in Pittsburgh, an amateurish attempt she described as their "little parade." "We were scared to death," she admitted. "There were about 200 women and a handful of men—fourteen, I think." The suffragists made their own flags and banners, which turned out to be too heavy, and the marchers staggered under their weight.[17] But as with much of the struggle for suffrage, the leaders learned and tested their tactics through trial and error to ensure that future efforts would be more successful.

* * *

On December 31, 1911, in the *Pittsburg Press*, propitiously placed on the page with the Automobile News, there appeared a foreboding headline: "Suffragists Will Nab the Bachelors in 1912, If They Don't Watch Out! Single Men Warned." What followed was a half-page diatribe that might have been characterized as satirical if the movement were not still so new and still eyed with such suspicion. Published on the eve of a leap year, a time when tradition held that gender norms might be reversed, the article suggested that the practice of women proposing marriage to men might no longer be confined to every four years. Rather, it warned, ". . . from now on, every year, nay every month and every day will fairly ooze matrimonial possibilities." The suffrage movement, according to the article, was only fueling the flames of romance:

If definite proof be required, ask the brainiest women of your acquaintance. Ten to one they are either announced suffragists or they are thoroughly in sympathy with the suffrage movement. They'll tell you in so many, oh so many, words, why women have just as much right to do the selecting of their husbands as men have in choosing their wives.

. . . Any unmarried man who thinks that suffragists are man haters and that they despise the married state, are sadly in error. The real, ardent suffragists is a firm believer [sic] in marriage; and they don't believe in allowing a man to have all the say in it either, before or after.

. . . Feeling this way about it, the Suffragists are inclined to avail themselves of the coming Leap Year, and to institute a mode of procedure that will fling conventionality to the winds, and rectify once and for all this lop-sided antiquated style of marriage proposal.

Three of the leading women in the movement also weighed in on the topic:

Suffragists want their husbands to love them as their equals. In marrying a suffragist a man can be reasonably sure that he is not marrying a fool, at least, for only seriously inclined women are numbered among the suffragists. . . . It is not too much to expect that before long public reason will not reel on her throne when woman lets man know that she is willing to enter into wedlock with him.

Miss Mary E. Bakewell

Do I believe in woman proposing marriage to man? I certainly do. They should be allowed to do this (propose to men) without in the least being considered indelicate or unwomanly.

Mrs. Enoch Rauh

Of course I believe in marriage, but I do not think that woman's sole end in life is marriage and rearing children. As long as women remain parasites, so long must they look forward to marriage as their only profession. But now that women are coming into their own, and have opportunities to be self-supporting, they are freed from the dreadful alternative which women too often are compelled to face, of enduring abject penury or accepting some man who is willing to marry them, and thus secure for themselves a means of support.... I am more interested in restricting it (marriage) than in urging suffragists to propose.

Miss Mary Flinn

"Forewarned is forearmed," the article concluded.[18] Happily married and delighted to be the mother of one-year-old Julian, Lucy remained decidedly silent on the subject.

7 LAUNCHING THE CAMPAIGN

The new year of 1912 opened with a bang. Literally. On January 8, at the Grand Opera House on Diamond Street, Mary Flinn fired the opening gun that marked the beginning of the formal suffrage campaign in Pittsburgh. Each day that week, a different speaker from the Equal Franchise Federation took the stage, both afternoon and evening, for ten minutes following the regular vaudeville performance of song and dance, pantomime, and comedy. With the use of a stereopticon projector to give three-dimensional impact to the images, these six young women showed photographs and cited statistics surrounding a number of issues relating to suffrage: child labor, the "ignorant vote," the result of the franchise in various states, the attitudes of men toward the movement, and "the influence of woman in the home, in the office, in the workshop and in public life."[1]

Clad in white and donning a "great picture hat," Mary Flinn opened on Monday before a full house of "fashionably gowned women" and an equal share of business men, many of whom filled "Peanut Heaven" and draped over the balcony railings. As one woman, Florence E. Little, described the scene later that week, "The masculine precinct up aloft was fairly dripping with good humor and smiling expectation of more slapstick comedy to come. It was evident that almost to a man they had been too busy to look at their programs, and were sitting in innocent and pathetic trustfulness that Harry Davis would 'send along another good one.' It was cruel to take advantage of this childlike attitude; therefore the shock was great."[2] As the crowd sat expectantly, the lights dimmed, all but one, into which stepped a "dainty golden-haired young girl exquisitely gowned." As the men leaned forward for a better look, Mary announced herself and her affiliation: "Equal Franchise Federation of Western Pennsylvania." At that, a thin man in the front row of the gallery threw himself back into his seat, slammed his legs onto the railing, and groaned, "Aw-aw, piffle!"[3] "A low felt masculine muttering rolled up and down the rows," and seven men reportedly slapped their felt derbies and bowlers on their heads and hastily walked out. But when Mary invoked Abraham Lincoln against the stirring backdrop of his portrait on the stereopticon, quoting his statement that "I go for all, sharing the privilege of the Government, who assist in bearing its burdens, by no means excluding women," the man in the front row sat up and took notice.[4]

The *Daily Post* reported the next day that Mary "spoke 10 minutes, but in those 10 minutes she told why she and a hundred thousand other women in Pennsylvania want the franchise, and why they think they can make Pennsylvania a greater, better more honest state, if they get it."[5] "The suffrage movement, ladies and gentlemen, will surely go marching on," Mary concluded, "but the pace will be faster, the goal will be reached quicker if you join it and help do a work for it until Liberty's torch shall not only enlighten New York harbor but this whole country."[6] Ida Morton spoke on Tuesday, Adele Shaw on Wednesday, Hannah Patterson on Thursday, and Mary Bakewell, the new president of the federation, on Friday.

It was Lucy who gave the closing arguments during the Saturday matinee and evening performances. In her characteristically deep, booming voice, she put forth the arguments that she would come to articulate countless times to countless crowds in the months and years to come. Her thundering rhetoric was difficult to ignore.

Lucy vigorously denied the argument that husbands, fathers, brothers, and sons represented women at the polls, and she refuted several of the common arguments against granting women the vote. "Some better reason must be found for depriving women of the ballot than the assertion that if they vote they ought to fight and do police duty. If it were true that no men were allowed to vote except those who are able and willing to do military and police service it might be consistent to debar women, but so long as the infirm, the old, the halt, the maimed and the blind are freely admitted to the ballot box this argument against woman's suffrage will not hold good." She went on. "Of the clergymen who denounce woman's suffrage, not one in 20 of their number is fit for military duty, of the teachers who oppose it not one in four could shoulder a musket, while of the lawyers who follow a case the majority could not be defenders of their country should the necessity arise."

It has been asserted that the ballot has been of no benefit to the laboring man. It is not right, if this is true, to blame the ballot; we should censure its poor use. Every political huckster seeks to control the labor vote, so the working man is assailed on all hands, and that he gets no fair recompense is not the fault of his enfranchisement. There are 20,000,000 women of voting age in the United States, and they ought to be allowed to vote. If they do get the ballot you will find that every professional politician in the land will be asking what he can do for women. If organized female labor is driven to work under conditions which produced the horrible Triangle Shirtwaist fire, such as inefficient factory inspection, inadequate protection from fire, it will not be because they were unprotected and helpless, but because they have not yet learned to use their ballot well. The responsibility for the death of 140 of the working girls in that fire now rests entirely upon the male voters in New York City and clearly proves that man cannot represent woman because he forces her to work under conditions against which she is rebelling and the dangers of which she clearly comprehends.

The most enthusiastic advocates of woman's suffrage do not anticipate that the ballot will cure all the evils from which we suffer, but they do believe that the exercise of the ballot will give woman a beneficial experience and a knowledge of political conditions which she cannot otherwise acquire. Justice will be worth more to women than chivalry, if they could not have both.[7]

Throughout the week, a cadre of eighteen young "society" women was on hand to collect informal ballots on the issue of suffrage from the public as they milled through the marathon event. Among them was Eliza, still home on Christmas break from her senior year at Vassar.

Reviews of the campaign kickoff at the Grand Opera House week were mixed. Certainly it garnered a great deal of attention. In a full-page article on the event for the *Sunday Post*, Florence Little maintained that the suffragists sought the vote for women "not as an end in itself, but as the quickest and most effective aid to securing just legislation in matters affecting women."[8] And in defense of the young women who dressed in their "prettiest gowns," Little quoted one of them: "We have got to stop those caricaturists from picturing us suffragists as 'frumps.'"[9] It remained to be seen if the stunt would prove effective. As one *Daily Post* headline quipped, "State Lawmakers in 1913 Will Decide If Play Is To Be Tragedy."[10]

That same early January week, Lucy hosted a most auspicious houseguest at 5400 Forbes Street. Beatrice Forbes-Robertson, a noted English actress and playwright in the Shakespearian tradition, and one of the organizers of the Actor's Suffrage League, had married a prominent New York lawyer, Swinden Hale, and left the footlights to devote her time to forwarding the cause as a "constitutional suffragist," the non-militant variety. On January 10, she spoke to the Twentieth Century Club in the morning and to the Equal Franchise Federation in Carnegie Lecture Hall in the evening.[11] The Twentieth Century Club meeting also included an opposing argument presented by Mrs. Horace Brock of Philadelphia. While the club leaned rather toward the anti side of the argument, enough members were suffragists that it was decided to offer a more balanced treatment of the topic. Each woman was given four minutes to speak.[12]

"Without votes," admitted Mrs. Hale, "women could ultimately achieve their ends, but . . . in one year women could do with the ballot what it would take ten years to do without it." "Politics is not in the business world only," she added. "The protection of the home needs the votes of the women. Politics concern the baby as well as the businessman." She went on to say, "There are two fundamental ideas held by the opposers of woman's suffrage. One is that woman is half angel and half child—too holy to be defiled and mentally undeveloped—and the other, that there are already too many voters. To an English woman the latter seems a sad commentary. Are Americans beginning to distrust their own splendid democracy?" She concluded with her hope "that man and woman, using their common intellect and experience will walk together, hand in hand, as brother and sister through this beautiful world which today is so full of muddles and mistakes."[13]

Mrs. Brock countered. She suggested that suffragists were "playing with dangerous things that they did not understand." A shudder ran through the room as she suggested that "Suffrage for women means women in politics whether they will or no. They will have to serve as jurors!" Loud applause followed as she added, "Men don't want you in the courts. You have other rights and privileges that men don't have. Men are supposed to support their wives. . . . Of what benefit is it going to be to the State to upset the existing order of things?" Finally she concluded, "A serious side of the suffrage question is the antagonism it will create between the sexes." "Men are made to do the rough things, but women the finer work of the world. Women stand for the ideal, the spiritual. The suffrage movement stands for materialism."[14] This was only the beginning of the battle between the suffragists and the women who would oppose them.

* * *

The biggest coup that winter of 1912 was unfettered access to the media . . . for a day. The management of the *Pittsburgh Sun* was sympathetic to the cause and offered the suffragists full control of the February 29 edition of the paper, from editorial, to production, to circulation. So it was that at eight o'clock on a fair February morning in 1912, sixteen women filed into the *Sun* offices at the corner of Wood Street and Liberty Avenue, dressed in long, slim, tailored suits and broad-brimmed, deep-crowned hats. With a couple exceptions, these women were not seasoned journalists. They were club and society women, debutantes, professional women, and housewives. But each one went straight to a desk in the newsroom, sat down, and went to work.

It was Leap Day, a day recognized as a time to turn the tables on traditional gender norms. In Irish tradition, it was known as Ladies' Privilege or Bachelor's Day, the one day when it was considered acceptable for a woman to propose marriage to a man. In Pittsburgh, as the women's suffrage movement was gaining momentum, it was a day for a cast of female characters to assume editorial leadership of the city's evening newspaper for one very special issue.[15]

Advance advertising promised "Something New Under the Sun for Women by Women! Once-in-Four-Years! . . . SO NOVEL, SO REMARKABLE IN ITS NATURE that it will mark an epoch in newspaper history, not alone of Pittsburgh, but of the United States." The ad admitted, "An Innovation is a Gamble." But newspapermen across the country watched with keen interest and placed advance orders for their copies of the "Women's Suffrage Edition." It was a unique moment in the history of journalism.

The women had visited the paper's offices in advance to observe the operation, so they knew exactly where to go to assume their assignments for the day. As the guest editors took their places, the regular staff watched with trepidation and wondered what, exactly, these interlopers would ask of them. They were only women, after all. But they were formidable women, all of them ardent members of the Equal Franchise Federation of Western Pennsylvania.

Euphemia Bakewell sat at the managing editor's desk. Newly married, she continued to use her maiden name as a regular contributor to the *Pittsburgh Daily Post* on the topic of women's suffrage. Her sister, Mary, federation president, was the editorial writer and contributed several poems and limericks. Jennie Bradley Roessing served as city editor. Lucy assumed the role of assistant city editor. Florence Little, a published writer and painter and a

WOMEN'S SUFFRAGE EDITION
OF THE
PITTSBURGH SUN
BY THE
Equal Franchise Federation
February 29th, 1912.

GOVERNMENT OF BY ⅋ FOR THE PEOPLE

ARE NOT WOMEN PEOPLE?

The special suffrage edition of the *Pittsburgh Sun* had the highest circulation in the paper's history.

director of the Women's Press Club, was named news editor. Hannah Patterson, who had contributed to the "Why I Am a Suffragist" series in the *Pittsburg Press* earlier that winter, was the business manager. Other women served as music, art, and drama critics and took charge of publicity, circulation, telegraph news, and the society and school pages.

Dozens more served as contributors from afar. Among them was Anna Howard Shaw, who called the band of sixteen "a splendid enthusiastic lot" who "ought to succeed in stirring things up."[16] Others included Lucy Anthony, niece of pioneering suffragist Susan B. Anthony; Jane Addams of Chicago, the renowned social worker and settlement activist who would go on in 1931 to be America's first woman to win the Nobel Peace Prize; Inez Milholland, the beautiful young lawyer who had been Eliza's contemporary at Vassar and who would ultimately die a martyr for the cause; and Alva Vanderbilt Belmont, leader of New York's "gilded suffragists," who declared that "to sweep, to dust, to scrub the household of political corruption is part of woman's new mission."[17]

The editors sought out the opinions of local politicians, businessmen, attorneys, doctors, and clergy. Mayor William A. Magee and most members of city council wrote statements in favor of suffrage with Magee declaring, "It is useless to debate the inevitable."[18] Cables and telegrams poured in from leaders and lawmakers in every corner of the world with messages of support and congratulations for the *Sun*'s journalistic triumph. School board member Taylor Allderdice and Shadyside Academy principal Dr. W. R. Crabbe were among the educators who provided pro-suffrage statements. With such a diversity of supportive voices, the paper represented the most comprehensive and effective suffrage propaganda piece produced to date anywhere in the country.

"From the first page to last page it was a paper of, by and for women," the *Pittsburgh Post* reported.[19] A woman's perspective was applied to every story, whether it originated in police court, the mayor's office, the governor's mansion, or the halls of Congress. They wrote news stories, editorials, and critical reviews. They conducted interviews. And they showcased the accomplishments of women in art, music, and drama alongside celebrity endorsements from the leading ladies of the day. One news item welcomed the first Colored Women's Equal Franchise League of Pittsburgh to the struggle, headed by Mrs. Israel S. Lee. Suffrage news from abroad cited progress in more than twenty countries.

Even the sporting editor was booted for the day, as Miss Emily McCreery focused on female athletes. A half column was devoted to world champion baseball star Miss Myrtle Rowe, who happened to come from New Kensington, twenty miles up the river from Pittsburgh. Another story profiled Miss Cora Livingston, champion wrestler. A survey of local girls' basketball teams pointed out that basketball promotes strong healthy bodies. "These strong healthy bodies will maintain intelligent virile brains fit to decide the burning issues of the day at the polls," commented a reporter the next day.[20] There were photos of golf champion Mrs. John Raymond Price and of a jubilant Helen Hathaway Robison Britton of St. Louis, the only woman in America to own a baseball team. Miss McCreery even managed to snag an interview with the usually reticent captain of the Pittsburgh Pirates, Fred Clarke, who provided plenty of pro-suffrage quotes for the sporting page.

Aside from naming women's suffrage as a matter of simple justice, the collective voices of endorsement cited numerous problems that women could address more effectively with access to the voting booth: impure food and water, unreasonably young ages of consent, child labor, white slavery, poor working conditions for women, vice, war, unsanitary tenement conditions, inefficient schools, and more.

The paper was not lacking in humor. On the front page, one of the lead stories carried the byline of "A Mere Man" and related the experience of working for a female taskmaster. "The most striking thing about suffragists when they publish a newspaper," wrote the author, "is that they do not remove their hats when they begin to work. This shows that they have good nerves. Their concentration is splendid. The fact that they could wade through the mass of news matter which develops during the course of a day, with plumes waving about their heads sometimes obstructing their vision, without their nervous temperament putting on a three-act show, is beyond man's understanding. But they did it."[21]

"Many of the staff had never before this written a line for the newspapers nor ever had their photographs in print," Euphemia Bakewell reported. "I think none of us had ever seen a newspaper plant before. It certainly interested us to see the great presses, the clicking linotypes, the matrix making and the other divisions of the work getting the paper out." [22]

When it came time to print, it was Euphemia Bakewell who went down to the pressroom, a union stronghold. There she found waiting for her a card of membership in the International Printing and Pressmen and Assistants' Union of North America: "This is to certify that Miss Euphemia Bakewell is entitled to work in the pressroom of *The Pittsburgh Sun* and is entitled to all union privileges for this one day. W. J. Smith, Secretary." With that validation, Euphemia threw the hefty lever that set the spinning rolls and whirring wheels in motion. And as the first damp paper came off the presses, she took hold of it triumphantly.

It then fell to the women to get the paper out to readers. In limousines and on foot, thousands of women armed with bundles of newspapers took to the streets, which grew more crowded as the word spread. The papers quickly sold for one cent each. The "suffrage newsies" even enlisted the help of the alluring celebrity mysticist, Anna Eva Fay, who peddled papers from an automobile in between her performances at the Grand Opera House. Groups gathered—on the streets, in cars and trains, theaters and shops, in homes—to discuss the contents of the unprecedented paper. The special issue contained more local advertising than any other Pittsburgh paper that day, and its circulation was the highest in the *Sun*'s history.

The suffragists anticipated that the paper might have even greater impact on women than on men. "We find it easier to convert men than women," Euphemia Bakewell explained. "That may seem strange, but it is easily explained. The man is used to politics, and is awake to the progress of the times. He can grasp political situations easily, and when they are brought to his notice, he can easily adapt himself to them. With the woman, who has hitherto had no experience in politics and who has not followed politics, all this is too new to her. Therefore, we are so confident with our newspaper venture. We know that the reading of the Thursday *Sun* will not only hold the interest of women but will confirm the vagrant views of some men, convert others, and make enthusiastic supporters of many." [23]

Lucy declared this first suffrage issue of any paper to be "a coup for both the suffrage organization and the *Pittsburgh Sun*." [24] Before they were through, the suffragists would garner the support of not only the *Morning Post* and the *Evening Sun* but also the *Pittsburgh Leader*, the *Pittsburgh Post*, the *Sun*

Telegraph, the *Chronicle Telegraph*, the *Pittsburg Press*, and the *Pittsburgh Dispatch*, the paper in which the renowned Nellie Bly published her investigative articles on female factory workers.[25]

The same week as the special edition of the *Sun*, the Pittsburgh papers reported on the militant activities of the suffragettes in England, who had smashed plate glass windows of large department stores, government buildings, and private clubs in London as a protest demonstration. Led by the infamous Emmeline Pankhurst, 120 women were arrested and sentenced to two months in prison. The Pittsburgh suffragists must have taken some pleasure in knowing that their peaceful but persuasive approach garnered more positive public attention than did the militant activities of their English sisters. Still, it would be another eight arduous years—a rollercoaster ride of buoyed hopes and dashing disappointments—before American women would win their battle, a battle that would employ the power of the press as just one of many ingenious tactics in a large and diversified arsenal.

The inaugural suffrage edition of the *Sun* was well timed. A legislative commission to revise the election laws of Pennsylvania was to hold a hearing on the question of woman suffrage in Philadelphia in three weeks, on March 22, 1912, to consider three questions: (1) Do the majority of women desire the right of suffrage, and what statistics are available as a basis of judgment on this question? (2) Will the right of suffrage, if granted, be exercised generally by women, and what statistics are available on this question? (3) Will the exercise of suffrage by women result in a benefit to the community, and what statistics are available on this question? In anticipation of this event, Frances Orr wrote in the *Pittsburgh Daily Post*, "The real question is, Can America, the free and civilized country we mean to have her, continue to countenance so palpable an injustice as the political discrimination against women?"[26] As it turned out, a small Pittsburgh contingent of five women from the Equal Franchise Federation, led by Mary Bakewell, went to the hearing, but Mary reported that time ran out and she was not able to speak.[27]

While the suffrage movement in Pennsylvania had originally focused on education, the Equal Franchise Federation eventually decided that it was time instead for political action to secure an amendment to the state Constitution. A constitutional amendment would require passage of a resolution at two successive sessions of the state legislature, in 1913 and then again in 1915, before being put to a public vote in November 1915. There was much work to be done.

With this in mind, a large delegation from Allegheny County led by

Jennie Roessing traveled to Philadelphia for the 1912 annual convention of the state suffrage organization. It was a "rather fusty" group, in Lucy's estimation, and the "radical" newcomers from Pittsburgh apparently made quite an impression. By the end of the convention, Jennie Roessing was president, Mary Bakewell was first vice president, Lucy was second vice president, and Hannah Patterson was chairman of the Women's Suffrage Committee. All of them under the age of thirty-one, with the exception of Mary Bakewell, they had seized the reins of the statewide movement.

Working with a number of attorneys volunteering from around the state, the group drafted an amendment and moved its headquarters to Harrisburg. "We were regarded as villains by the legislators," Lucy later recalled.[28] They faced considerable opposition from leaders in the Senate as well as the Republican governor, John K. Tener, whose successors over the ensuing decade—Martin Grove Brumbaugh and William Cameron Sproul—would not prove to be much more supportive.

In order to counter the opposition, securing the popular vote would necessitate a targeted grassroots movement, county by county, town by town, district by district, street corner by street corner. Recognizing this, Carrie Chapman Catt conceived of a strategy that would harness the energies of women on the local level and empower them to effect incremental influence.

Carrie Chapman Catt, who would serve as president of the National American Woman Suffrage Association from 1900 to 1904 and again from 1915 to 1920, became a mentor to Eliza.

Catt had been working as a political activist since 1886, when she joined the Iowa Woman Suffrage Association. Ultimately, she would succeed Susan B. Anthony as president of the National American Woman Suffrage Association, serving from 1900 to 1904, when Anna Howard Shaw took over, and again from 1915 until the Nineteenth Amendment was passed in 1920. In the meantime, her New York Suffrage School on Madison Avenue became a mecca for aspiring suffragists.[29]

Eager to enlist in the fight, and with the enthusiastic approval of both her parents, Eliza enrolled in a short course at Catt's school the fall following her 1912 Vassar graduation.[30] There she got to know the iconic woman who would become her mentor. Already twice widowed and well into middle age, Catt had deep-set soulful eyes with perpetual dark circles below and narrowly pursed lips. Her exuberant, wavy hair was tamed into two great white tufts, one on either side of her heart-shaped face. She stood a head taller than Anna Howard Shaw, and like Dr. Shaw, she would become something of a fixture on the local Pittsburgh suffrage scene and in the Kennedy household.

Also serving as the head of the International Woman Suffrage Alliance, which boasted an active presence on five continents, Catt brought a big-picture perspective to what was a decidedly grassroots campaign. To the ladies of the Equal Franchise Federation, her message of worldwide suffrage solidarity was inspiring and hopeful:

> When movements are new and weak, Parliaments laugh at them; when they are in their educational stages, Parliaments meet them with silent contempt; when they are ripe and ready to become law, Parliaments evade responsibility. Our movement has reached the last stage. The history of the past two years has demonstrated that fact beyond the shadow of a doubt. Parliaments have stopped laughing at woman suffrage, and politicians have begun to dodge. It is the inevitable premonition of coming victory.

> Statesmen, be it remembered, are men who serve their country and great causes regardless of consequences to themselves; politicians are men who serve their parties and themselves regardless of consequences to their country or great causes. The twentieth century has produced a far larger crop of politicians than statesmen, and it is the politicians who are creating the delay.[31]

* * *

Catt's inspiring rhetoric, backed by training in practical tactics, empowered the suffragists of the Equal Franchise Federation to embark on their own relentless campaign. "It was very fortunate that we knew very little about practical politics," Lucy would recall long after the vote had been won. "We wasted no time on attempting to pull wires at the court house or city hall, but took the cause directly to the people."[32] And they met the people wherever and whenever they could. Using a variety of clever tactics, the Kennedy sisters and their allies provided a glimpse of the tenacious political style for which they would come to be known . . . and ultimately feared.

Weather permitting, they held street meetings in every part of the county where they could secure permits. Few enough automobiles navigated the city streets that it was possible to set up in bustling locations like the center of downtown at Wood and Diamond, in the shadow of the Germania Savings Bank and the Mercantile Trust Company, or on the steps of H. H. Richardson's imposing Allegheny County Courthouse, or at the center of the fashionable East Liberty district at Highland and Penn. Lucy recalled that "sometimes it was possible to hold 100 meetings in one night, with every good speaker speaking five or six times from soap boxes and open automobiles."[33]

They placed advertisements in every streetcar in the county. They appeared in booths at every county fair, making speeches and passing out leaflets. They attended every picnic at Kennywood, the amusement park that had opened in 1899 as an attraction at the end of the Mellon family's Monongahela Street Railway. When the Ringling Brothers Circus came to town, the suffragists again had a booth.[34]

When the Pittsburgh Exposition was in session, with its three great halls dominating the confluence of the Allegheny and Monongahela Rivers to form the Ohio, the suffragists had another booth. The Exposition was a curious hybrid launched in 1889 that offered the down-home feel of a county fair coupled with the exotic intrigue of a world's fair. Poultry exhibits were comingled with fashion shows from New York and Paris as well as performances by the nation's best bands and orchestras, featuring the likes of Victor Herbert and John Philip Sousa. It offered a little something for everyone, a sort of one-stop accessibility to a broad cross section of the population—from working folk to socialites—with whom the suffragists could share their message. During the 1913 Exposition, that message attracted a thousand new members to the federation each week.[35]

When the Automobile Owners' Association of Pittsburgh opened its eighth annual automobile show in January 1914, the suffragists were there. Fifty glistening new machines valued at two million dollars were displayed amidst white pillars and light posts beneath a billowing canopy of soft-toned green touched with red and white. From motorcycles to limousines, "plebeian to aristocratic," foreign and domestic, gasoline and electric powered, the exhibits and "glib-tongued demonstrators" offered something for everyone. There was even a used car section in the basement. The women, it was reported, favored the electric models.[36]

Approaching labor, they secured engraved resolutions in favor of suffrage from nearly every one of the unions. The exceptions, Lucy ruefully noted, were the drivers of the beer wagons and the Bartenders Association. The suffragists visited every mill, catching both the morning and the evening shift changes as they spoke from automobiles and soapboxes at the factory gates, handing out pamphlets to the throngs of workers, exhausted and sweaty from their twelve-hour shifts and lugging their empty lunch pails home or to their neighborhood bars for refreshment.

They held meetings for the teachers in every school in Allegheny County, plying them with coffee and home-baked angel food cakes. Ultimately, some two thousand teachers enrolled as dues-paying members of the Equal Franchise Federation.[37]

They appeared at a socialist debate at the Labor Temple and at an agricultural fair at Duquesne Garden. There they maintained a booth, distributed literature, and delivered lectures amidst daily demonstrations of the slaughtering and dressing of poultry and exhibitions of the training and taming of wild and vicious horses in the garden's arena.[38]

They contacted every congregation of every denomination, and some six hundred became active supporters of the cause, with leadership from their clergy. Bishop Whitehead, head of the Episcopal Church, was among them. "It is a great thing to be living in these stirring times," he said, "when reforms of every sort are in the air, when every man and woman is needed, when each one must have responsibility, not transferable to anyone else, and when the personal participation of women in civic and municipal affairs is desirable and necessary."[39]

And wherever they went, the suffragists were armed with literature, hundreds of thousands of pamphlets and flyers and cards espousing their cause from every angle. Some of it was produced by the National American Woman Suffrage Association or the Interurban Woman Suffrage Council in New York. Some of it was supplied by the Pennsylvania Woman Suffrage Association. And some originated with the Equal Franchise Federation.

* * *

Toward the end of that year, on Friday evening, October 18, 1912, the Equal
Franchise Federation planned a large gathering in Old City Hall. Days earlier,
to promote the event, Lucy organized a tour of the county by ten automobiles.
Despite a downpour and "endangering of millinery," the motorcade left the
federation headquarters on Stanwix Street, draped in yellow with banners
flying and horns tooting, and paraded through downtown before disbanding,
each car to a different district, to distribute flyers. "We want the ballot and fear
of contracting a cold or spoiling millinery is no consideration," said Euphemia
Bakewell, who had charge of the upcoming meeting. Jennie Kennedy and
Mary Bakewell occupied the first car, followed by Mary Flinn and her mother.
Eliza was in car number seven.[40] Before the meeting, a band paraded the streets
accompanied by boys carrying illuminated signs.

It was still raining on the night of the meeting, which nonetheless drew
a crowd of fifteen hundred. That night, a new political party was established:
the nonpartisan Woman's Suffrage Party of Allegheny County. A huge blue
flag with six white stars representing the suffrage states was spread across the
platform, where Hannah Patterson welcomed the crowd.[41] Mary Bakewell
was greeted with cheers as she was elected chairman, and Jennie Roessing
was elected secretary. Bakewell and Roessing, along with Mary Flinn, had
attended the Republican State Convention in May to ask for a woman's suffrage plank in the party platform.

Representatives of the national parties—the Democratic, Republican,
Socialist, and newly formed progressive Bull Moose—spoke, as did Julian
Kennedy, William Flinn, and several other men. Mrs. Jean Nelson Penfield,
chairman of the New Work Woman Suffrage Party, was on hand to congratulate the fledgling organization: "A few years ago such a meeting as you have
here tonight would be considered almost incredible," she began.

> "It is a great privilege to be present at the birth of a new political
> party. . . . The democracy of women's suffrage is its greatest power.
> All men and women can meet in our party on equal terms. Some
> of us are rich and others poor, but it makes no difference. We are
> not all of the same religion, and we do not all believe the same as to
> methods; but it makes no difference. We are all bound together by
> the justice of women's suffrage. . . . If every man and woman who
> says that he or she stands for women's suffrage tonight will stand by
> this organization, Pennsylvania will soon follow Washington and

California, and you will vote for the President of the United States in 1916."[42]

A resolution was passed at this massive rally to hold a convention no later than September 15, 1913.

The object of the new party was to establish a leader in each legislative district. And savvy suffragists knew, as Mrs. Penfield advised, that "an amendment cannot be carried at the polls by a spectacular campaign, beginning a few months before election. Three years from this November [in 1915], we hope our amendment will go before the people for the popular vote."[43] Lucy would later recall that the battle was "contested at every step."[44]

Despite their prominence, the Pittsburgh society suffragists did not enjoy the height of celebrity status of their New York socialite sisters, who leveraged their star power to further the cause. Those "gilded suffragists" were the media darlings of their day, and the suffragists capitalized on the public's hunger to follow their clothes, their parties, and their travel.[45] The grand dame of them all was Mrs. A. H. K. Belmont, the former Mrs. William Vanderbilt. When the National Congressional Union held their first meeting and raised forty-one thousand dollars in fifteen minutes, ten thousand of it reportedly came from Mrs. Belmont.[46] She and her peers were women of considerable power and influence, and they knew how to use it.

What Lucy and Eliza and their cohort did have was access—to the media, to the men in power, to the women and men who could join them in the trenches, and to sufficient funding to fuel the effort. Through Julian's business connections and the family's rising social standing, they had garnered the support of newspapers, politicians in power, and the city's elite. And they were not afraid to use it.

* * *

As the suffrage movement gathered momentum, those who would thwart it were rallying their own troops. The National Association Opposed to Woman Suffrage (NAOWS) had been organized in 1911, with the support of some wealthy women, some Catholic clergy, and the distilling and brewing industries, who had every reason to fear the influence of women. At a luncheon in New York, the group had declared that they would "follow the activities of the suffragists step by step."[47] With the movement gaining traction in Pennsylvania, New Jersey, Maryland, Virginia, Ohio, Oregon, Kansas, Missouri, Kentucky, and New Hampshire, the anti-suffragists, or "antis," would be kept running to try and keep up with the "suffs." By the time of the first-round passage of the amendment in the state legislature, Lucy reported, "the opposition forces were now truly awake."[48]

In the wake of the January debate at the Twentieth Century Club, the antis launched a new organization and a strong presence in Pittsburgh. Supported by the national movement, they called themselves "home conservationists" and maintained that they did not raise their daughters to be voters. With Julia Morgan Harding and Eliza D. Armstrong leading the charge, the Pittsburgh Association Opposed to Woman Suffrage waged a fierce battle of its own. The group held its first meeting of fifty women at Hamilton Hall in Oakland on February 12, 1912. Their second meeting drew a hundred of the city's most fashionable women. By November, they had ten thousand signatures against suffrage in Pennsylvania.[49] By the end of the decade, the National Association Opposed to Woman Suffrage would claim a total membership of 700,000.[50]

The antis dismissed the suffragists and their activities as a "cult" and a "bluff." They insisted that suffrage was a privilege, not a right; that it had not benefitted women in the states and countries where they had the ballot; that women in politics would be a menace to society and the home; that it would introduce more immigrant, Negro, and immoral voices; that it would double the cost of elections; that the suffrage movement encouraged a state of neurotic unrest and hysteria; that women's views were already adequately represented by their fathers, brothers, husbands, and sons; that women could be more effective in advancing their interests "free and unfettered by political ties and obligations"; and that, quite simply, women did not want it.[51] "Indifference is a greater foe of the suffrage cause than the active manifestations of the anti-suffragists," they argued. "We cannot have manly men unless we preserve womanly women."[52] Julia Morgan, according to one report, had gone so far as to suggest that "suffragists should be spanked."[53] The antis accused their opponents of perpetrating "make-believe quotations" and "fake" news stories.[54] Like the suffs, the antis maintained a robust arsenal of badges and literature.

But to the members of the Equal Franchise Federation, the arguments of the antis seemed ludicrous. In her regular column in the *Post*, Euphemia Bakewell set forth the anti arguments and dismissed them one by one. She described suffrage as a duty of "transcendent importance," and asserted that women brought their own political gifts to the political process, that they could effect positive change, and that, ultimately, it was a matter of simple justice.[55]

A generation older than Lucy and most of her cohorts, Julia Morgan and Eliza Armstrong were unmarried women who righteously defended the sanctity of marriage and motherhood and the rightful place of women as being in the home. To Lucy, a happily married young mother, their arguments that suffrage would make women too masculine seemed particularly spurious. She predicted that woman suffrage would be "one of the great forces in the advance of civilization."[56]

Julia Morgan was from a political family, a descendant of Ebenezer Denny, the first mayor of Pittsburgh and of Harmar Denny, who had served in both the Pennsylvania House of Representatives and the US Congress. A former newspaperwoman, she had been active in the Daughters of the American Revolution and helped to found both the Twentieth Century Club and the Tuesday Musical Club. Julia was a close friend of Mrs. Bertha Rauh, head of the local chapter of the National Council of Jewish Women and an ardent suffragist.

Eliza Armstrong, also a member of the Twentieth Century Club, was the daughter of an Irish immigrant who had made his fortune in the coal and coke business. Her father, Charles, was infamous for a violent strike-breaking incident at his eponymous mine in Sewickley Township on November 29, 1874, an incident that involved a great deal of gunfire in which four men died and for which he was convicted of "aggravated riot" and fined.[57] As a young woman during the Civil War, Eliza had helped to organize relief efforts for local soldiers. Four decades later, emerging out of relative obscurity, she stepped up to a leadership role as the anti-suffrage movement was being launched. She would maintain her anti-suffrage stance until the day she died at the age of ninety in 1935. In 1912, when they began to go toe to toe with the women of the Equal Franchise Federation, Julia Morgan was fifty-eight and Eliza Armstrong was sixty-seven. Lucy was thirty-two.

Looking back at the events of the year, 1912 had been a particularly busy one, in Pittsburgh and beyond. The nation had added three new suffrage states through the November election—Arizona, Kansas, and Oregon—adding to the six existing ones and doubling the number of women voters to three million, as the suffrage block of the West expanded eastward. Colorado had just sworn in its first female state senator. Nevada's legislature was to decide whether to put the question on the 1914 ballot. New Hampshire and Ohio anticipated that their constitutional amendments would consider the issue. "Even conservative Massachusetts," the *Sunday Post* reported, was waging "an active campaign."[58] And a Men's League for Women's Suffrage had been formed at Dartmouth College. With four Pittsburghers at the helm of the Pennsylvania Woman Suffrage Association, the state headquarters had moved from Philadelphia to Harrisburg for proximity to the legislature.

In Pittsburgh, the Equal Franchise Federation had become a recognized force and had launched a campaign that drew widespread attention and admiration as well as constant media coverage. And when the editor of the *Daily Post* was asked to name two or three prominent suffragists, he listed three: Mary Bakewell, Mary Flinn, and Lucy.[59]

8 TAKING THE FIGHT
TO THE HALLS OF POWER

February 28, 1913, saw another special suffrage edition of the *Sun*. Then, the Pittsburgh suffragists went practically straight from the newspaper offices to the train station, boarding the overnight express for Washington, where a national parade was to take place on March 3, 1913, the day before Woodrow Wilson's inauguration. Celebrating the first change of administration in sixteen years, the monumental inauguration would include a parade of its own, but it did not include a place for suffragists. They would have to stage their own.

Joining the throng of some five thousand marchers, a contingent of Pittsburghers included several of the members of the core group that had met in the Kennedys' living room just a few years before. Lucy and Eliza were accompanied by eight of their compatriots: Jennie Roessing, Hannah Patterson, and Mary and Euphemia Bakewell, as well as Mrs. Cornelius D. Scully, Mrs. Robert Levin, Mrs. J. Booth Orr, and Miss Mary Cree Porter.[1] Like the New York parade they had joined on May 4, 1912, a thronging extravaganza of fifteen thousand marchers, the Washington parade offered the opportunity not only to show their support but also to learn.

As the day for the parade approached, tensions rose in Washington between the suffragists and the antis, who had established a headquarters near the parade-planning office at 1420 F Street. Two burly private watchmen paced back and forth between the opposing camps, each suspicious that the other might resort to violence.[2] The antis accused the suffs of slinging mud on the windows of their headquarters. The suffs flatly denied the allegations.[3]

Refusing to be relegated to the side streets, the suffragists had fought to get permission to parade down the tree-lined main thoroughfare of Pennsylvania Avenue on their way to a mass meeting in Continental Hall.[4] The route from the Peace Monument at the Capitol to the Treasury Building was two miles long, and streetcar operations were interrupted for the duration.[5] Neither President Taft nor President-elect Wilson was present that day, but Mrs. Taft took to the reviewing stand hoping to watch the thousands of women of all ages—and hundreds of men—march by, along with twenty-five floats and fifty mounted heralds, many decked out in colorful costumes and allegorical pageantry. Led by Grand Marshall Mrs. Richard Coke Burleson, mounted on a black charger, the parade had seven sections representing various aspects of the movement and presenting "a kaleidoscopic picture of ever-shifting color,"[6] a mélange of millinery.

Inez Milholland of New York, Eliza's Vassar contemporary, was dressed in purple astride a skittish horse and served as the herald whose trumpet blast signaled the start. Prominent placement was given to Lucy and Eliza's mentors, Anna Howard Shaw and Carrie Chapman Catt. Progress in the nine suffrage states as well as Norway, China, New Zealand, Finland, and Australia was also depicted. Interspersed were detachments of women farmers, manual workers, nurses, business people, college graduates, and homemakers.[7] Miss Anna Hall marched in fetters "after the most approved design of the Federal penitentiaries," to represent the bondage of women.[8] The Pennsylvania contingent with its ten Pittsburghers—including Lucy and Eliza—marched toward the rear, taking it all in, still dressed in their traveling clothes but draped with yellow and white ribbons bearing the word *Pennsylvania*.

This parade was not a simple procession of earnest women. It was a spectacle, a progressive pageant, enough to awe the small band of women from Pittsburgh.

But early on the spectacle took an ugly turn. With an estimated three hundred thousand spectators in attendance, the marchers had to fight their way through the crowds from the very beginning, and they took more than an hour to traverse the first ten blocks.[9] The hostile crowd climbed over and under the stout wire ropes that had been stretched the length of Pennsylvania Avenue. They swamped the marchers, taunting them with jibes and insults, tripping them, grabbing and pinching them, tearing their clothes, and spitting tobacco juice in their faces. Many of the women were reduced to tears. Mrs. Taft and her entourage were driven away by the bedlam before the parade even reached them. A few fought back, including one member of the prancing "Petticoat Cavalry" who "struck a hoodlum a stinging blow across the face with her riding crop in reply to a scurrilous remark."[10]

The police force of 575 men proved powerless against the surging crowds. The men in blue were at best indifferent, at worst encouraging the ruffians and laughing at the turmoil. One of the boy scouts who worked valiantly to drive the crowds back was reportedly beaten by police for interfering.[11] "We were more frightened by the police than by the crowds," one marcher reported.[12] Troops of cavalry from Fort Myer were finally brought in to bring order, pushing aside the district police and driving the mobs back off the street.[13]

To make matters worse, the parade was to culminate by passing a series of tableaux, where scantily clad women in thin drapery waited in bare feet on the cold, gray steps of the Treasury Building. There they would stage an allegorical representation of Columbia summoning to her side Justice, Charity, Liberty, Plenty, Peace, and Hope. The tableaux performances were to climax just as the parade reached them. As envisioned by the organizers, "To the crashing of cymbals and brass, a flying figure in glowing crimson appears—Liberty— unfettered and free among the great assemblage of women and children massed in tableaux on the steps. She poses for an instant at the top of the steps and then with swift running feet sweeps on the plaza below, beckoning her attendants to follow. Thereupon a company of gay and brave girls troop out from between the columns, and with floating scarfs of crimson, rose and gold, weave a glorious dance of joy and freedom."[14] As it turned out, the tableaux performers stood shivering for over an hour, waiting for the halting parade to reach them, until they finally took refuge within the Treasury Building.[15]

At the end of the day, some papers reported, more than three hundred women ended up in Washington hospitals suffering from hysteria, faint- ing, bruises, and shock after being crushed in the unprecedented crowds as the parade fought its way up Pennsylvania Avenue. The avenue, it was also reported, "was deeply littered with paper, parts of millinery, hat pins and other portions of feminine attire."[16] Helen Keller was to have spoken at a meeting in Continental Hall after the parade, but she was too exhausted and unnerved from the day's chaos to attend.

Those who did attend that evening turned the gathering from a suffrage demonstration to an indignation meeting. Their first order of business was to pass a resolution—to be presented to President Wilson after his inauguration the next day—calling on him to demand that Congress launch a thorough investigation of the causes for the poor police protection during the parade.[17] The resolution censured and denounced the "shameful conduct" of the police, "which denied to the marchers for suffrage their rights to parade freely and unmolested in the main streets of the capital, and subjected them to frequent ribald insults from the crowds which all but overwhelmed them."[18] Within two days, the resolution had been introduced in both the House and the

Senate and hearings were underway. Graphic testimony depicted the police behavior, and hundreds of women crowded the corridors and hissed at statements in defense of the blue coats.[19]

The Pennsylvania legislature piled on as well, issuing condemnations of the Washington police who had "scandalously insulted" the "women of character of this Commonwealth."[20] Some expressed sympathies for England's militant suffragists after feeling so thoroughly attacked during the parade. But sympathizing with Mrs. Pankhurst, just days after she and her crew had blown up the country home of Chancellor of the Exchequer David Lloyd George, seemed a bit extreme. Jennie Roessing, on behalf of the Pennsylvania Woman Suffrage Association, instead presented a resolution from the Association that it would continue to employ peaceful educational methods.[21]

A week after the parade debacle, Carrie Chapman Catt was in Pittsburgh, a house guest of the Kennedys, to speak to a crowd of nearly a thousand at Old City Hall and reflect on the Washington affair in the context of the United States and international suffrage movements.[22] In the end, three months later, the police were absolved of blame in the investigation—in fact were praised for their performance—but the suffragists had learned some valuable lessons and further fueled their resolve.[23]

Continuing on the heels of the inauguration, Alice Paul, at just twenty-eight years of age, led the National American Woman's Suffrage Association campaign for the federal amendment. Five hundred strong, Paul's army marched to the Capitol on April 7, through cleared streets and with a police guard almost as great in number. No one wanted a reprise of the March parade. Energized by the march, the women greeted their congressmen with petitions and fervent rhetoric. That day, formal resolutions proposing a constitutional amendment were introduced in both houses of Congress.[24] Suffragists stormed the Capitol repeatedly that month, bringing in their heaviest artillery. Anna Howard Shaw addressed the Senate committee charged with considering the suffrage issue, saying, "We are not afraid of the body of ladies who are going up and down the land opposing suffrage. They are just enough in number so that by holding out their skirts they can make a screen for the men operating dens of vice and iniquity and prostitution to hide behind."[25] The suffragists would go on that year to lobby for a standing committee on woman's suffrage in the House. For twenty-three years, they argued, suffrage bills had been sent to the Judiciary Committee, which had proven to be a "graveyard" for such measures.[26] By January 1914, the latest measure, too, would be dead.[27]

Explaining the move toward what she called a "shortcut" national approach, Alice Paul pointed out that the state-by-state approach had positioned the cause to benefit from the leverage of ten suffrage states, which represented one-fifth of the members of the Senate, one-seventh of the members of Congress, and one-sixth of the electoral vote. That leverage was strengthened by activities in the "campaign states" of Montana, Nevada, North Dakota, New York, Pennsylvania, and New Jersey.[28]

* * *

Even as the 1913 parade in Washington was progressing down Pennsylvania Avenue, the "Rockwell Resolution" for an amendment to the Pennsylvania constitution was progressing through the state legislature in Harrisburg. Pennsylvania was among four states in which the suffragists were pushing for amendments that year, along with New York, New Jersey, and Massachusetts. In Pennsylvania, the resolution had already passed the House, but Senator F. S. McIlhenny, chair of the Senate Judiciary Committee, was stalling in hopes that a vote late in the spring session might get lost in the inevitable chaos of the session's closing weeks. McIlhenny professed to be of open mind, but he delayed the hearing several weeks until March 18. Such sabotage seemed unnecessary, given that the measure was only the first step in a painfully protracted legislative process that would require passage by the legislative sessions of *both* 1913 and 1915 before going to a public referendum in fall 1915. The state amendment was far from a done deal.

In anticipation of the March 18 public hearing by the Senate judiciary committee, the suffragists were hard at work circulating petitions throughout the state. The day before the hearing, they turned out in force to hear Anna Howard Shaw. The crowd of some twelve hundred people crowded onto the floor, into the galleries, and along the side lines. They stood six deep in the lobby behind the rail. Even more were expected the next day, when the list of speakers would include Dr. Shaw and Mary Bakewell during the day and Julian Kennedy at the YMCA that evening. As the day's session opened, the legislature halls and galleries were choked with advocates of both sides, although the suffragists were reportedly in the majority by almost ten to one. It was the largest crowd at a legislative hearing that any of the oldest men in Harrisburg could remember.

The suffragists wore daffodils, while the antis wore red American Beauty roses, and "the red and yellow did not mix."[29] Yet as each side made its case during the two-hour hearing, the opponents were respectful, "except to snicker softly and sarcastically at times."[30] Senators also showed their colors; those who preferred not to display the daffodils or roses instead wore white carnations, or no flower at all.

At the daytime hearing, each side was to be given just one hour.[31] Both sides declared their concern for the welfare of children and working girls and women. Both purported to be intensely interested in good government and social service.

The antis, fewer in number, were not apologetic about their supporters' low turnout. "They are too busy attending to their babies and keeping watch over their homes," explained Grace Hamilton, one of the Pittsburgh contingent. "Our women and 92 percent of the women of the state. You hear this noisy, frothy 8 percent of the women who run around demanding the vote."[32] In the end, the vote was postponed yet again.

The resolution was introduced to the Senate on March 25, to be followed by a first reading, a second reading, and finally a vote. By April 2, the vote had still not occurred, and the Senate was split—21 to 21—on whether or not to postpone it, again, until four ill senators could return to the floor. Lieutenant Governor John M. Reynolds cast the deciding vote, moving the resolution to the postponed calendar. In less than a week, the suffragists lost one of their affirmative votes with the death of Senator Jacob C. Stineman of Cambria County.[33]

Prospects looked bleak for passage of the resolution, which required 26 affirmative votes to pass. "Suffrage bill is likely to be defeated," the newspapers reported, and a canvas of the senators showed 28 out of 50 opposed.[34] William Flinn, Mary's father, as the boss of the Republican State Convention, had done little to forward the cause with the party, although he purported to favor the resolution. It was delayed again April 7.

As the rollercoaster ride continued, the rhetoric continued unabated and the suffragists swung between rising hope and plunging despair. The *Pittsburgh Daily Post* editors contended that "the question is not whether women want the suffrage or not. There comes a time when men are not asked whether they wish to serve in the army. They must serve whether they will or not. The time has come for a draft upon the women of the nation to serve the nation and themselves—to serve the nation in every way in which citizenship can magnify and enrich the life of womanhood—as democracy has greatened the life of men."[35]

Finally, on the morning of April 22, the issue came to a vote in Harrisburg. The cards appeared to be stacked decisively in favor of the antis, and the suffragists had to be nervous. But just an hour before the vote, the president of the Central Labor Union of Scranton and the News Writers Union of Scranton, representing some seventy thousand voters, arrived in the office of one of the senators who opposed the resolution, Walter McNichols. His constituents, the man told McNichols, were strongly in favor of the resolution. Back out in the hallways, the senator promptly gave notice to some of his opposition allies that he might have to vote the other way. And when the votes were tallied just before lunch, the resolution passed, 26 to 22.[36]

Lucy was alone in the federation's offices when the news came in from the *Sun*, followed by a joyful telegram from Jennie Roessing. Stunned at the outcome, she had to do her initial celebrating alone, but there followed a full day of "hallelujah meetings" as the suffragists danced between shock and ecstasy.[37] They had cleared the first of three hurdles toward getting the state amendment. But victory was at best two and a half years away.

* * *

By fall 1913, the center of gravity for the Pennsylvania suffrage battle had shifted to Pittsburgh, and the Equal Franchise Federation hosted the forty-fifth annual statewide convention of the Pennsylvania Woman Suffrage Association for three days at the end of October. As the time approached, Julian made a speech to the New Era Club in which he made his own case for suffrage, summed up with a bold statement: "Women are very much more competent than men in certain lines. They have more courage in dealing with questions which should be solved contrary to custom. The objections toward reforms are all financial ones, those which men see first."[38]

Excitement mounted as the opening day approached. Shortly before noon on a Saturday just three days before the convention kickoff, a crowd gathered in the pouring rain outside May's drugstore at Liberty and Fifth Avenues downtown to watch an intriguing performance. Eliza sat alongside Mary Bakewell, smiling and turning over the leaves of a "voiceless speech," each page presenting a pro-suffrage argument in bold letters. "Women in factories are often underpaid and overworked under bad conditions," read one. Others cited additional wrongs that could be righted by women with the ballot. Before the day was out, both Kennedy sisters and both Bakewell sisters, along with six other prominent women, had delivered voiceless speeches, each pair spending an hour flipping through the charts and posters to make their points. In the window of the nearby Kingsbacher Jewelry Company, a beautiful miniature display included dolls representing each of the states and countries that already enjoyed women's suffrage, all standing "scornfully aloof" from a small party of "stay-at-home anti-suffragists" at a tiny bridge table.[39] Stars from local theaters joined federation members in selling plenty of collateral materials—buttons, badges, suffrage stamps, and literature. More than two and a half million stamps had been ordered, to be sold in books of 100, 250, 500, and 1,000.[40]

Lucy, Eliza, and their mother were among the hundreds of delegates representing some thirty thousand members of the state organization.[41] They gathered by day in the grand Fort Pitt Hotel, followed by mass meetings in the evenings in Old City Hall, Carnegie Music Hall, and the Soldiers Memorial. Miss Margaret Whitehead had designed a new banner, completed just in time for the convention, which featured a city seal and "Equal Franchise Federation" on a blue ground. It served as a backdrop as Lucy offered the welcoming address with a promise: "We are now going to show what we can do."[42]

Success would come in 1915, they all agreed, if only the suffragists could raise fifty thousand dollars for the cause, largely by "skimping" on luxuries of any kind—opera tickets, hat trimmings and furs, Christmas presents, and the like. Within five minutes, they had raised the first seventy-five hundred dollars, five thousand of it from Lucy on behalf of the federation. "Women all over the room gasped for breath, and then came a storm of applause."[43] Of the total, two thousand dollars was to be earmarked to help the election of legislators sympathetic to the cause, as well as three thousand for literature and seventy-five hundred for travel.[44] Both of the Allegheny County suffrage leagues organized by women of color made reports at the convention.[45] Resolutions established the suffragists' support of union initiatives, child labor laws, fair pay for women workers, arbitration for disputes among nations, and aid to victims of white slavery.[46] Lucy was reelected as an auditor of the state organization and also chosen as one of thirty delegates to the upcoming national convention, along with her mother.[47] If, as it seemed, Eliza was excluded, she must have been disappointed.

Festivities surrounding the convention included an automobile parade, a suffrage tea, suffrage moving pictures, a poster contest, and comedy routines. "I believe as an anti," one routine went, "Woman's place is in the home! . . . Woman should have her way, but she should not get it by the vote, but by more ladylike methods. Let her get her way by breaking up dishes, pounding pillows, making the home a hell on earth, but all this is ladylike and not the vulgar suffrage way of casing a ballot." Author Jesse Lynch Williams opened his act with sarcasm:

> In the Victorian period, the heroine of romance was a fragile, fluttering "female" who never did anything. She never even ate a square meal—except in private, where our sex could not see her do it. It would have disillusioned us. Women, we were to believe, are too good to eat.

> According to Jane Austen and other veracious depictors of the manners and customs of the period, she spent most of her time in the graceful pastime of fainting—except again in private, and for the same reason. Men considered her the most bewitching thing in the world, and, of course, she was—at that time.

> More recently, we fiction writers have played up oh, such a shockingly different type of heroine: A biped! One who can do 36 holes of golf—not only do it, but enjoy it (and this comes hard) even in some cases where there is nothing more masculine on the links than a 10-year-old caddy.[48]

In late November, Lucy and her mother joined the thousands of women who swarmed into Washington for the convention of the National Woman Suffrage Association. While they were there, Woodrow Wilson delivered his annual address to Congress, in which he made no mention of women's suffrage. In a resolution the next day, the convention collectively excoriated Wilson for his failure to "rise to the sublimest heights of democracy."[49] The resolution passed unanimously.[50] Carrie Chapman Catt called it "the greatest political mistake of his career."[51]

On the final day of the convention, a Friday, delegates participated in House hearings as to whether a standing committee on women's suffrage should be established, and fifty-five delegates committed to staying in town until Wilson, who was reportedly under the weather with "la grippe," might be well enough to meet with them.[52] He agreed to an appointment at the White House the following Monday. That cold, blustery morning, eighty-eight women marched by twos and fours, banners waving, in the face of a bitter gale wind to meet with the president. As they circled around him in his private office, Anna Howard Shaw stepped forward to make their case. But the appointment proved to be a disappointment. Wilson was evasive and avoided revealing his personal views and instead toed the party line, refusing to endorse a plank that was not in the Democratic platform. As the women filed out of Wilson's office, a number of them refused to shake his hand.[53]

Lucy returned immediately to her campaign back in Pittsburgh, speaking daily in various venues.[54] And within a month, on a Tuesday afternoon in January 1914, about a hundred women packed into the offices of the Equal Franchise Federation for the first class of the six-week School for Suffrage Workers. On the blackboard were written five topics for the day: "Get in touch with your audience," "Brief explanation of suffrage," "Arguments against suffrage," "Why women want suffrage," and "What suffrage has done." Introduced by Lucy and led by Mary Bakewell, by now the vice president of the statewide organization, the school met two afternoons per week. Each two-hour class provided training in public speaking and armed the speakers with plenty of information. They were taught how to avoid panic, overcome self-consciousness, and breathe properly to achieve the proper tone. They were also tutored in the history of the movement and women's rights, constitutional law, labor and industry, taxation, municipal administration, and election rules. Tuition was set at twenty-five cents per class or a dollar fifty for the course, which came to be known by some as Lucy Miller's Suffrage School.[55] Fashioned after Carrie Chapman Catt's school, which Eliza had attended, it was also to include training in "How best to hold a crowd" and simulation of a street meeting in which the class was instructed to simulate a mob and "to make as much unruly disturbance as possible."[56] Steeled to perform in the face of whatever hecklers might hurl at them in the way of insults and invectives, the graduates were unflappable and fully prepared to march back into battle.

9 TAKING IT TO THE STREETS OF PITTSBURGH

By the time Suffrage Day rolled around again on May 2, 1914, the ladies of the Equal Franchise Federation had seen enough large-scale parades that they knew how to stage a spectacle of their own. By two o'clock that afternoon, under fair skies, an enthusiastic crowd had already formed along the sloping shores of the Monongahela Wharf for the first event, a motorcade of more than a hundred vehicles. Festooned with yellow bunting and flowers, American flags, and banners bearing "Votes for Women" and "Victory in 1915," the cars ranged "from six-year-old models of obsolete makes to the latest and most luxurious limousines and electric broughams."[1] At the head of the fleet was Jennie Kennedy, the "Boss of the Road." Both Lucy and John were also pictured in the paper, as "generals."[2] Shimmering in the hot sun, the motorcade wound its way through downtown, then across the Allegheny River to the North Side, and back through downtown to the East End, ultimately returning to the Jenkins Arcade to join the pedestrian march. Stores and houses all along the route were decorated in honor of the day.

At four o'clock, the marchers spilled out of the Arcade into the midst of "an immense throng," a swarming hoard of some ten thousand spectators who lined the streets, hung out of cars, and leaned perilously from the windows of offices and shops. Many downtown streets had been blocked in anticipation of even greater throngs, from Penn to Ninth to Liberty to Wood to the corner of Fifth and Grant. The chaotic crowd of suffragists quickly coalesced into a carefully orchestrated lineup that showcased the breadth of support that was developing for the cause, with some two thousand marchers, five hundred of them men. A brigade of motorcycle policemen "spurted ahead of the charging phalanx," followed by a contingent of policemen on horseback.[3] Next in line, carrying a large silk American flag, was one of the Bakewell sisters.[4] Miss Bakewell, whichever one it was, as the *Gazette Times* recounted the next day,

Pittsburgh's first suffrage parade in 1914 began with a festive motorcade of more than a hundred vehicles. From the *Pittsburg Press*, May 3, 1914

"bore up" well under the weight of the large American flag.[5] There followed a group of ten girls in white dresses with yellow sashes representing the ten states that already had granted suffrage to women: Wyoming, Colorado, Utah, Idaho, Washington, California, Oregon, Arizona, Kansas, and Illinois. One additional girl represented the lone suffrage territory, Alaska.

Next in line was the Pennsylvania state division, a band of luminaries—including Hannah Patterson, by now acting president of the state organization, and Jennie Roessing, its former head. Behind them, Danny Nirella's brass band kept the lineup moving with its rousing marches. The musicians of another group, the Eighteenth Regiment Band, "whooped up 'No Wedding Bells for Me,'" a song choice they insisted was not intended as a commentary on the single suffragists' marriage prospects.[6]

Lucy followed, carrying the suffrage banner and leading the "Grandmother's Brigade." Among the grandmothers was one of the wealthiest women in Pittsburgh, marching arm in arm with her laundress.[7] Then came the Music Club and the Allegheny County Suffrage Party.

A contingent of Black women from the Anna Howard Shaw and Lucy Stone Suffrage Leagues marched in the middle of the parade. Contrary to the common practice in some cities, this group led by Julia Craig was not relegated to the end of the line.

Next came a delegation of college women in full academic regalia, their dark gowns and mortarboards a stark contrast to the profusion of white and brightly colored dresses. Toward the end of the parade were the Camp Fire Girls, a kindergarten delegation, and four Boy Scout buglers.

Finally, bringing up the rear was the men's contingent, around five hundred strong and led by Herbert DuPuy and Julian Kennedy. As the parade spilled out of the Jenkins Arcade, the men had gotten separated and they had "a strenuous time" to catch up with their mothers, sisters, wives, and daughters. Among them were a number of "prominent men," including three city councilmen praised for their courage as they "scorned possible criticism on the part of their brothers and joined with their sisters."[8] Despite minimal support from city council, the organizers nonetheless also managed to decorate City Hall with streamers and flags.[9]

Some of the individual marchers received applause as they were recognized, the papers reported. Among those celebrity suffragists were renowned author Mary Roberts Rinehart . . . and all three Kennedy women. Crowds also applauded the ten young women who represented the ten suffrage states. One policeman was overheard to exclaim, "And they say suffragists are homely. Not these!"[10]

Demonstrating that suffrage would not jeopardize their feminine appeal, many of the marchers were dressed to impress. In addition to the requisite suffrage white, they sported a rainbow of colors and the latest in styles. A new fashion trend introduced that spring was what would soon come to be known as the "war crinoline," which featured a mid-calf, bell-shaped skirt with a wide over-skirt. Slightly less cumbersome than the wasp-waisted Gibson Girl costumes or the slim, stride-restricting "hobble skirts" of the preceding years, the war crinoline offered a more nimble profile for marching through the streets. A short-lived fad, the ankle-revealing war crinoline violated standards of modesty and wartime fabric conservation, but it was deemed to be a morale booster, prompting a popular slogan: "The war is long, but the skirts are short."[11]

The antis, of course, had a presence as well. Streetcars carried cards voicing anti-suffrage sentiments: "She who wishes the vote and knows why she wishes it, is a feminist—Oppose her. She who wishes the vote and does not know why she wishes it, is a suffragist—Pity her. She who does not wish the vote and does not know why she does not wish it, is asleep—Awake her. She who does not wish the vote and knows why she does not wish it, is an anti—Follow her."[12] Mrs. John B. Heron of the National Association Opposed to Woman Suffrage offered an interview in which she predicted that the movement would fall to the "heaviest defeat it ever has known" that year in Pennsylvania: "Woman suffrage is not sure to come. It can be restricted within its present limits by the energetic and concerted action of the men and women who are opposed to it. It is now on its way to defeat at the polls in several of the most important states in the Union. From the boastfulness of the suffragists, it might be supposed that the suffrage movement is sweeping everything before it. But this is not true."[13]

The parade route concluded at the site where Henry Clay Frick's enormous Union Arcade would soon be built, at the corner of Fifth and Grant Streets. There, from wooden platforms and automobiles, some thirty speakers spoke, six at a time, lending the proceedings an effect described by one reporter as "rather worse than the average three-ringed circus" as spectators strained to listen to the simultaneous speeches.[14] Lucy and her father were among the speakers who "hurled oratorical bombs"[15] at the crowds that afternoon, along with a host of other women and a handful of prominent local pastors. Climbing onto her platform as the crowd shifted its attention to her, Lucy presented a pair of resolutions that reflected the shift already afoot in the movement, a shift from a statewide to a national effort:

> Whereas, A resolution providing for the submission of a constitutional amendment enfranchising the women of Pennsylvania passed the legislature of 1913; and
>
> Whereas, This resolution must pass the Legislature of 1915 before it can be submitted to the voters of the state for their decision;
>
> Be it Resolved, That this mass meeting hereby endorses woman suffrage and urges every candidate for the legislature from this county, to pledge himself, if elected, to vote for the submission of a constitutional amendment enfranchising the women of Pennsylvania; And be it further Resolved, That a copy of this resolution be mailed

to every candidate who aspires to represent this district in the next legislature.[16]

There followed a resolution addressed to the US Congress:

We, the citizens of Pennsylvania have assembled here today to voice our demands that women, as citizens of the United States, be accorded the full right of such citizenship. We congratulate the 4,000,000 women voters who have won their right to the ballot in 10 states, and confidently expect to see five more states under the franchise banner after the November elections.

We hereby declare that suffrage for women has become a national, as well as a local issue, and we urge our senators and representatives in Congress to enact federal legislation which will insure to women political equal rights with men.

We therefore ask the Congress of the United States to proceed without delay in the most feasible and practical manner to remove the barriers which prevent American women from the exercise of full franchise and to make our country not a government in which half the people are denied the right of participation, but in truth and reality a democracy.[17]

Lucy's speech was met with hearty cheering and thunderous applause from the crowd.[18] She would later thank the mayor, director of public safety, and director of public works for their support, noting that the police protection "was in marked contrast to the policing given in our national capital March 3, 1913."[19]

In fact, the papers reported, the crowd maintained a respectful attitude. "The whole parade and the mass meeting afterward seemed steeped in an atmosphere of democracy" as "women of culture stood side by side with poorly dressed working-women."[20] "All the women, young or old, had a certain air about them that impressed the spectators in spite of themselves. There was nothing of boldness nor flaunting; just a sweet sincerity and honest, modest determination to go through with their undertaking that shone in every face."[21]

Five hours after the extravaganza had begun, the crowd finally began to disperse, enthralled and exhausted. Parades occurred in at least sixty Pennsylvania towns that day, as well as in other major cities, including Chicago, Philadelphia, and Boston. But as one local editorial noted, "In looking over the reports of the celebration in other cities there is no indication of a more enthusiastic turnout in proportion to population than Pittsburgh provided."[22] The Pittsburgh parade was deemed "a thrilling affair," "a glorious, gorgeous success,"[23] and May 2, 1914, memorialized as "a great day for suffrage." Moving pictures of the day's events were used to promote the cause for months to come.[24]

Some ten thousand suffragists from all over the country would be back in the capital the next Saturday, marching to present the resolutions passed in their respective cities and towns.

10 SACRIFICE AND NEW STRATEGIES

With nearly a year until the next state legislature vote and nearly eighteen months until a possible public referendum, there could be no letup in the campaign. In the month that followed the parade, Eliza as the federation's office manager oversaw the distribution of thirty-seven thousand letters as well as thousands of cards and pamphlets.[1] The now familiar yellow slips that supporters were asked to sign flooded into the Jenkins Arcade offices at a rate of about seven hundred per week.[2] In July, Lucy launched a fifteen-week campaign on behalf of the Woman's Suffrage Party.[3] One component of the campaign was the Orphan's Picnic at Kennywood Park, where the suffragists and the antis debated amidst a crowd of forty thousand people.[4]

A small victory came when the state Democratic platform, adopted June 3, 1914, included a suffrage plank: "The denial of the right of suffrage of the women of our state has aroused a deep feeling that they are deprived of those equal rights, to which, as American citizens, we believe they are entitled. We favor an immediate referendum on this important question."[5] The Bull Moose Party also adopted a suffrage plank.[6] The Republicans remained curiously silent on the topic.[7] Nationally, the Democrats and their leader, the president, refused to endorse suffrage.

* * *

By the end of July, Anna Howard Shaw and the NAWSA were asking women to melt down their jewelry and other heirlooms to support the seven states facing suffrage votes that fall: "A little of what you treasure, an ornament of beauty, a tribute of friendship—something prized because of its place in household life—put it in the melting pot; send it to the suffrage campaign committee."[8] The proceeds, anticipated to be in excess of $50,000 nationwide, were to be allocated to Ohio, Missouri, Nebraska, Nevada, Montana, and the two Dakotas.[9]

In Pittsburgh, the crucible at the federation headquarters quickly filled with thimbles, watches, lockets, jewelry, and souvenirs from seaside resorts, the collection raising some $400.[10] The "Suffrage Melting Pot," as it was called, would be used again in 1915, and the suffragists obtained a copyright on "Melting Pot Day."[11]

A nationwide campaign promoted "Sacrifice Day" on Saturday, August 15, encouraging supporters to earn money, give something up, or just make an outright cash contribution. From working as newspaper reporters in Philadelphia to setting up a manicure salon on Nantucket, the Pittsburgh suffragists were prepared to do what they could, wherever they happened to be. The papers were particularly intrigued by Lucy's contribution, as she was ensconced for the summer season on Crusoe Island in Beaumaris. She committed to "fish all day Saturday, sell her catch and give the money for the Cause." One *Pittsburg Press* reporter was amused. "As Mrs. Miller never has fished before, some fun is anticipated by the members of the party which will go with her—all suffragists, by the way. Rumor has it that already Mrs. Miller has engaged a good-sized string of fish, to be kept by one of the fish markets in the vicinity, in case she is not successful. But she stoutly denies this. 'I will try to earn the money,' she says, 'and if I am not successful, the Cause must take my labor as my offering.'"[12]

Momentum built as early September 1914 found the federation women back for the twenty-sixth annual season at the Pittsburgh Exposition. Their booth sat near the entrance to the auditorium in the central corridor and featured posters, a large map, plenty of novelties for sale, and a procession of "suffrage dolls," each representing an American state or foreign country where women already had the vote. From that central location, they had access to the tens of thousands who flocked to see the exhibit on the Philippines, the model homes, and the production in the Hippodrome, "Fighting the Flames," a visualization of a great fire on New York's East Side.[13] Also at the Exposition, the Woman Suffrage Party of Allegheny County, by now boasting a membership of twenty thousand, distributed flyers for an essay contest for public school students, both boys and girls.[14]

On September 15, federation members marched with their own float in a Peace Parade through downtown. The day before, they had sold twenty-six hundred peace buttons.[15] At the nineteenth annual meeting of the State Federation of Pennsylvania Women in October, a hotly contested battle ended with a strong majority vote—350 to 28—in favor of endorsing equal suffrage.

When Election Day rolled around on November 4, 250 poll watchers turned out, keeping the required fifty-foot distance from the polls, handing out literature and collecting signatures to drum up support for the referendum hoped for in 1915. Taking a page from the playbook of their Philadelphia sisters, the federation in late November launched a "Flying Yellow Squadron" of decorated automobiles canvassing door to door with literature.

Later that month, the 1914 state convention in Scranton offered programming for six days. The statewide movement at that point was led by Jennie Roessing as president of the Pennsylvania Women Suffrage Association and Hannah Patterson as chair of the state Woman Suffrage Party. Mary Flinn Lawrence, the state treasurer, collected free-will pledges toward the $100,000 projected budget for the 1915 campaign, and they came in every form imaginable. "I'll pledge five dollars for the husband I haven't got and never will get," one woman said. "Here's thirty cents for each of the husbands I have refused," said one Philadelphia woman. "It's all they're worth." "Here's twenty-five cents for an opinion expressed by an Anti that we suffragists are crazy," said another, throwing in a quarter. "It's all their opinions are worth," said Jennie Roessing as she tossed the quarter to the treasurer. Cash pledges that day exceeded twenty-five thousand dollars. A poor farmer's wife pledged a pig. One woman donated her cottage cheese and strawberry crops for the next year, another her sweet corn, another the apple and cherry crops from her Bedford County farm.[16] Before the end of the convention, the three hundred delegates would affirm their nonpartisan status, would refuse to permit the reading of a letter from the militant Mrs. Pankhurst, exiled from her native London, and would pass a resolution deploring the European war and contending that winning the ballot for women would mean the end of all wars.[17] On the final evening of the convention, the state Men's League held a mass meeting at which Julian Kennedy spoke.[18] All in all, the Pittsburgh contingent returned home noting that "our suffrage motors have received a new charge."[19]

* * *

They put the charge to work as 1915 opened, with ten months of intense campaigning ahead. At the age of thirty-five, Lucy was being quoted in the newspapers several times a week, which seemed to embolden her. Eliza and Julian came to be widely known players in the public saga as well.

In Washington, the national effort was also in full gear as the new year dawned. By this point, President Wilson, no friend to the suffragists, had received nearly a dozen delegations at the White House but held firm in his stance: "I am deeply impressed with the woman suffrage question, but I believe it can best be worked out by state rather than by attempting a change of the fundamental law of the nation. Such a change would run too far and too fast ahead of the general public opinion of the country."[20]

Nonetheless, several alternative bills were forwarded in Congress. The primary distinctions among them lay in whether they sought a federal amendment or tossed the issue back upon the states to decide for themselves. As between the two primary alternatives, the Bristow-Mondell Amendment would grant suffrage at once in all the states, at least once three-quarters of the states had ratified it, while the Shafroth Amendment would force a referendum in each state whenever 8 percent of a state's voters requested such a vote. Another federal measure proposed permitting women to vote just for senators and representatives.

When the proposed Bristow-Mondell Amendment came before the House on January 12, it was defeated 204 to 174. Anti-suffragist leader Mrs. Arthur M. Dodge commented, "It means that the suffrage movement fostered by hysterical women is on the wane."[21] But many contended that the suffragists were expecting not victory but rather enlightenment. And with 174 votes in their favor, enlightenment would seem to have been on the rise, an encouraging glimpse at the prospect of ultimate victory. Yet Congress took little further action on these resolutions for the rest of 1915.

* * *

Meanwhile back in Pennsylvania, the Legislature was preparing for its second round of voting on a state amendment that spring of 1915. The 1913 resolution had passed the House by a large margin, 131 to 70, but had barely escaped defeat in the Senate, 26 to 22.[22] To be safe, the campaign this time around would have to be more aggressive, notwithstanding that the Republicans had already included a suffrage plank in their platform the previous August.

The campaign had begun even before the resolution was introduced the last week of January. New York had just passed its resolution, for the second time, on February 4. On the eve of the Pittsburgh vote, Julian Kennedy had wired all of the Allegheny County members of the legislature soliciting their votes.[23] The resolution had passed the House by 170 to 31 on February 9, despite weak support from the Allegheny County reps, who voted 8 for and 16 against. Valentines that year were suffrage themed: "Love Me, Love My Vote."[24]

But the resolution stalled in the Senate and lumbered along until March 15. That night, the galleries were full when the resolution passed by 37 to 11, and the response was so positive that the lieutenant governor, Frank B. McClain, presiding with a suffrage yellow boutonnière, broke a piece of ivory from his gavel trying to restore order in the midst of thunderous applause. In the face of complaints about the chaos that evening, McClain replied with a broad smile, "Do the senators forget that this is ladies' night in the senate?"[25]

Not long after the successful state senate vote, the Equal Franchise Federation hosted a speaker who would galvanize audiences around the issue of vice. Miss Rose Livingston, known to many as "the angel of Chinatown," told harrowing stories of her work trying to save women and girls from "the coteries of men who live on the earnings of women" in a system rife with deception and heartless cruelty. In her encounters with men of the underworld, she had been stabbed three times, been shot once, had her jaw broken, had sixteen teeth knocked out, had both arms broken, and had both ankles broken. Sitting in the sanctuary of Trinity Methodist Episcopal Church on the North Side, four hundred women fixed their attention on Miss Livingston, a diminutive woman of less than a hundred pounds, as she recounted an instance in which she was released from the hospital at about the same time one of her assailants was released from his prison sentence for assaulting her. Later she found herself standing near a polling place on election day watching enviously while that same assailant voted. "Fifty thousand girls of the underworld are crying out for help . . . these girls are your little lost sisters whether you want to acknowledge them or not," she said. "The only way in which the white slave evil will be eradicated will be for women to obtain the right to vote," she repeated over and over. Making her headquarters at 5400 Forbes, Miss Livingstone shared her message with guests of the Kennedys as well, including a thousand public school teachers hosted by Eliza.[26]

By the time the Pennsylvania legislature had opened the way for a referendum in the fall, the Equal Franchise Federation was the largest suffrage organization in the United States, with a membership of two thousand[27] and a payroll of seven organizers, three or four stenographers, and a switchboard boy. The Woman's Suffrage Party, which the federation took "under their guidance," boasted twenty thousand members.[28] Likewise, their brother organization, the Men's League for Woman Suffrage, boasted more than twenty thousand members, and they put themselves at Lucy's disposal, accompanying the women on their campaigns into the countryside and speaking wherever they were asked. At the top of the speakers list was Julian.[29] It was estimated that the speakers reached more than a hundred thousand people that year.

Now, with a statewide referendum planned for the fall, the "strenuous campaign" had to be taken to the people. The *Post-Gazette* published photos of the three women they expected to lead the charge: Jennie Roessing as president of the Pennsylvania Women Suffrage Association, Mrs. George A. Piersol, chair of the Woman Suffrage Party in Philadelphia, and Lucy as president of the Equal Franchise Federation.[30] At a two-day conference in April, 150 women planned their strategy, which kept the federation busy throughout that spring, summer, and fall. Despite that the "Great War" had been raging for more than a year, the Pittsburgh crusade was sufficiently aggressive that suffrage news often vied for first-page placement with President Woodrow Wilson and news of the fighting overseas.

Pennsylvania was now at the center of a veritable suffrage storm as sixty-two of its sixty-seven counties had organized by the end of March and concurrent campaigns were occurring in the bordering states of New York, New Jersey, and West Virginia, as well as more distantly in Massachusetts. Collectively, these states constituted more than a quarter of the nation's population. Anna Howard Shaw was in town on a regular basis, speaking at "town hall" meetings and riding in public processions. Like Carrie Chapman Catt and the Kennedys, who hosted her each time she came to town, Shaw considered suffrage to be a matter of justice, "a fundamental principle of democracy." "I believe in woman suffrage," she said, "whether all the women vote or no women vote; whether all women vote right or all women vote wrong; whether women will love their husbands after they vote or forsake them; whether they will neglect their children or have any children." She equated its importance with that of the war. "The time has come when the theory of divine right of sex is as obsolete as the theory of the divine right of kings. The battle of the one is being fought to the death in this country today by women suffragists. The battle to the death of the other is being fought across the sea."[31]

Shaw maintained that suffrage was an issue whose time had arrived.

That year, suffrage had come before the legislative bodies in every one of the thirty-six non-suffrage states. And like the Kennedys, Shaw was optimistic but ready for a fight. Pennsylvania, she said, was "the keystone of the national situation" and would be her last battleground before retiring.[32]

* * *

Saturday, May 1, 1915, found the suffragists once again lining up to parade through the city. This time, a lineup of eighteen automobiles traversed downtown and the North Side, horns blaring and flags waving, led by a police escort and a brass band, on their way to a vacant square next to the courthouse, the site where the new City-County Building would soon be built. There, five of the "machines" were parked to serve as platforms for a cadre of twenty-five speakers who made their case for two hours. Included among them were Lucy, Eliza, and Julian as well as a woman speaking entirely in German. It was not nearly so much of a production as the 1914 parade had been. They were saving that sort of affair for a time closer to Election Day.[33] For now, their attention turned to widening their circle of allies.

Suffragists and Socialists joined hands the next day as Julian spoke on behalf of the Men's League for Woman Suffrage at a Socialists' event on International Labor Day. His plea, he said, was based upon justice. "It is not our business what the women will do with the vote in the future. Since democracy has the force to alleviate men's troubles, it will do as much for women."[34]

Mrs. Yee Quil, a Chinese woman married to an American-born Chinese man, made history—and front-page news—when she shook Lucy's hand and joined the Equal Franchise Federation, along with her son and her sister-in-law. Federal law specified that a woman marrying an American assumes American citizenship without naturalization. Mrs. Quil's assignment as one of the foreign-language speakers on the federation roster was to gain support from Pittsburgh's American Chinese Progressive Club. In her speeches on the subject, she noted that the idea of women's suffrage was "spreading swiftly" back in China.[35]

There were more theater speeches, with both Lucy and Eliza participating. When Mme. Alla Nazimova came to perform Marion Craig Wentworth's one-act feminist drama, "War Brides," at the Grand, the suffragists purchased three hundred reserved seats on the first floor, as well as all the boxes on the first and second tiers, all draped in suffrage yellow. The Kennedy box was a family affair hosted by Lucy and included her parents along with Eliza and young Julian, both accompanied by their love interests. It was said to be the largest single theater party ever held in Pittsburgh.[36] The powerful play told the story of a pregnant war widow who commits suicide rather than bear more children for a nation that allows her no say in decision making. One of the most successful plays of 1915, War Brides toured the country for several months before being made into a silent film in 1916 with Nazimova in the lead role. With its decidedly pacifist message, the play was banned in some cities and states, and it was withdrawn from circulation in 1917. The suffragists did not shrink from controversy.

* * *

The end of spring always promised garden parties, and in 1915 the one to see was the two-day "fête-dansante" in early June at "Cairncarque," the palatial home of Mr. and Mrs. Robert Pitcairn. The house sat at the center of a sprawling estate in Shadyside, and the rolling green lawns were filled with festive activity. Ten tents with striped awnings featured Venetian masks. Fortune-telling booths housed "Suffragina, the Queen of the Gypsies" and "Enfranchiser, the Living Wonder."[37] Other booths and a country store were selling everything from gold fish to sporting goods. Multiple orchestras were tucked away amidst the shrubbery. A sweeping dance floor was occupied all afternoon and evening, and exhibition dancing offered prizes. A vaudeville tent "was the scene of riotous hilarity."[38] There were moving pictures, a Japanese tearoom, a Punch and Judy puppet show, and plenty of food.[39] In a mock voting booth, women could pay a "poll tax" of five cents, vote for or against suffrage, and—to lend a light-hearted air to the proceedings—register their preference of candidates for the "suffrage president of the United States," the two options being Anna Howard Shaw and Lucy.[40] The spectacle was all a bit too much for Lucy. "If Dr. Shaw could only see us now," she gasped. "She would never accuse us of neglecting the more frivolous appeals to the votes of this end of the state."[41] Nonetheless, the fête was a success far beyond their expectations, attracting more than three thousand people and raising thousands of dollars for the cause.

In each of the county's sixty-eight townships and 675 political precincts, suffragists knocked on doors day and evening to secure the promise of votes in November.[42] When ten thousand men volunteered to work alongside the laborers of the county road department to improve the county's 1,270 miles of dirt roads on Good Roads Day, May 26, the suffragists equipped four trucks with stoves and waffle irons and traveled around delivering lunch and coffee in suffrage souvenir cups.[43] Those dirt roads, which represented three-quarters of the roads in the county, would become particularly important to the movement in the months to come. Recognizing the importance of rural voters, an additional campaign targeted nine thousand farmers and their families across the county with packages of suffrage materials.[44]

Lucy, Eliza, and their cohorts spoke at countless women's clubs, men's clubs, churches, lodges, union halls, YMCAs, theaters, public spaces, and private homes as well as on hundreds of street corners and at open-air assemblies and playgrounds. Lucy, in particular, was in great demand. Her message was straightforward, particularly as she delivered it to male audiences: "We do not come to you pleadingly, we do not come to you subserviently, we are not humble—we come to you as earth beings of one sex to equal earth beings of the opposite sex, asking you what you are going to do about granting equal suffrage after the decades you have been declaring to us, unofficially, as it were, that we are equals."[45]

Speaking from a North Side pulpit in mid-May, Lucy likened the plight of the disenfranchised woman to that of the good Samaritan in the biblical parable, who had no voice in Israel's government and was a political outcast yet had cared selflessly for one in need. She had been invited by the pastor, who had encouraged attendees to wear suffrage yellow.[46]

Addressing a large crowd at the "Prosperity Carnival Made in U.S.A." that same week in Motor Square Garden was Senator Moses Clapp of Minnesota. "They say politics are too corrupt for women to mix in," he said. "Well, if that is true, then it is certainly time that women get in and help to clean politics up. If political meetings are too corrupt for women to go into, they are too corrupt for self-respecting men to go into. It is due time, then, that we have woman's refinement as a vitalizing influence in public affairs."[47] Lucy and Eliza listened intently.

For Eliza, who became more engaged as a speaker as time went on, the issue was also one of education and expediency, which would become her watchwords. "By contact with the world of affairs, women themselves and through them their families will become cognizant of events of which they would otherwise remain ignorant, and this will produce a more intelligent class of people, and a better world in general," she said. "We now prepare children for the world, and we want the right to prepare the world for the children."[48]

Along with their sisters in nine other states,[49] federation members distributed tens of thousands of seed packets that would blanket public and private gardens alike with the signature suffrage yellow. To promote the effort, Lucy, Eliza, and other suffrage leaders joined in the planting, at least long enough to be captured in publicity photos. "Stinging blisters have been raised on many unaccustomed hands and aching backs are common cause at headquarters," the *Daily Post* reported. "But everyone is cheerful, because it is for 'the cause.'"[50]

The particular varieties of flowers were rechristened with names symbolic of the movement's hope and confidence:

> Golden Dawn *(Eschscholtzia)*, the first to bloom in the spring
> Advance *(Calliopsis)*
> Persistence *(Calendula)*
> Conquest *(Mignonette)*
> Victory *(Zinnia)*
> Jubilee *(Crysanthemum)*, the last to bloom in the fall[51]

Playing to the sometimes competitive nature of gardeners, the promotion promised that the five best gardens were to receive prizes of either a hundred fine yellow tulips or a hundred yellow daffodils. One supporter planned a garden with an outline of the United States in which all the suffrage states were planted in brilliant yellow while all the others were filled with somber, non-flowering plants. To further their reach, Lucy also announced that the flowers would be distributed to hospitals, orphanages, and "the desks of recalcitrant voters."[52]

Lucy appealed to clergymen throughout the county. In March, her voice thundering through the telephone lines, she contacted a hundred Protestant ministers, Roman Catholic priests, and Jewish rabbis in an effort to secure recognition of May 9 as Suffrage Sunday. In the process, she determined that seventy of the clergymen favored women's suffrage and were willing to publicly state their support.[53] By May, she claimed that two hundred clergymen marked Mother's Day by advocating votes for women in their sermons. The message generally focused on "the vital part mothers take in the upbuilding and the perpetuation of the republic, with the declaration that with the ballot women might become even a greater and more useful influence." Responding to the

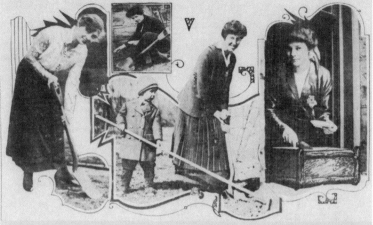

Suffragists Are Busy With Spade, Rake and Garden Trowel
Golden Flower Beds Will Advertise Campaign for Votes

Lucy (second from right) and Eliza (crouched) posed for publicity photos to promote the suffrage cause through gardening. From the *Pittsburgh Daily Post*.

antis' contention that discussing suffrage from the pulpit was sacrilegious, Lucy argued that if that were true, it would be sacrilegious to bring any secular topic into the pulpit. "When the abolition of slavery was being discussed, Henry Ward Beecher and other great pulpit orators were similarly assailed by Southern sympathizers for their 'sacrilegious use of the pulpit,'" she said. "But they persisted, and the infamous institution of slavery was finally abolished."[54] By July, a canvas of 300 ministers revealed 260 in favor and only fourteen opposed.[55]

One Catholic priest went so far as to say that it seemed to be "in accordance with the church to be in sympathy with this movement, for the spirit and trend of the church has ever been to elevate woman to her proper dignity and to give her every right to which she is entitled." Noting that Catholics were "free to act as they choose without hindrance from ecclesiastical authorities," he nonetheless offered a ringing endorsement:

> Neither man nor woman has an inherent right to vote or rule, but they obtain this right by having the necessary qualifications. Both have by nature equal faculties and ability to vote or to rule; they have the same intelligence, and if there is any advantage anywhere between the sexes it is on the woman's side, as the majority of women

have a higher standard of morality than men. . . . If we wish to be
up with the spirit of the age, the spirit of progress; if we wish our
descendants to be proud of us, if we wish to be considered as great
and broad by future generations, . . . then we will vote unselfishly in
November . . .[56]

No fewer than sixty teas were planned, an average of two per week, hosted
by society leaders including Mrs. Howard Heinz, Mrs. Herbert DuPuy, and
Mrs. Clinton Childs.

* * *

The Equal Franchise Federation's *Suffrage Cook Book* doled out equal parts propaganda, sarcasm, and prescriptive advice for the home chef.

Perhaps in an effort to counter the contention by some that voting would prove too much of a distraction from women's domestic duties, the federation used food as an effective instrument for raising money and awareness. What began with bake sales and bazaars "to seek man's vote through his stomach"[57] ultimately culminated in the 1915 publication of the *Suffrage Cook Book*. The federation's cookbook was one of at least a half dozen such volumes published around the country in support of the "Great Cause."[58]

The charity cookbook as a fundraising tool had been introduced after the Civil War, when the proceeds were used to help war victims and support church-related issues.[59] The first one dedicated to the cause of women's suffrage had appeared in 1886 at a sold-out launch party in the Boston Music Hall: *The Woman Suffrage Cook Book, Containing*

Thoroughly Tested and Reliable Recipes for Cooking, Directions for the Care of the Sick, and Practical Suggestions Contributed Especially for this Work. Coming from across the country in Seattle, the *Washington Women's Cook Book* of 1908 opened with a legend on the title page: "Give us the vote and we will cook, The better for a wide outlook."[60]

Contributors to the federation's cookbook included forty-five women—and twelve men—from Fair Hope, Alaska, to London, half of them from Western Pennsylvania. Interspersed among the recipes were pro-suffrage testimonials from six governors of states where women were already successfully exercising the right. Also among the contributors was Irvin S. Cobb, a New York journalist and humorist who contended that "Women cannot make a worse mess of voting than men have."[61]

Concocted of equal parts propaganda, sarcasm, and prescriptive advice for the home chef, the *Suffrage Cook Book* was not written solely for the kitchen. The pastry section featured an entry that was unattributed but strongly flavored with Lucy's brand of humor:

> "Pie for a Suffragist's Doubting Husband"
> 1 qt milk human kindness
> 8 Reasons:
>> War
>> White Slavery
>> Child Labor
>> 8,000,000 working Women
>> Bad Roads
>> Poisonous Water
>> Impure Food
>
> Mix the crust with tact and velvet gloves, using no sarcasm, especially with the upper crust. Upper Crusts must be handled with extreme care for they quickly sour if manipulated roughly.

The cover design featured Uncle Sam holding a scale on which the sexes rested in balance, along with a wheel whose twelve-and-a-half spokes represented the states, plus the territory of Alaska, where women had been granted suffrage. (The half spoke represented Illinois, where women enjoyed just partial suffrage.) Lucy was one of two women to whom the book was dedicated, along with Mrs. Henry Villard, wife of the renowned financier

Lucy was one of two women to whom the 1915 *Suffrage Cook Book* was dedicated.

and owner of *The New York Evening Post* and *The Nation*. Despite that neither Lucy nor Eliza were noted for their culinary talents, and that both had always been served by cooks at home, Eliza staunchly insisted that anyone who could read could also cook. Lucy was pictured in a full-page photograph with her first two children, Julian and Eliza, opposite her "Baked Ham a la Miller," a dish "fit for the greatest epicure." Likewise, Eliza appeared in a photographic portrait opposite her "Suffrage Angel Cake a la Kennedy," although it seemed unlikely that Eliza's busy schedule would actually permit her the time to sift the flour nine times and the sugar seven times before adding them to the batter, as the recipe prescribed.

Jane Addams, renowned for her activism in the realm of settlement and social work and the second woman to win a Nobel peace prize, was pictured in a pensive pose opposite her words of encouragement to the women in the four campaign states:

> You are working not only toward your own enfranchisement but toward the enfranchisement of the women in all the non-suffrage states in the union. Your victory means victory in other states. You are our leaders at this crucial time and thousands of women are looking to you....[62]

Even author and activist Jack London, whose popularity had soared with the publication of *The Call of the Wild* in 1903, weighed in with an offering. From aboard his yacht Roamer while cruising off the West Coast, he offered best wishes and a recipe for roast duck. Fans were shocked by his untimely death a year later at the age of forty.

Offered for a dollar apiece, the two thousand copies of the first edition sold out almost immediately.[63] Mrs. Kleber and a trio of others reportedly boosted sales by traveling around the county on a horse-drawn prairie schooner, making speeches, distributing literature, and selling cookbooks.[64]

* * *

Without a doubt the greatest stunt that summer of 1915 was the Justice Bell, also known as the Woman's Liberty Bell. The bell was an exact replica of the Liberty Bell, with two differences. First, the original inscription, "Proclaim Liberty Throughout the Land to All the Inhabitants Thereof" was augmented with two simple words: "Establish Justice." And there was no crack in the Justice Bell. In a dramatic bit of showmanship, the bell's clapper was bound by massive bronze chains and padlocked to render it silent until women had a voice through the vote. As one account explained the bell's impact, "It made them realize that the women of Pennsylvania who are asking for the ballot today are prompted by the same patriotic impulses and motives that stirred the men of this state in 1776."[65]

The bell had been the brainchild of Mrs. Katharine Wentworth Ruschenberger of Strafford, Pennsylvania, who had introduced a two hundred-pound prototype in 1914 and then paid the full cost of fabricating a two-ton version. The casting took place on March 31 at the Meneely Bell Company in Troy, New York. Jennie Roessing and a delegation of suffragists from around the state watched as the molten metal was poured and the white-hot mold covered with sand. The event was captured on film by the Pathe, Mutual, and Hearst-Selig film companies, three of the nation's largest, for their *News Weekly* reels.[66]

Mounted on the back of an open truck, accompanied by a "plucky little band of women,"[67] the bell began its statewide tour on June 23, leaving the town of Sayre in Bradford County and zigzagging across the northern counties, down through the western tier, and eastward en route to its ultimate destination at Philadelphia's Independence Square on election night.[68] Covering some fifty miles a day, it visited every one of the state's sixty-seven county seats and as many rural towns as possible, resting on Sundays. As it crossed each county line, it was met by cheering crowds, sometimes a brass band, and always a new escort of automobiles packed with suffragists, horns blaring, that would accompany it to the next county line. It was enthusiastically received in dozens of small towns where spectators listened with rapt attention to the suffragists' speeches, prompting headlines such as "Woman's Liberty Bell Tongue-Tied: But the Belles Who Tell Its Message Have No Lingual Impediments."[69]

The Liberty Bell truck provided a perfect platform for speeches. When the truck reached Sewickley, down the Ohio River from Pittsburgh, Lucy joined Jennie Roessing to address the crowd. "This bell," she began, "which will not sound until the men of Pennsylvania have given the women the right of franchise, could have come on no more appropriate time than on the eve of Independence Day. It must not be confused with the old bell in Philadelphia. That bell rang out liberty for men. This will ring equality for women. It is carrying a silent message through the state, an appeal for the men to unloose its tongue, to let it proclaim that equality after the election in November." [70]

As the bell made its way closer to Pittsburgh, it took its requisite sabbath rest on the Fourth of July, and rolled into Oakland on the Fifth for National Americanization Day, which was being celebrated on Flagstaff Hill in Schenley Park. It was the first Americanization Day that Pittsburgh had ever seen. More than ten thousand adults watched nearly a thousand school children sing patriotic songs as they formed a giant American flag to one side of the bandstand. The hillside was a sea of straw boaters and festive summer hats, waving handheld flags, and bobbing balloons. During the celebration, which struck a decidedly inclusive tone, Mayor Armstrong welcomed the new citizens, and prominent Pittsburgh attorney and former Secretary of State Philander Knox spoke extensively on the meaning of citizenship. He contrasted the natural-born citizens—who might be "orientals, anarchists, polygamists, assisted paupers, public charges, avowed enemies of social order given to evil practices and associations"—with naturalized citizens, who hold "a judicial degree of fitness." He argued that America is a land "in which absolute equality exists." And he noted that "those who come from countries in which they have had no part in matters governmental or political, in which they have had no voice in the making, judging or enforcing of the laws, now come where they may cast their votes for those whom they desire to represent and serve them. Every vote so cast counts such as any other vote. . . ." [71]

The irony of Knox's remarks was not lost on the women of the Equal Franchise Federation. They had surreptitiously gathered at 5400 Forbes and then discreetly ridden in automobiles into the park. Led by Lucy and Mary Flinn Lawrence, they suddenly emerged from the automobiles, coalesced into a long line, and marched up and around Flagstaff Hill—society women, business women, doctors, nurses, social workers, artists, and writers. They were native- and foreign-born, maids, young mothers, matrons, and grandmothers. All were dressed in white dresses and caps and gowns with their signature yellow sashes. But what distinguished this demonstration from others was that it was silent. The crowds were moved. "As score after score of the wordless protestants filed by, the throng of thousands assembled for the exercises was hushed into a silence as impressive as that of the marchers." They stood in a semicircle around the crowd for a full fifteen minutes, holding aloft the huge banners that spoke for them in the midst of their silence. Each group carried its own sign: "We are grandmothers; will our sons, the native sons of this state, and the naturalized sons of other lands deny us the right to vote?" "Silent greetings to naturalized foreigners from the suffragists of Allegheny County. We are glad you have the right to vote. Vote to give us the same right." "We are young mothers. We are rearing sons to vote. Give us the vote to aid in passing laws that govern the home." "We are unmarried taxpayers. Taxation without representation is still tyranny. Who represents us?" A particularly large group comprised women who were transplants from suffrage states: "We represent suffrage states. Give us back the vote we lost when we came to Pennsylvania."[72]

Then, as quietly as they had come, the protestors marched away, past Carnegie Institute and down Forbes Street, where the Justice Bell sat, on its truck, beneath a canopy. There they broke their silence as one after another jumped up on the truck to speak. Unlike the other stunts the suffragists had pulled, this one came with no advance notice. Only the marchers themselves knew that it was coming.[73] Lucy thought it all "a marvelous stunt."[74]

The next week, the Equal Franchise Federation issued an open letter, signed by Lucy, to all candidates for city and county offices. The letter called for a public "confession of faith" relative to votes for women, characterizing suffrage as the most "trenchant, sweeping question" on the ballot and stating that this was a duty of the candidates that "must be faced and cannot be evaded." Hoping that November would be the last election in which they were denied the vote, they wanted the candidates to go on record for future reference. They promised to inform the public of the responses.[75]

It would seem that these tactics had some impact. At the next big celebration in Schenley Park, held on Labor Day, Anna Howard Shaw was given the podium for an hour-long speech.

* * *

On August 31, telephone operators frantically tried to keep up with the calls as the Equal Franchise Federation conducted a straw poll by telephone. They called judges, physicians, lawyers, ministers, Catholic priests, city officials, engineers, and officials of the board of trade and chamber of commerce. Many calls were made from the federation's Jenkins Arcade headquarters, but an army of two thousand supporters also agreed to call ten men each on their private residence phones. By the end of the day, twelve thousand calls had been made, with three-quarters of those reached favoring suffrage and pledging their support.[76]

Meanwhile, Eliza had taken on the role as head of the Women's Suffrage Party from 1912 to 1915, through which she maintained the records of some seventy-five thousand signers to the suffrage cause, which had to be districted according to their voting precincts. In the process, she became intimately familiar with the mechanics of the voting process in Allegheny County, a knowledge that would later stand her in good stead. She also served as membership chair of the Equal Franchise Federation, and that summer of 1915, she published several articles on suffrage in the *Pittsburg Press*.[77]

* * *

The antis campaigned vigorously throughout those eight months. These women were a thorn in the side of the federation, to be sure. But they also kept Lucy and her cohorts on their toes and forced them to hone their message. The antis opened a new headquarters on Wood Street. The suffragists followed suit. Both had booths at the Exposition.

Like the suffragists, the antis had their share of teas and lectures that year, and their dance at the Rittenhouse Hotel in late May attracted more than eight hundred.[78] They gave countless lectures and voiced their opinions frequently in the local papers. Their arguments had not changed, but they became more strident, even ominous. Suffrage would cause women to neglect their homes and families. Suffrage would increase the divorce rate. Women—at least the seventy-five percent who were married—were already represented in the votes of their husbands. Suffrage would force women into jury duty, for which they were unfit. Suffrage would draw women into the tawdry political arena, which was not befitting their delicate constitutions. Suffrage had not improved working conditions for women in states that already permitted them to vote. Suffrage would double the cost of elections. And women wouldn't vote anyway. Only ten percent of women wanted the vote, they said. They cited the failures of suffrage states to pass progressive, humanitarian legislation and boasted that Pennsylvania, without the benefit of women's votes, had passed "the best mothers' pension act in the United States," with its thirty-seven-and-a-half-hour work week for children, twelve hours less than the national child labor committee had ever recommended.[79]

"If the brass bands, torchlight parades, haranguing from automobiles, old-fashioned rallies and soap box oratory on street corners by women are a sample of women's participation in politics it is quite apparent that woman would be degraded rather than elevated by the exercise of the ballot. . . ," one anti wrote. "In politics there is struggle, strife, contentions, bitterness, excitement, agitation, everything which is averse to the true character of woman. . . . The political woman would be a menace to society, to the home and to the state."[80]

The antis criticized the suffs for their close affinity with the Socialist Party, which had wholeheartedly endorsed them with planks in their state and national platforms. In a two-page spread in the *Gazette Times*, one anti asserted, "Woman suffrage was ceasing to be a live issue in this country when it was revived by a movement that is now attacking the constitutional monarchies of the world with the violence that it exhibited in 1848. That movement is Socialism." "It is incontrovertible that suffragettes and Socialists go hand in hand," another added. "The result is self-evident."[81] The Socialist bond was considered so strong that national speaker Mrs. Frank L. Goodwin, along with several of her cohorts, refused an invitation to debate the subject at a party meeting. "We have no time to spend in ways that promise no return," she said.[82]

The antis also tried to link the suffs to the issue of prohibition, which Lucy flatly denied. "Some prohibitionists do and some do not favor the enfranchisement of women," she said. "And some suffragists favor prohibition, and some are opposed to it. Each party is confident that its cause will stand upon its own merits."[83] Ultimately, she contended, women with the ballot would decide on the issue according to their individual consciences.

Lucy later admitted that at times the struggle seemed hopeless.

11 ELEVENTH INNING PITCHES FOR SUFFRAGE

As the summer of 1915 slipped into fall and the countdown began to November 2, the battle between the suffragists and the antis intensified, with each side using every weapon in its arsenal. Alongside them, America was indulging its infatuation with the national pastime as baseball teams fought battles of their own. For the Equal Franchise Federation, whose members shared a mutual admiration with the Pirates, this posed yet another promotional opportunity. The federation was full of baseball fans. It also had its fair share of *aspiring* fans. They planned a special Suffrage Day at the ballpark and formed the Suffrage Baseball Boosters and Writers Association, which held its first meeting in boxes at Forbes Field. It was to be a training session for the suffragists, a place where they could learn how to talk about "fan stuff" and know "when to whoop and when to moan" on Suffrage Day.[1]

The Pirates' manager, Fred Clarke, had already proven himself to be a fan of the cause. Clarke hailed from the suffrage state of Kansas, and his wife was a registered voter there. "I favor suffrage for women," he said. "because it seems to me one of the most natural things in the world. . . . They are every bit as capable of coping with the voting end of politics as men. I'm in favor of woman suffrage first, last, and all the time."[2] Owner Barney Dreyfuss and star player Honus Wagner were also very vocal in their support of the movement, and the other players seemed amenable.

Suffrage Day ticket sales drew big crowds as the federation opened a new auxiliary headquarters on Wood Street on September 15 and arranged a whole day of festivities around the game, which was scheduled for the next afternoon at Forbes Field, just outside Schenley Park and next to Carnegie Institute. The million-dollar ballpark, the first steel and concrete stadium in the country, had opened in 1909 as the third home of the Pittsburgh Pirates, and it would become the first home of the Pittsburgh Steelers in 1933.

The newspaper clipping reads:

SUFFAGISTS RELEASING BALLOONS AND SOME OF THE FINDERS WHO WILL BE THEIR GUESTS TOMORROW

Balloons Carry
Admittance to
Baseball Game

Finders of Tickets Will Be Guests of Suffragists in Forbes Field Tomorrow.

PRAISE FOR WOMEN VOTERS

Upper, left to right—Miss Sarah Hillman, Miss Louise G. Taylor, Miss Sarah M. Bennett, Miss Lois Rankin and Miss Elizabeth Ogden. Below, left—Sol Ackerman, office boy at Suffragist headquarters; right, Max Bermen, who captured prizes after sharp race along Liberty avenue to Sixth street.

Miles Theater Opens
With "The Melting Pot"

Walker Whitesides in Photo-play and an Elaborate Musical Program Opens Season.

OCEAN INTELLIGENCE.

On Suffrage Day 1915, yellow balloons released into the air carried vouchers for free baseball tickets that could be redeemed at the Equal Franchise Federation's new headquarters. From *Pittsburgh Gazette Times*

Two days before the Suffrage Day game, the sky over downtown was dotted with yellow balloons carrying streamers and vouchers for free reserved tickets that could be redeemed at the new headquarters.[3] On hand to help sell tickets was renowned actress and singer Lillian Russell, who had retired from the stage to marry her fourth husband, *Pittsburgh Leader* owner and future ambassador to Spain Alexander Pollock Moore.[4] When game time rolled around the next day, Miss Russell threw out the first ball just as the players on both teams released yellow balloons into the air. Women in white and yellow filled the banner-draped stands, and many, Eliza among them, were on hand to canvas the fans, asking them to pledge support for the suffrage amendment, distributing literature, and selling souvenirs.[5] The federation offered five dollars for every run scored by a Pittsburgh player, and they were to receive a percentage of the gate receipts.[6] With the Pirates losing to the Giants 8-4, the federation doled out sixty dollars that day. But it was a win for the suffragists, who drummed up public support with their hospitality, festive atmosphere, and spirited enthusiasm.[7]

Within days the federation opened another auxiliary headquarters nearby in the former Antler Hotel. Originally built in 1885 as an office building, the hotel had gone out of business, and the empty building had been purchased by Herbert Dupuy, a successful business entrepreneur and a social peer of the Kennedys. His Pennsylvania Rubber Company, founded in 1899, had pioneered the development and manufacturing of tennis balls and would become the world's leading producer for nearly seventy years. DuPuy had parlayed his success in the rubber business into a real estate development empire with holdings in Pittsburgh and was purported to be one of the largest real estate holders in New York City. His success made it possible for him to be a generous supporter of the cause, and his wife and daughters were active in the Equal Franchise Federation. Dupuy agreed to allow the federation use of the building during the fall campaign.[8]

The Antler was a narrow building that stretched through the middle of the block between two main streets, Fifth and Oliver Avenues. The block was anchored on one end by City Hall and on the other by Farmer's Deposit National Bank. Across Fifth Avenue was the Grand Opera House. In the block across Oliver Avenue stood the gloriously Gothic First Presbyterian and Trinity Episcopal churches, along with the Oliver Building, a relatively new office skyscraper by famed Chicago architect Daniel Burnham that rivaled Frick's Burnham-designed building a few blocks away. Well located and with steady traffic seven days a week, the hotel would prove to be a busy thoroughfare and a perfect production space.

The new "Suffrage Arcade" drew opening day crowds on Saturday, September 25 with an art competition described in one report as "a pot-pourri of art, music, and suffrage oratory."[9] When the doors opened at ten o'clock that morning, the walls had been lined with green cloth, upon which were mounted brown paper rectangles just waiting for the artists' touch. The charge to the artists was to produce suffrage-themed posters, "either sedate or ludicrous."[10] The artists—a young group, some twenty of them by one report—worked for two hours on posters and cartoons with the strains of phonograph music playing in the background. The space was festooned with yellow flowers, and plenty of suffrage literature was on hand.

"The artists worked in view of the passing Saturday crowds," the *Post-Gazette* reported the next day, "and no sooner had the first made a few strokes with his brush on his paper, than the pedestrians began to stop and gather. It was as good as a vaudeville show to some, better to most. For here they saw pencil vying with brush and crayon, a score of artists busy at once in a contest, all with the same subject: suffrage."[11]

After two hours of feverish work by the artists, with some five thousand spectators funneling through the space, the official judging began. While awaiting the outcome, a free "Bohemian lunch" was served to three hundred guests, who were treated to a live recital with piano, violins, a tenor, and a soprano. Miss Sarah Hillman was responsible for the event, aided by more than thirty women suffragists.[12] And of course there were speeches, with Lucy, Eliza, and Helen Allen each making a fervent pitch for suffrage.

The winning entry, by a twenty-one-year-old artist named Porter Woodruff, depicted a draped female figure, crouching, her hands manacled with a ball and chain, and a boldly lettered title at the top: "Until She Gets the VOTE!" Woodruff was awarded a ten-dollar gold piece for his efforts, and his poster was printed in the paper the next day. Woodruff and Norman Kennedy, another contestant in the day's competition, had given a lecture earlier that year at the Carnegie Institute on "The Art of the Poster."[13] Woodruff would go on to create covers for *House and Garden* magazine and to become one of five American fashion illustrators *Vogue* magazine had based in Paris in the early 1920s.[14]

Among the prominent visitors that day were Bishop Cortlandt Whitehead, the leader of the Episcopal Diocese of Pittsburgh, and his wife. The bishop would have a notable altercation with Lucy the next year. But for now, he spoke on behalf of the cause in an address that was widely circulated from the new headquarters. "Man obtained suffrage by taking it—by forcing it," he said. "Woman asks and petitions for it. It is the right of both. There is no question about that. The trouble is that man, having obtained his right, refuses to share it. Justice, common justice, demands that he do so. . . . It is ridiculous that he should class his helpmate with imbeciles, lunatics and others who are deprived of franchise."[15]

Then, with less than a month to go, the cause was given a great boost by the announcement of President Wilson that he would be voting for the suffrage amendment in his home state of New Jersey. It was suggested that, with three daughters who favored the amendment, the president could hardly do otherwise. Wilson qualified his endorsement, however, saying "I shall vote, not as the leader of my party in the nation, but only upon my private conviction as a citizen of New Jersey." Nonetheless, Anna Howard Shaw, Carrie Chapman Catt, and other leaders of the cause took it to be very promising news indeed. Catt declared, "It is a source of great gratification to suffragists that the foremost man in the country, perhaps in the world, and the greatest living authority on the true principles of democracy should stand before the country as a professed suffragist." "This is the greatest single victory we have had this year," Lucy exclaimed exultantly. Eliza ecstatically declared it to mean "The East for woman suffrage." Triumph felt imminent, and "Wilson Days" were declared downtown on October 7 and in Oakland on October 9. Lucy's nemesis with the antis, Julia Morgan Harding, simply commented, "This is not the first mistake the President has made."[16]

Other endorsements came in at the eleventh hour from former Pennsylvania governors Samuel W. Pennypacker and William A. Stone, current governor Martin G. Brumbaugh, Theodore Roosevelt, and a majority of Wilson's cabinet. Conferences of Methodists and Baptists had endorsed them, as did the Pennsylvania Federation of Women, representing forty-five thousand women. The suffragists were euphoric.

* * *

As October opened, World Series fever was spreading across the nation, and Pittsburghers geared up for a contest that would pit the Boston Red Sox against the Philadelphia Phillies, who had just won their first National League pennant.

Pittsburghers had a special affinity for the World Series contest, which had been born twelve years earlier, in 1903, out of an agreement between the Pirates' owner, Barney Dreyfuss, and the owner of the Boston Red Sox, Henry Killilea. Dreyfuss represented the established National League and Killilea the fledgling American League. Together, they negotiated a peace treaty to ensure success for both leagues. They established a single set of rules, brokered agreements with the minor leagues, and introduced cooperative scheduling. They also agreed to stage a playoff for the "world championship." The Red Sox had won that first contest in 1903 and prevailed again in 1912.

By now the World Series was a national sensation. But short of sitting in the stands, fans found it difficult to follow their favorite teams. In Manhattan, the *New York Times* sponsored a giant scoreboard in Times Square to showcase a real-time mechanical re-creation of the first game. The paper reported that a crowd of ten thousand packed into the square. Philadelphia, too, posted game reports on a giant scoreboard outside City Hall.

In Pittsburgh, however, there was no such reporting mechanism, and radio would not be widely available until 1919 (despite having been invented as a communications medium in the 1890s). Twice daily reports published in the local newspapers were inadequate to meet the urgent demand for play-by-play accounts of the games. The *Morning Post* and the *Evening Sun* satisfied the call for immediacy by pasting large posters in their storefront windows every few minutes. The street in front of each office teemed with throngs of people, mostly men, straining for the first glimpse of each new update.

Before long, the enthusiastic crowds became a problem. They blocked passersby on the sidewalks, forcing pedestrians into the street. Congestion in the streets interfered with the regular flow of electric trolleys, automobiles, and the occasional horse-drawn carriage. The entire traffic situation became so unmanageable that city council invoked an ordinance it had passed in October 1912 regulating "all street parades, processions and street assemblages or meetings occupying, marching or assembling upon any highway, street, lane, alley, wharf, or public square of the City of Pittsburgh, to the interference, interruption or exclusion of other citizens in their legal right to the use thereof . . ."[17] The ordinance went on to cite its objective of preventing obstruction of said public ways as well as "the preservation of peace and good order." The accompanying red tape—and the consequences for violating it— made it difficult for the newspapers to continue posting play-by-play accounts during subsequent World Series contests. A fine of up to a hundred dollars plus costs, or a sentence of up to thirty days in jail or the county workhouse, made the notion of incurring violations just to keep up with baseball scores seem less than prudent.

With the statewide suffrage referendum on the horizon, the suffragists recognized an opportunity inherent in the city's restrictions. They looked at the throng of clamoring baseball fans and saw a crowd of voters with the potential to support their cause. So the ladies turned to a couple newspaper men who were already sympathetic to suffrage. Hart Given, owner of the Pittsburgh *Morning Post* and *Evening Sun,* and Arthur Braun, who managed both papers, agreed to supply regular play-by-play accounts by telephone. The updates could then be announced to the assembled crowds in the arcade on the first floor of the Antler Hotel.

On the morning of October 8, when the first game was to be played, the police lieutenant of the district came into the Equal Franchise Federation office. Anticipating that Lucy might have gone too far in one of her antics, the office was abuzz with excitement. Perhaps she was due to be arrested, they thought. The lieutenant's mission, however, was to find out if the building had been inspected as a safety measure, and to secure some assurance that the floor would hold up under the strain of the expected crowds. Lucy promised him that they would immediately have the building inspected. By game time later that day, she insisted, safety provisions would be made. Under Lucy's direction, the ladies convinced a team of contractors to come to their immediate rescue. The contractors made a thorough examination and shored up several places in the building. "These

"Objections Answered," a booklet printed by the Pennsylvania Woman Suffrage Association in 1914, was small enough to tuck neatly into a proper lady's diminutive evening bag.

men cooperated so effectively," Lucy later wrote, "that by two o'clock the floor would have carried several heavily loaded freight trains."[18]

Newly reinforced, the spacious arcade could hold as many as two thousand people at a time. And the crowds came. Men leaned in to hear amidst the din, waving their straw boaters and shouting as they cheered on their favorite players and teams.

* * *

In advance of the 1915 Series, Phillies' president William F. Baker had won the coin toss to determine which team would host the first game. His Baker Bowl, with seating for some eighteen thousand people, became the setting for a wet and gloomy opening day. In order to pack in more spectators, Baker had additional seats added in the left and center fields, a move that would ultimately disadvantage the Phillies. Their ace pitcher, Grover Cleveland "Pete" Alexander, faced Sox starter Ernie Shore. The Phillies also had power

hitter Gavvy Cravath. Alexander did not allow the Sox to score a run until
the eighth inning.

* * *

After an uneventful start to the first game, Lucy hopped onto her soapbox in
the arcade to fill the empty air. "It is fair and right," she began, "that the people
who must obey the laws should have a choice in choosing the law-makers, and
that those who must pay the taxes should have a voice as to the amount of the
tax, and the way in which the money shall be spent . . . In taking a vote to get
at the wish of the majority, certain classes of persons are passed over, whose
opinions for one reason or another are thought not to be worth counting. In
most of our states, these classes are children, aliens, idiots, lunatics, criminals
. . . and women. There are good and obvious reasons for making all these
exceptions . . . all but the last."[19] Every lull in the action that day was similarly
filled with a message from the suffragists.

* * *

The score was tied until the bottom of the eighth, when a pair of runs gave
Philly the final margin. It was during that game that a twenty-year-old Red
Sox pitcher named Babe Ruth made his only appearance in the Series, stepping
in as a pinch hitter. "In the bottom of the ninth, with one on and one out,"
the report read, "Alexander pitches to Boston's leading home-run hitter, Babe
Ruth. Ruth grounds out and Alexander gets Harry Hooper on a game-ending
pop fly." Philly emerged victorious, 3-1.[20]

* * *

Lucy broke in amidst the cheers. "Some would argue that women are already
represented by their husbands, fathers, and brothers," she bellowed. "But we
say that this so-called representation bears no proportion to numbers. Here
is a man who has a wife, a widowed mother, four or five unmarried sisters,
and half a dozen unmarried daughters. His vote represents himself and all
these women, and it counts as one; while the vote of his bachelor neighbor
next door, without a female relative in the world, counts just as much. Since
the object of taking a vote is to get at the wish of the majority, it is clear that

the only fair and accurate way is for each grown person to have one vote, and cast it to represent himself or herself. . . . Unless men and women should ever become just alike—which would be regrettable and monotonous—women must either go unrepresented or represent themselves."

* * *

Game 2 was held again at Baker Bowl, with President Woodrow Wilson throwing out the first ball. His appearance marked the first by a chief executive at the Series, and the widowed president created a sensation as he arrived from New York at one o'clock with his fiancée, the elegant, forty-three-year-old Edith Galt, also widowed. Scheduled to be married later that year, the two drew a crowd of some fifty thousand Philadelphians on their way to the ballpark. The president was reportedly distracted through much of the game as he directed his attention to his fiancée, so distracted, some said, that when the band broke into "The Star-Spangled Banner," it wasn't until the final few bars that he rose and removed his light-gray fedora.

Boston's Rube Foster, who had led the club with twenty regular-season victories, took the limelight in that second game and allowed just three hits while Erskine Mayer permitted ten. Yet the score was just 1-1 after eight innings.

* * *

Back in Pittsburgh, another suffragist seized the lull between innings. "To those who would say that women are already over-burdened and that a woman would not have time to perform her political duties, we say, how much time must she spend on her political duties? If she belongs to the well-to-do class, and hires others to do her work, she has time for whatever interests her most. . . . If she does her own housework, she can take ten minutes to stop on her way to market and vote once or twice a year. She can find half an hour a day for the newspapers and other means of information. She can talk with family and friends about what she reads. . . . If she does this reading and talking, she will be better informed than the majority of voters are now."

* * *

Then, in the top of the ninth, the announcement came, "With three hits already, Foster drives Larry Gardner home with a single." The president and his future first lady watched as Boston closed the game with a 2-1 victory that tied the Series at one game apiece.

Game 3 shifted the contest to Boston, where the Red Sox management moved from Fenway Park, their home field of four seasons, to the city's mammoth new Braves Field.[21] Braves Field did not just provide seating for some forty thousand fans, more than twice the capacity of the Baker Bowl. It also featured deeper outfields—410 feet on the left and right sides and 550 feet down the center—which would work to Boston's favor. When it opened in August that year, baseball legend Ty Cobb commented, "No one will ever hit a home run out of here." The particularly deep outfield provided plenty of space for the talented Red Sox outfielders to work their magic. Braves Field also introduced an unprecedented amenity in a ballpark: special compartments next to the dugouts to accommodate motion picture cameras. Baseball was indeed looking to the future.

Pitchers Pete Alexander and Dutch Leonard battled to a 1-1 standoff in game 3, until the bottom of the ninth.

* * *

Seizing the moment back in the arcade, another suffragist made her case. "Some would argue that women's suffrage would double the ignorant vote," she began. "But statistics published by the National Bureau of Education show that the high schools of every state in the Union are graduating more girls than boys—some of them twice and three times as many. Because of the growing tendency to take boys out of school early in order to put them into business, girls are getting more schooling than boys. Equal suffrage would increase the proportion of voters who have received more than a mere elementary education."

* * *

Turning their attention back to Boston and the ninth inning of game 3, the Sox's Duffy Lewis hit a single over second base, sending Harry Hooper home with the winning run and ending the game at 2-1.

It was more of the same in game 4, with Boston securing its third straight

2-1 win. Pitcher Ernie Shore was instrumental in the win, with Philly only making one run on seven hits.

Returning to their home field for game 5, the Phillies commanded a 4-2 lead after seven innings, largely due to three RBIs by Fred Luderus. But the suspense began to build in the eighth inning. The Sox's Lewis tied the game as he hit a two-run homer into the center-field bleachers.

* * *

And once again, Lucy was on her soapbox, emboldened by the cheering crowd. "To those who would argue that if women vote they ought to fight and do police duty," she roared, "we say that so long as the old, the infirm, the halt, the lame and the blind are freely admitted to the ballot box, some better reason must be found for excluding women than the fact that they do not fight. All men over forty-five are exempt from military service, yet they vote." She quoted the venerable Lucy Stone, who had been a leader in the women's rights movement as early as 1847, adding that "some woman risks her life whenever a soldier is brought into the world," and closed that segment with another quote, this time from British activist Lady Henry Somerset: "She who bears soldiers does not need to bear arms!"

* * *

With game 5 tied, it remained to be seen if the Series would continue to a sixth game. Then, in the ninth inning, the Sox's Hooper belted his second home run of the game, bouncing the ball into the extra seats in left field and putting the Sox on top, 5-4.

That was it. The Series was decided in five games, and the Red Sox emerged victorious, as they would again in 1916 and 1918. The Phillies would not win another postseason game for sixty-two years. Meanwhile, with the Pittsburgh suffragists running a continuous campaign from ten o'clock in the morning until ten o'clock at night, their makeshift forum saw as many as ten thousand people pass through its doors daily. And the response was positive. "It was a Roman Holiday for the suffragist," according to Lucy.[22] "A good-natured, appeased crowd went out," she recalled, "feeling that women who could put on that kind of a show ought to have the vote."

It was a home run for suffrage. The game, however, was far from over.

12   A PIVOTAL VOTE

As November 1915 approached, the suffragists had decided to augment the free news publicity they were getting with full-page advertisements in each Pittsburgh paper. It was Lucy who made the rounds to the men in control. By the time she was through, every paper except the *Press* had agreed to give them a full page without charge either the day of or the day before the vote. The *Press* asked instead if the Equal Franchise Federation would be satisfied with a front-page column every day for six weeks, written by Miss Gertie Gordon. This was, of course, an even better option, and ultimately, not to be outdone by its peer papers, the *Press* succumbed to running a full-page advertisement as well.

The ads featured copy by John Brashear, who had been voted "the most popular man in Pennsylvania," setting forth his reasons for wanting women to have the vote. They also included a facsimile of the ballot, "showing just where you could mark your yes or no." Additional ballot facsimiles—three hundred thousand of them—followed on large postal cards mailed out just before Election Day.

* * *

There was no time for the suffragists to catch their breath. With just seventeen days to go until Election Day, it was time for one last spectacular parade. This was to be the greatest ever held in Pittsburgh. The planning committee, headed by Lucy, brought together all constituencies and included Mrs. Wilfred Holmes and Mrs. Paul Laurence Dunbar, widow of the renowned poet, to represent Black women.

Parade day, October 16, arrived with a flurry of anticipation. Threatening skies cleared just in time for the procession to leave the Monongahela Wharf on the mile-long march, which wended its way through downtown and across the Allegheny River. Seven thousand women joined the great yellow column, a sea of white dresses and yellow parasols. For nearly an hour, they passed at the rate of a hundred per minute. A hundred thousand spectators cheered them on as businesses closed for the duration. Small by New York standards, where tens of thousands of women and men would march later that month, with half a million spectators, it was nonetheless a spectacle for Pittsburgh.

Mary Flinn Lawrence, an accomplished equestrian, headed the horseback delegation.[1] The first float represented a kitchen, representing how politics enters the home through issues of sanitation, food supply, water supply, garbage removal, and more. "Back to the Kitchen? We Never Left It," the banner read. Spectators were charmed by a "garden" of children dressed as yellow daisies: "Women prepare children for the world. Let women prepare the world for children." The marchers were confident and said so: "Woman Suffrage is inevitable—eventually, why not now?" As in past parades, the men brought up the rear.

Finally, the parade dispersed at the North Side's West Park, where a rally ensued, with Lucy presiding and her father among the speakers. Lucy called it "visible evidence of our earnestness." Jennie Roessing declared it one of the best parades ever in Pennsylvania. As the sun set on the rally, it was said that the big ball of yellow symbolized their goal, "just over the hill." [2]

Victory on Election Day would not only mean a reward for all the Equal Franchise Federation's hard work. If all four states in contention were to win, it would mean thirteen million women voters in the country, a dramatic increase over the four million in the existing eleven suffrage states. The stakes were high, and the federation women pulled out all the stops, as did the women of the Pittsburgh Association Opposed to Woman Suffrage. Rhetoric on both sides became heated, with "verbal bombshells and cannonballs of contradiction" flying. At a luncheon in the Fort Pitt Hotel, Helen Allen spoke of the "indirect influence" favored by the antis. "Have you ever known indirect influence that wasn't crooked?" she asked. Eliza Armstrong indignantly defended herself and stormed out, refusing to "be pulled to pieces."[3] Helen asserted that the anti literature was "laden with generalities which do not glitter, half truths, near quotations, partial statistics and faulty data."[4] An attorney visiting from New Jersey, John A. Matthews, countered, saying, "I have never heard any good reasons advanced in favor of woman suffrage. Little is heard today of the reasons formerly advanced by the suffragists as to why women should have the vote. About the only thing they have left is that purely effeminate 'because.' Their whole argument is in that one word. They want the vote 'because.'"[5]

Both sides still foresaw victory when President Wilson got off the train in Princeton on October 19 for an early Election Day and walked around the corner to the fire hall, where he purportedly cast his vote for suffrage. It wasn't until ten thirty that evening that the New Jersey results were conclusive. The amendment had been soundly defeated in every big city and in nearly every town.[6]

Eliza Armstrong and her cronies, naturally, were delighted by the defeat in New Jersey. One might have expected the women of the federation to be discouraged. But it only seemed to fuel their resolve. "There never was any great reform gained without years of hard work. We are working for suffrage now, and we will keep on working until we get it—whether that be November 2 or years from then," said Mrs. Franklin Irish.[7] Their new cry, "Pennsylvania will be the first of the original thirteen states to vote favorably for suffrage," was rooted in a refusal to interpret New Jersey's rejection as prophetic and a conviction that, ultimately, right was on their side.[8] A favorable vote for suffrage on November 2, they argued, would eliminate the necessity of another five-year campaign. Regardless of the outcome, however, they were not going to give up.

The only pause in the contentious final days before the November 2 vote came incident to a tragic factory fire at the Union Paper Box Company on the North Side in which thirteen young women perished. It was a horrific flashback to the Triangle Shirtwaist Factory fire four years earlier in New York. Immediate accusations of gross negligence and code violations would grow into full-scale investigations.[9] Both sides tearfully expressed heartfelt sympathy and contributed relief funds for the victims and their families. Lucy, however, just couldn't resist inserting a pitch: "Is it likely that the women working under those conditions would have been forced to continue so had each one of them been able to cast a ballot and been affiliated with thousands of other women entitled to vote?" she asked.[10] "In this day of tragedy for working girls of Pittsburgh, words of sympathy help little. What is needed for the protection of working women is direct power to improve conditions under which they work."[11]

On the heels of that grisly incident, thousands of ministers engaged in Supplication Day across Pennsylvania, an idea conceived by Jennie Roessing.

Clergy of all denominations prayed from their pulpits for men to pass the state amendment.[12]

That week, suffrage speakers addressed some five thousand meetings in nearly every city precinct and county borough. Some two hundred thousand leaflets were distributed. A fifty-mile automobile parade snaked through dozens of small towns. The federation headquarters hosted two ten-hour marathon days of speeches in addition to their regular program. Both sides were still targeting the mills, even as the federation believed that they had labor interests firmly on their side. Eleventh-hour endorsements came in from the United Mine Workers of America, the American Federation of Labor, and the Pennsylvania Federation of Labor.[13]

The proposed Pennsylvania amendment was one of six issues up for consideration on that November 2 of 1915: the election of five nonpartisan candidates for city council and a minority place on the board of county commissioners, plus four proposed amendments to the constitution. Three of the amendments were widely supported and expected to pass: for the extension of Philadelphia's borrowing capacity, for the enforcement of workmen's compensation for injuries and occupational diseases, and for a system of registering and guaranteeing land titles by the state or counties.[14]

But the proposed first amendment, the suffrage question, consumed most of the press leading into the election. The *Gazette Times*, in its Sunday morning rotogravure picture section, featured a full page of portraits of sixteen active advocates of suffrage, "their reasons tersely told." Lucy, photographed on her porch with young Julian and baby Eliza, was quoted as saying, "Countrywide suffrage for women is inevitable because the desire was born of intelligence and reason. It will prevail in Pennsylvania, its men believing in fair play." Eliza appeared in an earnest-looking portrait with the quote, "I forecast with confidence that day when women now professing to be opposed to us will add their votes to ours for improvement of laws governing our homes."[15]

Julia Morgan Harding countered with "Nothing could be more dangerous than the injection into the electorate at such a time, of an immense element of temperamental instability."[16]

Speaking for the Equal Franchise Federation, Mary Hay said, ". . . their entire supply of ammunition is distortion and fiction. It could all be pigeonholed under one title, but that word is taboo in polite society." She went on to detail just how the data had been distorted. "Either the professional mouthpieces of the opposition know they are making false statements—or

Lucy managed to maintain a busy schedule with the Equal Franchise Federation even as she tended to a young family at home. From *Pittsburgh Gazette Times*

they are ignorant of the facts and therefore unreliable propagandists."[17]

It was Lucy who had the last word. "For five years, we have been making our arguments," she said. "Tuesday the women of Allegheny County will appear for judgment before their political peers, and those political peers are supposed to render their decision upon the merits of the case. . . . Herewith, we close our case, and await the verdict."[18]

There was of course gambling on the issue. Odds in Philadelphia were three to two that the amendment would fail. One advertiser in Pittsburgh offered a new kitchen cabinet for the woman who could guess the outcome and the number of votes by which the referendum would pass or fail.[19]

The "suffragents" were also active in the weeks leading to Election Day as the Men's League weighed in with their support.[20] Senator William Flinn, Mary's father, was working hard for clean election laws and proved to be a particular ally. He rallied his many friends among the "old line politicians," and Joseph Guffey of the "then meager" Democratic Party and Alexander Moore also lent active support for the cause. Even those who opposed suffrage "vied with each other to be nice to the women watchers" on Election Day.[21]

November 2 dawned with fair skies, cold temperatures, and biting winds. That did not deter the suffragists from poll-stalking. For four or five weeks, Lucy recalled, they had held meetings for poll workers, "instructing them in every possible contingency and requesting them wherever possible to get from the Judge of Election, after the counting of the ballot, the number of votes for and against suffrage so that there could be no skull-duggery later."[22] On Election Day, they had an army of more than two thousand volunteers to ensure that each polling place in the city had a woman present from seven o'clock in the morning until the ballots had been counted.

Reports were that, for the most part, the suffragists were courteously received by the men on duty, some of whom passed their smoke and lunch breaks with the women.[23] Eliza, watching the polls that day, commented, "Some of the polls I saw today were dingy, but, when we women have the right to go into them, we'll take our mops and brooms along."[24] To Eliza, who was looking forward to marriage and homemaking, politics was public housekeeping, and she planned to run a tidy house.

When it came time to tally the votes, the *Gazette Times* boasted that it had developed an innovative relay system for processing the returns as they came in. The system made use of Remington accounting and Burroughs adding machines specially constructed for the purpose. Returns would be called in from the districts to a corps of telephone operators and then relayed by messenger boy to the machine operators. Manufactured for use in all kinds of business, these devices were said to be "infallible in results" and could do the work of two or three active clerks. With their inclined keyboards of as many as seventeen columns of keys, and their complex inner workings, the machines could be as costly as a new car.[25] The particular models used for this election were large enough to show all candidates' names and were equipped with "totalizers" to add each individual column separately. "In short," the paper explained, "as this remarkable machine typewrites all the figures, it completes the computation of all the election returns under various sub-headings, which are composed of all the different sections where the votes are cast and counted."[26]

As the returns came in, it seemed that all the hard work might have been worth the effort and that victory was at hand. "City Hall gasped," Lucy recalled, as they carried even the third ward, which had been "one of the worst" in terms of machine-controlled politics.[27]

Yet at midnight it looked as though the amendment vote had been lost.

By ten o'clock the next morning, victory in Allegheny County again seemed certain. "If we carry Pittsburgh and Allegheny County," Lucy exclaimed, "it will be the first time in the history of suffrage that any city the size of Pittsburgh or any county the size of Allegheny has gone pro-suffrage."[28]

The closing count was slow in coming. Even though final returns would not come in for another two weeks, it was quickly evident that the amendment had won in Allegheny County but lost in Pittsburgh and statewide. They received a particularly heavy vote in the industrial districts, reflecting the support of labor.[29] In the end, the huge victory in Allegheny County was not enough to carry the day, and the amendment was defeated by some fifty-three thousand votes across the state.[30]

Lucy was mad. And she told the papers so. Hearing more than fifty reports of "irregularities and illegalities" on Election Day, she had complained to the District Attorney, who sent investigators. In some locations, liquor was being distributed. In some, official ballots were permitted to be taken outside the polling place. One suffrage worker told Lucy she saw money change hands in sight of the polling place. Whether it was in exchange for votes she could not say. She also reported seeing the same persons go into the polling place many times. Many counts alleged that "fake" sample ballots had been distributed that appeared to be designed to confuse voters. The suffragists and the antis each charged the other with responsibility.[31] Lucy decried these "desperate" measures.[32] The district attorney called it "willful fraud." He added, "It is disgusting to think anyone would resort to such tactics. I am frank to say that although I have seen nearly all the political tricks worked, this is the first time I ever encountered anything of this kind—it's a new one on me. These women watched the election like hawks. They're hustlers. You've got to give them credit."[33] A grand jury charged with investigating the matter, however, concluded that there was no punishable offense.[34]

Worse yet, Lucy contended that they had been double-crossed in Philadelphia by State Senator Edwin H. Vare. Vare was popularly referred to as one of the three "Dukes of South Philadelphia," who held the city's political machine in their hands. Son of a pig farmer, coal dealer, and garbage and excavation hauler, Vare had served briefly in the State House of Representatives before entering into a contracting partnership with his two brothers—a highly successful venture, albeit plagued with numerous civil complaints and indictments. In his 1908 Senate campaign, he had won 80 percent of the Republican vote in the city's first district and begun a political reign that controlled the courts and power brokers across the Commonwealth. The story is told that he would stand at the top of the imposing marble staircase in the Capitol Rotunda looking down with an inspecting glare as each freshman senator climbed the steps for the first time as if to claim them as his vassals. Vare's stronghold would last until his death in 1922.

According to Lucy, Vare had publicly stated that he would support the suffrage cause but at the last minute issued orders to the Philadelphia machine to get out an adverse electorate to vote against the amendment. So despite having overcome the opposition in all the unfavorable counties, more than thirty of them, the pro-suffrage majority was overcome by an unfavorable vote in Philadelphia. Anna Howard Shaw agreed that the machine had intervened, although Jennie Roessing did not.[35] But Lucy felt betrayed. Ironically, Vare's wife Flora went on to become the first elected woman state senator five years after her husband's death.[36]

New York and Massachusetts also suffered defeats that day. The suffragists could find consolation and a modicum of hope, however, in comparing the votes for suffrage with votes cast in the 1912 presidential election three years earlier. In Pennsylvania, suffrage received more than 109,000 more votes than Taft, 10,000 to 30,000 more than Wilson, and nearly as many as Roosevelt, who had carried the state. In New York and in Massachusetts, suffrage received more votes than either Taft or Roosevelt.[37]

The battle was lost, but the war was still on. By law, the suffrage question could not come before the people again for another five years. That was five years in which the suffragists could argue their case. In a calmer moment, Lucy insisted, "We are not discouraged. Nothing big comes easily. In any case we have won thousands and thousands of splendid men and women to our standard. We have educated thousands of young men in high schools who . . . five years from now will cast their votes for us. We have discovered what ignoble tactics are being used against us. And all the knowledge we have gained in this campaign is behind us for the one we are taking up immediately. Discouraged—well, no!"[38]

Jennie Roessing declared, "If our opponents are laboring under the delusion that they have dealt us a death blow by defeating our amendment this year, they have a sad shock in store for them. . . . Woman suffrage has not been defeated in Pennsylvania. It has merely been postponed."[39]

The *Gazette Times* said,

> Unquestionably they displayed political capacity and acumen. They must naturally be disappointed at the outcome, but they need not be ashamed or apologetic. Allegheny County, with more than 1,000,000 population and a great industrial center, presents for contemplation perhaps the biggest surprise in all the four states named. The suffragists emerge from the contest in such strength as to amaze all political prophets. They have carried the county. The assumption that woman's suffrage would have indifferent support in a community where there is a vast army of working people

is completely dissipated. There are felicitations due the energetic women who made the campaign in this county upon so striking an exhibition of efficiency and concentrated effort.[40]

"So we were back where we started from," Lucy later recalled, "with all the work to do over again."[41] Both the Equal Franchise Federation and the Pittsburgh Association Opposed to Woman Suffrage headquarters were open for business on November 3 as though there had been no election at all.

13 TIME OUT FOR LOVE
AND MARRIAGE

As the suffrage campaign leading to the watershed November 1915 election waged on full force, Eliza was understandably distracted. She was in love. The final election returns appeared on the same page in the *Gazette Times* as the announcement of Eliza's upcoming wedding.

The object of her affection—a 1910 Cornell graduate named R. Templeton Smith—was equally smitten. They had met as small children in the First United Presbyterian Church of Pittsburgh, and their families knew and liked one another, although Temp's family did not run in the same social circles as the Kennedys. After she had returned from her initial suffrage training in New York, sometime in 1913, Temp asked Eliza to a dance, and they were immediately drawn to one another—he to her beauty, brains, and quiet strength; she to his classic good looks, hard-working entrepreneurial spirit, and unshakable optimism. They had begun a courtship and correspondence soon after that first date, and as the relationship unfolded, Eliza kept one foot in the suffrage battle and one in the life of a socialite.

Temp and Eliza's letters doled out equal parts local gossip and news, progressive political commentary, and declarations of love, albeit circumspect by twenty-first-century standards. She shared drafts of her suffrage speeches and recounted her exploits on the road back to Vassar College and on suffrage business in New York. He shared his triumphs and frustrations as a buyer traveling for the H. J. Heinz Company. By June 1914 they were secretly planning to marry, and Temp wrote, "Dearest Sweetheart, . . . I am overwhelmingly in love. I have to write it down not once but times without end."[1]

"Honestly sometimes I think I really must be dreaming," Eliza wrote back, "when I think of the past months and the wonderful part is that I find when I pinch myself that I am really awake."[2] They chuckled about how they managed to fool the world and keep their "little secret," even from their families, and

Eliza and Temp had been secretly engaged for a year when she was photographed for the *Suffrage Cook Book*.

they schemed about their future life together, a life that they envisioned as simpler, more family focused and less social, than that of Eliza's parents.

Not infrequently, the letters would end with "P.S. Burn this letter quickly." But they were too precious to burn. "Dear Eliza," Temp once wrote, "Your admonition to burn a perfectly scrumptious letter has not been heeded. Fact is, I may read it again."[3]

Nonetheless, they were able to keep their engagement under wraps for more than a year. Eliza, in the process, acquired a skill that later would stand her in good stead in the world of politics. She was learning to bluff. Writing of one friend who was suspicious of a romance, Eliza said, "She claims I showed an unusually keen interest in the subject [of marriage] and therefore there must be a reason. I told her that there most assuredly was and put on a few flourishes to color it up a bit. She didn't believe a word. I knew she wouldn't, but I thought it would be nice to remind her of it when I really did tell her."[4]

Even as late as July of the year they were to be married, Eliza enjoyed carrying on the ruse. Describing an encounter at a dance in Beaumaris, she recounted, "One man violently discussed suffrage with me and warned me that I was lessening the possibilities of matrimony. The poor man didn't know that I am so nearly married now. I didn't tell him because it seemed like such a good joke and I wanted him to make as many remarks as possible.... I shall take a great deal of pleasure in introducing the young gentleman to you."[5]

Another man with anti-suffrage leanings whom Eliza encountered at a party while visiting friends in Long Island, knowing that she was engaged, suggested that Temp was in for "an awful life."

We had quite a discussion last night about a wife being home to welcome her husband when he comes home in the evening.... I am glad I won't have that idea to live up to . . . I'm afraid dear I can never reach those heights of devotion. What do you think about it? Will it worry you if you come home some evenings and find I'm still out to a suffrage meeting? It might even mean that your dinner would be late. Could you still love me under those circumstances dear? I can hear right now just what you would say, you dear sweet boy. I tell you I'm an awfully lucky little girl to have such a wonderful, wonderful sweetheart. Let's not ever get in the state where we are so narrow minded that we cannot get a good broad point of view.[6]

As love letters, Eliza and Temp's correspondence was sweet, not steamy but instead rather formal in expression—exactly what one might expect in polite Edwardian society. Eliza herself admitted to a somewhat reserved nature: "In my letters as well as in my conversation I am a person of few words in regard to my inmost feelings. What they are you will have to find by reading between the lines. The thought waves are all there if you know where to find them."[7] "There are things I feel that you know so well that it seems foolish to write them down. Imagine them, if you will, written just right here. Lovingly, Eliza."[8] "Somehow I never get over the feeling that the paper is a third party and they are things which I want to whisper in your ear alone."[9] "The paper is such an arduous chaperone."[10]

Eliza was drawn to the handsome young R. Templeton Smith in 1913, and their devotion would last more than fifty years.

Temp was a bit more given to rushes of endearment, though still constrained by decorum. "Dearest Sweetheart," he wrote early on, "To be perfectly frank with you, and in unvarnished language so to speak, I would like terribly much to see you right now."[11] . . . "So, dear, dear girl, when a certain kind of feeling begins to creep in, I drift away in spirit and lo! I am gloriously happy."[12] . . . "If you were here or I were there, there would be a wedding tonight. That is my state of mind."[13]

Writing from the Hotel Martha Washington in New York, Eliza told of passing her time visiting various suffrage headquarters, where she secured much new literature and "ammunition for suffrage speeches."[14] "I wish you could have seen us today marching down Ewington Street . . . with our banners unfurled . . . Votes for Women . . . we advertised the cause as well as seeing the famous streets of the East Side. . . . We visited the fish market under the bridge, stopped at a couple of fascinating brass shops, a playground and baseball park and the Henry Street Settlement House."[15]

July 1914 found Eliza once again in Beaumaris, eagerly anticipating the August house party that would bring Temp to her side for ten days, his first visit to the island oasis. "Here's hoping we get at least half a chance for a few brief conversations unchaperoned and unobserved as it were. Isn't it selfish of me to want to run off in that fashion with the handsomest man at the house party? I shouldn't blame the others a bit for being peeved at a hostess who would do such a thing."[16]

Temp, too, was excited at the prospect of their time together. "Regarding those ten days in August, I dare not think too long of the possibility of your unadulterated society for that time, wings might grow, and they would be inconvenient here. This is earth, I am told."[17]

"You're the dearest, sweetest boy in all the world."[18]

"You are the dearest best girl in a.t.w. . . . I love you so much that it seems my very life comes from you."[19]

By January 1915, Eliza had returned to Pittsburgh, visiting schools and making suffrage pitches to children, parents, and teachers. After visiting one poorly equipped school in a "low" district, she remarked that it would be better if the equipment were cut off in the better districts rather than the low ones because the children of privilege had more in their homes and didn't rely as much on amenities in the schools.[20] It was a seemingly endless schedule of speeches as they visited every school, some more than once. "Today they invited me to come back and speak at a mother's meeting of the kindergarten. . . . My same old speech is getting worn so threadbare that I should have to get busy and write something new. I have terrible qualms when I go to speak where I have been before."[21] It was also providing a glimpse into yet another area of civic life that would benefit from reform.

As Temp's ardor grew, so too did his commitment to her cause. "I'll be the 'goat' for a tryout of your new suffrage gleanings. I'll place myself on the sacrificial altar. You can, you may say the new speech to me first . . . thus enabling you to watch the effect on an audience before you meet them en masse. That's noble, is it not?"[22] In fact, his unflagging support reached almost comic proportions in the eyes of others. Eliza reported the ribbing she received from one family friend: "Said one of my near neighbors had told him I had a suitor and that this suitor 'had always been regarded as a very respectable, cautious, quiet and careful (etc.) young gentleman, becomes suddenly and very enthusiastically absorbed in a strange subject to wit the suffrage of women, for no extraneously explicable reason. And the young gentleman in question, it seems, so runs the story, moved by the spirit, arises in an eminently frivolous or unimportant social gathering and exclaims heroically 'Give me five minutes and I'll tell you why women should vote!'"[23]

As their November 1915 wedding approached, Eliza's letters to Temp from Beaumaris described a leisurely oasis that must have seemed worlds away from the suffrage battle raging back home. "This certainly is a lazy life that I lead here and I am hoping that I will gain about thirty pounds."[24] When she was not golfing, boating, or socializing, she spent idle moments playing with her nephew Julian or hemming linens for her "hope chest." There was no mention of the World Series or the upcoming election.

She was not, however, unmindful of current affairs and had her strong opinions about justice, fairness, and greed. In the aftermath of the scandal in which the young millionaire Harry Thaw was acquitted for the murder of architect Stanford White in Madison Square Garden, a murder at the center of a steamy love triangle that involved Thaw's wife, the beautiful actress Evelyn Nesbitt, Eliza was not sympathetic to the defendant, who had recently been released after seven years in an asylum for the insane. "Harry Thaw I see is now residing in Pittsburgh, a great honor for the smoky city. It seems terrible that just because he has millions behind him that he is able to get out when a poor man would have had to stay in. When we read of things like that and the conditions at the Colorado Fuel and Iron it doesn't seem as if we had much democracy in this country but a moneyed aristocracy that is ruling the country."[25] The 1914 incident she referenced, known as the Ludlow Massacre, had pitted the Colorado National Guard against a tent colony of twelve hundred striking miners and their families. When the machine gun fire was over, some twenty-one men, women, and children were dead. The owner of the mine, John D. Rockefeller, was widely blamed.

"When we think of the great fuss they are making over the sinking of the Lusitania," she wrote in another letter, "they are through negligence allowing some equally criminal things to happen here in the U.S.A. The awful accident in the Chicago River cost almost as many lives as the Lusitania. We can't blame it on the Germans either. We must put the full blame on inefficiency in our own country. After the Slocum disaster in New York, it was thought that it would be impossible for such an accident to occur again. But here we have a similar instance and probably will in the history of our country as long as there is so much greed."[26] In the General Slocum disaster on June 15, 1904, the sidewheel steamship had caught fire and sunk in the East River, killing more than a thousand of the thirteen hundred-some people aboard for a church picnic. It was the worst disaster in the New York area prior to the September 11, 2001, attacks. The Chicago River accident on July 24, 1915, involved the S.S. Eastland, a passenger ship that rolled onto her side while tied to a dock, killing 844 passengers and crew members, the largest loss of life from a single shipwreck on the Great Lakes.

Eliza and Temp's correspondence also captured the eager anticipation that had been building even before their "secret" had been publicly announced earlier that year. One evening, on a boat ride "in the most perfect moonlight," Eliza confessed that "I was left alone with my thoughts." She went on,

> Without overworking your imagination, I think you can guess somewhat the nature of those thoughts even though you could not figure exactly what they were. I had time to meditate on many things that have happened, many bright and happy hours spent in the society of a beloved boy. Is it strange that my thoughts flew back to a certain Memorial Day when we took a trip to a little Pennsylvania town. Then there seemed to spread out before me all the wonderful hours that we have spent together. Oh! But I did want you then. I just longed to have you here for a little while so that I might give to you some things which you very much deserve, you darling. . . . Dear I wish you could realize how blissfully happy you have made me. The fact that you love me simply thrills me . . . I am just as dippy as ever, you might even say I am worse, but it's all your fault for making me love you so much.[27]

"As always you'll find lots of love between the lines as well as on the lines from someone who loves you better than anyone else i.a.t.w."[28]

Less than two months before the wedding, Eliza reported on an incident that tested her mettle. Writing from the Hotel Martha Washington, she reported on her train ride into the city and the unwanted advances from another passenger. "About one o'clock it seemed to me advisable to call the Pullman conductor to my berth and ask that as a matter of safety either my berth or that of the 'gent' above be changed. The conductor thought it best to change me where said 'gent' would have no idea of my whereabouts. Therefore at one a.m. I moved myself and my belongings two cars forward." Eliza was livid. "Needless to say, my nerves were slightly disturbed due to a state of extreme wrath," she went on. "I fear said 'gent' did not reckon that he was dealing with a 'strong minded' suffragette for I don't think he felt that anyone in authority would be called." She then delivered the most damning commentary on the "gent" involved: "I'll bet he wouldn't even approve of women having the vote." Eliza chose not to take further action, although the conductor told her she might, but one can only imagine the tongue lashing the "gent" received over his inappropriate behavior. "This incident has proved one thing, that I can take care of myself although I must confess I was a bit frightened but my anger overcame every trace of fear. It made me so boiling mad (I use that word advisedly) that I was fairly frothing at the mouth."[29]

Temp, too, was predictably incensed. "Dearest, best, gal, The thing that had the upper berth infuriates me. It makes me too angry for expression. There's no limit to the punishment that creature could get at my hands. My dear, dear girl the thought that anybody would annoy you—oh, I'm mad!"[30]

As the 1915 World Series contest was unfolding, Eliza and Temp were counting down the days until their November 24 wedding at the Big House on Forbes Street. After attending his cousin Florence's wedding in October, Temp wrote, "Dearest girl, it is wonderful beyond measure to think that six weeks from tonight we will be married. The ceremony was fine last night. I wish we could have one just like it, only . . . no 'obey,' no 'forsake,' none of the gloomy features in it."[31]

The wedding unfolded as a large and elaborate affair, with a processional march that began on the second floor and proceeded slowly down the broad semicircular staircase around the music room. Eliza's gown was a loose-fitting, layered confection of ivory satin, tulle, and lace with a train of moderate length. Her brown hair was pulled back simply under a rose point lace veil held in place with a ring of delicate flowers, and she wore a triple strand of tiny pearls. Gone was the Gibson Girl silhouette with its piled-high pompadour and corseted wasp waist. This was a woman of the new age. In her formal portraits for the occasion, Eliza looked squarely into the camera, demure but confident, even if perhaps a bit out of place in such frillery.

Lucy served as a bridesmaid and their mother as matron of honor.

Eliza's brother Joe and nephew Julian wore white suits for the occasion.[32] Music, flowers, and food were reportedly lavish, and a great display of wedding gifts filled the living room. Among them were a linenfold Tiffany lamp from H. J. Heinz and a teak wood chest full of antique Indian artifacts from Dorabji Tata of Jamshedpur, India, where Julian had built the country's first steel mill.

The couple honeymooned in New Orleans before returning to take up residence with Eliza's parents at 5400 Forbes Street. Lucy and John had

Eliza looked the part of a demure bride for her 1915 wedding.

moved out to a comfortable home of their own before building a grander home in nearby Murdoch Farms for their family of five. Even so, the Big House ultimately would prove not to be big enough to contain the personalities of four strong-willed adults, and Eliza and Temp were eager to move out.

As the Great War drew in the United States in 1917, Temp volunteered as a first lieutenant in the army and was assigned to a gas defense plant at Flushing, New York, on Long Island, where he oversaw a staff of two thousand. Eliza went with him. Ensconced in a small apartment, their first home of their own, Eliza became a housewife and taught herself to cook, a skill that she mastered for that temporary setting but one which she would never enthusiastically embrace. When the war ended, Eliza and Temp returned to 5400, more intent than ever on finding a home of their own in Pittsburgh. They had long discussed finding a small house, something they might rent for forty-five dollars or so a month. But they were still living with her parents when Eliza gave birth to their first son, Templeton Jr., on August 19, 1919. Only when Tempie, as they called him, was a year old would they finally establish their domestic independence by buying their own home. By then, the suffrage battle would be nearing its end. But in 1915, on the eve of their marriage, the Pennsylvania amendment had just been soundly defeated and the battle raged on.

14 NEW GAME PLANS IN THE WAKE OF DEFEAT

In the face of the crushing defeat of November 1915, the suffragists of Western Pennsylvania knew just what they had to do first. They had to celebrate. At a big rally in Exposition Hall the next week, they drew a crowd of three thousand, about half of them men. In the public invitation for the event, Lucy opened the doors to friends and foes alike. "Every suffragist in the county and every person who voted for our amendment will be welcome at our meeting," she said. "It is primarily to celebrate our Allegheny County victory. In addition, we will welcome just as heartily those who failed to vote for us this time and those who endeavored to defeat us. We know most of them will be with us during the next fight."[1] Anna Howard Shaw, Jennie Roessing, Hannah Patterson, and Lucy all spoke that evening. Shaw heaped high praise on Lucy, saying, "No woman in the country has devoted more brains and more heart to the cause of suffrage than Mrs. John O. Miller, who led your Allegheny County forces to such a glorious triumph a week ago last Tuesday. The county, the state and the nation owe Mrs. Miller and her faithful coworkers a heavy debt."[2] Hannah advised, "The suffrage ranks know no quitters. But you must realize that a hard five years is before you, and you must never relax one bit of effort until we have won our state to victory."[3]

Along with their counterparts in New Jersey, New York, Massachusetts, and Ohio, the Pennsylvania suffragists would have to retrench and try again. Undaunted, Lucy believed that their educational work had not been in vain but rather had laid the groundwork for the next round of battle. Their plan was to hold suffrage conventions in every borough and township.

Two days after the November 2 election, Jennie Roessing and Lucy were already discussing their options with legal experts in Harrisburg. A lawyer there laid out three avenues for pursuing suffrage in the months and years ahead. The first was to resubmit the state amendment and champion it through the three-step process all over again. The second was to join the national movement for an amendment to the federal constitution. The third would be to call a state constitutional convention, a move that had been discussed for ten years and that Governor Brumbaugh favored. The constitutional convention option would secure the vote for Pennsylvania women in 1919.[4] The other options would mean that suffrage could not be achieved until 1920.

At this juncture, the state and national suffrage organizations both underwent upheavals in leadership. Women had been socially conditioned to avoid conflict, yet now as a new generation of leadership was emerging, they found themselves at odds with one another. The suffragists, both nationally and locally, would need to somehow address the shifts and fissures in their ranks before proceeding with the next phase of their campaign.

Anna Howard Shaw, after eleven years at the helm of the National American Woman Suffrage Association and thirty years of campaigning, surprised her constituents by announcing her retirement. She had given 198 speeches before Election Day, and she was ready to take a break.[5] Carrie Chapman Catt reluctantly returned as president, saying, "I am an unwilling victim. I accepted this office because no one else would take it. I did not want it, but since it has been forced on me I am going to exact a pledge from every one of you—'get together.'"[6] Still stinging from the last defeat, Catt maintained, "We would have won the last campaign if every woman had done her part, instead of running off to the seashore, the mountains or going to bridge parties and on automobile rides."[7]

NAWSA leaders announced their intention of turning their upcoming national convention in Washington into a study of "the psychological moment in the history of suffrage." This was Anna Howard Shaw's phrase, used to convey that "the time is right for a big advance, both in state campaigns and for the federal amendment."[8] As Jennie Roessing stepped up to become first vice president of NAWSA and Hannah Patterson to serve as its corresponding secretary, the women in Pittsburgh were proud to have two of their own in national positions. But dissent was occurring within the national ranks, which were now torn between two different proposed national amendments.[9] The NAWSA's favored option, the Shafroth Amendment, would require that states put suffrage on the ballot if eight percent of voters petitioned for it. The alternative Susan B. Anthony Amendment sought to grant the ballot outright to women across the nation. Still more discord emerged over the issue of whether to wage a nonpartisan campaign or hold the dominant political party responsible.[10]

Jennie Roessing's ascension to national office left a void at the state level, and the Pennsylvania Woman Suffrage Association elected new leaders as well. In a hotly disputed contest, Mrs. George B. Orlady of Huntingdon, wife of a superior court judge, was elected president on a ticket heavy with candidates from the western regions of the state that included Lucy as first vice president. An alternate slate, forwarded by "insurgents" from Philadelphia, featured an eastern contingent. Roessing, chairing the meeting for her last time, had difficulty keeping order. Lucy made her position quite clear as she delivered her ultimatum: "I came to Philadelphia representing Allegheny County," she said, "which we carried and which has borne more than one-half of the financial burden of the campaign. I know what part Allegheny will play in the next campaign, and I cannot see that I can take a part unless the ticket of the nominating committee goes through." Bryn Mawr College president M. Carey Thomas, on the slate as second vice president, echoed Lucy's remarks. At the end of it all, the Philadelphia contingent reportedly was "smarting under their defeat" by the Western Pennsylvania group.[11] A power block of fifty-nine delegates, led by none other than Mary Bakewell, characterized Lucy as a "steamroller." Lucy preferred to call herself a general.[12]

Heading to Washington to promote the Anthony resolution, suffragists from every state were armed with a three-mile-long petition of half a million signatures from voters in enfranchised states. The eighteen thousand-foot petition had been driven three thousand miles cross-country by a pair of women from California and Oregon, and during the trip, thousands of signatures from non-suffrage states had been added. Sadly, after surviving the grueling car trip, the petition was somehow "lost" as it was being shipped from Wilmington to Washington, and they had to make do with a substitute. After presenting the petition to a hundred congressmen on the steps of the capitol, the parade of a thousand women headed to the White House as the impressive document "undulated like a Chinese dragon" in the raw winter wind.[13] There they were met by a slightly more tractable Wilson than the one who had met them in 1913. He told them that it was too late to add suffrage to his annual address but that he would maintain an open mind about the issue.

Thus began the first national convention of the Congressional Union for Woman Suffrage. Anna Howard Shaw pointed out, "We have introduced this self-same resolution in every Congress for the last 47 years."[14] While in Washington, convention representatives also appealed to members of the Democratic and Republican National Committees to include suffrage in their next platforms. They would proceed to organize regional conferences, one of them comprising the Mid-Atlantic states.

The antis of the National Society Opposed to Woman Suffrage were of course there as well.[15] They condemned the suffragists for continuing to "torment Congress" during a national and international crisis and for "uselessly annoying" the president.[16]

Yet the campaign to torment Congress had potential. Senator Charles S. Thomas of Colorado acknowledged that the suffragists had reduced his former majority of forty-five thousand to a little more than a thousand. "While perhaps the men we have opposed may not like us very well, they pay much more attention to our requests afterward," according to Miss Margery Ross of the Congressional Union.[17]

So when the Senate Judiciary Committee voted 10 to 9 in March 1916 to kill all proposed suffrage amendments, as well as all related to prohibition, the suffragists were understandably disappointed.[18]

* * *

Back in Pittsburgh, the antis immediately doubled down with meetings to establish their position and craft their message, beginning with a January luncheon for three hundred. Unlike their suffragist sisters, they argued, it was not *more* votes they were seeking, but *better* votes, not a *doubled* electorate, but a *better* electorate. "We can get a better electorate only from better homes, better homes only from better mothers, and better mothers only by women giving more time and thought to the home and motherly duties." So said a male attorney visiting from New Jersey. As for the female perspective, the visiting head of the New York State antis simply dismissed the whole movement as "mostly hysteria." "Suffrage is going, not coming, but it will take a long while to chase it out of sight," was the general sentiment of the group, articulated by national anti leader Mrs. Arthur M. Dodge.[19] They favored a focus on military preparedness for the conflict overseas, just as women's clubs in general were rallying around the organization of auxiliaries to "drill the fair sex" in telegraphy, radio, nursing, motor driving, and more.[20]

Lucy single-mindedly responded with a statement that "the most advanced form of civic and domestic preparedness in a country claiming to be a government for the people and by the people" was, of course, equal suffrage. "We, the women of the nation, ever have been the ones to prepare. . . . This is nothing more or less than asking us to rally to the support of a nation which, in part, denies us support." Dripping with sarcasm, she added, "It is truly flattering that the nation feels need of us," then concluded reassuringly, "As individuals, we will aid in any emergency which arises. Always we have, always we will." But regardless of their personal views for or against preparedness, the focus of the Equal Franchise Federation as an organization was on only one thing—getting to legislators, both state and federal, who would support votes for women, what Lucy called "political preparedness."[21] What they had learned from the 1915 defeat was the need to enter more earnestly into the political arena, albeit in a nonpartisan way, and preferably in the primaries.

To get the statewide effort rolling, in February Pennsylvania's top suffrage leaders—Mrs. Orlady of the Woman Suffrage Association and her counterpart at the Woman Suffrage Party, Mrs. George W. Dibert—made their first official visit to Pittsburgh. Staying at 5400 Forbes, they planned a campaign with fifteen county chairmen. Lucy and her mother then attended a two-day meeting in early March as delegates of the statewide organization in Harrisburg, where the group agreed to dedicate forty thousand dollars in 1916 toward the election of legislators favorable to suffrage amendments.[22]

Out of that meeting came new resolve and a new game plan: "Suffragists will reopen their fight in Pennsylvania by introducing at the next legislature an amendment to the state constitution to grant the right of suffrage to women. This action will be preceded by work in the May primaries in every county to secure endorsement and pledges of support from candidates of all parties."[23] Within a month of the Harrisburg meeting, Mrs. Dibert resigned for health reasons, and Lucy was unanimously elected to chair the state party. Like Carrie Chapman Catt when she found herself returning to the presidency of the national organization, Lucy was reluctant. "I am accepting the office only because there are now, well under way, plans which cannot be stayed even for a little while."[24] The thirty-five-year-old mother of two found herself as head of the Equal Franchise Federation, chair of the state Woman Suffrage Party, and first vice president of the overall state woman's suffrage organization.

Eager to take on new assignments, the federation women engaged with a new round of promotional activities. They had a strong presence at the Pittsburg Pure Food and Industrial Show at Motor Square Garden, including a cooking demonstration of how to bake the now iconic suffrage angel cake.[25] They staged a grand costume ball in the two-story, white and gold ballroom of the new William Penn Hotel. Recalling an old English May Day tradition, they distributed three thousand blooming pansy plants in baskets to immigrant children in crowded districts.

But increasingly the focus under Lucy's leadership was on direct political action. The Equal Franchise Federation moved to larger quarters in the Jenkins Arcade and geared up for the fight ahead, while grassroots campaigns under the auspices of the Woman Suffrage Party were germinating in neighborhoods and towns all over the county.

The federation launched a Bread and Butter Club, a luncheon and dinner speaker series that included politicians who were asked to provide their views on suffrage. In a surprising move, the federation debuted the new club with a dinner at the William Penn Hotel on April 29 at which the infamously militant British suffragette, Emmeline Pankhurst, was invited to speak. Long considered a thorn in the side of the English cabinet and derided by the American suffragists for her violent tactics, Pankhurst had redeemed herself by halting her militance at the start of the war. Instead, she turned her energies to convincing thousands of men to enlist and thousands of women to engage in patriotic national service. Mrs. Pankhurst was now considered "one of the greatest assets of the English government." They had to turn the crowds away after the ballroom and balcony of the William Penn Hotel had filled to overflow capacity. A thousand people—both suffragists and antis—had turned up to hear the famous suffragette.

Lucy introduced her as the foremost figure of woman's emancipation of the last two decades. "To be frank," Lucy said, "certain methods followed by the suffragists in England are not approved by the women of the United States. . . . But be our opinions what they may in this connection, we must admire the spirit actuating the English women. In the furtherance of what they believed their just cause they invited that which they knew would cause them to endure physical suffering and made personal sacrifices such as men patriots of various lands suffered in what they believed were worthy causes necessary to the progress of their races." Finally, she said, "You may criticize those who wage war, if you will. You may condemn those whose labor in any way contributes to war, if you desire, but the war now being waged right or wrong, from your various viewpoints, has shown that women, aye even suffragists, are just as patriotic as the other sex."[26]

With that, Mrs. Pankhurst took the podium and began to tell her story. It was a story that everyone had been reading in the newspapers for years with horror and disgust, a story filled with bombs and broken glass, arrests and prison, hunger strikes and force feeding. But now here she was, the featured speaker in Pittsburgh's most elegant new venue, endorsed by its most revered suffragist. "We used the only weapon that the unrepresented have," she began. "After 60 years of patient working and waiting we were tired—do you blame us? So we adopted the men's methods, except that they were milder because women are milder than men." Turning to her work recruiting for the war, Pankhurst said that the war had restored her faith in men. "Suffragists and anti-suffragists have forgotten their differences and are working in a common cause. We of the militant organizations were ready first, because we were thoroughly organized, and had very capable leaders particularly suited to military work." Finally, she talked about her work with "war babies," the illegitimate children who seemed to be an inevitable byproduct of war, many of whom she was committed to saving herself and caring for at her spacious home in the English countryside. It was a wildly successful evening.[27]

* * *

In Washington, the suffragists were supplementing their messages to the congressional judicial committee with white and yellow boutonnieres hung on their doors, with bonbons, with valentines, and with cakes. "A wonderful white, yellow and purple frosted cake with fifty-nine candles was borne through the rotunda of the Capitol to the door of the house of representatives and there presented to Representative Williams of Illinois, on his fifty-ninth anniversary. The message which accompanied it wished him many happy returns, and the passage of the Susan B. Anthony amendment." Caught between two opposing constituencies, the committee members weren't sure if they resembled "heroes or boobs."[28] On May 16, envoys of the Congressional Union for Women Suffrage made their final plea to about fifty senators and representatives in the Capitol rotunda, whom they encircled with rope and yellow ribbon, a captive audience to the case for a federal amendment.[29]

Yet NAWSA president Carrie Chapman Catt suggested that the efforts at a federal amendment were futile and that the state-by-state approach would still be more effective. "Don't try to deceive yourselves into believing we are going to get the suffrage amendment from the present Congress," she told one gathering. "You might as well know that half of Congress is owned by somebody else and we must influence those 'somebody' else [sic] first."[30]

With the federal suffrage amendments set aside by the congressional judicial committee until at least the end of the year, the next plan of attack was to infiltrate the 1916 Republican and Democratic conventions. Both were held in June. The Republicans had chosen Chicago and the Democrats St. Louis. The Progressive or Bull Moose Party, which sought reunification with the Republicans but with Teddy Roosevelt as the presidential candidate, also met in Chicago.

Suffragists converged from across the country, tens of thousands of them, for the national conventions. In Chicago, it turned out, the regular delegates to the convention had booked all available hotel rooms. It was feared that the thirty to fifty thousand women suffragists expected to attend might have to "bunk on boats" if accommodations could not be found nearby in Milwaukee. They were prepared to charter lake steamers if necessary. They might engage Pullman berths on trains parked in the terminals. Or they might appeal to their suffrage sisters in Chicago for accommodations in private homes.[31]

As the time approached, Pennsylvania suffragists held a Go-to-Chicago Shoe Rummage to raise money by selling their "second best shoes." Pittsburgh papers reported, "High boots that lace in the back, low boots that lace on the side, button boots, pumps, walking slippers, all those made in the blithesome colors of the 1916 fashions, will be thrown into the heap and sold as second-hand shoes or for the leather they contain."[32]

Just before the convention, the Equal Franchise Federation held its election to determine the leadership for the next two years. Lucy and Mary Hay were reelected as president and secretary. Vice presidents were Mrs. Herbert DuPuy, Mrs. Robert Pitcairn, Mrs. William Thaw Jr., and Mrs. John G. Pontefract. Eliza was now elevated to the executive leadership as treasurer and Mary Flinn Lawrence and Mary Roberts Rinehart as auditors.[33]

With pennants flying, balloons soaring, and crowds cheering, suffrage supporters gathered at the Pennsylvania Station to bid Godspeed to Lucy and Mary Flinn Lawrence, along with their old friends Jennie Roessing and Hannah Patterson, as they boarded the June 5 night train to Chicago in a group of twenty-some Pittsburgh delegates. They traveled on the "Suffrage Special" in reserved Pullman cars, delivering flyers and speeches from the rear platform at stops along the way. More than fifty from Philadelphia were doing the same.[34]

The Republican and Progressive National Conventions drew the biggest crowd to Chicago since the 1893 World's Columbian Exposition, the world's fair that boasted attendance of twenty-seven million. At this convention, the 985 Republican delegates and seven hundred Progressive delegates, all with their alternates, along with the two thousand officials and staff members necessary to pull off the affair, were expected to be handily outnumbered by the twenty-five thousand suffragists and one hundred thousand other visitors.[35]

In the days just prior to the National Convention, the two rival suffrage organizations met separately, each seeking to accomplish the same end by different means. Led by Alice Paul, the Congressional Union for Woman Suffrage held a one-day convention at the Blackstone Theater. It was followed by a two-day conference of the National American Woman Suffrage Association at the Princess Theater, led by Carrie Chapman Catt. Both sought party endorsement of suffrage. But the Congressional Union sought to accomplish their objectives by establishing a national Women's Suffrage Party. Helen Keller was a notable supporter and witness of that effort.[36]

Speaking on behalf of NAWSA, Anna Howard Shaw criticized the idea of a party. "They fight to substitute a method for a principle," she said. "We are fighting for a principle, and our plank is distinctly for a principle." She went on to say, "The Woman's Party is a great hindrance to suffrage. You can't organize the women to fight the men on one point nationally, and then expect these same men to co-operate with women on other points which are of vital importance."[37]

Carrie Chapman Catt went even further. She blasted the Woman's Party's insistence on getting the Republicans and Democrats to include an amendment in their platforms, calling it "suicidal" for the suffrage cause. If the Republicans included the amendment in their platform, she explained, the Democrats would be compelled to take the opposite stance, making it a partisan issue. If instead they endorsed suffrage without specifying a method for attaining it, the Democrats might take a similar approach.[38]

The culminating event of the three-day suffrage extravaganza was, not surprisingly, a parade.[39] The spectacle would unfold just as delegates were arriving for the first day of the Republican Convention. Excitement intensified at a ball the night before hosted by the Chicago Equal Suffrage Association at one of the Michigan lakefront estates of Edith Rockefeller McCormick (Mrs. Harold McCormick).[40] The daughter of oil baron John D. Rockefeller, Edith had married the heir to a fortune built on the mechanical reaper that had transformed farming and would become the nucleus of International Harvester. Their dynasties thus merged, the McCormicks had become the wealthiest and most influential couple in Chicago.

At four o'clock on the afternoon after the McCormicks' party, the parade mobilized on the Lake Shore in Grant Park. It was expected that thirty thousand women would march. As it turned out, the parade was reduced by a torrential downpour to an intrepid core crowd of fewer than six thousand, Lucy among them, who marched for two hours and two miles through the city's muddy streets. Many of them were decked out in matching white pique skirts and white shirtwaists, with yellow sashes and twenty-five-cent straw hats with yellow bands. There were twenty-five bands, two fife-and-drum corps, and fifty-two automobiles, according to one report. Brass players poured the rainwater out of their instruments periodically as they marched. A partial canopy of bobbing umbrellas provided insufficient protection. Before they were through, the streets were littered with the remains of umbrellas that had turned inside out as they were wrested from the marchers' grips by the whipping wind. The parading women all looked like "drowned rats" by the end, Lucy recalled.[41] "Clothing wet, ardour undamped," the *Chicago Tribune* headline read.[42] One wry Chicago observer suggested that the suffragists revise their motto to "Boats for Women!"[43]

Wherever possible, the state presidents headed their delegations in the parade, so Lucy was front and center for Pennsylvania, carrying the state banner. Marching alongside her was Cornelia Bryce Pinchot (Mrs. Gifford Pinchot), who shortly thereafter joined the state board and whose husband would become governor of Pennsylvania in 1923 and serve two non-consecutive terms.[44] The rest of the Pennsylvania delegation carried staffs topped by blue keystones with "Pennsylvania" lettered in gold and yellow "Votes for Women" pennants fluttering in the cold west wind.[45] The Woman's Liberty Bell on its truck rolled silently alongside the crowd.[46]

A baby elephant—the G.O.P. symbol since Civil War times—led the eastern delegation, carrying a wooden plank bearing the words "woman suffrage," a literal and none-too-subtle message to the convention delegates as they were constructing their platform.[47] It had been suggested at one point that mascots from the suffrage states, draped in yellow finery, should be in the lineup: a grizzly bear from California, a buffalo from Wyoming, a mountain goat from Colorado, a porcupine from Utah, a black bear from Idaho, a cinnamon bear from Oregon, an eagle from Washington, a lizard from Arizona, a pig from

Kansas, a mountain lion from Montana, and a mustang from Nevada.[48] And there was the uncooperative parrot, who refused to say "Votes for Women" and reportedly was returned to the bird store.[49] In the end, it seems, all but the elephant were spared the deluge.[50]

The five thousand-some women marching in the parade were not just a showing of hopeful future voters. They also served as a reminder of the four million women now enfranchised to vote in the upcoming November election by the twelve states that already enjoyed presidential suffrage. Those women claimed to control one-fifth of the electoral college and one-third of the vote necessary to elect the next president. The bedraggled, but determined horde in their drenched white dresses and limp, beribboned straw hats—undaunted by the wind and rain—was a particularly compelling visual for the Republican delegates as they entered the Coliseum for their opening meeting.

By the end of the convention, the Republicans were ready to present their platform. The anxious women in the convention hall represented all three factions on the issue: the conservative NAWSA, the radical Congressional Union, and the oppositional antis. All leaned in as Senator Henry Cabot Lodge, chair of the resolutions committee, read, "The Republican party, reaffirming its faith in government of the people, by the people, and for the people, as a measure of justice to one-half the adult people of this country, favors the extension of suffrage to women . . ." The crowd, a portion of it at least, erupted in cheers and frenetic waving of hats and flags. Only when the commotion subsided could Lodge continue, "but recognizes the right of each state to settle this question for itself."[51]

In the rival camps of suffragists, this news was received differently. The members of the new women's party, who wanted explicit support for the Susan B. Anthony amendment, were clearly disappointed. The officers of the NAWSA, on the other hand, were entirely satisfied. "The action of the convention is all we wished," said Anna Howard Shaw.[52]

That same week in Chicago, the Progressives tied their suffrage plank to the issue of preparedness. "We believe in preparedness for defense, but never for aggression. We must not sacrifice the lives of men for the glory or gain of military conquest. And we believe that the women of the country, who share with men the burdens of government in times of peace and make equal sacrifice in times of war, should be given the full political right of suffrage, either by state or federal action."[53]

Next stop was the Gateway to the West. The day after the Republicans concluded in Chicago, suffragists began pouring into St. Louis to try for Democratic endorsement of a federal amendment. The plank NAWSA presented to the Democrats was simple: "Believing that governments derive their just powers from the consent of the governed, we acknowledge the right of women to participate in government and favor their enfranchisement."[54] The Woman's Party faction was less concerned with the platform and more concerned with influencing the delegates to pressure their congressmen to pass the Anthony Amendment as soon as possible.

The accompanying spectacle planned for this convention was the "Golden Lane," in which thousands of women with yellow sashes, hats, and parasols lined the twelve city blocks through which Democrats would have to pass between their headquarters at the Jefferson Hotel and the convention hall in the Coliseum. The plan was for the women to stand silently during those two hours. Reports differed as to how successful the women were at keeping their vow of silence. Some suggested that such a prolonged a period of silence proved to be too tall an order for a group of six to eight thousand excited women and that, standing and sitting along the cobblestone streets in the sweltering St. Louis summer heat, they talked quietly among themselves as the delegates paraded past.[55]

Midway through the Golden Lane, a tableau was staged on the steps of the old Art Museum Building. It included a Goddess of Liberty figure bearing a torch, along with representatives of the twelve states and the countries around the world where women could vote—Australia, Denmark, Finland, Iceland, the Isle of Man, New Zealand, Norway, and Tasmania. To either side were women dressed in black and heavily veiled, representing the states where suffrage had been denied. Like the parade in Chicago, this demonstration included a party mascot. The miniature donkey selected for the job kicked and brayed its way through the streets, causing considerable commotion.[56]

The Democratic plank, read by Senator William J. Stone of Missouri, was a disappointment to both the Woman's Party and the NAWSA, an even greater disappointment than the Republican one. Approved only after a close vote in committee, a contentious ruckus on the floor, and a vote of 888 ½ to 181 ½, the plank read simply, "We recommend the extension of the franchise to the women of the country by the states upon the same terms as to men." It was reported that a straight federal amendment proposal had lost in committee by just two votes. Wilson had gotten his way.[57]

The two factions of suffragists finally had something upon which they could agree. Carrie Chapman Catt's statement held nothing back: "No suffragist who was present at the convention today could misinterpret either the speeches or the action taken by the Democratic party in adopting the alleged woman suffrage plank in its national platform. The Democrats admitted freely in their speeches that 'political exigency demanded some kind of a suffrage plank,' and they thought to hoodwink the women by a jumble of words that were designed to meet the situation, but in no sense succeeded. The so-called suffrage plank which they adopted, after bursts of eloquence that were far more frank than intelligent, cannot be expected to win the presidential campaign for them. But it may well be expected to win the antagonism of millions of men and women voters in all parts of the country." She concluded by saying that the world could justly accuse the president of "descending to the tricks of the cheapest politicians."[58] With four million women voters, a chest of five hundred thousand dollars, and a determined spirit, the suffragists vowed to return to Washington and resume the fight.

The canvasing of all candidates for the US Congress and House of Representatives began almost immediately. The suffragists were seeking accountability and transparency, one candidate at a time, as they asked three questions: "(1) Are you in favor of woman suffrage? (2) If elected will you vote in Congress to submit to the states a federal amendment to enfranchise the women of this country? (3) If appointed on a committee in whose jurisdiction such an amendment should fall, will you do all in your power to expedite the passage of such a measure?"[59] They would ultimately report that 370 congressional candidates supported a federal amendment, thirty-six opposed it, and twenty-nine were undecided or noncommittal.[60] As the November election approached, Pennsylvania suffragists pressed their legislators for commitments to a federal amendment.

That same week, a rally drew more than six hundred suffragists from eleven Pennsylvania counties to Suanlinber, the country home of Mr. and Mrs. Edward E. Kiernan in Somerset, with many making speeches from their automobiles en route. At the meeting, a new suffrage flag and slogan were adopted. The flag had a yellow field with a blue keystone surrounded by eleven stars to represent the suffrage states. The slogan: "Suffrage first; safety will follow." Lucy spoke on "The Indifferent Woman," urging those who are interested in foreign missions to begin by gaining a voice at home and then helping foreign women to get the vote in their own lands.[61]

* * *

The *Sunday Post* on September 3, 1916, reported "Busy Schedule for Suffragists: Autumn and Winter Season Will Be Crowded with Vote-Seeking
Activities."[62] With alliances set and foes identified, the ladies of the Equal
Franchise Federation and their national counterparts were prepared to enter
the 1916 election season armed and loaded for bear. A great divergence of
battles on many fronts were waiting to be fought, but all of them could be
waged in the name of securing the ballot.

When Carrie Chapman Catt pledged the entire NAWSA organization at
the disposal of the federal government in fighting infantile paralysis, Lucy had
jumped in, saying, "Nothing appeals to the women of our county organization
to a greater degree than the welfare of the babies. I know of no work at this
time in which our organization as a whole, and as individuals, will be more
interested, or for which they will work harder."[63]

As the polio epidemic threatened to spread from New York into the hin-
terlands, the women of the federation offered their energy and influence to distribute warning bulletins in several languages at schools and theaters and on
playgrounds, to push for health and sanitation regulations in every borough,
and to organize "plague fighting squads" with nurses and other volunteers to
investigate and clean up unsanitary conditions in congested districts of the
city.[64] Their findings of open and clogged sewers, refuse dumps, and other
health hazards were an embarrassment to city council, whom Lucy excoriated,
with an entourage of thirty women on hand to back her up. "We have come to
tell you you are not good municipal housekeepers," she said. "We will furnish
you with autos, we will go along with you and show you the plague spots. We
will back you up in any course you may take to remedy the conditions, and if
you cannot do it we will show you how it can be done."[65]

When National Guard soldiers were stationed on the Mexican border
to subdue the paramilitary forces of Mexican revolutionary Pancho Villa,
federation volunteers wrapped fifty-four hundred packages of tobacco to
send to "Allegheny's Soldier Boys on the Border." The dodgers, wrapped with
the bundles of tobacco and cigarette papers along with cigars for the officers,
read, "Women being women know a soldier likes his smoke." They were boldly
branded with the federation's identity.[66]

And when the annual Pittsburgh Exposition opened again in September, the suffragists turned out in droves. Included in their prominent corner booth this year was a modern voting machine on which attendees could "vote" for state or federal suffrage amendments or voice their preference among the Republican, Democratic, Socialist, and Prohibition parties based on their expressed commitments with regard to women's suffrage.[67] With both men and women voting, the final results indicated a close race between Wilson (1,625 votes) and Hughes (1,582 votes). Votes for state versus federal amendments, on the other hand, were not close at all, with the state option receiving 2,189 for and 80 against and the federal option receiving 1,065 for and 45 against. The vote in favor of installing voting machines was 2,441 to 16. The new innovation seemed a streamlined replacement for paper ballots, which in Allegheny County alone would consume thirty-one thousand pounds of paper.[68] Anna Howard Shaw spoke at the Expo, as did Hughes, who was curiously silent on the subject of suffrage.[69] The federation also had a presence at the thirteenth automobile show in October at Motor Square Garden, which enjoyed record crowds.[70]

The watershed moment of that fall of 1916 was a special national meeting of "loyal suffrage soldiers" of the NAWSA on September 6–10 in Atlantic City. The emergency meeting was to preempt the usual November meeting, which would come *after* the election. Carrie Chapman Catt had issued the call for the meeting, declaring the situation a "crisis" created by the two party conventions and asking delegates to "prepare for the most important meeting in the annals of our movement."[71] There they would decide whether to pursue a national campaign, a state campaign, or both.

But before they could come up with a game plan, there was more upheaval in the Association's leadership. Jennie Roessing and Hannah Patterson announced their resignations from national office and their plans to return to Pittsburgh. Lucy's name was floated as a candidate, but she had no aspirations for a national office and had made it clear that she would not accept if nominated.[72] NAWSA would have to build a new leadership team on the fly at the meeting in Atlantic City.

As the meeting opened on September 6, a thousand delegates representing every state poured into Atlantic City. On the very first day, a triangular debate took up the question of whether to pursue a state, a national, or a combined agenda for securing the vote. After several stormy sessions, the delegates voted to continue lobbying in Washington for a federal amendment, to be supported by a program in the states of "education, agitation, organization and publicity."

They called it "The Winning Plan" and devised a million-dollar campaign over the coming year to support it, with Pennsylvania pledging $125,000. It was also decided to maintain strict neutrality in the upcoming presidential election and not to endorse any party or candidate.[73]

Carrie Chapman Catt delivered a rallying cry to the crowd: "The woman's hour has struck!" Looking at the worldwide context, she exhorted the women to recognize the present opportunity, which, "if seized with vigor, enthusiasm and will, means the final victory of our great cause in the very near future." She described the change of heart in the ranks of their adversaries. "In Great Britain hundreds of bitter, active opponents have confessed their conversion on account of the war services of women. Above the roar of the cannon, the scream of shrapnel, and the whirr of the aeroplanes, one who listens may hear the cracking of fetters which have long bound the European woman to out-worn conventions. The woman's hour has struck. It has struck for the women of Europe and for those of all the world. If our own people possess the sense of nationality which should be the inheritance of an American, they will not wait until the war is ended, but will boldly lead in the inevitable march of democracy, our own American specialty."[74] Both Hughes and Wilson prom-ised their support.

Lucy was one of the six delegates from Pittsburgh who proudly presented a new national flag based on the Pennsylvania suffrage flag. It bore an eagle with outstretched wings, standing on a globe and set on a yellow field, surrounded by eleven stars.

After they joined the emergency national meeting, the state organization held its four-day convention in Williamsport in late November, where another state suffrage amendment would be crafted. At that meeting, Lucy resigned her position as chair of the Woman Suffrage Party of Pennsylvania. It seemed that as first vice president of the other statewide organization, as chair of the Woman Suffrage Party in Allegheny County, and as president of the local Equal Franchise Federation, not to mention two young children at home, her plate was too full.

But in the meantime, there was an election to work on. Almost all of the candidates in Pennsylvania had already gone on record in favor of a second referendum in 1920, and the Allegheny County voters had proven their sup-port in 1915, so the task before the local federation suffragists would seem to be achievable. Sporting their yellow sashes, some two hundred women visited about a hundred polling places on Election Day merely to cheer the voters, thank them for their support in 1915, distribute literature, and discourage votes for the one or two candidates who were known to oppose suffrage.[75] The women were well received and secured signatures in favor of suffrage from a majority of men. The personal touch seemed to allay any fears that the men might have had about the negative impact of voting on the women of Allegheny County. "We find . . . many men have a picture in their minds of the strident, mannish suffragist—the celibate who is supposed to think of nothing else but the vote," reported one poll watcher. "When they met us and saw that we were real women with womanly cares and interest, I know they felt more favorably towards us. We had no difficulty in getting them to sign their names to our petitions."[76]

In a close race, President Wilson was reelected by a margin of just six electoral college votes, 272 to 259, with 266 required to win. Pennsylvania had the largest number of electoral college votes, which had been thrown behind Hughes.

* * *

In Pittsburgh, the climax of that fall suffrage season came on the evening of Friday, November 10, 1916, when thousands of people poured into Motor Square Garden for an evening of merriment and moneymaking. The big-domed building was ablaze with lights, and spirits were high. It was the long-awaited Shirtwaist Ball, and it was billed as "the Most Democratic Fête ever attempted in Pittsburgh."[77]

Organized by the Equal Franchise Federation to draw broad support for suffrage from all sectors of society, the event was conceived not as a showy display of fine ball gowns and tailcoats but rather as an egalitarian assemblage of shirtwaists and men's daywear. Among the festivities was to be a contest to design the best shirtwaists, still a staple of every woman's wardrobe, regardless of class or economic status, just as it had been during Lucy and Eliza's days at Vassar.

Active suffragists had been charged with selling tickets to the ball in advance to ensure a good turnout. A flyer addressed to "Fellow Suffragist" spared no hyperbole in promoting the event: "We want you to help a joyful cause!" It promised "Joy, Merriment, Cheer, Pleasure, Melody, Color and The Rhythm of Motion." This Is to be a Whirl and Swirl through Hours of Happiness." "Under the auspices of Suffrage will be brought together, Girls from the

THIS FESTIVE DEMOCRACY
HER HOPE —
HIS OPPORTUNITY

Suffrage
Shirtwaist
Ball
50¢
NO EXTRA CHARGE FOR DANCING
NOV. 10
MOTOR SQUARE GARDEN

The Shirtwaist Ball drew 3,000 suffrage supporters from all walks of life. From Detre Library and
Archives, Senator John Heinz History Center

big stores, from the factories, from the shops; Union Girls, College Girls, Society Girls and Suffrage Girls. There will also be Young Men in large numbers, and we want them all—young women and young men—to be merry under the auspices of Suffrage. We expect this evening to have something of the Spirit of New Year's Day, of Christmas, of Hallowe'en—of ALL the times when ALL are merry. To do this, Suffragists must labor hard and long as only Suffragists can and have; and the PART WE ASK YOU TO DO is to dispose of the two tickets enclosed."

The organizers sold all twenty-eight boxes available for a premium ticket price to a cadre of the city's most prominent citizens. The Babcocks, Dupuys, Flinns, Kennedys, Rineharts, and Thaws were all there, along with the Men's League.[78] Mayor Joseph G. Armstrong was also in attendance. Lucy, Eliza, and the rest of the federation's executive board acted as the reception committee.

Even in the wake of Wilson's reelection earlier that week and continual updates on the foreign war, the ball made front-page news. "3,000 Attend Suffrage Shirt Waist Ball."[79] "Debutantes and shop girls, clubmen and mill workers, lawyers, stenographers, doctors, nurses, educators, students, society matrons and housewives, and men and women in every walk of life in Pittsburgh forgot social distinctions for several pleasant hours last night and mingled freely in a cheering festival of democracy given under the auspices of the Equal Franchise Federation in Motor Square Garden."[80]

"Hundreds of couples gliding about the hall, scores of women selling favors. . . ." Attendees "purchased and wore white-and-yellow Russian turbans, neck ruffs, boutonnieres, shoulder sashes, hatbands and other favors."

The entries in the shirtwaist contest, most of them yellow, were of linen and silk and voile and satin, embroidered and lace trimmed and frilled and plain. Prizes were awarded for "the most attractive waist made by the wearer" and "the most attractive garment whether made by the wearer or not." In place of the "usual grand march" that opened most balls of the period, the Shirtwaist Ball opened with vaudeville featuring a series of dance performances, from an English country dance to a "social fox trot."[81] One worker at the event explained, "We dispensed with that [the grand march] because the dancers march and march and don't get anywhere. The great aim of the suffrage association is to get somewhere."[82]

Right after the Shirtwaist Ball, NAWSA announced its new national slogan. "Votes for Women" was deemed to be getting old and unpopular and was to be supplanted by the alliterative "Ballots for Both." Lucy was proud that the winner of the national slogan contest had come out of her own Woman Suffrage Party of Pennsylvania.[83]

The year closed with another kerfuffle among factions of the movement. Ten members of the militant Congressional Union had heckled President Wilson during his eighteen-minute congressional address on December 5 by unfurling from the gallery a large yellow silk banner, mid-speech, with the words, "Mr. President, what will you do for woman suffrage?" Lucy joined Anna Howard Shaw in censuring the move. "It was inevitable," Lucy said, "that the comparatively small organization, the working field force of which consists of hardly more than a dozen women, should veer more and more toward the spectacular, being led, as this small force is, by a woman [Alice Paul] who engaged in hunger strikes in England as a follower of Mrs. Pankhurst, without having the broad vision of that leader, who has declared a truce with her government, and has planned a more dignified method of procedure. Incidentally, Mrs. Pankhurst criticized the methods of the Congressional Union while in this country." Lucy went on, "Every activity, almost without exception that has been staged by this small body has been colored by the English way of thinking and acting, and opposed in every detail to the American. That the action of the union is unpalatable, politically speaking, to the American women, is shown by the fact that all their campaigns have been failures, and being failures, must be born of a warped trend of perspective that must satiate itself with the spectacular. So true does this seem that color is given to the frequently-made statement that although they may not in fact be working with forces opposed to suffrage, they undoubtedly give to the opponents the best weapons used to delay the enfranchisement of women."[84] Lucy did not mince words. But the women of the Congressional Union would not be deterred.

15 WARRIORS ON THE HOME FRONT

On New Year's Day 1917, NAWSA mailed each representative and senator a postcard with New Year's greetings and a poem: "And what so good a gift can be / As freedom? Won't you set us free? Vote for the federal amendment."[1]

While NAWSA was meeting in Washington, Alice Paul and the militants of the Congressional Union were following up on their December disruption of the president's congressional address. "There is a royal blaze of color at the White House gates these ripping winter days," *The Suffragist* reported in mid-January 1917. "For the first time in history, the President of the United States is being picketed."[2] The picketers carried with them the same banner they had unfurled in Congress, along with others: "Mr. President, how long must women wait?" The demonstration had begun on January 10, and Wilson would have to pass by the silent sentinels each time he went out for his morning round of golf, smiling and saluting them as he passed. They refused his invitations to come in and get warm.

Lucy, Eliza, and the rest of the Equal Franchise Federation continued to "deplore" the militants.[3] Just to be sure that her position was clear, Lucy wrote directly to the president:

> Honored Sir: The Pennsylvania Woman Suffrage Association, appreciating all that which you have done as a citizen to advance the cause of suffrage and having explicit confidence in all that which you voiced as President before our national convention, begs permission to make plain that neither it nor any of its members are in any way connected with the Congressional Union now picketing the White House with the so called "silent sentinels." . . . the National Woman Suffrage Association, with which we are affiliated, does not resort to such "mildly militant" or sensational methods. . . . Our object in

writing at this time is to preclude the confusing of suffrage identi-
ties, and to express as a state organization our fealty to you as Chief
Executive of the United States, and our gratitude to you for what
you have done for the suffrage cause.[4]

The new year also brought a renewed charge toward passage of the state
amendment with the goal of another public referendum in 1920.[5] The state
organization supplemented its strong leadership with its first paid lobbyist,
Antoinette Funk, a lawyer from Chicago who had been associated with the
successful Illinois Campaign in 1912, as well as Mrs. George Bass, who later
became chairman of the Women's Democratic Committee under Woodrow
Wilson, and a Mrs. Fairbanks, another Illinois operative. With their headquarters still in Harrisburg, the women set about securing written pledges in
favor of the Constitutional amendment, just as they had in 1915.[6]

* * *

When war had broken out in Europe in 1914, the United States had watched
anxiously from the sidelines as President Wilson promoted a policy of neu-
trality. But now, in 1917—still stunned by the sinking of the Lusitania in May
of 1915—the situation appeared sufficiently dire for Congress to appropriate
$250 million for arms to ensure that America was at the ready.

With the conflict commanding the attention of all Americans, the suffrage cause had to take a back seat. But the suffragists, seizing the moment,
would find ways to respond to the country's clarion call while continuing to
build their own political capital. On behalf of the state organization, Lucy
telegrammed the governor with a formal offer to the state, and to the country:
"The Pennsylvania Woman Suffrage Association places at your disposal the
entire strength and all the resources of its organization to be used by you or
through you at the direction of the President of the United States in any way
deemed advisable toward preparing for any eventuality connected with the
severing of diplomatic relations with the government of Germany."[7]

Lucy then headed to a national meeting in Washington called by Carrie
Chapman Catt to consider what they could do.[8] While advocating against
war, the NAWSA nonetheless pledged the strength of its membership of more
than two million.[9] It was less than two months later that Wilson would call
for a declaration of war.

Carrie Chapman Catt, speaking in a syndicated interview on behalf of the national and international suffrage organizations she headed, said that—even as a pacifist—she would be willing to die for her country. "No power can wage successful war without the organized aid of its women," she said. Urging the United States to learn from the experience of war-torn European countries, she recommended a committee of women's organizations that could serve as a clearinghouse for wartime service, from bandage rolling to munitions work, to street cleaning, to ensuring an adequate food supply for families left behind by active servicemen. The burdens of war would offer a chance to prove by deeds what all the words spoken from soapboxes had failed to achieve. Ultimately, she concluded, "The enfranchisement of women is sure to follow the restoration of peace."[10]

Given the circumstances that the country now found itself in, Wilson asked that this inauguration be a simple one. There was a parade and, for the first time, suffragists were welcome to participate, a move that officials perceived as heading off a separate, distracting demonstration like the debacle of 1913. "Will Not Be Permitted in Inaugural Parade Unless They Promise to be Good" read the *Gazette Times* headline.[11] The suffragists did, in fact, behave. Under the threat of impending war, the entire march was primarily a showing of patriotism in a fluttering sea of red, white, and blue.

As spring blossomed, there was something else to celebrate. On Monday, April 2, Representative Jeannette Rankin of Montana, the first woman elected to federal office, reported for her first day in Congress. The small, slender NAWSA field secretary bore "the enthusiasm of a zealot"[12] as she championed suffrage nationwide and had succeeded in winning not only a seat in Congress but also the admiration of the Pittsburgh papers for her womanly proficiencies: "First Congresswoman Good Cook; Trims Her Own Hats."[13] Frequently captured without a hat, Rankin's long face was topped by a close cap of dark curls, and she dressed simply. She was attractive enough, but not too attractive, to comfortably take her place among her male colleagues. Rankin was known as "the best stump speaker in Montana," and she was headed to Washington at the age of thirty-six to promote a platform of eight-hour workdays and wage parity for women.[14]

At a breakfast in Rankin's honor that morning, the two national suffrage factions had gathered in harmony to support their sister. Rivals Carrie Chapman Catt and Alice Paul sat on either side of the congresswoman, who asked for solidarity. "The day of our deliverance is at hand" was the central message of Mrs. Catt's speech that morning. "I want you to know how much I feel this responsibility," the congresswoman said in her reply. "There will be many times when I shall make mistakes and it means a great deal to me to know that I have your encouragement and support." Buoyed by the sisterhood rallying around her, Rankin walked confidently into the House chambers, where she was met with uproarious cheering and applause. Every member on the floor and everybody in the crowded galleries rose as she entered, wearing a dark dress and no hat but carrying one of the scores of bouquets she had received in her new office. Colleagues rushed over to greet her. A second outburst of applause came as her name was called on the roll, and she blushed conspicuously as she replied "present." The ovation went on until finally she stood and bowed.[15] Her first vote, a highly controversial one, came at the end of the week as she voted her conscience against the resolution that a state of war existed between the United States and Germany.[16] Rankin would go on to serve two separate terms, the only congressperson to vote against both World Wars.

Meanwhile, the picketers outside the White House kept up their vigil, denouncing the president as the only obstacle to the passage of the federal amendment.[17] Their demonstration would continue into the next year. One day at the end of June, upon the arrival of the new Russian ambassador, their banners charged that the president was deceiving Russia by saying that the United States was a democracy. That day, they were charged by an angry mob, who tore all their banners to shreds.[18] And, for the first time, there were arrests. On Bastille Day, July 14, they adopted the cry of the French Revolution: "Liberty, Equality, and Fraternity" and added a cry of their own: "Mr. President, How long must America wait for Liberty?"[19] By the end of July, there were sixteen women sentenced to sixty days in the workhouse in Occoquan, Virginia, and subsequently pardoned by the president, much to their chagrin. He declared that they could continue to picket the White House unmolested, as long as their banner messages stopped short of treason, but that he was much too busy with the war to push the suffrage amendment through Congress.[20]

The picketers had hoped for a bit more drama, with more confrontations and arrests. And they got what they wanted. The day they unfurled the "Kaiser Wilson" flags in front of the White House, a mob of three thousand men, women, and children attacked the suffrage headquarters a block away, tearing down their banners and pelting the women on the balcony with eggs. The only banner that survived was one that one of the women wrapped herself in after the angry crowd ripped off her clothing. When the kerfuffle had settled, six of the militants were arrested for obstructing traffic and sent to the workhouse for thirty days of heavy gardening, sewing, and laundry. More arrests followed into November, as many as forty-one at a time, including Alice Paul herself, who was sentenced to seven months in prison.[21] Like her English heroines, Miss Paul resorted to a hunger strike and was reportedly force-fed at the Asylum Hospital in Washington along with her companion.[22] With Lucy's support, the Pittsburgh papers published scathing editorials against the militants, asserting that their actions discredited the rest of the movement.[23]

* * *

Back in Pennsylvania, the suffrage amendment was slated for a vote on April 18. With optimistic anticipation, the suffragists arrived in Harrisburg with a thousand feet of petition, signed by more than fifty-six thousand persons, as well as petitions from 268 labor unions. The gallery was full of women, the suffragists wearing yellow gardenias, the antis red roses.[24] They had every reason to be hopeful, having garnered so much support the last time around and with so many pledges from current legislators.

It was that much more of a devastating disappointment, then, when the House voted 101 to 94 against the resolution, just three votes shy of the majority required to pass. Even a motion to reconsider the original vote—which prompted two hours of bitter debate—could not resurrect the dead resolution. At best, it would be 1921 before women would have full franchise under the Pennsylvania constitution.[25]

It was not over, however, for Lucy and her band of warriors. Infuriated, Lucy called on the members of the state House who had pledged to suffrage but were absent. She demanded an explanation for their absences and excoriated those who had voted contrary to their pledges. The Pennsylvania Woman Suffrage Association immediately proposed to push a bill for suffrage in presidential races only, which would not require a referendum. That measure, the Mitchell Bill, was introduced in the state House on April 30. The suffragists were not naïve about its chances of passing, particularly as the women continued to speak their minds.[26] As one member of the House reportedly said, letters directed at the legislators had been "vindictive and insulting, unladylike and presumptuous." The governor tried in vain to mediate by recommending passage of the presidential suffrage resolution.[27]

At both the state and national levels, the suffragists also committed to fight the liquor interests, whom many blamed for the defeat in Pennsylvania, by playing the rationing card and passing a resolution urging the president, the US Congress, and the state legislature to "devise laws preventing the use of grains for the manufacture of liquors or other beverages, and to conserve the same for the making of foodstuffs for the duration of the war."[28] For Lucy, this was not a moral battle but rather a political one.

Then, finally putting their disappointment behind them, the women of the Equal Franchise Federation turned to putting Mrs. Catt's words into action. In an address to the membership, Lucy declared that the slogan of "Votes for Women" should be supplanted by "Patriotism, thrift and efficiency." New committees set about promoting war gardening, teaching domestic science, and providing school children with a daily supplemental meal. Volunteers around the county reclaimed vacant lots and established community gardens, where they grew potatoes, corn, beets, radishes, carrots, and more on hundreds of plots, large and small. Mrs. Kleber, the woman behind the *Suffrage Cook Book*, was the mastermind of this effort as well, and she advocated a spirit of democracy. "It will do us all good to lower the arched eye-brow," she said, as young women from all walks of life worked side by side. The gardeners wore overalls, a new and still controversial clothing option for women that advertisers touted as a most practical innovation. One particularly enthusiastic gardener wrote a song to accompany the gardening and harvest: "The Battle Cry of Feed 'Em." Working with the Board of Education, the federation set up a hundred weekly classes in the best methods of eliminating waste and extravagance in food preparation. Lucy advised the women of the federation not to spread themselves out too thinly but rather to "choose one thing and stick to it."[29]

The thing that the Equal Franchise Federation and the state organization stuck to most fervently, their most ambitious wartime strategy by far, was the Liberty Bond initiative. The plan was put in motion by their lobbyist, Antoinette Funk, according to Lucy. A particular friend of Secretary of the Treasury William McAdoo, Mrs. Funk convinced him—and the board of the state suffrage organization—that they should swing the suffrage effort into the loan campaign. She assured the secretary that the women alone could raise a million dollars.

On April 28, 1917, Lucy received a letter from Secretary McAdoo to come to Washington for a conference. Upon her arrival, she found a small cadre of familiar faces assembled in the secretary's private office. There and then, they organized the National Women's Liberty Loan Campaign Committee, chaired by the president's daughter, Eleanor Wilson McAdoo, with Mrs. Funk as vice chairman and Mrs. George Bass as treasurer. Lucy became a member of the National Committee and chairman for the state of Pennsylvania, and she reported that the committee was granted "absolutely independent status" from the men's committee as well as its own appropriation.[30] This was another opportunity that even women of small means could support, "those whose savings have been put carefully away in a blue teapot or stocking, who can not only be of service to the Government in buying bonds, but will have their savings in a safer place."[31]

Before they were through, the suffragists had unleashed their energetic network on a series of Liberty Loan campaigns, five in all. Lucy was allotted the sum of $19,000 for the Second Liberty Loan effort, which engaged sixty-five of the state's sixty-seven counties and employed five paid organizers. The fifty- and hundred-dollar bonds, set to mature in ten to twenty-five years at a four percent interest rate, were offered for outright cash, through four installments, or on a weekly club plan for forty-nine weeks. The Women's Liberty Loan Committee of Pittsburgh reported to the Equal Franchise Federation at a meeting at the Kennedy house on October 27, 1917, where Lucy offered encouraging words: "An ingenious woman can devise a hundred ways to attract purchasers." As one journalist wrote, Liberty Bonds offered "a splendid opportunity to invest in a gilt-edged security and at the same time experience the thrill of patriotism which comes with the realization that one is helping one's Government in its time of stress, helping to uphold the nation's honor."[32]

As it turned out, Mrs. Funk had underestimated the abilities of the women of Pennsylvania. With an allowance of less than $130,000, but with a volunteer force more than a hundred thousand strong, they sold seven hundred million dollars' worth of bonds in the five loan initiatives, two hundred million more than New York State, which boasted the second largest success in the country. The successful campaign not only fueled the war effort but also boosted the suffragists' stock. These were women who could get things done.

The suffragists would subsequently launch a "suffrage auxiliary" of the Pittsburgh Chapter of the American Red Cross.[33] Eliza presided over the organizational meeting, and she was on the advisory committee, which Lucy headed. The federation's executive board called upon the members "to throw their every ounce of energy, not already being expended in other patriotic service, toward assisting the Red Cross in meeting the increased demands being made upon that organization for surgical dressings and hospital supplies." The auxiliary set up workrooms downtown, where they rolled bandages and organized supplies. Nearly seven hundred women and girls signed up to work, and in a single session, eighty girls could turn out twelve hundred dressings. Their first order included 36,400 articles.[34] Also participating was the Negro Auxiliary of the Pittsburgh Chapter of the American Red Cross. Jennie Kennedy was in charge of equipment. "Around half a score of tables, in the spacious room with its rows of windows on three sides, its two storerooms on the fourth, the workers, in the sheer white robes of the Red Cross, the white coifs with their simple insignia, the women wielded scissors and yardsticks, cutting machines and other implements, in swift production of surgical dressings." By the end of the year, the federation volunteers reported that they had made seventy-eight thousand surgical dressings in eight months.[35]

The auxiliary also offered dinner and music to a hundred officers and men of the motor supply transport of the Army en route from Detroit to Baltimore, an event they called a "Gloomless Sunday."[36] To serve the dinner, Lucy, her mother, and a dozen others dressed as Red Cross nurses. Lucy was the only speaker that evening: "We welcome you in the name of our federation, for you are going out to fight for the same thing that we have been fighting for these many years, the spirit of democracy. The first line we women are going to try to take is the Senate. If any of you can help us before you go, we'll be awfully glad. We are glad to have you here and we hope you will have a good time and a good dinner. We are going to fight just as hard for democracy here at home as you are for the same thing over there."[37] The Red Cross auxiliary also held night classes and taught German, Italian, and French.

The suffrage Red Cross auxiliary also pitched in to the campaign to raise four million dollars in Allegheny County. They set up an outdoor fundraiser with entertainment and hosted an auction of paintings donated by the Associated Artists of Pittsburgh. They even collected from inmates in the county jail, where one man in murderer's row declared that he was willing to go without tobacco money to "relieve the succor of our boys over there."[38]

As the nation and the Equal Franchise Federation were throwing themselves headlong into the war effort, the Kennedys were stunned by a devastating family loss. Tom, the youngest son, had married the radiant Eugenia Mason, a recent Phi Beta Kappa Vassar graduate, on August 3, 1917. Crushed when Eugenia's beloved brother had been killed in an aeroplane accident in France just a day or two before the date set for the wedding, the couple had simplified their plans and delayed their departure on an automobile honeymoon through the East. They were then to settle in Flushing, New York, for Tom to commence his war work. One Saturday evening in September, after visiting friends near Kearney, New Jersey, they were driving home, with Eugenia at the wheel. As they approached a train crossing, Eugenia, apparently a somewhat aggres-

Jennie Kennedy paused during her work with the suffragists' Red Cross Auxiliary to pose with her first two grandchildren.

sive driver, confidently declared that she thought they could make the crossing before the train did. She miscalculated. Eugenia was killed instantly when the Erie Express struck their car, and Tom was severely injured.[39] He would remarry in 1921, but complications from the accident took his life within a year. The tragedy cast a pall over the family from which it would not soon recover. But somehow their suffrage activities continued.

Later that fall, a success in New York—making it the fourteenth state to enfranchise women, the twelfth to do so fully—was a victory for suffragists nationwide. It notably gave both Anna Howard Shaw and Carrie Chapman Catt, New York natives, access to the voting booth, along with nearly two million other women, whose power and energies could now be unleashed to help their sisters nationwide.

Buoyed by the success in New York, the Pennsylvania Woman Suffrage Association Convention later that month in Pittsburgh opened with an air of celebration and promise. Lucy was ecstatic. "We were surprised, there is no use in saying anything else," she said in her rousing opening remarks. "We had hoped and hoped for so long and then to have the victory handed us so completely, to have the big state come on our side, was almost overwhelming. It means encouragement for the suffragists in the rest of the states which so far have not recognized true democracy. It means that now we are a power. That is seen already in the claims made by the various parties that they are responsible for the big suffrage vote."[40]

Noting that New York gave the suffragists forty-five electoral votes, Lucy announced, "We are now putting all our efforts on the federal amendment." Finally, she said, "We have proven ourselves to be an absolute necessity. We have shown that we are not hysterical creatures of impulses, but sensible helpers in a most difficult situation. Men who never would have paid any attention to us, now are admiring us because of the tireless work done by millions of women not only in our own country but in the European countries. The war has made men see what we can do and how necessary our help is. It was an easy transition from seeing how we were needed in such a tremendous issue as war, to realize how we are needed in all big issues."[41]

Lucy boasted that the Pennsylvania suffrage organization had been the first woman's organization to offer its services to the US government after war had been declared, and she laid out a plan by which every woman in the state would be registered as to her ability—stenographers, automobile drivers, writers, speakers, shop girls, executives, even singers and painters—so that if Uncle Sam needed a certain number of workers for a certain type of work, he would know just where to find them. She also, as always, got in her gibes about the petty, grafting politicians who got away with their shady shenanigans while the nation was focused on the war. "Inefficiency in city and state government means help for Germany," she declared.[42]

The first evening of the statewide gathering, Lucy hosted several hundred of the convention delegates for an opening dinner at the Twentieth Century Club, with all of her loyal accomplices by her side in the receiving line. A "War Time Supper" for eight hundred the next night at the William Penn Hotel included a keynote by Anna Howard Shaw as well as a riveting speech by Col. Swartzkopensky of the Russian army. The colonel, after serving the czar for twenty years, had been banished to Siberia for refusing to order troops to shoot innocent men and women on Bloody Sunday, then tramped twenty-five hundred miles in shackles, spent a year in a dungeon, and lived ninety-six days in the wilderness before making his way to Count Leo Tolstoi, who hid him for seven weeks before helping him to leave the country, only to return later to work on behalf of the revolutionary party. After such a harrowing tale, the patriotic singalong at the close of the evening must have been an upbeat relief.[43]

In addition to the suffrage cause, much of the state convention program was dedicated to the topics of war and food conservation.[44] With women pledging their wardrobe allowances and others stepping up with significant donations, they raised fifteen thousand dollars during the convention. They pinned a twelfth star on the state suffrage flag to honor the New York victory. They endorsed household economy so that that savings could be used to buy war bonds. And they reelected Lucy president.[45]

Lucy went next to Washington for the NAWSA annual convention, where they endorsed both a suffrage amendment and a prohibition amendment. Part of the program was for the delegates, in groups of as many as a hundred, to "make pilgrimages to the shrines of their state congressional representatives." An informal poll of the Senate after the visits showed twenty-eight Republicans and twenty-three Democrats for the amendment, twelve Republicans and twenty-five Democrats against it, and eight doubtful. Even if the eight doubtfuls were added to the affirmative votes, they would still come up five short of a majority. Given those prospects, NAWSA was relieved when they learned that there would be no vote on the issue until at least January. That would buy them a little more lobbying time. Within a few days, another poll indicated seven more votes than a two-thirds majority.[46] With a vote scheduled for January 10, and a perceived change in sentiment among the Pennsylvania members of Congress, things were looking good.[47] The year ended on an optimistic note, with victory seeming imminent.

16 THE BISHOP AND
MR. BABCOCK

As the suffrage message was being shared in the most genteel of settings—at picnics and teas, in parlors and churches—Pittsburgh was teeming with vice. Later dubbed the "Metropolis of Corruption" by journalist Walter Liggett, the city was a hotbed of bootlegging, prostitution, graft, and hardhanded machine politics dominated by tough ward bosses.[1] Downtown had no fewer than four hundred houses of prostitution and more than a hundred known "bed-houses," with an estimated three thousand "public women" and more than five hundred "male hangers-on." And that was just downtown. Four other districts were similarly infested. "Liquor is sold in such places without hindrance," one report went on to say, "and the wildest kind of orgies ensue."[2] Combined with the swelling presence of gambling establishments, this made for a seamy underbelly that respectable citizens looked to the mayor to solve.

But neither the mayor nor the rest of the political establishment were likely to help. Liggett went so far as to say, "It is very doubtful whether anywhere else in America there exists such debauched, dishonest or utterly incompetent public officials as these [sic] comprise the political machine which mismanages the affairs and systematically loots the treasuries of Pittsburgh and Allegheny County." And there were those who refused to recognize the problem lest it give the city a "black eye."[3]

Mayor William A. Magee, who had taken office in 1910, seemed unable or unwilling to contain the vice problem, and in the eyes of many, had instead permitted its proliferation. Julian Kennedy had spoken out six months into Magee's term:

> Disorderly houses have quadrupled in the last six months under
> Magee. These houses used to be run in a very modest way, so to
> speak, but now they are very aggressive. Today you cannot walk

where they are without having them thrust upon you. They have given us a wide-open town—that is not what they promised us. About a year ago [1909] a bulletin was put forward in this city by the Voters' League in reference to Mayor Magee. He announced himself against a wide-open town and said he would go farther than had Mayor Guthrie.[4]

Magee had defended himself, saying simply, "They are my inheritance, not my creation."[5]

It was now 1917, and the mayor's seat was once again up for grabs after a term under Joseph G. Armstrong. Magee was back, running against Edward Vose Babcock and Dr. J. P. Kerr on a nonpartisan ballot. Before long, the race narrowed to just Babcock and Magee. The ladies of the Equal Franchise Federation had become acquainted with Mr. Babcock, known to the public as E. V., when he had headed a committee of a hundred that backed Armstrong. "Many citizens felt that Armstrong's term as Mayor has been anything but successful," Lucy later wrote, "and joined the ranks against his former chairman."[6] At the same time, Magee was under pressure for his leniency during his time in the mayor's office. It was a hotly contested campaign of mudslinging and personal attacks. Lucy jumped right in. It would be her first toe-to-toe battle for what she described as integrity in government.

For this particular fight, Lucy and her comrades chose to employ the power of the press. Their own press. They incorporated a paper under the name of *Publicity*, with Lucy as president, Mary Hay as secretary, and Eliza as treasurer. Lucy reported that the political cartoons were the anonymous contribution of Cy Hungerford, employed at the time by *The Pittsburgh Sun* but later known for his fifty years with the *Pittsburgh Post-Gazette* beginning in 1927. *Publicity* carried stories and pictures of Mr. Babcock's lumber camp in Georgia, showing his use of prison labor and his exploitation of workers through their coerced use of his company store. The *Publicity* staff also secured, from a former director of the Federal National Bank, all the data on the failure of the bank, of which Mr. Babcock had been a director and a large stockholder.[7]

Now, with Magee vying for another chance in the mayor's office and Babcock his fiercest competitor, the issue of vice was again coming under public scrutiny. The Ministerial Union of Pittsburgh examined both men, with about 150 pastors present as Babcock made a speech and Magee answered questions. Both noted that the matter of morals was a private matter, more in the purview of the pastoral inquisitors than of the mayor. But each took a stance against vice. "I have said repeatedly to the people of this city that I stand for a clean city morally and a sound city financially," Babcock said. "You cannot have a city beautiful if you have social and moral cankers eating at its vitals."[8] At least one local editor would praise Babcock for his realistic position: "The refusal of Mr. Babcock to guarantee the eradication in four years of an evil that has existed through the ages shows that he is not making a scramble for office with anything that might gain a vote from the unthinking."[9]

Despite Lucy's challenges to his candidacy, Edward Vose Babcock served as Pittsburgh's mayor from 1918 to 1922.

Still, the public wanted some assurances. The candidates were also approached by a committee of men headed by James A. Gray, later a judge in the county courts. Each was again asked to articulate his stand on prostitution. The results of the interviews were to be printed as statements in *Publicity*. After the Babcock interview, however, as Lucy recounted, it seems that the men were unwilling to share the candidate's position, indicating that it was too scandalous to repeat. The ladies characteristically persisted, but the committee members remained firm in their refusal.[10]

Then, as Election Day approached, three prominent clergymen were quoted in the newspapers in support of Babcock's candidacy: Bishop Cortlandt Whitehead of the Episcopal Diocese; Hugh Thomson Kerr, pastor of Shadyside Presbyterian Church; and William L. McEwan, pastor of the Third Presbyterian Church. Not mere clergymen, these three represented the highest moral ground to the most influential Pittsburghers of the day. Frontpage stories with large headlines—"Babcock Held in High Esteem by Churchmen" and "Pastors Favor E. V. Babcock as Next Mayor"—reported that the three "indorsed E. V. Babcock's moral standing and expressed confidence in his ability and purpose to give Pittsburgh a clean city morally." McEwan said that he had known Babcock very well for a long time and described him as a "big, strong, clean, upstanding man." Kerr, who was Babcock's own pastor, pronounced him to be his personal friend and a Christian gentleman. The bishop "expressed surprise that there should be anyone in Pittsburgh who would impugn the motives or moral purpose of E. V. Babcock," whom he

Cortlandt Whitehead was bishop of the Episcopal Diocese of Pittsburgh from 1882 until his death in 1922.

called "a man of irreproachable character, a man of force, of judgment, of executive ability and business experience." He was, in their collective estimation, a man of "religious impulses and philanthropic disposition," regularly hosting Sunday school picnics and charity events at his farm, Vosemary, six miles north of the city.[11]

This endorsement in the face of Babcock's questionable behavior was more than Lucy could stand. Her blood boiling, she returned to the committee and insisted that they share the results of their interviews with the candidates. "I told them," she later wrote, "that if they were too shy to tell me they could write it down and sign it, because I was calling upon these three clergymen." Like so many, the committee members found Lucy impossible to refuse, and provided her with the quote from Babcock that she needed: "Houses of prostitution are as necessary as water closets, but I will prohibit more than one girl in a room." Armed with this statement, along with ten corroborating signatures, Lucy made her appointments.

Bishop Whitehead had backed the suffrage cause, but for Lucy, past support was no guarantee of future immunity from scrutiny and criticism. With her mother in tow, Lucy first called upon the bishop at his residence. Much to their embarrassment, the ladies were greeted at the door by Mrs. Whitehead, who of course had no knowledge of the purpose of the visit, and ushered them into the living room for tea.

It was only some time later that the bishop finally appeared, a rather benign looking man with a plump, benevolent face, balding, with gray hair and whiskers. He wore bishop's gaiters, buttoned up the side, an anachronistic remnant of the days when Anglican clergy needed to protect their trousers and stockings from the splash of mud as they traveled on horseback to visit all corners of their jurisdictions. More than two decades later, the conversation was vividly etched in Lucy's memory.

"I apologize for my delay," the bishop said.

"That's quite alright, sir," Lucy replied. "We would be happy to adjourn to your study for our discussion."

"And I would be happy to join the discussion," added Mrs. Whitehead eagerly. "After all, I am a member of the Equal Franchise Association."

Racking her brains for a graceful out, Lucy simply replied, "Perhaps this is a discussion we should have with the bishop alone."

Finally settled into the bishop's private study, the door closed, Lucy began to weave her web. "I have come to see you about your endorsement of Mr. Babcock and your interview in the papers."

"I have known Mr. Babcock for

Lucy was a young mother when she went toe-to-toe with Bishop Whitehead over the mayoral candidate E. V. Babcock.

a good many years," he responded. "We are both members of the board of trustees of the University of Pittsburgh, and I have always had a very high regard for him." He added, "I don't think endorsement is the proper term to use. As a clergyman, I am too remote and aloof from politics to endorse any candidate. I think of it more as a friendly recommendation."[12]

"Did you know that Mr. Babcock is backed by Senator Penrose?" Lucy asked, adding, "What do you think of Senator Penrose?"

"I do not like Mr. Penrose," he replied, "nor was I aware that he is backing Mr. Babcock."

"You were not aware, then, that Mr. Babcock held a large political meeting in honor of Mr. Penrose at Vosemary?" Further questioning, Lucy recalled, would reveal the bishop's general ignorance and naivete with regard to political matters.

Lucy then handed the bishop the offending statement from the men's committee. His response was visceral and immediate, his face blustering a deep crimson and the veins in his temple pulsing hard. A bit daunted by the bishop's distress, Lucy nonetheless forged ahead.

"Do you believe it, Bishop?"

"Mrs. Miller, I could not fail to believe it when it is signed by such a committee."

"Well, then, what are you going to do about it, Bishop?"

Bishop Whitehead pushed his chair back from his imposing desk and hesitated before answering. "I am always telling people what they should do. Now I am going to ask you to tell me what I should do."[13]

Seizing the moment, Lucy replied without hesitation. "There are two things which you might do. You might get in touch with the editors of the various newspapers and tell them what you have told me, that you are so remote and aloof from politics that you are not competent to make statements regarding the candidates' suitability, and that since the public has been led to believe that you are really endorsing Mr. Babcock for mayor, you want to withdraw any statement that you have made. This would be the easy way out. But do you want to know what I would do if I were Bishop Whitehead?"

Intrigued, but with some trepidation, he answered, "Yes."

"I would call the editors and tell them that since making the endorsement I have been given some very authentic information that makes me feel that not only am I against Mr. Babcock for Mayor, but that I feel he would be an absolute menace to the City if elected." The bishop did not take either the news or the advice with a great deal of grace, and he finally dismissed Lucy and her mother, promising that he would consider the issue from every angle, discuss it with his friends, and give her an answer in the morning.

The ladies' next stop was Dr. Hugh Thomson Kerr. As the venerable pastor of the Shadyside Presbyterian Church, and spiritual guide to many of the city's first families, Kerr commanded a powerful position. He had only come to the post in 1913 but would ultimately stay there until 1945. Sitting in the rounded bay window of his paneled office overlooking the expansive and well-kept church lawn, Dr. Kerr looked the part of a prosperous, conservative cleric, his intense eyes glaring over pursed lips. Surely he would have an interest in propriety and decorum. He told the ladies that Mr. Babcock was a member of his congregation, that he had known him intimately for a number of years, and that he thought Babcock to be a very fine man.

"Are you aware that Mr. Babcock is noted for having a rather scurrilous tongue?" Lucy asked.

"I've never heard him use language that was unbecoming to a gentleman."

"Well, then," replied Lucy, "if he is elected Mayor, you had better stay by his side at all times, lest he be tempted. That way you might spare the people of Pittsburgh a lot of unsavory language."

At this point, Lucy produced the statement from the men's committee. After an initial perusal, Dr. Kerr's piercing eyes and strong jaw seemed to freeze in a stony glare. He shook his head and flatly refused to believe it.

"Do you think I forged it?" she asked.

"No, but I still don't believe it."

Lucy paused only briefly. "Dr. Kerr, do you believe in the miracles of *The Bible*?" she countered.

"Yes, of course I do."

"Well, you believe them on much less evidence than you hold in your hands right now."

Lucy had met with a stalemate. They sat face-to-face in Kerr's office, both knowing that he intended to do nothing about his statement. The only difference between them was that Kerr was rendered uneasy by the situation, while Lucy was only rendered more resolute.

She returned home to discuss the matter with her father. Julian Kennedy knew Bishop Whitehead very well, as they had been classmates at Yale. He offered a bit of additional ammunition to Lucy's arsenal. Julian had heard another story about Babcock regarding his remarks at the opening session of a Lumbermen's Convention in Pittsburgh.[14]

Lumbering, it seemed, converged quite nicely with the prostitution that was rampant in the city. It so happened that Mr. H. D. W. English, the head of the Berkshire Life Insurance Company in Pittsburgh and also a pillar of Bishop Whitehead's church, had actually been present at the Lumbermen's Convention and was able to substantiate the story about Mr. Babcock. Apparently in his zeal to welcome the delegates, Mr. Babcock had announced, "The lid is down tight on the town, but if you boys want to have a good time, Joe here has the addresses. We can furnish the taxicabs, but don't ask me to go with you because I have a young and frisky wife at home."

At Lucy's behest, her father asked Mr. English to give the bishop an unexpurgated account of the incident, which he promised to do. The very next morning, as Lucy was headed for the Equal Franchise office in the Jenkins Arcade, she happened to meet the bishop on the way to his office in the same building. In characteristic form, she seized the moment.

"Have you made your decision?" she asked him squarely.

He evaded her eyes, trying to contain his embarrassment. "I've written you a note and mailed it to your house."

Not one to be put off, Lucy came right back at him. "Could you tell me verbally," she asked, "as I will not be home until late this evening and will not have the note in hand until then." The bishop shuffled and hesitated, but could see that Lucy was not to be easily dismissed.

"My friends agree with me," he began, "that my remarks in the paper were not really an endorsement, and I can do nothing further about it."

"Have you talked with your parishioner Mr. English about his recollections from the Lumbermen's Convention?"

"I have."

"Do you have the unexpurgated statement?"

"I do."

"Do you believe it?"

"Given the source, I cannot help but believe it."

"From what you know, then, Bishop Whitehead, do you think that Mr. Babcock would make a good Mayor for the City of Pittsburgh?"

She had him now, or so she thought. "I do not," was the bishop's reply, adding, "but I am not going to do anything about my endorsement."

At that point, Lucy let loose on him. She didn't even try to contain herself. Stretching to her full height, she looked the bishop squarely in the eye. "You are the bishop of this Diocese and have no business getting into politics when you do not have the courage to stand behind your convictions! I am going to tell you exactly what I think of you!" Standing a bit taller, she added, "You are a spineless jellyfish!"

"I'm sorry to know that you feel that way," was his cold reply.

"That's exactly how I feel," sputtered Lucy, turning on her heel. The bishop and Lucy never spoke again.

Lucy went straight to her office and telephoned Mr. English, telling him exactly what she thought of his bishop. Mr. English asked somewhat helplessly what he could do about it. She suggested that he could put on his hat, go to the bishop, and tell him exactly what he thought of him. Later gossip, Lucy heard, was that the incident nearly cost the bishop his job. But only nearly.

* * *

As Election Day approached, Magee's campaign manager solicited the support of the Equal Franchise Federation and its endorsement in *Publicity*, and his supporters proposed to finance one hundred sixty thousand free copies every week. Lucy warned them that the federation was not enthusiastic about either candidate. The most they would say about Magee was that he was the lesser of two evils. They also stipulated that the Magee campaign could not interfere with *Publicity*'s message and that payment had to be made one week in advance of each issue to cover printing and mailing.

In the end, Babcock prevailed, although he attributed the small size of his victory margin to the negative coverage in *Publicity*. He was inaugurated in January 1918. Just three days after the inauguration, Lucy received a telegram from a Mr. Ashe, who had been head of the Recreational Bureau, which managed the city's playgrounds. With Jennie Roessing as treasurer, Ashe had quickly built the bureau into a large organization before the city took it over. Drafted into the war effort, Ashe had then been sent as recreational director to one of the southern camps, from which he sent the telegram. He asked Lucy if she would please try to prevent the appointment of Roy D. Schooley as head of the bureau and if she could recommend another qualified candidate. "I know of no one else who could carry on the fight," the telegram stated. She agreed to take it on.

Lucy, having earned no favor with Babcock during his mayoral campaign, recognized that he controlled five of the nine votes among city council members, who would make the appointment. She did, however, have the ear of J. P. Kerr, council president, who arranged a meeting with Babcock for Lucy and Mrs. H. Talbot Peterson, an active federation member, with the stated intention that the only item on the agenda would be the playgrounds. Lucy warned Mrs. Peterson that it would likely be an unpleasant interview. She was not mistaken. As they were ushered into the mayor's office in the monumental new City-County Building, he shouted, "How dare you cross my threshold!" But cross they did, and the mayor asked them to be seated, their backs to the window. Lucy launched into a discussion of the playground program, which was still in its infancy, and how its success or failure depended upon the right bureau chief. "It seems too bad," she began, "that a recreational bureau dealing with children and employing especially trained educators should be under the supervision of the Department of Public Works. It just does not seem to be the happiest possible set-up."

"It's not under the Department of Public Works," the mayor replied. "It's under the Department of Health." "Anyway," he added, "I can't believe a word you say on any subject after all the lies you told about me in that dirty rotten sheet of yours."

"I have come to talk about playgrounds," Lucy responded, "only playgrounds. Besides, we could talk for weeks about the statements made in my 'dirty rotten sheet' and we would never agree." Getting back to the issue of who controlled the playgrounds, Lucy said, "I could verify my statements by looking in the little book on your desk." The book apparently contained copies of city files and "set-ups" of the city government. The mayor fumbled for some time though the book without success, that is, until Lucy found the right page for him.

"By jove you are right," he conceded.

"I usually am," she replied.

"You have the most colossal nerve of anyone I have ever known."

"It should not take colossal nerve for any citizen to come to see his mayor."

That was the end of the conversation. Mr. Schooley did not receive the appointment.

Lucy would not encounter the mayor again until March, when they were both addressing a mass meeting of citizens in front of the Old City Hall on Smithfield Street. As they both stood on the balcony, Babcock expressed his annoyance at it being an outdoor meeting, wondering how he would make himself heard. "I just told him to yell," Lucy later recalled, "and told him he would be alright." They brought him out a little soapbox. But as Babcock, a man of substantial height and girth, stepped up onto the box, it cracked, and "he was again in a flutter." Having had considerable experience with soapboxes herself, Lucy leaned over and advised him to spread his weight by positioning his feet at either end of the box. Firmly planted, Babcock then delivered his opening in stentorian terms: "Ladies and Gentlemen, I want to assure you that I am patriotic from the crown of my head to my toe nails." Lucy couldn't help chuckling.

17 VICTORY AT LAST!

As the new year of 1918 opened, the sacrifice associated with the war was rendered slightly less demoralizing by the promise of a possible suffrage success in the nation's capital. Lucy led the Pennsylvania delegation that campaigned right up until the US House vote with a message of "democracy at home as well as throughout the world." Telegrams and letters poured in to back up the women in Washington. They carried with them the support of numerous labor leaders and organizations as well as prominent business and professional men and were counting on their Congressmen, "without exception," to vote in their favor.[1] Never mind that the suffrage issue was tangled up with the prohibition issue as legislators traded favors and penalties in their negotiations. And never mind that the southern Democrats, who feared the flood of Black women voters into the electorate, were lobbying against them.

On the eve of the scheduled January 10 vote, Wilson surprised everyone by coming out squarely for the Anthony Amendment.[2] With that long-elusive endorsement, the suffragists and anti-suffragists alike were certain it would pass, and Carrie Chapman Catt predicted ratification by the spring of 1919. Lucy was among the jubilant crowd that swarmed into the House galleries the next day to witness the historic moment.[3]

It was a full day, with five hours of fierce debate, appropriately opened by Jeannette Rankin. In the midst of the wrangling, Representative Decker of Missouri shouted, "I'll tell you why women should be given a hand now—because they have more courage, more grit, more sheer, determined bravery than men. The world knows it."[4]

In the end, the bill barely garnered a two-thirds majority, 274 to 136, with two of the supporting representatives rising from their sick beds in order to vote. The speaker made no effort to quell the burst of wild applause in the galleries, as the women embraced and shouted, "Glory, Glory Hallelujah."

Every attempt to modify the language of the amendment was defeated, so it read as originally proposed: "The right of citizens of the United States to vote shall not be denied or abridged by the United States or by any state on account of sex." [5] With a House victory and the endorsements of the president and both major parties, the suffragists now turned to the Senate with complete confidence. Their thoughts had already pivoted to the process for securing ratification by the states.

By February 17, with no date set, the bill needed just two more votes in the Senate. Only three senators from suffrage states remained unpledged. One of them was Senator Wadsworth of New York, whose wife was president of the National Association Opposed to Woman Suffrage, and another was a lifelong opponent. But there were other senators who could be swayed from their negative stances. Plus, there were the vacancies due to deaths of senators from Wisconsin and New Jersey, and the Republican governors of those states were expected to appoint suffrage supporters to fill those seats. [6]

Would it be triumph or disappointment? As one columnist wrote, "They pray that the amendment may go through, but one gathers that they would not be overcome with discouragement if it didn't. One gathers, in fact, that a good suffragist is never confused or disconcerted by a snub or disappointment—for the woman suffrage movement has been raised on snubs." [7]

On May 6, the Senate voted down a motion to take up the Anthony Amendment the following Friday. The suffragists lacked just one vote to move the action forward. [8] June 14, the president was still hopeful. [9] Lucy was at home on a four-month furlough recovering from a "strenuous season" and anticipating the birth of her third child, Barbara, who arrived on June 30. She would have to be content with watching from the sidelines as the day-by-day accounts of the Senate's seemingly interminable gyrations unfolded for the rest of the month. [10]

In Pittsburgh, Anna Howard Shaw spoke at the Equal Franchise Federation annual meeting that May, at which Lucy was reelected president. Dr. Shaw encouraged a continued push for suffrage as a natural way to support the fight for democracy, as being squarely in line with the national mission in a time of war. "It is our patriotic duty to fight on," she declared. [11] Women's suffrage also offered practical strategic impact, she said. "The bravest and best are being taken from us, while the incapacitated, the feeble, the pro-German, the pacifist and the I. W. W.'s [Industrial Workers of the World] are being left behind." Instead of ceding the government into the hands of this "undesirable group," she urged that the ballot might better be given to loyal, patriotic women who would work to keep the country's institutions "pure."[12]

On June 24, acting federation president Mary Hay wrote to Senator Philander Knox, imploring him to vote in favor of the amendment. "The members of our organization have regretted that as one of our senatorial representatives you have not voiced any expression which could be taken as an indorsement of the Federal woman suffrage amendment," she chided. Pointing out the contributions of Pennsylvania women in particular—forty thousand war workers, Red Cross workers, war savings stamp campaigners, Liberty Loan workers with hundreds of millions in sales, and others—she asked him to state his position.[13] No record survives of any response from Knox.

Finally, on June 27, there was news from Washington. "Suffragists lose round as Senate defers vote on measure," the headlines read. The action, or inaction as it were, came on the heels of three hours of heated debate in which priority was given to twenty billion dollars in war appropriations.[14] Alice Paul, watching from the gallery, summed up the general sentiment that day: "The patience of American women cannot be much longer taxed."[15] Within days, the militant pickets would be back in Lafayette Park opposite the White House, and more arrests would follow.[16]

In the meantime, somehow the women of the Equal Franchise Federation had to swallow their disappointment on that day of deferment in Washington as they opened their long-awaited carnival back home in the Oakland civic center of Pittsburgh. Commandeering eight hundred feet of the major thoroughfare of Bellefield Avenue between Fifth and Forbes, in the shadow of the grand Schenley Hotel, the mammoth midway was "a mass of surging humanity" as some fifteen thousand people turned out to benefit a recreation fund for soldiers stationed in Pittsburgh. There was plenty to attract them—dancing, vaudeville, athletic contests, Nirella's brass band, and booths. One booth featured an exhibition of the "wonderful American submarine." In another, for a nickel, "anybody could throw bombs at Berlin." Others showcased menageries, the Wild Men from Borneo, the Oriental Gazer, the Magic Entertainer, Salome and her Snakes, and "Negroes rendering the melodic compositions of the Southland." With sideshow barkers, lemonade, peanuts, multi-colored confetti, strings of red, white, and blue lights, balloons and bunting and rattles, it was a loud and colorful whirl of activity. Admission was by thrift stamps for all but the soldiers, who were admitted for free.[17] With the three thousand dollars raised by the event, the suffragists extended hospitality to visiting soldiers by setting up information booths—fashioned to look like giant gun shells—on downtown streets and by furnishing various "suffrage service huts" where the soldiers could relax, listen to music, snack, smoke, read, and write letters home. They even provided a shopping service, with free delivery within the hour on orders placed with local merchants.[18]

On August 24, 1918, with some sense that they would emerge victorious, the anti-suffragists in the US Senate introduced a resolution demanding action on the suffrage amendment.[19] In response to a group of Democratic women who called on him in mid-September, Wilson vowed to urge a Senate vote as early as he could, promoting the amendment as a war measure.[20] A date of September 26 was set.[21] After some last-minute calls on doubtful senators early in the day, the suffragists and antis poured into the galleries for choice seats to watch the historic vote, which would rest on one or two senators who had kept everyone puzzled. Both sides anticipated victory by safe margins.[22]

What they apparently didn't foresee was the bitter debate over attempts to modify the amendment on the floor. Senator John Sharp Williams of Mississippi declared that if his amendment to prevent Black women voting were adopted, "two-thirds of the southern opposition to suffrage will disappear."[23] Senator Theodore Frelinghuysen of New Jersey proposed requiring American citizenship of women voters. While advocates hoped for a vote and opponents threatened a filibuster to delay until all their allies were present, the outcome hung in the balance for days. Finally, on October 1, after five days of "bitter debate, corridor conferences and cloakroom negotiations," the tally was in. The Susan B. Anthony federal amendment resolution, enacted by the House in January, was defeated in the Senate 54 to 30, just two votes shy of the necessary two-thirds majority, with twelve senators not voting. Technically, this left the resolution pending on the Senate calendar, in position for reconsideration after the November elections. It had been forty years since the amendment was first advanced, and four since it had last been defeated in the Senate. Charges and countercharges of blame for the outcome were hurled back and forth.[24] It seemed inconceivable, insulting, impossible, but not insurmountable.

* * *

As if a World War was not enough of an interruption, in the midst of the state and national suffrage campaigns of 1918 there arrived a deadly threat, an invisible adversary that neither traditional warfare nor strategic politicking could defeat. When the *Pittsburgh Gazette Times* announced the city's first case of the Spanish influenza on October 1, no one was particularly concerned, despite that it was already reaching epidemic proportions across the state in Philadelphia. Within weeks, however, there was ample cause for alarm.

In the first ten days, more than thirteen hundred Pittsburghers contracted the flu. A week later, it was 4,445, and it kept climbing. Reportedly, 1,221 people died in a single week alone. Conditions in the city's overcrowded tenements only exacerbated the situation, as did overflowing hospitals. The Red Cross recruited nurses. All across the county, volunteers stepped up to help with institutional and at-home care. By the end of the month, after fifty-three students and two teachers had died, schools were closed.

The Pennsylvania Acting Commissioner of Health, Dr. Benjamin Franklin Royer, issued a statewide closure order for saloons, theaters and movie houses, and other places of amusement. Large assemblies and parades were banned. Social distancing and masks were the order of the day. No one balked until Royer added a ban on liquor sales by any outlet other than a drug store. Locally, Mayor E. V. Babcock extended the closure order to churches. But generally hostile to orders from above, Mayor Babcock resisted enforcement of the lockdown and battled with officials in Harrisburg to reopen. The Pittsburgh bans lasted only a little over a month, but the epidemic would continue for seven.

The pandemic put the brakes on suffrage activities, at least temporarily. Carrie Chapman Catt was stricken, as were many lawmakers in Washington. In Pittsburgh, more than twenty-five thousand Pittsburghers had contracted influenza by the beginning of February, and the city's reported death rate reportedly surpassed that of most other major cities.[25] Experts were baffled. No one, publicly at least, was suggesting that the city's poor air quality might have something to do with it. Not yet.[26]

* * *

By year's end, Michigan, Oklahoma, and South Dakota had been added to the list of suffrage states, and the suffragists had managed to get enough allies elected to the US Senate that success once again seemed possible, perhaps even before this Senate session was scheduled to conclude on March 4, 1919. Suffragists targeted state legislatures, asking them to request that their US Senators vote for adoption of the amendment. Wilson reportedly pressured

the senators from the South to vote yes. Another vote was scheduled for
Monday, February 10.

On the eve of the vote, in anticipation of a negative outcome, the militants
outside the White House pushed the limits of propriety further still. They
created an effigy of the president, which they carried to the front of the White
House in a procession of nearly a hundred women. Several thousand spectators
watched as they held the three-foot-tall paper likeness of the president over
a blazing caldron, reducing it to ashes. Sixty-five women were arrested that
night.[27] To the women of the mainstream movement, including the Equal
Franchise Federation, and certainly to the general public, it hardly seemed an
effective strategy for winning over hesitant senators.

Finally, the big day arrived. On February 10, 1919, the US Senate convened to vote for the fourth time on the suffrage amendment. Surprisingly,
the papers reported minimal fanfare around the long-awaited vote. Women
filled the galleries, but there was no drama, no demonstration. They simply
watched quietly as, for the fourth time, the resolution was defeated, this time
by 55 to 29, one vote short.[28] One week later, it was reintroduced.[29] In a last
ditch effort on March 2, an alternative amendment was proposed that would
leave enforcement to the states.[30] That bill died in filibuster on the last day,
along with ten others.[31]

That was it for this session of Congress. The amendment would have to
wait until the Sixty-Sixth Congress convened on May 19, 1919, when the
Republicans would control both the House and the Senate. If it passed, it
would then have to go to the states for ratification.

After repeated near misses, every single vote was more critical than ever
as Congress reconvened in May. The resolution passed the US House easily
this time, 304 to 89, a considerably larger margin than in January 1918, with
Republicans favoring it almost two-to-one over Democrats. But they needed
54 votes in the Senate before the amendment could go on to be ratified by
the state legislatures. As the days went on, it looked promising. Of the forty-eight states, nineteen were solidly in favor of the amendment, eighteen had
a friendly majority, seven in the south had majorities against, and four were
divided. Only one, Alabama, was solidly against. A tribute to the work of Lucy
and her colleagues across the state, Pennsylvania was in the majority column,
although Senators Knox and Penrose were against.[32] Remembering how the
same resolution had failed in the Senate in 1887, in 1914, in 1918, and again
in February, the suffragists were understandably on edge.

Then, finally, on the afternoon of June 4, 1919, the US Senate made its historic vote in favor of the Susan B. Anthony Amendment, 56 to 25, with two votes to spare.[33]

Eliza Armstrong sat alone that day in the gallery, the only anti-suffragist to witness the watershed moment. Surrounded by her opponents in the fight, she at least had the satisfaction of hearing a glowing tribute from one Allegheny County senator, who praised the "dear old lady" for her persistence.[34] Eliza sat back at home in Pittsburgh, seven months pregnant with her first child.

Suffrage leaders were "in high glee," according to the papers.[35] It was all over but the ratification. They would need thirty-six of the forty-eight states, and most of the state legislatures met only biennially, in odd-numbered years. Suffragists at every level of the battle, from the local to the national, would have to scramble. Some state legislatures would be asked to convene in special sessions to get the job done.

It was predicted by some that Pennsylvania could be the first state to ratify, and Lucy left for Harrisburg, hopeful of putting the whole decade-long struggle behind her. What she met there was one more disappointment. Despite encouragement from the governor and having already voted to move the state amendment forward, the leaders of the House and Senate seemed reluctant to rush ratification of the federal amendment before they adjourned at the end of the month. Instead, Wisconsin, Illinois, and Michigan were the first to ratify, quickly followed by Kansas, New York, and Ohio.

Then came Pennsylvania's turn. The Senate approved it by 31 to 6. Then, on June 24, hundreds of women crowded into the House galleries, where finally, by a vote of 153 to 44, the Keystone State became the seventh to ratify the amendment. The response from the galleries was explosive as the legislature took a two-minute recess to allow Lucy, who was introduced as "that womanly woman,"[36] to offer remarks of gratitude for the action. Amidst thunderous applause, Lucy was escorted to the speaker's chair, where her booming bass voice recaptured the attention of all present:

> When New York granted suffrage to its women in 1917 in the midst of the rejoicing for the victory, the Pennsylvania women felt chagrined that their great state had not seen fit to deal out an equal measure of justice to them. But they all realized that the passage of the referendum bill in the State of New York meant a speedy victory in Congress because, with the gain of this largest state in the

Union, it meant that the suffragists could bring enough pressure to
bear on Congress to successfully pass their measure.

Pennsylvania today has taken her place by the side of New York
because she has made possible by the ratification today the speedy
ratification of the necessary 36 states. A year ago, when an analysis
of ratification possibilities was made by Mrs. Catt, president of the
National Woman Suffrage Association, Pennsylvania was rated as
the most difficult of the 36.

The pendulum has swung so far, and it means that when this great
Republican stronghold has come out for ratification that every
other Republican state will fall into line. Furthermore, it means
that the Democrats in the southern states will be forced to do
equally as well unless they expect to see the prize of the votes of
more than 15,000,000 women who already have been enfranchised
snatched away from them in the presidential election of 1920.

The Pennsylvania Woman Suffrage Association takes this opportunity of thanking its old friends, who have been with it when it
was not so pleasant to be a suffragist; its new friends who for some
reason or other have not been with us in the past; our governor, to
whom we feel the greatest debt of gratitude for the ratification ... [37]

Lucy went on to thank particular senators who had helped squire the
bill through to passage and presented a plaque declaring gratitude for the
historic action. The wooden gavel used to pronounce the successful vote was
then presented to her for safekeeping.

Lucy and her entourage from the Equal Franchise Federation and the
state organization spent the rest of the day basking in the glow of success
and accolades, first at the governor's office and later at a celebratory dinner in
the Penn-Harris Hotel. Still estranged, even in victory, the militants of the
National Woman's Party, now headed by Lucy's former ally Mary Bakewell,
had a victory celebration of their own elsewhere in the hotel.[38] It was a great
day for the cause and a great day for Lucy, who received congratulatory
telegrams from Susan B. Anthony's niece Lucy and from her mentor, Anna
Howard Shaw. Lucy Anthony had been Dr. Shaw's companion for thirty years

THE GAZETTE TIMES.

Founded July 29, 1786

PITTSBURGH'S ONE BIG NEWSPAPER

The Weather Partly Cloudy

TWO CENTS A COPY

PITTSBURGH, THURSDAY MORNING, JUNE 5, 1919.

TWELVE CENTS A WEEK

SENATE PASSES WOMAN SUFFRAGE AMENDMENT

TREATIES IN BALANCE AS ALLIES FAIL TO AGREE

CITY WELCOMES 80TH UNITS TODAY

WILL ARRIVE IN PITTSBURGH FOR PARADE

MOVE IN SENATE TO INQUIRE HOW BUSINESSMEN GOT PACT; PEACE ENVOYS MAY BE CALLED

Resolution Introduced by Hitchcock Is Backed by Lodge and Borah. Latter Threatens to Place Copy of Pact in Congressional Record, Thus Giving It to Public.

WILSON YIELDS FOR SAKE OF ALLIED UNITY

RESOLUTION ADOPTED BY VOTE OF 56 TO 25; NOW GOES TO STATES

Pennsylvania Legislature May Be First to Ratify Anthony Amendment—Party Lines Split in Balloting—36 Republicans and 20 Democrats For, While Eight Republicans and 17 Democrats Are Against Measure.

Police Remain Without Clue In Bomb Plots

Peace Terms Unacceptable, Austria Says

Nation League Is Advocated By Notables

SUFFRAGE LEADERS IN HIGH GLEE AS RESULT OF VICTORY

LEAP THROUGH AIR PREVENTS SUICIDE

GREEK MASSACRE URGED IN THRACE

PLAN TO MAKE HOURS WORK EXTRA HOUR

Bunkies in France Meet Again, One a Copper, Other a Burglar; "Stop Thief!" Causes Reunion

ROLL CALL IN SENATE ON SUFFRAGE MEASURE

LEGISLATORS WORRY OVER LACK OF HEAT

The passage of the 19th Amendment took top billing in the Pittsburgh papers on June 5, 1919. But it would not become law for another year. From *Pittsburgh Gazette Times*

and was at her bedside when, a week later, the doyenne of women's suffrage died at the age of seventy-two.

By the time Eliza had given birth to her first son, Templeton Smith, on August 19, fourteen states had ratified the federal amendment, and to some at least, the way seemed clear to passage in 1920. But each state faced its own set of challenges. Some argued that special legislative sessions would be too expensive, despite that suffragists offered to raise whatever was necessary to cover costs. Some worried that the amendment might not be fully ratified in time for women to register or pay their poll taxes in advance of the November 1920 election. By the end of September, just seventeen states had ratified. By Christmas, the number was up to twenty-two, but skeptics still questioned the inevitability of passage. With the jury still out, the Rochester Twentieth

Century Club just outside Pittsburgh that month held another debate on the subject of women's suffrage.[39]

Nonetheless, the women of Pennsylvania were confident enough of a successful outcome that on November 10, 1919, the Pennsylvania Women's Suffrage Association voted to change its name to the Pennsylvania League of Women Citizens. They elected Lucy chairman of the new organization, which within a year would be renamed the Pennsylvania League of Women Voters.[40] As an added tribute to "the woman to whom, more than to any other, we owe the triumph of our cause in this state," they established a new endowment, which they named the Lucy Kennedy Miller Fund. Lucy was deeply touched.[41]

The state league immediately began issuing its monthly *Bulletin*, encouraging summer picnic rallies and setting forth an aggressive educational campaign and legislative agenda. In just seven months, their membership had swelled to more than thirteen thousand. In calling their first annual convention, Lucy's league declared, "New duties, new responsibilities, confront us. Millions of women look to us for guidance. We must formulate a program of activities at the forthcoming convention which will set the standard for the women of Pennsylvania to follow. We must prove our pledges to have been given in good faith."[42]

Likewise, the Equal Franchise Federation transitioned into the League of Women Citizens of Allegheny County, with branches established according to election district, whose purpose was to promote voting on the basis of principles and the merits of candidates rather than on a partisan bias. At first, Lucy was the head of the county as well as the state league. That would eventually prove to be too much for her.

On the national level, the NAWSA planned its fifty-first and final convention for February in Chicago, where only one woman was present who had attended the original 1869 convention—eighty-five-year-old Dr. Olympia Brown. The Association had every expectation of merging its membership into the new League of Women Voters once the thirty-sixth state had ratified.

As 1920 opened, additional states stepped up to ratify the amendment, and the air was full of speculation about its fate. By early March, thirty-three states had ratified, with ten states left to vote. Alabama, Georgia, Maryland, South Carolina, and Virginia had already rejected it. West Virginia and Tennessee were unlikely—some said "hopeless"—given constitutional technicalities in those states. Prospects were also not good for the remaining states in the "solid south"—Florida, Louisiana, North Carolina, and Mississippi. That left four states from which the last three votes might most realistically come—Connecticut, Delaware, Vermont, and Washington. It was going to be close.

In a surprise twist, West Virginia came through before the end of March. The West Virginia Senate vote occurred in a special session and hung on the arrival, at the eleventh hour, of tobacco magnate Senator Jesse Bloch, who cut his Pacific-coast vacation short and made a record-breaking trip across the continent from California to Charleston. There he was met at the station in the wee hours of the morning by a cheering crowd of suffrage supporters who escorted him to the capital the next afternoon in time to cast the deciding vote. "I'm not a suffragist," Bloch said, "and I have no personal axe to grind, but if the women want to vote, why not let them?" Spending five thousand dollars in the Chicago-to-Cincinnati train leg alone, Bloch opted for a special express train in lieu of taking one of the earliest "airborne limousines." It seems that his wife had balked at the peril involved in the nascent commercial aviation industry. The excitement in Charleston was compounded as another West Virginian, A. R. Montgomery, attempted to rescind his resignation from the Senate the previous summer and have his seat restored in order to cast a vote in opposition. Lucy and the rest of the league watched the drama with the greatest of interest. In the end, Montgomery was denied a seat, Bloch cast his vote, and the resolution passed, 15 to 14.[43]

Washington and Delaware seemed the next most likely to ratify, both in special session. Vermont and Connecticut were still also considered possibilities, but only if they convened special sessions. Some even held out hope for the southern bastions of Louisiana and North Carolina. Washington, the fifth state to have extended suffrage to women, passed it unanimously on March 22. In Delaware, the issue was more contentious, caught in the midst of heated political jockeying and ultimately failing in the House on April 1, failing in the Senate on May 5, and failing to get another vote in the House on June 2, despite pressure from the president.[44] In the meantime, as expected, Mississippi defeated it soundly. The situation was further complicated by the fact that the Maryland and Ohio votes had been challenged legally. In the case of Ohio, it had gone all the way to the US Supreme Court.

Now it was down to just one state. One state that could forever claim credit for casting the pivotal ratification vote. One state that would finally put the issue of women's suffrage to rest. Carrie Chapman Catt declared,

"Suffrage is won. The words are simple, but they thrill as few words do or can."[45] The fact remained, however, that one state needed to step up. By the beginning of April, six contenders were left: Connecticut, Florida, Louisiana, North Carolina, Tennessee, and Vermont. At the same time, suffragists were actively seeking a reversal of the vote in Delaware.

As speculation brewed and people looked for reliable predictions, the latest ratification reports appeared in the *Pittsburg Press*, curiously, alongside a Kaufmann's Department Store advertisement for the popular Ouija Board, claiming "no scarcity here, despite the great demand."[46] Rooted in nineteenth-century mysticism and condemned by some as a tool of the devil, the "magical" device purported to answer questions "about the past, present and future with marvelous accuracy," along with "never-failing amusement and recreation for all the classes."[47] Not even a Ouija Board could predict what came next.

In Chicago, the Republican National Committee unanimously adopted a resolution calling on the remaining Republican states to ratify the Anthony Amendment.[48] But the support seemed hollow, given that the Republican legislature of Delaware failed to ratify and the Republican governors of Connecticut and Vermont, the last two Republican holdouts, refused to call special sessions to consider the issue.[49] Nor would the Republican presidential nominee, Warren G. Harding, agree to pressure the governors, citing a violation of states' rights.[50] Out came Alice Paul and 125 National Women's Party militants to protest, albeit quietly, all in white and carrying their signature tri-color banners.[51]

Then, on June 23, just before the Democratic National Convention in San Francisco and in response to a telegram from the president, Governor Roberts of Tennessee announced that he would call a special session of his state legislature. If a Democratic state should consummate the suffrage deal, party leaders believed that they could win the bulk of the women's votes as a show of gratitude. Not to be out-maneuvered by the Democrats, the Republicans turned to Governor Clement of Vermont to hold a special session there. He again refused.[52]

Carrie Chapman Catt settled into Nashville for the duration, certain that Tennessee would be the thirty-sixth state. By the time the special session began on August 9, both the suffragists and the antis had been ensconced in the city's finest hotel, the Hermitage, for the better part of a month.[53] Tirelessly, they assessed their odds and lobbied the legislators, thirty-three in the Senate and ninety-nine in the House.[54] Here again, both sides were in for a roller-coaster ride. A resolution was defeated to delay the vote until mass meetings could be held in all counties. But it was defeated only narrowly.[55] Then protracted committee deliberations over constitutional issues delayed the vote.[56]

Messaging on both sides of the suffrage issue was caught in the swirl of presidential campaign rhetoric from the Republican team of Harding and Coolidge and their Democratic challengers, Cox and Roosevelt, as they charged toward the November election. Roosevelt accused Harding of jumping on the suffrage bandwagon late in the game when he voted yes in the Senate on June 4, 1919.[57] Harding's supporters countered by pointing out that twenty-nine of the ratifying states were Republican strongholds.

On August 14, the Tennessee Senate voted 25 to 4 in favor of ratification and passed it to the House. In the days leading up to the August 18 House vote, suffrage leaders confidently claimed to have sixty of the ninety-nine House members in their camp. The antis were equally certain of victory as rumors spread that members pledged to support ratification might be weakening.[58] Among those who were wavering was twenty-four-year-old Harry Thomas Burn, the youngest member of the legislature, who had been pressured by party leaders to vote against ratification. It was ultimately a letter from his mother that turned the tide. "Don't forget to be a good boy and help Mrs. Thomas Catt with her 'Rats,'" she wrote. Young Burn would later say, "I knew that a mother's advice is always safest for a boy to follow. . . ."[59] So it was that after two days of debate, when the Tennessee House called the question and the vote looked like a tie at 48 to 48, young Burn cast the deciding vote to pass the ratification, 49 to 47. In a last-ditch effort to have the motion reconsidered, the speaker subsequently changed his vote, yielding a final count of 50 to 46. It was never reconsidered.

Victory at last! After seventy-one years of organized work and through countless twists and turns in the road, the Nineteenth Amendment was finally the law of the land. First introduced in 1878 as the Sixteenth Amendment, the Susan B. Anthony Amendment had been before Congress longer than any other amendment in the Constitution's history. Within days, opponents from Tennessee, New Hampshire, Missouri, West Virginia, and Arkansas would begin a series of challenges that would go as far as the US Supreme Court, but to no avail.

It would take more than sixty years for the remaining twelve states to ratify the amendment. Mississippi would be the last to do so, holding out until March 22, 1984.

Final ratification was the stuff of sensational headlines, but Lucy would have liked more of a live-action spectacle. Secretary of State Bainbridge Colby's actual signing of the amendment and his public announcement proved to be a disappointing nonevent, with none of the pomp and pageantry that might have seemed fitting for such a momentous occasion. He simply put his moniker on the proclamation at his home at eight o'clock the morning of August 26, just a few hours after he had heard from the governor of Tennessee. No women witnesses were present. Colby insisted that he had wanted to avoid the limelight and the possibility of arousing controversy over who would be invited to attend a signing ceremony. Still, it was disappointing.[60] Nonetheless, Lucy headed home from Canada immediately upon hearing the news.

Just a few days later, back in Pittsburgh, Mayor Babcock also gave the moment its due. He issued a proclamation and called for a public celebration:

> After a valiant struggle lasting through three-quarters of a century, under the leadership of Susan B. Anthony and other devoted and patriotic women, American womanhood has finally achieved its emancipation and enjoys for the first time full citizenship in the republic.
>
> No greater moral or political victory has ever been won in the world's history than the triumph of the woman's suffrage cause. Like all great reforms, it has encountered bitter and persistent opposition, often unfair and unjust, but now that the great end has been attained and American manhood has recognized the fellow-citizenship of their womanhood, who can doubt that the participation of women in full political rights will contribute vastly to all that makes a country great?
>
> Now, therefore, I, E. V. Babcock, mayor of the city of Pittsburgh, ask all our industrial concerns and all others where possible, at 12 o'clock noon, Saturday, August 28, 1920, to cause the blowing of whistles and the ringing of bells and other like joyous demonstrations in celebration and recognition of this great victory, one of the most important events in our history.[61]

The very next day, at noontime, the air in Pittsburgh reverberated with the sound of celebration. Ringing church bells, factory whistles, car horns, and joyous shouting echoed throughout the city. Amidst the din, thousands of women lined up at the Allegheny County Courthouse to celebrate the hard-won victory in the most appropriate way they could—by being assessed and registered to vote. The county's stringent registration requirements, however, were certain to thin the crowds. Not only did a woman need to produce proof of age, residency, and citizenship (her own or her husband's). She also had to present a state or county tax receipt or pay a special assessment. In Pittsburgh, the assessment totaled forty-nine cents for county tax, thirty cents for road tax, and nineteen cents for poor tax. Elsewhere in the county the taxes totaled ninety-eight cents. The registration was made even more difficult by the fact that only three days were available on which to register, two in September and one in October.[62]

A month later, on a sunny autumn Saturday, September 25, in Philadelphia's Independence Square, Lucy found the spectacle she had been craving. She joined a thronging crowd of her suffrage sisters, with the Justice Bell as the centerpiece. The lengthy program began with singing, accompanied by the police band, the repertoire combining old favorites from the earliest days of the battle to "some of the new jazzy affairs that mark the era of syncopation." The mayor proclaimed that the nation could expect "better things because of the advent of women into the realm of American citizenship." He spoke of the duty that accompanied the ballot. The governor asserted that the granting of equal franchise was the latest of the four "paramount and historic events in American history," along with the Declaration of Independence, the acceptance of the Constitution, and the Civil War. Both men couldn't help highlighting woman's underlying duty to the home even as she took on this new role. There followed speeches by Mrs. Maud Wood Park, the Radcliffe-educated suffragist who had been tapped as the first president of the new National League of Women Voters; Miss M. Carey Thomas, president of Bryn Mawr College; and Lucy. In an allegorical pageant that included forty-eight women and girls in white dresses with sashes indicating their home states, a Justice figure clad in a flowing green robe with a coronet of oak leaves unloosed the chains that had held the bell's clapper silent for five years. Finally, Miss Catherine Wentworth, the beautiful young niece of bell patron Katherine Wentworth Ruschenberger, stepped up to the bell in a simple white frock and no hat, accompanied by a dozen little flower girls carrying armfuls of yellow marigolds. She and a sequence of others pulled the rope forty-eight times—once for each state—as the ringing resounded throughout Independence Square and beyond. The crowd of triumphant warriors watched and cheered with orderly jubilance.[63]

Eliza Armstrong and the antis did not go down without a fight. The Pittsburgh Association Opposed to Woman Suffrage vowed to keep their organization going even after the amendment was enacted into law, although Eliza did cast her first vote in 1924. But she never backed down. Even on her deathbed in 1935, lying weak on a lace pillow with her wispy white hair framing her tired face, Eliza Armstrong would remain resolute, declaring that "Women haven't done any good with the vote."[64]

Immediately upon ratification in Tennessee, Carrie Chapman Catt had laid down the task ahead of the newly enfranchised. "Since votes for women is now an accomplished fact," she said, "what are the women going to do with the vote? Are they going to draw back their skirts in disdain from all interest in politics on the ground that it is corrupt? Are they going to join the army of kid-gloved men slackers whom I have heard proudly boast that they would not touch politics with a 10-foot pole? Or are they going to be of those who will help America's army of voters, who put conscience and thought into the scales with party politics and party candidates?"[65] "That vote has been costly. Prize it!"[66] At sixty-one, Catt was still very much on the scene. She would capture the suffrage story in her 1923 *Woman Suffrage and Politics: The Inner Story of the Suffrage Movement* and establish the national League of Women Voters, then live to the age of eighty-eight in New Rochelle, New York, with her partner, Mary Hay.

Speaking for the militant faction of the movement, Alice Paul argued that the "real fight," the one to bring women to full economic as well as political equality with men, had just begun. "What we have thus far accomplished after years of strenuous effort has after all been merely preliminary," she said.[67]

Likewise, Lucy and Eliza knew that their work was not over. Thrilling as the victory was, passage of the Nineteenth Amendment was not the ultimate goal of the Equal Franchise Federation. It was merely a means to it. They had a longer-range objective—education of the newly enfranchised female electorate so that they might use their individual and collective voices to bring some integrity, efficiency, and reason to local government. This was a tall order in the "Metropolis of Corruption." It was not the kind of job one might expect to be taken on by two well-heeled, happily married women with four young children at home and another baby on the way. But Lucy and Eliza were resolute and would prove to be equally relentless.

IV The Battle for Good Government

18 LIFE AND THE LEAGUES

In the dog days of summer 1920, the office on the seventh floor of the Jenkins Arcade was as bustling as ever, the heavy wooden desks packed closely together and the walls lined with file cabinets stacked high with pamphlets and papers. The thick, hot air reverberated with the loud clicking of Underwood typewriters and slamming of file drawers as stenographers kept up with growing mountains of correspondence and other paperwork. Even before the August 28 celebration of the Nineteenth Amendment in Pittsburgh, the women of the new Allegheny County League of Women Voters (the successor to the League of Women Citizens) had wasted no time in shifting gears. Likewise, the Pennsylvania League of Women Voters had launched into a busy agenda under Lucy's leadership. The suffrage battle effectively won, they turned their energies to a new mission: putting the vote to work through education and promotion of good government.

Even as the ratification process continued to stumble along, state by state, the new leagues—Allegheny County and Pennsylvania—confidently forged ahead on the assumption that ratification was only a matter of time. "Equal Franchise Federation Dies," the headline read on January 14, 1920. With Lucy presiding over the organization's "parliamentary death," a crowd of more than a thousand women of all classes, creeds, and races gathered in the ballroom of the William Penn Hotel and voted unanimously to disband the federation. Amidst vigorous applause, Eliza then presented a resolution to form the Allegheny County League of Women Citizens with Mrs. Clifton A. Verner as chairman. Eliza was elected secretary. The new organization carried a tagline of "Not Politics But Citizenship."[1] Lucy declared, "There will be no attempt made to influence the members' votes." Nor was it an attempt to establish a women's party, she insisted. "We couldn't do it if we tried," she said, adding that the federation had always benefitted from the combined wisdom of men and women. She also welcomed antisuffragists into the new league. Eliza Armstrong, head of the local antis group, declined the invitation.

Lucy suggested that the new league embrace education as one of its priorities, not only the education of its membership but also improvements to public education, including better pay for teachers and the election of at least two women to every school board. Among other agenda priorities named were child welfare and women in industry. The organization was slated to be renamed the Allegheny County League of Women Voters immediately upon full ratification of the Nineteenth Amendment. Lucy was among the delegates from Allegheny County who attended the final convention of the National Women Suffrage Association in Chicago.[2]

Embracing their new vocation with characteristic gusto, the two Kennedy sisters worked in tandem from the outset, earning them the nickname of "political twins." Eliza was in the Pittsburgh office every day and returned home each night full of stories. Lucy was back and forth to Philadelphia on the train, juggling her engagement with both organizations.

Eliza stayed behind to plan the league's first six-class Citizenship School in March. The school was designed to instruct women in the fundamentals of American government, with daytime classes at the Moose Temple downtown and evening classes at Schenley High School in Oakland. The classes covered the workings of Congress, election laws, the party system, local governments, the judiciary system, and the public schools. The program culminated with a lecture on "Problems that Await Us."[3] Participants paid seventy-five cents per session. Correspondence courses were also available.

An aggressive membership campaign followed in May, accompanied by a straw vote on the Republican and Democratic candidates for the upcoming election.[4] Hundreds of small, gaily striped red-white-and-blue ballot boxes were placed in shops, in railroad stations, in public buildings, and on street corners to gauge the sentiments of the prospective new voters. The women favored former Secretary of the Treasury William G. McAdoo for the Democrats, with President Wilson coming in second. For the Republican ticket, they favored General Leonard Wood, with Herbert Hoover a distant second.[5] The local league had sixty-nine hundred members by August, when the amendment was finally ratified.[6] Speaking on behalf of the league, Eliza was elated. "It seems impossible to realize," she said, "that after so many years of work, we actually have the vote at last. American men are the best in the world and American women will prove that they should have had the ballot long ago."[7] The membership would continue to grow over the years.

The mood was festive on November 2, 1920, when some ten million women across the country voted in elections for the first time, in every state except Mississippi and Georgia. The second most populous state, Pennsylvania was fourth in terms of votes cast, more than two million, even with only 21 percent of voters participating.[8] But the turnout was a bit disappointing to those who had fought so hard. Two out of three women stayed home, and an estimated three women voted for every five men.[9]

It would be another two years before women could run for the Pennsylvania General Assembly. But they seized the earliest opportunity. In 1922 eight women would be elected to the House of Representatives, and in 1924 Pennsylvania would elect its first woman to the State Senate. Ironically, the first woman senator in the state was Flora Morris Vare, the widow of the man who had subverted the 1915 popular vote on suffrage. She would serve from 1925 to 1928.

Rumors persisted that Lucy would run for mayor, and some feared that Pittsburgh would go the way of Yoncalla, Oregon, where women captured all of the municipal offices that year. Others speculated that she might later run for State Senate. But Lucy had other goals in mind.

The leagues did not sponsor or recommend candidates. They studied issues and worked for selected legislation. Their shared belief was that political education and active participation in government are essential to success in a democracy.

Yet both Lucy and Eliza made it clear from the outset that they would not shy away from the shenanigans of local politicians. They were neither intimidated by those in power nor charmed by local heroes. "City government was not organized to provide an arena where so-called political gladiators display their prowess or their tricks," Lucy wrote. It is organized to carry on the business of the city government."[10]

When the baton was passed to Eliza to take over as chair of the county league in 1923, little did she know that she would hold the position for the next forty years. She wasted no time in launching an aggressive campaign, setting forth the philosophy that would guide the league during her tenure:

> It is my purpose to sound a warning to the women voters of Pittsburgh and Allegheny County against the efforts which will be made to weaken, and possibly make actually ineffective, the . . . strength of the Republican and Democratic women. . . . The league is not a partisan organization; it is all-partisan, in that members of

any party may become members. The distinct purpose is to assist women voters in becoming forceful factors in their party, rather than mere adjuncts to party machines. The league has no interest in cliques, factions or groups. It is concerned only in getting facts so that women may base their actions in the party on solid, enduring ground, instead of on the plea of "organization." The league aims to substitute reason and judgement on the part of individual women for the personal preferences and ambitions of individuals aspiring to leadership and even to so-called bossism. . . .

Experience proves that those who work only in party organizations tend to become more or less bound to candidacies and issues even though developments plainly indicate that the welfare of the party, the city or the state, demands the taking of another course. Rather than be bound in advance, under the plea of organization, it is better for women voters to insist on learning all the facts before they commit themselves.

Our aim in one sense, is to substitute facts for factions. We will want all the facts we can get about candidates to be chosen this fall.[11]

For Eliza in particular, life and the league became intertwined in a way that would seal her identity for the rest of her life.

The twenties were not a time of great drama for the county league, just hard work on education, fact gathering, and lobbying for more efficient and honest government. To get at the facts, the league scheduled public meetings and issued questionnaires to all candidates for city and county office, asking pointed questions like "Will it be your intention to give your entire time to the conduct of the office or have you any outside interests that would divide your activities?" or "Do you think the affairs of the office can be conducted more economically and if so, point out where a reduction of expenses can be made?" The league demanded to know the views, plans, and records of all candidates. "Public offices are not the private property of any clique or faction," a league statement insisted. "They are the property of the whole electorate."[12]

League luncheons could attract as many as a thousand women hungry for facts. Throughout the decade, Lucy and Eliza were kept busy speaking at dozens of smaller meetings held by neighborhood branches of the league. The state league's call for its 1925 convention stated it simply: "Democracy's problem is not solved by the ballot alone but by the ballot in the hands of the informed. . . . Public opinion and not political bosses should guide our lawmakers."[13]

The county league's Friday Morning Club offered a speakers' series featuring distinguished men and women leaders of state, national, and even international fame. Out of the series emerged a new movement to get ordinary women, particularly housewives, more involved in politics. Eliza summarized the thinking behind the movement: "Women must get into politics if they are to win back their age-old supremacy in their own homes."[14] The series would continue for fifty years.

By 1927, the Allegheny County League of Women Voters had the largest membership of any county league in the United States. The league's record of remaining impartial and nonpartisan "confounded skeptics," according to one *Pittsburgh Post* editorial that described the league as "an experiment in politics," a "sober, determined, even dogged adventure to use the voting capacity of a great body of citizens for the largest public service—namely, helping the Government to work as was intended when the fathers of the Nation drew up its constitution."[15] Eliza maintained that "women are more independent voters than men. . . . They are more interested in intelligent reform of election methods and the abolition of election frauds than they are in upholding the party machine."[16]

Some selected issues seemed worthy of an elevated intensity of combat during the course of that first decade. February 1921 saw them protesting Mayor Babcock's proposal to exempt city department heads from civil service law, removing them from the merit system and placing them instead under a spoils system, in which political allies could be rewarded with public jobs. November that year saw them investigating city council, the county commissioners, and the criminal, juvenile, and morals courts.

In 1925, the county league went after the office of the collector of delinquent county taxes, an appointment controlled by the county treasurer, which Eliza called "a prize political plum" and which afforded its lucky recipients hundreds of thousands of dollars in fees. "The exorbitant fees paid for the collections of so-called delinquent taxes mean that those who pay the taxes are in reality contributing toward paying a superfluous salary to an office holder," she argued. "Taxes are not collected in these days for the purpose of rearing a luxurious race of office holders . . . We all know that one of the fundamental evils indicative of a decaying and dissolving civilization was the practice of farming out taxes."[17] In 1922 alone, the Allegheny County delinquent tax collector had collected $110,000 in fees, Eliza would discover, while the president of the United States was paid just $75,000.[18] Statewide, the fee-grabbing strategy was estimated to cost taxpayers between three and four million dollars. Lucy took up the same fight for a bill to eliminate the fee system under consideration in the state legislature. "Big Fight Looms on Ludlow Tax Bill," the headline read. The tax collectors joined forces to fight the bill. The fee system had even caught the attention of President Coolidge, who in his inaugural address said, "It is nothing more nor less than legalized larceny." Lucy called the practice "legalized graft" and dubbed their lobby "the most avaricious, selfish body which ever dared to scorn decent public opinion." [19]

As much as Eliza was revered for her command of the facts, Lucy was feared for her scathing attacks on wasteful government officials. In an address to the annual Allegheny County League Convention in November 1925, she tackled the topic of "Skeletons in the Court House" and spared no venom as she laid out the transgressions of county officials. "The million-dollar maintenance fee in addition to the $77,000 for new automobiles would seem to indicate that the county officials in all capacities suffered the loss of leg locomotion immediately after election." Citing expenditures such as hefty insurance premiums for old automobiles while the courthouse and City-County Building remained uninsured, or awarding a ballot-printing contract to the highest bidder, Lucy in her more charitable moments described the county operation as "haphazard and loose."[20]

In another local battle, Lucy turned her acerbic tongue to the issue of playgrounds, for which the county commissioners had purchased twenty-five hundred acres at a cost of $750,000, a move the *Pittsburgh Post* characterized as a "spending orgy." Urging public scrutiny of this move before an audience of five hundred at the league's annual banquet, she declared, "The czarism, studied indifference to public opinion and utter disregard of the effect of their actions on the cost of living for taxpayers which have heretofore been the conspicuous characteristic of the county commissioners invite this attention and study if indeed they do not arouse actual suspicion of their plans. . . . Tremendous sums have been spent for children's playgrounds, but children get no real benefit. . . . For too long have citizens in other parts of this state looked upon Pittsburgh and Allegheny County as the "playground of the politicians." Lucy's concern was with a bill pending in the state legislature that would have lifted spending limits and provided "plenty of play room for Mr. Armstrong and his political play boys of western Pennsylvania." Her contention was that the playgrounds were merely a cover for building up the political machine.[21]

At that same banquet, league members heard a talk by the former head of Amherst College and a professor at the University of Wisconsin in which he denounced Americans for their intolerance of differences of opinion, which he described as "a matter of friendship." The conflict of ideas and opinions, he contended, was the only means by which truth can be reached. This was a philosophy that both the sisters embraced.

Widely feared in the public arena, Lucy had a tender side for her family—Eliza and Barbara shown in c.1923—and for children in general.

On another spending issue, the league questioned plans for a forty-three-million-dollar bond issue to pay for a modern airport, a convention hall, and other large-scale capital projects. Eliza issued a list of twenty-two questions probing into such issues as the results of a previous twenty-nine-million-dollar bond in 1924 as well as the county's financial condition, the actual cost to taxpayers of interest and taxes on the projects, the allocation of the funds, and the bonding power of the county. In presenting her questions to the president of the People's Bond Issue Association in a letter, Eliza insisted, "It is not in any captious spirit, but with a sincere desire to bring out information that the voters should have before passing upon an issue so far reaching in its effects as the one now facing them." Yet her probe was detailed and pointedly called out perceived flaws in the plans. "Under existing business stagnation, unemployment, and high taxes, do you consider it sound business policy to construct scenic boulevards which will cost approximately $9,000,000?" she asked. "In view of the fact that the maximum life of a hard-surfaced road is admittedly less than 15 years, why is the public asked to approve 30-year bonds . . . ?" "In view of the fact that request is now made for $2,550,000 for a county office building, may I ask if it is not a fact that the commissioners knew in 1924, when they asked for only $1,100,000 for such purpose, that the building and ground was to cost $3,650,000?" "What was the annual salary and wage payroll in the county department of public works when the people approved the bond issue of 1924? What was the annual salary and wage payroll in the same department in 1926 and 1927?" Eliza's questions concluded with "Does your committee feel that one month's notice of these items gives ample time for intelligent discussion?" Clearly she did not think that it did.[22]

Eliza maintained that a convention center would benefit downtown corporate interests at the expense of individual taxpayers, "particularly so at this time of widespread business depression and unemployment, when any such addition to the tax burden must tremendously accentuate the already hazardous situation of the less wealthy class of taxpayers, who are struggling to hold onto what little they have."[23] She contended that county officials were bowing to the pressure of large investors who were seeking tax-free bonds.[24]

And so the sparring began. County officials squirmed a bit under Eliza's scrutiny but promptly fired back a response, question by question.[25] Forced into accountability by this group of insistent women and their unstoppable leader, they were learning just how thorough and vigilant these watchdogs would be as they came up against them in the decades to come.

In another skirmish, Eliza laid blame at the door of the county commissioners for the condition of the "assessment books," which contained the voter rolls and which she contended listed thousands of "phantom" names. "We do most strongly protest the fraudulent assessment of fictitious persons upon the county assessment books. You, as the ultimate custodian of the books, we hold strictly accountable." Dismissing the commissioners' allocation of twenty-five thousand dollars to investigate the fraud, she wrote, "It cannot be that you are not aware of their frauds, and as the public officers responsible for our elections it is your duty to take such measures as will prevent this corruption. Our organization cannot tolerate such flagrant abuse of the right of suffrage."[26] This would not be the last time the league took up this issue.

In response to the various questionable expenditures they observed in county politics, the league called for an audit of the county's books in early 1928. In time, audits would become one of the most effective weapons in the league's arsenal.

By the early thirties, the county league's priorities and active work were summed up by its seven committees: city government, county government, education, child welfare, living costs, international cooperation to prevent war, and courts.[27]

* * *

Meanwhile, representing the newly enfranchised women statewide, Lucy and the Pennsylvania league planned to pursue a clear agenda as it launched into the 1920s. In its clarion call to the membership to attend the state league's first annual convention, dubbed "THE MOST IMPORTANT ASSEMBLY The Women of Pennsylvania Ever Held," the Executive Committee declared, ". . . as everyone connected with the suffrage movement is aware, it was never ENTIRELY absorbed with the mere gaining of the franchise. In the course of its growth, the organization assumed other functions and adopted other aims. It undertook to educate the womanhood of America in the ideals of citizenship, to bring about the professional, economic and social advancement of woman, in addition to promoting her political equality. Have all these aims been accomplished? Most assuredly, they have not." The announcement went on, "Literally millions of women even now do not realize what the vote means. It is our duty to instruct them. Aside from partisan politics there are still dozens of problems affecting women and children which women must take the lead in solving." For Lucy, the newly enfranchised had an obligation to participate, particularly in public affairs "in which women are naturally most interested, such as laws affecting morality, the home and the school."[28] Each year, the annual convention of the state league would set forth a new agenda in the course of "many colorful sessions . . . of sparkling debate, vivacious wit, reasoned argument and unexpected political sagacity."[29]

Lucy's league supported the county leagues across Pennsylvania with conferences, citizenship schools, and a speakers' bureau that fielded and fulfilled daily requests for presenters. They flooded the state each year with thousands of personal letters and with more than a hundred and fifty thousand flyers, manuals, bulletins, and reports, including weekly legislative letters.

The Pennsylvania league's slogan in 1921 was "a woman on every school board." By 1923, the number had increased from eighty to a thousand. They continued to press for more female representation on poor boards and in other public offices and commissions. They successfully lobbied for increased appropriations for Mothers' Pensions, securing an increase of $350,000, for instance, between 1919–1920 and 1921–1922. They blocked a bill that would prevent women from serving on juries.

Having proven through the suffrage fight that she had the tenacity to pursue a contested goal over the course of many years, Lucy as head of the state organization took particular interest in continuing the campaign to call a constitutional convention. She had been one of two women who served on the twenty-five-member Commission on Constitutional Revision and Amendment authorized by the state legislature and appointed by the governor in June 1919. A convention, it was hoped, would allow for a revision of the state constitution of 1874, which by now was woefully out of date, as evidenced by the fact that it had been amended twenty-eight times in fifty years. She also served as the only woman on a seven-person Commission for the Reorganization of the State Government beginning in 1922, which sought to simplify Pennsylvania's administrative functions and establish an effective budget system.

The *Pittsburgh Sun* published a series of articles, later reconstituted as a pamphlet, *The Pennsylvania Papers*, making the case for a new constitution. Lucy's contribution, "From Women's Viewpoint," noted that the commission's work had been done "with none of the political twistings and subterfuge so often found in government."[30] Aside from the obvious revisions made necessary to accommodate the newly enfranchised female population, her particular rationale for advocating for a new constitution was rooted in a desire for an efficient budget process, a justice system that would be more equitable for the poor, a more impartial administration of the more than fifteen million dollars in state allocation to charities each year, and a more simplified state departmental organization. Fixated on the subject of the constitutional convention, Lucy campaigned vigorously to sway legislative and public sentiment. March 1923 found her delivering a series of lectures to a packed house in the Carnegie Lecture Hall in Oakland on "The State Constitution, Its Strength and Weakness," "Machinery of the State Administration," "Taxation," and "County Government."

The commission crafted a sample of what a new constitution might look like. In 1921 and 1923, a proposal passed the Senate and the House, setting the stage for a public referendum later that year. Ultimately, the proposal did not pass, and neither Lucy nor Eliza would live to see a new constitution. The 1873 constitution would continue in force and amended continually right up until it was replaced with a new one in 1968.[31]

They also took an interest in tax reform, election law reform, national immigration policy, and the League of Nations and World Court as a means of mitigating conflict. They cosponsored a conference in Pittsburgh on the Cause and Cure of War, similar to conferences held in every state in the Union.[32] Carrie Chapman Catt, still actively involved with the two sisters, was among those who spoke in favor of the World Court.

Election reform activities called for a constitutional amendment and a campaign waged by the Citizens' Voting Machine Campaign Committee, on which both Lucy and Eliza served, to promote a public referendum on adoption of voting machines that would increase efficiency, accuracy, honesty, and economy in the balloting process. The issue of voting machines would continue to capture the sisters' attention for the rest of their careers.

* * *

Lucy continued to lead the state league through the end of 1928. Both leagues waged aggressive drives to encourage citizens to vote and sought elimination of the poll tax as an obstacle to full enfranchisement. "Often plans of this sort," Lucy warned, "amount to nothing more than pretty gestures and empty words. It will be our aim to work out the details of an intensive campaign which will stir the minds and enthusiasm of men and women sufficiently to get them interested enough to enter the polling places." Explaining that the national goal was to increase the number of voters by 25 percent, she added, "As it is, only about half of the eligible voters cast their ballots. This is a pure waste of democracy."[33] In an eleventh-hour rallying cry before the 1923 election, Eliza said, "If you don't vote, then you are wasting your opportunities and you are unfaithful to the obligations of a citizen for the proper conduct of public affairs. . . . Go to the polls and vote and show that women are in earnest in their interest in politics and public affairs. Show that women have more than academic interest in public questions."[34]

Harkening back to the suffrage campaign of 1915, a "Get-Out-the-Vote" caravan traversed the state. The Justice Bell was resurrected and prominently placed in the lineup. The caravan was welcomed in each new community by a local parade of automobiles and a rally.[35] The sisters were on board for some of the journey, and Lucy had plenty to say as the caravan rolled into Pittsburgh and swelled into a parade of more than two hundred automobiles:

> Do we want to have our governmental institutions drift into the control of a small minority of the whole number of citizens? Of course not. But we should thoroughly appreciate the fact that in

times of peace the security of the republic rests upon the foundation
of active citizenship. If the indications are that this foundation is
tending toward weakness, it is the duty of the patriot to strengthen
it. . . .

Since 1896 the number of eligible voters who cast their ballots in
presidential campaigns has been steadily decreasing. . . . In 1896,
80 percent of the eligible voters cast ballots; in 1900, 78 percent; in
1908, 66 percent; in 1912, 62 percent; in 1920, less than 50 percent.

Reflect upon this: If less than 50 percent of the voters go to the
polls, then it is possible for about 25 percent of the eligible voters
to constitute a majority and control the elections and, therefore, the
government.[36]

At a luncheon that followed, Eliza opened the program, in which much
was said on the issue of voter suppression. Mayor Magee cited the complex
system required to qualify voters and suggested that the league work to "strike
away the limitations upon qualification which . . . turn out to be serious
incumbrances." The mayor spoke specifically of the tax qualification, which
was sufficiently onerous to serve as a deterrent to prospective voters. David
Lawrence, who was chairman of the Democratic Committee of Allegheny
County at the time, concurred with the mayor.[37] The county league concurred
with both of them.

* * *

As the league was establishing itself and its mission, Eliza and Temp had
purchased a home on Shady Avenue just a mile away from 5400 Forbes, and
it was there that they welcomed their second son, Kennedy, or Kenny, on July
12, 1922. Their nanny, Eva Suffall, had come shortly after Tempie was born
and would stay with them, in various capacities, for the next forty years. Eva's
reliable presence with the two little boys allowed Eliza to turn her attention
to matters beyond motherhood. It also enabled Eliza and Temp to slip away
on a six-week European trip in the summer of 1924.

Upon their return, with their family complete and their wanderlust satisfied, Eliza purchased the vacant lot next door, and they began planning for

construction of their ideal family home. Eliza took the lead in determining the character of the new house, which was designed not for grand entertaining but for the rather private upbringing of two boys. The boys and Eva had the entire third floor, which was provided with two bedrooms and a spacious playroom that would later double as a schoolroom when they were quarantined with Kenny's scarlet fever in 1929. The nerve center of the house was a second-floor den, where

Family came first for Eliza, pictured at home with Tempie and his little brother Kenny, c.1923.

the family gathered nightly after dinner and where many corruption battles and political schemes were conceived and debated. The den contained two phones, one reserved exclusively for politics. The first floor had a gracious living room, lined with bookshelves, a small dining room, and back-of-the-house facilities to accommodate a small staff. They moved in just before Christmas in 1925.

The family ate very well but not lavishly. In addition to their own vegetable garden, they had groceries delivered from a top family-owned store, Emery Specialty Grocery Company. Milk arrived daily in a horse-drawn wagon. Frank Phillipo offered fresh fruits and vegetables from a mule cart twice a week. The iceman came regularly to replenish the ice box. All cakes, pies, cookies, noodles, and ice cream were made at home.

Life at 1336 Shady Avenue was family focused but overshadowed by constant conversation about government and political reform. Eliza went daily to her office in the Jenkins Arcade downtown. At home, the phone rang off the hook with politicians seeking her support and league members and others asking her advice on how to vote or her help in addressing various political scandals or injustices. Her escapades in fighting for government integrity and accountability would become the topic of dinner table conversations and near daily newspaper coverage.

Around the edges, Eliza found time to serve as president of the Western Pennsylvania League of Girls' Clubs, which operated a summer camp and organized more than a dozen local clubs, and she served in the Women's Auxiliary of the Pittsburgh Hospital and on the board of the Curtis Home for Girls.

The summer of 1926, Lucy and Eliza, along with their mother and 16-year-old Julian, boarded the *SS Belgenland* and embarked on a three-month European tour, a trip similar to the one Eliza had done with Temp two years earlier. The 697-foot ship had been newly renovated after its wartime service, and it was the Red Star Line's most luxurious vessel, fitted with rich woodwork and elegant fixtures and accommodations for 350 first class passengers. They left on June 25 and returned September 25, just in time for Julian to return to boarding school at Taft. The Grand Tour was to be part of his education. No one seemed concerned that they left behind their husbands and four other children for the duration.

They took with them their "machine," a Buick sedan motor car that had been simonized to protect it from the sea weather, and they hired a private driver, putting more than four thousand miles on the car as they made their way around England and across the continent—Paris, Toulouse, Carcassonne, Venice, Florence, Pisa, Monte Carlo, Vienna, Prague, Brugges, Brussels, and back to London for the return voyage.

In her travel diary, Eliza kept meticulous records of their purchases—coats at Burberry's, scarves at Liberty's, and an entire winter wardrobe of a dozen day and evening ensembles for Eliza from Madame Rose at the fashion house of Olivan-Brevet in Paris, supplier of dresses to British and Russian royalty, for which she paid more than five hundred dollars. "I shall be so gorgeous this winter my friends will not know me," she wrote in her travel diary. Writing to Temp about her new "glad rags," she said "For once in my life I'm going to be really dressy."[38]

While in England, they visited Beatrice Forbes-Robertson Hale, who since their suffrage days together had returned to her native England, divorced, and written *What's Wrong with Our Girls?* Mrs. Hale's answer to that question was simple: urban life. From Chichester they ventured out to Bognor Regis on the coast to visit another old suffrage friend who had rented a seaside house for the summer, Mrs. Caspar Whitney (Florence Canfield Whitney).

Mrs. Whitney was president of the National League for Women's Service, a cofounder of the League of Women Voters, and wife of the renowned explorer and author who had originated the concept of the All-American team in college football while working for *Harper's Magazine*. Everywhere they went, Lucy and Eliza relished the beautiful landscapes, particularly those around the stately country homes of England, gathering inspiration for their own gardens back home. Eliza also took particular interest in the dungeons at Château de Loches in the Loire Valley and described in gruesome detail some of the torture techniques used there. She was not at all squeamish. Along the way, the traveling foursome also looked at colleges in England and seaside houses they might rent in Brittany if they were to bring the rest of the children over for a holiday.

Jennie, less enamored of it all, was not an easy travel companion. "Mother began one of her tirades," Lucy wrote to John. "But you know Mother. The only thing she really enjoys is eating. . . . Outside of that she thinks the trip is very dull. . . . In spite of her we are having a good time." Three weeks before they were to return, she wrote, "The going is good if we could just ship Mother home. She is getting a little more difficult every day." Lucy no longer idolized "Spirit." Eliza reported, "Nothing ever pleases her very long at a time but we are getting along much better than we expected to."[39] "Mother is really having a very good time but as usual she hates to admit it."[40] . . . "Grandma is in a terrible rage . . . wouldn't speak to us."[41] "She wears herself out getting excited about little things, fusses and stews about her baggage getting to her room and nearly falls on her nose turning around to see if we are following her."[42] "We get quite weary sometimes hearing about the perfections of the U.S.A. and 5400."[43]

Toward the end of the trip, Eliza wrote to Temp, fretting a bit about a widower friend who remarried after what she apparently considered too brief an interval. "It doesn't pay does it to be too devoted a wife, you might as well have a good time while here, for few husbands remember long. I think perhaps long periods of travel are a good thing and then one's husband gets used to being alone and then if one passes on he is better able to adjust himself. Lucy says she thinks we should just go on to Naples and Rome for another three months to get you and John trained for the future."[44]

* * *

Lucy and John's grand manor house at Emerson Point on the Eastern Shore commanded a broad view of the Miles River.

Lucy had long dreamed of living on a farm. In 1928, she found her version of paradise, Emerson Point Farm on Maryland's Eastern Shore. On 220 acres with a broad water view over the Miles River, she built a six-bedroom manor house surrounded by elegant boxwood mazes, grandiflora magnolia, loblolly pines, and cedars. The house stood at the end of a mile-long, tree-lined lane. A boathouse on their private cove was a short ride away on a bicycle or in the family's Ford woody station wagon, which Lucy never learned to drive, although Eliza did. Lucy's expectation was that she and John would eventually retire there. In the meantime, she built an idyllic and rarified world for her family to escape the smoky city in the summer.

Quickly realizing that she needed the comfort and companionship of her sister nearby, Lucy convinced Eliza to build her own house on the farm. Eliza and Temp arranged for two weathered cottages on the property to be moved to a waterfront location and joined into a rambling white frame assemblage centered around a large screened-in porch with a generous sleeping porch above.

Thunderstorms on the Chesapeake Bay were violent affairs, often knocking out the electricity. As the first rumblings would begin to rattle the house and her nerves, Lucy would call Eliza on the party line and insist that she come over and sit by her side. She worried incessantly about the dangers that awaited her children, and eventually her grandchildren, outside the stately Emerson Point house—leaky boats and fickle winds, jellyfish and horseshoe crabs, poison ivy and thorny bushes, mosquitoes and ticks, wasps and hornets, rabid raccoons and all types of snakes, rusty nails and hazardous farm machinery. Lucy was fearless until it came to things she couldn't control.[45]

Inside the house, a wide front hall extended from front to back, allowing a water view as one entered. To the right a formal living room stretched the full

Eliza and Temp's house at the farm was a far more informal affair.

depth of the house, dominated by an enormous rug, a Steinway concert grand piano, and an imposing portrait of Lucy. To the left, the dining room was more foreboding than inviting, with the kind of heavy chairs that made sitting down to a meal—even breakfast—feel like a major commitment.

Lucy exerted control over a daily agenda that was very formal and not particularly child-friendly, Breakfast, lunch, and dinner were served punctually at set times in the dining room, with sterling utensils on the massive mahogany table. Everyone was expected to dress properly and to maintain decorum as Lucy held forth. Waving her left hand with abandon, a lit cigarette between two fingers, she commanded the conversation, which generally centered around politics and almost never included the children.

Nearby, Eliza sat serenely on the porch swing of her more relaxed domain, doing needlework and crossword puzzles as children charged in and out, the humidity-warped wooden screen doors slapping shut behind them. They had free run of hundreds of acres and miles of shoreline, where they could build forts, shoot bows and arrows, build model boats, sail and swim, fish and crab, ride horses, and race pony carts along wooded paths and through fields of specimen holly trees. Days at the farm passed at an unmeasured pace, one slipping into the next over the course of long, leisurely summers.

A steady stream of houseguests, many of them associated with the league, would come and go all summer long. It seemed that Eliza was able to strike an enviable balance between her public persona and her private life. But for the occasional country club dance or yacht club regatta, it was a quiet and very private life, an oasis of calm far removed from the limelight glare of Pittsburgh. The farm would remain their cherished escape for the rest of their lives.

Life at the farm was carefree for Eliza's two sons, Tempie (right) and Kenny.

By the end of the decade, both Lucy and Eliza had their lives and their local league established. Lucy had stepped down as head of the Pennsylvania league. Eliza was just getting warmed up with the county league. The family had weathered the stock market crash with their finances intact, both sisters had built their Pittsburgh and Eastern Shore homes, and their children were all launched into good private schools. Now thoroughly settled into their routine as full-time unpaid political reformers, the sisters were ready for their next big battle.

19 SHE DEVILS AT THE DOOR

It started with a few cases of canned red salmon. The year was 1931, and the Great Depression had turned the world sideways. Unemployment in Pennsylvania was already taking its toll and would climb to 40 percent by 1933. Economizing was on most everyone's mind, even those who were not so hard hit. Even though the Pittsburgh corporate community was adding several new iconic skyscrapers to the city's skyline—Gulf Oil Tower, the Koppers Building, and the Grant Building—a general sense of frugal stewardship prevailed. Canned salmon was a fish for the frugal.

The mayor, however, was not known for his frugality. Charles H. Kline was a prosperous-looking man of sixty-one. A tall and imposing figure, he had a broad, aquiline nose and a full, square face, his prominent chin set against a thicker, second chin below, crowned by a well-groomed head of graying hair. He had a pronounced dignity about him and enjoyed the finer things in life as well as the accoutrements that came with being mayor. His eyes twinkled when he smiled at his own good fortune.

The women of the Equal Franchise Federation had gotten to know Kline during his days in the Pennsylvania Senate. An 1897 law graduate of the University of Pennsylvania, he had served one term as a state representative, three terms as a state senator, and seven years as a common pleas judge before he took office as mayor in 1926. He was elected president pro tempore of the Senate and had presided as the suffrage amendment stumbled through to approval in the spring of 1915. Like Lucy and Eliza, he was a staunch Republican.

Nearly twenty years later, with Kline firmly ensconced in the mayor's office, Lucy and Eliza had new business with the ambitious politician. As the community struggled with the devastation of the Depression, the Allegheny County League of Women Voters was recognized as a go-to source for help in dealing with municipal problems and political blarney. Eliza as chair remained committed to the league's work even as the membership declined and many remaining members, strapped for cash, neglected to pay their dues. The second phone at the Smith household, the one reserved for league business, still routinely rang off the hook.

One of the requests for help came in early 1931 from John Houston, a wholesale grocer in the city, who had been submitting bids to supply canned goods for city establishments and had repeatedly been denied the business. Frustrated, he finally learned from an honest city employee that the contracts—including a considerable amount for canned salmon—had been going to an out-of-town supplier at much higher prices. Houston had tried reaching out to city council in a letter, but the matter was referred to Mayor Kline, who held a secret meeting with the city controller, James P. Kerr, and the head of the department of supplies, Bertram L. Succop. The mayor attempted to dismiss the whole affair by firing Succop for "visible irregularities" and "using poor judgment" and promising that the city would, in the future, buy the more economical—and equally nourishing—pink salmon instead of red. Newspaper editorials couldn't resist punning about the mayor's distraction tactic: ". . . the consumption of red salmon is not the explanation of the wasting of thousands of dollars of the taxpayers' money through the supplies department and must not be permitted to be drawn as a *red herring* across the path of Council in its duty to bring out all the facts. . . . The taxpayers still see *red* every time they think of the wasting of their money in this case. . . ."[1] Despite the problem being brought to light, suspicions remained that something was still awry in city purchasing.

Not knowing what to do next, Houston appealed to Eliza for help. She listened carefully and then enlisted Lucy's assistance. Both women had skills as amateur auditors, and they descended upon the City-County Building demanding to see the books. At first, they were turned away. They had no right "to poke their noses into the city books," they were told. But Eliza advised those who were blocking her path that not only would the courts protect her rights as a citizen but the newspapers were "hungry for juicy stories."[2] And they were. As Eliza and Lucy proceeded with their tenacious bird-dogging, the papers had a field day with the sparring between the two amateur sleuths and the political hacks in the building. Feeling under siege by this pair of middle-aged matrons, whom some referred to as "the Silk Stocking Advisors," the row office occupants were terrified. The moment Eliza and Lucy would cross the threshold, the word would spread up and down the halls, through the row offices, into the dark recesses where the business of city government could privately fall prey to shady dealings: "The She Devils are at the door!"

Make Own Probe of City's Buying Methods

Eliza (left) and Lucy worked side by side to conduct their own independent audit of the city and county purchasing records. From *Pittsburgh Press*, February 28, 1933

"Food Probe Pressed by Women," the *Sun-Telegraph* headline read. The league presented a resolution to city council requesting a public investigation of six years of food and supply contracts, looking for "any irregularities or dishonesties," and suggesting that council should see that the money be returned to the treasury and that the culprit receive "the full penalty of the law." The resolution went on to say, "Since both the Mayor and the Director of the Department of Supplies, in this case, are involved, it would seem both impossible and absurd for the Mayor to investigate himself. . . ." In response to the mayor's apparent attempt at self-defense, the resolution added, "His Honor drags a red salmon across the trail by stating that no one would be so hard-hearted as to deprive the inmates of Mayview of nourishing food. Pathos is usually the resort of one who has no justifiable excuse to make and we have all heard it used many times in our courts and legislative halls. After scanning the Mayview menus and the money that has been expended for food for the same institution, we certainly cannot feel that the citizens have been hard-hearted. . . ." Playing upon the sentiment of public solidarity that grew out of the shared economic crisis, the resolution added, "In these times of great unemployment and suffering our public servants in every capacity should be conserving the resources of the city wherever possible instead of squandering them with the apparent audacity that has been used in this particular instance."[3]

Finally, the resolution praised Mr. Houston for stepping forward as a whistleblower. "It requires courage for a citizen of Allegheny County to bring before any of our public bodies evidences of irregularities and dishonesties, even though this dishonesty is based upon incontrovertible facts. There is, and has been, a tendency on the part of some of the servants of the city and of the county to attempt to make that citizen the culprit in a case of this sort. In this and in similar cases, we have noticed a tendency for certain public servants to become not only flippant but insolent when a citizen asks for the redress of a grievance." The resolution was signed by Eliza as league chair, with the backing of more than twelve hundred league members.[4] With that, she had thrown down the gauntlet to the mayor, and she would not be stopped.

Eliza and Lucy's quick and dirty investigation had revealed sufficient irregularities that council authorized a full audit by public accountants of six years' worth of city purchasing practices under Mayor Kline. The Food Probe, as it was called, put the mayor's entire record up for critical examination. Enlisting the support of the Civic Club of Allegheny County and the Exchange Club of Pittsburgh, Eliza organized a Citizens Committee, which assembled many prominent citizens who could not be intimidated or dismissed by politicians. The committee supported Eliza's demand for an audit, and she set about raising the money to pay for it. City council voted seven to two not to cooperate.

Eliza was not at all surprised by council's reluctance to cooperate. "It was exactly what I expected," she said. "My feeling is that council hopes that, if it can weather the blast for a week or two, the storm of public opinion will have blown over and things will go on much as they have in the past. I believe they do not appreciate that it is more difficult to scorn public opinion in hard times than it is in good. There are too many people suffering want and lack of employment for an outrageous waste of public funds to be tolerated." She concluded, "Council is simply putting off the evil day and the longer they put it off the worse it looks."[5]

Mayor Kline didn't help matters with his extravagant ways. The *Pittsburgh Press* reported in March that Kline spent seventeen thousand dollars on luxuries for his office, most of them without bids. The purchases included $1,350—nearly one and a half times the average annual pay of an unskilled worker—for an oversized, eighteen-by-twenty-foot Persian carpet for his office, and nearly two thousand dollars for another, as well as eight thousand dollars for radio-tone pictures, photos engraved on copper plates, of preceding mayors.[6] A dapper dresser with expensive tastes, he was one of the last men to continue wearing bowlers and spats—also known as spatterdashes or spatter guards—which had fallen out of favor during the 1920s. Kline rode in a top-of-the-line limousine. He loved lavishly entertaining visiting dignitaries and was proud of his photos with Charles Lindbergh after his famed New York-to-Paris flight, with Admiral Richard Byrd after his exploration of the North and South Poles, and with President Calvin Coolidge. He delighted at hosting the star of western films, Tom Mix, as well as the Miss America of Aviation, Ruth Elder, and champion boxer, Gene Tunney.

Kerr, recognizing that he couldn't stop the citizens' group, announced that he would conduct his own audit as controller. So it was that two teams of public accountants pored concurrently over the city's books, sniffing for improprieties. Appealing to the public for information,

The *Press* political cartoonist poked fun at the mayor for his extravagances. From *Pittsburgh Press*, March 8, 1931

the league announced, "It might be that city employes [sic] would like to tell things. They are taxpayers as well as the rest of us, and many of them resent this orgy of extravagance."[7] Promising anonymity, the appeal immediately evoked "a tremendous response," Eliza reported.[8]

By summer, the matter had been taken to a grand jury. The inquiries ultimately reached far beyond just food purchases to include police cars, asphalt trucks, bridge iron, rubber goods, soap chips, and more, with new revelations emerging almost daily.

As the investigations continued, Eliza was becoming daily, headline news. The more city council and the mayor tried to squirm out of the limelight, the more the probe dug in. Experts speculated as to how to right the systemic wrongs that spawned the scandal. "Ways Out of Pittsburgh's Civic Mess," read the headline of one two-page spread, which praised the probe as "a magnificent piece of public service."[9] It was not surprising, then, when nine-year-old Kenny commented one evening, "What's wrong, Muvie? Your picture isn't on the front page today."[10]

Then, in late 1931, the grand jury indicted Kline on forty-eight counts of malfeasance for fraudulently approving contracts that had cost the local taxpayers millions of dollars, and Succop on forty-six counts of malfeasance for fraudulently issuing them. The case was taken to adjacent Butler County for a trial, in which the jury convicted Kline on May 14, 1932, and ordered him to resign and serve a six-month prison term. Succop, already out of office, was sentenced to one year. An editorial in the *Pittsburgh Press* exalted, "Yes, it can be done! The people can smash the most unscrupulous political machines, and dethrone the most powerful bosses. They can make public office a public trust, and elect public officials responsive to their will. They can get decent, economical and efficient government—if they want it, and are willing to fight for it."[11]

Mayor Kline appealed the case on the basis of his poor health, and the battle was back on.[12] On September 15, 1932, Judge Thomas D. Finletter set aside the jury's verdict on Kline, on the condition that he resign, and suspended the six-month jail term with the following revised sentence: "That the defendant be ousted and removed from the office of mayor of the city of Pittsburgh, and that he pay a fine of $5,000 to the use of the commonwealth, and that he stand committed until this sentence is complied with."[13] Yet somehow Kline was allowed to return to his office for "political fence mending."[14]

The *Press* called it a "Mercy Deal."[15]

Many in the city just wanted Kline gone. Paul Block, publisher of the *Post-Gazette*, said, "The fight has not been directed against the Mayor as an individual, but as an official. The record justifies the public's lack of confidence in him as chief executive of the city, but there is no personal bitterness involved. . . . His resignation—without further penalty—would no doubt satisfy the great majority of our citizenship."[16]

For some, though, particularly those closest to the dealings, the case was not over when the trial ended. They continued to litigate it in the papers. They questioned just how Kline's diagnosis—"hardening of the arteries, with specific involvement of the vessels of the central nervous system and peripheral circulation, the heart, and the kidneys"—might have endangered his life during a prison term.[17] Three of the doctors who had said he was too ill for prison reportedly received anonymous death threats by mail.[18] Certainly Eliza and Lucy had trouble letting it go. Waste in the face of a depression was particularly egregious. Unforgiveable. Besides, the recounting of Kline's demise made such a good object lesson.

After seven years in office, Kline finally resigned in disgrace on March 31, 1933, "broken in influence, reputation and health."[19] "Clinging to the last shred of dignity attaching to his office," one reporter wrote, "he makes no mention of the fact that his resignation was forced by the court."[20] When the resignation finally occurred, the *Post-Gazette* was again quick to distinguish between Kline's role as a public official and his status as a private citizen, and the editors expressed satisfaction simply that he had been removed from office. They also commended the Citizens' Committee and others who aided in the investigation, noting that the outcome demonstrated "the power of public opinion, once it is aroused...."[21]

Disgraced and broken, Kline quietly said good-bye to his cabinet. He died four months later, on July 22, of a paralytic stroke.

In death, much of Kline's dignity was restored, to an extent. In his obituaries, he was recalled as a larger-than-life figure who had welcomed screen stars, royalty, and air heroes with golden keys to the city during his seven years as mayor. He, in turn, had been honored by government officials in Hungary, Italy, and Sweden. A full page in the *Sun-Telegraph* recounted an exemplary career with a meteoric rise to power cut short by an abrupt, self-inflicted demise fueled by greed and graft. "Seldom have the political heights and 'paths of glory' led so surely and deeply and swiftly into the tangle of the political dismal swamps as they did for former Mayor Charles H. Kline," the report began. It described him as "a political boss whose individual word was law within the Republican organization of Pittsburgh and, to a large extent, in Allegheny County." It recounted the creation of "a political machine without precedent in Pittsburgh, a machine as answerable to the will of a single man as was any political organization ever built in the United States." Kline, the article contended, "instituted the unquestioned rule of the ward chairmen, and every ward chairman was a man of his own picking. Concessions, patronage, whatever was the best medium of winning and holding votes in their ward, were thrown their way. And in return they furnished the money and the ballots which kept the Kline machine running smoothly." Kline controlled city council as well, the article said, making it his puppet.[22] The *Post-Gazette* suggested that "an evil star reigned over the Kline regime."[23]

There were of course words of praise from Kline's loyal following. And Bertram Succop, awaiting a pardon in his Allegheny County jail cell, said, "Mayor Kline was a fine type man, one of the finest men I have ever met in public life. Now that death has called, the many good deeds and great accomplishments of his career are revived with an appreciation of his many fine qualities.... I sincerely believe and hope from this time forward animosities will be forgotten...."[24]

The next day, municipal offices were closed, city flags flew at half-mast, and police and fire stations were draped in mourning for the man who some contended lost his way when he traded a seat on the bench as a brilliant and respected Common Pleas Judge for the high-backed mayor's chair, where he was subject to constant criticism for his vanity, arrogance, and loyalty to a group of "profiteering henchmen." Judge Kline was the esteemed jurist who wrote fifteen volumes—forty-five hundred pages—on the principles of civil and criminal law. His alter ego was the mayor who "walked into office and beckoned the ward leaders and the ward-heelers to follow him."[25]

In the short term, Kline's successor was John S. Herron, who ascended from his office as president of city council to temporarily take the reins.

The Food Probe investigation had not been rooted in partisan politics. Lucy and Eliza were, in fact, staunch Republicans who supported a second term for President Hoover rather than the alternative "cure-alls" and "ill-advised fields of social experimentation" proposed by his opponent in the 1932 election.[26] Unlike the majority of the electorate, they viewed him not as callous and insensitive but rather as fiscally conservative. But as they traveled the speakers' circuit and made speeches on the radio, they urged all women—regardless of their political stripes—to vote in the historic 1932 election. The league's programs presented divergent views, including positive reviews of Franklin D. Roosevelt's administration.[27] On the eve of the November 8 vote, when the Debating Society of the University of Pittsburgh arranged a symposium to consider the Republican, Democrat, and Socialist party stances, Eliza presided.[28]

Machine politics, graft, and corruption were not unique to Pittsburgh. Dozens of cities nationwide fell prey in the early twentieth century to patronage—from crooked contracts on purchasing and infrastructure projects, to vote buying, job selling, bribes, kickbacks, and "straight-up" embezzlement—as their elected officials notoriously used their power to control and extract revenue from the public coffers. The police were often complicit, turning a blind eye to practices that fed the business of vice by failing to enforce the laws governing drugs and alcohol, gambling, and prostitution or, worse yet, by selling protection. Some infractions progressed to the level of criminal investigations and prosecutions of local politicians, but the corruption continued nonetheless, most notably in Minneapolis, St. Louis, Philadelphia, Chicago, and New York, as well as in Pittsburgh.[29] Some contended that working through the machine structure was easier than dealing directly with representatives in the municipal legislatures.[30]

Writing for *McClure's Magazine* in 1903, muckraker Lincoln Steffens drew attention to the public's complicity in allowing both financial and police corruption to continue. "Pittsburg: A City Ashamed" focused light on the partnership between the city's late boss, Christopher L. Magee, and William Flinn, whose firm, Booth & Flinn, received virtually all of the city's paving contracts between 1887 and 1896, even as he continued to serve in the state Senate.

"Angry and ashamed," Steffens wrote, "Pittsburg is a type of the city that has tried to be free and failed."[31] It would seem that Lucy and Eliza were up against a powerful and longstanding national epidemic that was too rampant to rein in. But that didn't stop them from trying.

As an antidote to the problem of corruption, Eliza and her allies advocated for the city manager form of government, in which an appointed executive is answerable to a proportionally elected council. Such a model already existed in Cleveland, Cincinnati, Dayton, Des Moines, Kansas City, and Rochester, and it had proven to improve services, they maintained, while eliminating public graft and reducing taxes. A bill was pending in the state legislature that would have given each municipality the choice to adopt such a government. Objections to the model were plentiful, however, many of them coming from big business.[32]

In response to the objections, Lucy and Eliza visited Cincinnati to do a thorough analysis with the same accountants they had used for the Food Probe. Eliza then published a series of three articles in the *Press* outlining how and why the model could work for Pittsburgh. Had Pittsburgh followed the efficient city manager model in 1930 through 1932, she contended, the savings would have been in excess of eleven million dollars, with tax millage at half the rate Pittsburghers were paying.[33] A mass meeting on the subject drew thousands of public supporters as well as an appearance and endorsement by Charles Taft II, the former president's son and an active Ohio politician. But the city manager proposal never gained much traction.

* * *

While they were still ensnared with the Kline investigation, Lucy and Eliza continued to scan the scene for other infractions and found a whole other set of irregularities that they contended cost taxpayers millions of dollars.

The Commonwealth and the county had been considering the use of voting machines as early as 1923, and after a county referendum in 1929 approved the notion, they began to shop in earnest. In 1931, as the county commissioners were considering alternative machines for the September primaries, the sisters called attention to certain abnormalities in the bids submitted. Given that the county was ordering a thousand machines at more than a thousand dollars apiece, the matter warranted their attention.[34] The county had already paid seven hundred thousand dollars to the Poole Engineering and Manufacturing Company of Baltimore, an enterprise that the papers noted had no previous experience in the production of voting machines.[35]

The Poole Machines were first put into use for the general election on November 3, 1931. Shortly thereafter, Lucy and Eliza delivered a letter to the county commissioners charging that not only did fifty-three of the 186 machines fail to properly function on Election Day but also that Poole's "Electromatic" machine had jammed in a subsequent test. With twenty-eight thousand parts, the machines were arguably destined to malfunction in some way. "It took the Poole experts three hours," the letter said, "to change the machine from the original setup to the setup required by the Allegheny County ballot sheet. Out of 47 votes cast, the machine failed to perform six times. The levers jammed so that it could not be operated until adjustments were made by mechanics."[36]

Those who opposed the machines blamed the failures on the machines themselves. Those who favored them blamed human error and mismanagement on the part of the elections bureau and the elections board operatives, who had not followed the operating instructions. In some cases, the ineptitude was as simple as failing to plug in the machines. In a few instances, critics alleged malicious tampering. In others, the problem was attributed to inadequate instructions to voters, who unwittingly jammed the machines.

For the next two years, repeated attempts to refurbish and retest the machines appeared to be throwing good money after bad. That was just the sort of fiasco that kept the sisters engaged. In May 1932, they were photographed alongside the three attorneys associated with the investigation of the Poole machines.[37] By the end of the year, it seemed that perhaps the operating problems had been resolved.[38]

In March 1933, Lucy and Eliza were both present at the new County Office Building to witness demonstrations of two of the original Poole machines, which had been refurbished yet again. Their job, as they saw it, was to inspect the machines and ensure that they were "fool proof and vote thief proof."[39] It was understood that only after they were satisfied with the remodeled machines could the remaining eleven hundred faulty machines be reconstructed by the National Cash Register Company. When inspection of the two sample machines turned out to require four mechanics working for ten hours to setup and adjust their inner workings, the sisters and two of their league compatriots, who joined the vigil, were undaunted. "We'll stick and see it done," Lucy declared.[40] They also attended a demonstration of sample alternative machines manufactured by the Automatic Voting Machine Company of Jamestown, New York, who had first introduced the machines in 1892.[41] But after a thorough inspection, the sisters were not impressed, and in a letter to the county commissioners, Eliza called it "a reckless expenditure of public money" and advocated instead a return to paper ballots.[42]

Nonetheless, that summer of 1933, the Thomas Spacing Machine Company of Glenshaw was retained to make repairs to the eleven hundred machines, working under the watchful eyes of a corps of armed guards. Some 125 mechanics made an estimated two hundred changes to the machines—thirty-five machines per day on an assembly line—at an additional investment of $125,000.

The kerfuffle over the voting machines carried on throughout that year. While Republican officials were trying to block use of the suspect machines, the county election officials were making plans to send them into all the districts in Pittsburgh as well as nearby McKeesport and Clairton. A force of 924 unemployed National Guardsmen and ex-servicemen were lined up to carry the machines to the polling places and guard them around the clock. An additional force of 464 machine inspectors were to step in on Primary Day, September 19.

As an added measure, the county commissioners ordered that a guide to operating the machine be printed in all daily and foreign language newspapers in the county. A full-page photo ran in some five hundred thousand copies of the papers with the headline, "It's Easy to Operate a Voting Machine—Just Observe These Simple Instructions." Included was a text bubble, pointing to a button, that read "Push this button to close curtains and set machine when you enter. Push it again after you've voted."[43] It all seemed straightforward enough.

In practice, however, the equipment was a bit more problematic. "Machines Jam, Snarl Voting" . . . "Brawls Mark Balloting," the evening headlines of the *Sun-Telegraph* declared. It had been a heated day at the polls, as fighting and bullying had brought state and local police in to calm the commotion over the county's most contentious political race in years. Many voters and election officials struggled to figure out how to operate the machines. Matters were complicated by the fact that many of the machines broke down, and thousands of voters were thwarted during the morning hours. Eliza joined a group that stormed the Bureau of Elections to complain. Many suspected sabotage. Others charged incompetence in operating the machines, compounded by panic. "Unutterable confusion reigned" all morning until noon when, under court order, truckloads of paper ballots were frantically dispatched to the polling places using every possible conveyance. Police cars, taxicabs, county work trucks rushed to all corners of the city and county. District Attorney Andrew T. Park called it "the worst managed election in the county's history." In some districts, not a single vote was cast before four o'clock in the afternoon. "Thousands of eleventh-hour voters veritably stampeded the polls as the primaries came to a close . . . in a realm of confusion." Anger and confusion prompted nonpartisan talk about a new election. In the midst of the melee, some lawyers declared that it was legal for voters to write their own ballots.[44]

A subsequent three-week investigation generated hundreds of pages of testimony by some two hundred witnesses. Lucy and Eliza were invited to appear and make a statement. Testing of the machines revealed that "by using the 'straight party lever' forcefully, the interior mechanism could be so thrown out of alignment that it would thenceforth be easy to cheat with . . . two buttons. . . . if one moderately clever and willful voter were to enter the booth early in the day, force this 'straight party lever' and manipulate the buttons, it would then be easy for his less cunning followers to 'beat' the same machine all day."[45] The story was told that Eliza demonstrated just how vulnerable the pinion gears were, using a hairpin to jam them and cast multiple votes for a single candidate. During the inquiry, one state senator insinuated that Lucy and Eliza had received money from the Automatic Voting Machine Corporation, the rival concern whose machines had been rejected in favor of the Poole machines, an accusation that the sisters flatly denied.[46] They also bristled at accusations that they had been "voting machine obstructionists," reminding the investigators that they had spent ten years trying to get voting machines in Allegheny County.[47]

This time, the investigation concluded that the debacle represented an unfortunate convergence of defective machines, slipshod performance by election workers, and inexperience on the part of voters. Despite the failure in the primaries, however, the machines were deemed safe for use in the general election with just three minor mechanical fixes, which would require a workforce of forty-two mechanics and sixty laborers. Then, just days before the November 1933 election, the $1.1 million worth of voting machines were scrapped. The entire contest was tallied using paper ballots. Eliza and Lucy were not surprised to

Telling Probers What's Wrong With Vote Machines

Eliza testified about the defects in the new voting machines, calling them a "reckless expenditure of public money." From *Pittsburgh Sun-Telegraph*, October 17, 1933

learn that the Poole Engineering and Manufacturing Company was bankrupt.

Still, the county continued their efforts to salvage the faulty machines. By the end of February 1934, three years and $1.3 million after the initial purchase, Secretary of the Commonwealth Richard J. Beamish gave his official approval of the eleven hundred machines, once they could be refurbished by Westinghouse Electric Engineers. That was expected to cost yet another four to six hundred thousand dollars. It was not until later that year that the machines were finally deemed satisfactory.

* * *

Lucy and Eliza's crusade against corruption was not without risk. One couldn't help but shudder as another front-page news item on February 28, 1931, adjacent to a voting machine article, depicted a beautiful young woman, "reputed to be a prominent figure in the night life" of New York, who was found strangled in a gulley in the Bronx on the eve of her testifying in a vice and graft investigation. And gangster "Scarface" Al Capone was sparring with authorities in Chicago over his own unsavory activities. Skulduggery was the order of the day. But if Lucy and Eliza were threatened in any way, they never let on to their families.

They were, however, threatened by at least one attempt at a reputational smear. In March 1933, state representative Joseph G. Steedle, MD, publicly accused the sisters of tax evasion, of failing to pay county personal property taxes in excess of a hundred thousand dollars.[48] In a scathing riposte, just days later, Lucy cleared the air and then abruptly turned the tables on their accuser. "My father, the late Julian Kennedy, . . . made a return to the Tax Revision Board of Allegheny County and paid the tax ever since the law went into effect in 1913. I, myself, have paid the four-mill personal tax for the past eight years. . . . My sister . . . has made a return and paid the tax for the past six years. My mother, the late Jennie E. Kennedy, . . . never made a return. Upon her death the executors of her estate made a return for five years, as required by law, and paid the tax and the penalties." But she didn't stop there. "If, as chairman of the Appropriations Committee, you are as inaccurate in your figures and facts as you have shown yourself to be in this statement it must be a great handicap to the work of that most important committee," she charged. "If you will take the same trouble in regard to your own returns, you will find that from 1928 to 1932 you never made a return—that you did make one in 1933. It would seem to me a little unkind to criticize an aged woman who is no longer here to defend herself, when there are thousands of women and businessmen who made their returns for the first time in 1933 and when you, yourself, the Chairman of the Appropriations Committee of the Pennsylvania Legislature, are guilty of the same offense." Lucy concluded, "I appreciate that owing to your constitutional rights as a member of the House it is impossible for me to secure any redress for the injustice you have done me and my family by making this misleading and untruthful statement."[49] Her message was almost biblical in its clarity: let him who is without sin cast the first stone. As one citizen wrote to the *Press* editors, "More power to your pen, Mrs. Miller. . . . I hold no brief for the Kennedy's nor does Mrs. J. O. Miller need any help, apparently, in a fight where Dr. Steedle is her opponent, but the 'Sage of McKees Rocks' [Steedle] may learn that thrice armed is he or she whose cause is just. Thanks, Mrs. Miller, for the heartiest laugh the writer has had since the world turned blue three years ago."[50] The day after Lucy cleared the air, the two sisters were invited to participate in a mass meeting on the steps of the State Capitol by none other than the Tax Justice League of Pennsylvania.[51] Steedle did not seek reelection after his term ended the next year, and nothing more was said of the matter.

The league took up a number of other matters, including the foster home system as administered by the juvenile courts. In an investigation of abuse and neglect in foster homes, the league found fifty-six out of 162 to be unsatisfactory, and they lobbied for more trained social workers, a psychiatric clinic, and reform of the juvenile court system to be more protective of the children's best interests.[52] And in the midst of her political muckraking, Eliza threw her support behind the Family-Help-Family project to address the problem of hunger, which plagued some twenty-eight thousand families in Allegheny County.[53] As county chairman and a member of its executive committee, she worked with an army of 3,000 women who volunteered to raise money in order to supplement public funding for the most destitute.

With the Kline fiasco still fresh in their minds, the sisters also joined forces with a committee of 150 men and women who sought to establish good government in Pittsburgh and Allegheny County. Their primary targets were Kline's successor, Mayor John S. Herron, and State Senator James J. Coyne. The chair of the effort, Leslie M. Johnston, said, "Graft and corruption in the operation of city government is out of date. Taxpayers of all classes are sick and tired of the wasteful and inefficient methods and abuses which have grown out of and are part of the spoils system. The time has come to replace all inefficiency with modern methods of honesty, efficiency and economy."[54] The largest vote ever recorded in the county, the committee contended, drew just 38 percent of the electorate, "which allowed the 'gang' to control the county with only 20 percent of the people."[55] Citizen participation through voting was clearly one of the most powerful tools in battling the machine. Another was the relentless watchdogging of the women who had worked so hard to secure the vote in the first place. Hannah Patterson was the committee's first vice chairman. Joining Lucy and Eliza on the women's committee were their longstanding allies from their suffrage days, Jennie Roessing and Mary Flinn Lawrence.

Yet even as they were targeting Herron's misdeeds and the bootlegging activities of another candidate, Joseph N. Mackrell, the league hosted a luncheon for 450 people in early September to allow each of the five mayoral candidates to present on his own behalf. It was the first, and perhaps only, time that all five candidates appeared on the same platform. Recognizing the potential public appeal in this spectacle, the *Post-Gazette* sent not just the general news reporter but also the sports editor and the movie critic. The editor wondered, "Is this a show? . . . or a new indoor sport?"[56]

The sports reporter called it "an elimination series of bouts designed to name the next heavyweight political champion of Pittsburgh," staged before "the largest crowd of fair fans (that fair referring to the gender in this case) ever to attend a bare knuckle fight in the history of the town." "Mrs. R. Templeton Smith, the big shot of the league, took the part of Joe Humphries, the famous announcer," he reported. "Although the lads posed for pre-fight pictures before entering the ring and exchanged pleasantries, there was no punch-pulling or stalling once the bouts started.... Each battler at the ringside had an unofficial second in his corner, a sedate lady armed figuratively with water bucket and smelling salts."[57]

The movie critic declared, "The late Mr. Ziegfeld would have called it a 'Follies.' The equally late Mr. Phineas T. Barnum might have labeled it 'The Greatest Show on Earth.' Hollywood would have tacked on such superlatives as 'colossal,' 'stupendous' and 'spectacular.'" "It is an expensive production, this 'Meet the Mayor,' ably directed by Mrs. R. Templeton Smith." "Briefly," he went on, "'Meet the Mayor' tells of the mild confusion in a big-city electorate as they approach the day of reckoning. However, the confusion that accompanies the selection of the candidates is nothing compared to the confusion that results once the candidates have stated their platforms.... In the realm of sheer spectacle there has been nothing to approach [it] ... never again will there be another entertainment quite like it ... thank goodness."[58]

Of the five candidates on the stage, only Mayor Herron was interrupted by boos from the audience. Eliza insisted afterward that it was not league members who were discourteous.

William M. McNair, who read his speech, declared that efficiency and economy in government were impossible if men are elected to council and the mayor's office who "can see no evil ... when powerful utility or political racketeers are involved."[59] Come the September primaries, McNair won the Democratic nomination. Then, on November 7, 1933, a Democratic landslide carried McNair into the mayor's office, the first Democrat in twenty-five years to hold that office, launching a Democratic reign in Pittsburgh that would remain unbroken for the rest of the century and beyond. Eliza would quickly find herself by his side.

* * *

Even as Lucy and Eliza were steering an aggressive course through the Food Probe, the mayor's demise, the ensuing election scuffle, the voting machine debacle, and a host of other of other situations that demanded their attention, the Kennedy family was navigating major personal losses on the home front. Jennie Eliza Kennedy died on February 7, 1930, in St. Petersburg, Florida, and Julian Kennedy on May 28, 1932, of a heart attack at home. She was seventy-five, and he was eighty. Both of their funerals were held at 5400 Forbes Street.

With that, the generational baton had been passed. On her deathbed, Jennie had warned her daughters, "Beware of Joe." As it turned out, the sisters would tussle mightily with their brothers over control of family affairs. The 5400 Forbes Street property would eventually be turned over to salvage liquidators to sell off any architectural artifacts of value before its demolition in July 1937, just thirty years after it had been completed. "Wrecking! $450,000 mansion of the late Julian Kennedy," the ad read.[60] In the meantime, a public lawsuit over disposition of the estate between the two sisters and their two surviving brothers, Julian and Joe, would fracture the family even as it further cemented the bond between Lucy and Eliza. That rift would not be repaired for eighty-five years.

20 VIGILANCE IN THE HALLS OF POWER

By the time Mayor Kline left office under a cloud of scandal, the She Devils were well-recognized forces to be reckoned with for anyone in public office, particularly anyone involved in dishonest dealings. Far from the statuesque, wasp-waisted Gibson girls they had been at the start of the suffrage battle, Lucy and Eliza were now middle-aged matrons. They now generally wore conservative, loose-fitting dresses and sensible shoes. Their uncoiffed hair was swept up beneath understated hats, and they wore wire-rimmed or rimless glasses, minimal jewelry, and no makeup. One might legitimately describe them as dowdy. But one could not help but take them seriously.

The two sisters were a perpetual presence in the City-County Building as well as in the papers. They would pass hours reading city books and listening to deliberations in the council chambers, waiting to challenge the councilmen and other public officials at every turn. Paneled with intricately inlaid wood and fabric, and lit by soaring two-story windows and massive, ornate chandeliers, the imposing chambers could imbue anyone holding forth in them with the kind of outsized sense of importance that might encourage even a reticent speaker to pontificate. To occupy the long hours of listening as debates droned on and on, Eliza brought her knitting. The Smith children, and later the grandchildren, came to be well supplied with dozens of handmade sweaters.

By this time, the limelight was beginning to shift from Lucy to Eliza, who was now the ever-present voice in the media. Lucy was still a board member, still had things to say, but it was now Eliza's turn to shine. Hardly a debate in city council occurred without her chiming in, always calm but often with an acerbic tongue. She was not the grandstander that Lucy was, but she commanded the attention of the men in the room and the reporters covering each new political tussle. They knew that she would not be easily dismissed.

From their perch, the She Devils watched closely as Mayor Kline was succeeded briefly by John Herron, city council president, who inherited the ruins of the Kline machine and the tarnished reputation of his Republican party. Meanwhile, Allegheny County Democratic Chair David L. Lawrence was building a political machine of his own and tapped William Nissley McNair to run against Herron on the Democratic ticket. A young patrician lawyer with a ready wit, McNair had name recognition, having run for local office five different times, albeit unsuccessfully. To the Democratic machine, he seemed like an innocuous choice for the office, one who could be molded to serve his party's agenda. To Eliza, who only endorsed him a day before the election, he seemed an unsullied innocent who could be trained to be a responsible caretaker of the mayor's office.[1] Before he was through, he would disappoint them all.

Within two weeks of McNair's election as mayor, the headlines read, "M'Nair Names Woman as His Budget Aide: Mrs. R. Templeton Smith to be Council Observer for Mayor-Elect." "Beseiged by citizens" in his office, McNair was befuddled by the 1934 city budget and particularly concerned about the projected two-million-dollar increase as well as the three-million-dollar deficit. But there was also a more immediate problem: City council needed to find $1.2 million to cover current expenses and payrolls through the rest of the year.

Recognizing Eliza's facility with figures, McNair had asked her to act as his representative at the city budget sessions. "I know that you have spent many years in studying this phase of our city's problems," he wrote. "For this reason I feel that you can be of great assistance to me in formulating my policies."[2] She had accepted, employing the technical advice of the same accountant who had worked with her on the fateful Food Probe. Delighted to have Eliza on board, McNair requested that Mayor Herron give her full access to all city records, effective immediately, even before he was to take office on January 1.

"Woman is Power Behind McNair," the *Press* announced the day after the appointment. Confident in her role, Eliza knew exactly what data she was after: the city's cash position and outstanding obligations; an understanding of the city's personnel, their duties and compensation; the proposed 1934 budget; delinquent taxes on the books; the status of the city treasury; and more. She proposed to take on the task and to secure the necessary technical advice at no cost to the city.

The *Press* described Eliza as "a woman with an insatiable flair for figures" and "one of the most powerful influences" behind the mayor-elect. "And this

Want Ad Headquarters, Court 0000   THE PITTSBURGH PRESS   Other Press Departments

Woman Becomes Financial Power Behind New Mayor; Budget Aide Hunts For Payroll Drones

Mrs. R. Templeton Smith Is Daughter of Late Julian Kennedy

Pioneer Worker, With Sister, Mrs. J. O. Miller, in Suffrage Work

MRS. R. TEMPLETON SMITH

Shortly after his election, Mayor McNair tapped Eliza to be his budget advisor. From *Pittsburgh Press*, November 21, 1933

fact was causing both consternation and wonder at City Hall today," the paper reported. "For Mrs. Smith has long been a dreaded figure in the ranks of machine politics and city payrollers. With her sister, Mrs. J. O. Miller, she has been a close student of city finances with a particular ability for digging out disagreeable facts." There was particular dread of her close examination of payroll, with "an eye out for drones, for favoritism in compensation and for useless jobs." Explaining the long political history of the Kennedy sisters, the article noted that the two had been called "political twins." "And many other things, too," Eliza responded with a wry smile.[3]

The new "budget boss" and her accountant were given two adjoining offices on the fifth floor of the City-County Building. In due course, Eliza produced a quarter-inch thick booklet entitled "Recommendations to the Mayor on the Budget of the City of Pittsburgh for the year 1934." She pruned the budget to eliminate $1.8 million in expenditures. Her proposal was promptly rejected by council.

As part of their effort to streamline the operation of local government, Eliza and the league advocated for a single-tax plan. Such a plan would combine revenue collection for the city, county, and school district, along with coordinated purchasing and a modern system of accounting.

As she recommended the elimination of political appointee jobs, Eliza aroused the ire of many. Her frantic foes, it was said, demanded to know where *her* salary was hidden in the budget and that *it* be cut. Told that she was a volunteer, one of the threatened bureaucrats reportedly declared, "No one but a damn fool would work that hard without pay." A politician who knew her well replied, "That's the kind of damn fool she's been all her life." Reserved but thick-skinned, Eliza let the frequent verbal abuse she received roll off. She didn't seem to care as she was called uncharitable names and as unflattering photos were published in the newspapers, often with her mouth open.

"It is only by eternal vigilance," Eliza wrote in 1935, "that we can attain success. We must stay awake all the time, back the best issues and the best candidates, and gradually we shall see a finer type of person seeking office and going into government service. This alertness, or wide-awakeness," she went on, "must be maintained by the citizen with no hope of personal reward except the benefits that may accrue to him as part of a well-governed community."[4]

Despite her privileged circumstances, thriftiness came naturally to Eliza. At home, she was just as frugal as she was in her city office. The family's finances had not suffered during the Depression, with Temp even securing a new position as executive vice president of Pittsburgh Coal, doubling his salary. They nonetheless did what they could to economize. She loved to tell about the time she was "arrested" while driving downtown. Her old Franklin had begun to look a little dingy, so she had decided to paint it herself. "I gave it nine coats of enamel, rubbed down between coats with fine pumice stone. I was arrested for driving a new car with old plates. I was mighty proud of that paint job!"[5]

It was during the McNair years that Eliza and the league began to be immortalized in Cy Hungerford's clever political cartoons. Hungerford had honed his craft during fifteen years with the *Pittsburgh Sun*. Later, on staff at the *Pittsburgh Post-Gazette*, he produced daily cartoons from 1927 until his retirement in 1977.[6] One, during the height of Eliza's budget machinations, appeared on March 13, 1934, under the title of "A Tough Spot for Eliza." The cartoon harkened back to illustrations from various editions of Harriet Beecher Stowe's epic anti-slavery novel, *Uncle Tom's Cabin*, that depicted the fugitive slave Eliza crossing the ice floes of the Ohio River to freedom, her baby in her arms. In his cartoon, Hungerford cast Eliza as frantic and bedraggled, running from a vicious and mangy dog labeled "Deficit," carrying a baby labeled "City Finances," and encumbered by a tight skirt labeled "City Council." She is pictured in midair as she leaps desperately across two floes labeled "Delinquent Tax Collections" and "Bond Issue."

Two weeks later, as Eliza's budget was being presented to city council, the *Sun-Telegraph* published an image by Quin Hall, made famous by his cartoons in *The New Yorker*. Hall's cartoon depicts a woman labeled "League of Women Voters" walking in on a scene of chaos—a family living room in which McNair as a young boy is sliding down the bannister labeled "Single Tax" as a man labeled "Council" sits by helplessly on a sofa. Strewn about at his feet are a mop, pail, and brooms as well as papers labeled "City Affairs," "Payroll," "City Finances," and "Garbage

A Tough Spot For Eliza—By Hungerford

Cartoonist Cy Hungerford captured Eliza's struggles with city council to balance the city budget. From *Pittsburgh Post-Gazette*, March 13, 1934, original in author's collection

Contract." In the foreground, a dog runs off with the "Budget" in his mouth. The league woman calls out, "HUH!! And I thought you were going to clean this mess up!"[7]

By the time the 1936 budget came up for review, McNair had decided not to solicit Eliza's help again. "I hate to ask her to do it," he said. "Last year she saved Council two million dollars and they threw it out the window. So what's the use?"[8] Eliza, however, would continue to act as a self-appointed watchdog of the city budget for the rest of her life.

McNair's term in office would turn out to be a stormy one. His defiance of the Democratic machine was ultimately ineffective, and he resigned in October 1936 after less than three years in office, with a dramatic announcement in the rotunda of the City-County Building. "That's a load off my chest," he quipped.[9]

When he died twelve years later in 1948 at the age of just sixty-seven, collapsing in the St. Louis's Union Station from a fatal heart attack, McNair was charitably eulogized as a trustworthy politician. A *Post-Gazette* reporter

Cartoonist Quin Hall captured the chaos surrounding the city budget process. From *Pittsburgh Sun-Telegraph*, March 30, 1934, in author's collection

wrote, "His name was anathema to gamblers, racketeers and others of the easy-money gentry who found money tight because he insisted on running a clean and honest administration. Whatever vice existed flourished on a small scale in sporadic spots in the city, but not with his approval." The accolades went on, "He left his office as a man noted about the nation for his witticisms, his eccentricities, his defiance of a powerful Democratic machine and bold and open criticisms of even the President of the United States."

And yet, the *Post-Gazette* went on, "He left it, too, in a tragic vein, confessing inability to fight the forces aligned against his plans of civic betterment." The tumultuous turnover in his cabinet and other appointments were the brunt of criticism. Ultimately, the paper concluded, "He left city hall as he had kept it during his administration—in turmoil." [10] Eliza and Lucy would have to contend with yet another new administration. McNair was succeeded by City Council President Cornelius D. Scully, who would serve for ten years.

In the years following the Kline debacle and the brief McNair administration, Eliza and the league remained as tenacious as ever, hounding the mayor, city council, and just about everyone else in power, doggedly pursuing integrity and accountability in government. For the most part, these were not dramatic battles. They had little of the spectacle of the battle for suffrage of two decades earlier. They did not lead to any indictments or convictions. Instead, they served as a constant, nagging reminder to those who would abuse their offices that someone—someone unrelenting and scrupulously well-informed—was watching their every move and ready to pounce at any moment.

It was no surprise, then, to find Eliza in 1934 behind the wheel of her old Franklin, with Lucy in the passenger seat, skulking around before dawn in pursuit of loaded garbage trucks making their rounds. Public attention had been drawn to the fact that two private companies had held a virtual monopoly on garbage and rubbish collection and disposal for at least thirty years. They were paid between six and eight dollars per ton. Suspicious as to why Pittsburgh's costs for the service came in as much as five times higher than what industry experts said they should, Eliza and Lucy had decided to do some wee-hour sleuthing. What they found was appalling but not shocking. On their way to the weigh station, the truckers would stop just long enough to hose down the garbage and rubbish with water. Both sisters reported these and other findings to council. Lucy advised the councilmen that if they had bothered to investigate on their own, "You, too, might learn more than can be seen from the Council Chambers."[11] Eliza told them, "I've followed garbage collectors, not once, but many times, to see how they work. I wonder how many Councilmen have done the same thing. With proper inspectors, considerable savings could be made."[12]

The city had responded, in part, with a plan to take control of the garbage situation. A bond issue circa 1934 was conceived to pay for a municipal incinerating plant, although Eliza was quick to point out that they had failed to budget for trucks to collect the garbage and rubbish. The new million-dollar facility was not operational until 1940. Again, Eliza was on the case. Granted, the new facility had cut costs somewhat. But it was being mismanaged and the service was still shoddy, she said. Neighborhood surveys and spot checks by a corps of league volunteers had revealed collection delays as long as three weeks. Eliza laid the blame at the feet of politicians, who used the facility as a place to award patronage jobs. "Our city officials are treating the new incinerator like a toy," she announced. "They have put men at work at the plant who are wholly unfitted for the job; men who, if they had to be taken care of because they can swing a few votes, should have been given a polished desk in some office." Meanwhile, complaints poured into the league headquarters as garbage piled up in the streets. Eliza dubbed the whole situation a "bungle."[13] The complaints continued through the 1940s, when Eliza was still railing against the city's ineptitude. "The army of rats which is infesting our city, we believe, can never be eliminated until the garbage and rubbish situation is solved."[14] Eliza continued to berate city officials, writing to City Council President Thomas Kilgallen, "The collection of garbage and refuse is a problem of city housekeeping and at present we are very bad housekeepers. Nobody knows better than the women of this district just how bad it is."[15]

The garbage situation was symptomatic of a deeper problem rooted in the structure of city government, Eliza contended. "The City has been mired in the bog of personal ambitions and ward heelers too long," she declared as she continued to advocate for home rule and the city manager form of government.[16] Home rule, under consideration through the Edmonds Home Rule Bill in the state legislature, would allow for each of Pennsylvania's forty-nine cities to write its own charter and adopt its own governmental structure. According to Eliza, it would also eliminate more than 55 percent of the bills before the state legislature, which dealt with matters of local government.[17] The proposal was heartily endorsed by civic organizations such as the Taxpayers' League, the Pittsburgh Real Estate Board, the Legislative Council of Western Pennsylvania, and the Young Republicans of Allegheny County. The Democrats, firmly in control of Pittsburgh, were less than enthused about how the proposed bill might shake up the status quo. Opponents maintained that proportional representation would only serve as "a method whereby [a minority] may constantly harass and annoy duly-elected officials."[18]

As co-chair of the Pittsburgh Charter Committee, Eliza cited Cincinnati as an exemplar of the city manager model: "The interesting part of Cincinnati's record lies not so much in its excellent financial condition as in the constantly increasing number and quality of its services," she said. "Cincinnati's government shows what may be achieved through careful planning, study and adoption of the most efficient methods and careful supervision and administration with regard always for the two interests of the taxpayer—his welfare and his pocketbook."[19] Touting the system's merits in removing party politics from city management, Cincinnati Councilman Albert Cash declared, ". . . We have a personal responsibility in being members of council without regard to whether we are Democrats or Republicans."[20] With its proportional representation, placing all power and responsibility with a city council elected by district, the city manager model would also render disenfranchisement of minorities impossible, Eliza argued.[21]

* * *

In October 1940, the league launched a "Jury School" to teach citizens proper procedure in case they were called to serve. The first class of the "school" was convened at the courthouse on a Tuesday evening, where they staged a reenactment of a criminal trial involving a drunk driver, with a real judge presiding, a real assistant district attorney arguing for the prosecution, a jury selected from among the spectators, and witnesses represented by league members who had studied the case."[22] A subsequent reenactment focused on an arson case. Setting forth the curriculum for further sessions, Eliza couldn't help but think back to the argument posed, with horror, by the anti-suffragists twenty years earlier that if women were granted the vote, they would have to serve on juries. They had come a long way.

The league's Friday Morning Club would continue to be active in the 1940s, with lectures in Carnegie Music Hall. The club invited speakers on topics ranging from a primer on taxation and national defense to a debate on the plight of migrant farmworkers in California. Once the United States was drawn into the conflict in Europe, the group welcomed the former president of the League of Nations Assembly, a Swedish journalist, and war correspondent Upton Close. After the war was over, in 1946, *New York Times* foreign correspondent Hallett Abend and William Mandell, an authority on Russia, debated "Is Russia a Force for Peace?" The league also took up the issue of birth control.

As council wrestled with the issue of bond refinancing to balance the city's 1941 budget, Eliza declared, "If I were sitting in your chairs I could and would cut the budget and reduce taxes. I don't care if you don't raise the wages of the police, if they don't do a better job than they do now." Asked what she would cut from the budget, Eliza replied, "I don't know. I only got it 10 minutes before I came up here. What should we do—sue the Mayor for malfeasance in office?" There followed a deep silence, according to the *Sun-Telegraph*'s reporter in the room that day.[23]

Voter fraud would continue to be a consistent thread through Eliza's career. This particular year, a dispute over the mayoral race centered on alleged fraud in twenty-one city districts and a controversy over whether those districts should be thrown out entirely. Eliza thought they should.[24]

21 DIRTY AIR AND DIRTY DEALINGS

Returning home from the Eastern Shore at the end of each idyllic summer on the farm brought into stark contrast the dark smoky veil that had hung over Pittsburgh for decades. As workers streamed into downtown each day, the hovering smoke blocked the morning sun and the city's streets were as dark as night. Headlights, streetlamps, and neon signs glared all day long through the swirling, blurry haze. Professional women wore only dark clothing. Professional men carried spare shirts to change into midday when the stains around their collars became intolerable. Housewives struggled mightily to keep up with the soot on their windowsills and furniture. Bright new civic and commercial buildings quickly became tarnished by the grimy stuff, which corroded their masonry and metal. When Eliza and Temp had taken young Tempie and Kenny to Washington in the 1920s, the boys had marveled at how the entire gleaming white city could have been built in the space of one year. In their experience, any building that wasn't blackened had to be less than a year old. By 1941, those two small boys were completing their Harvard educations, and it was about time to do something about the smoke.

The wealth of bituminous coal in the steep hills around Pittsburgh had spawned a smoke problem from the city's earliest days, when the residents of Fort Pitt burned the soft, highly volatile fuel extracted from the region's first mine. Sulphur fumes and airborne particulates filled the air. General Presley Neville had written that "the peace and harmony of the inhabitants depend upon the speedy measures being adopted to remedy this nuisance."[1] That was in 1804. By the outbreak of the Civil War, with a growing population and hundreds of factories producing nearly half of the glass and iron in the country, along with vigorous railroad and steamboat traffic, Pittsburgh was consuming more than two hundred thousand tons of coal annually. One of the city's earliest periodicals had described the scene in which "the smoke . . .

Pittsburgh earned its title as the Smoky City, with the air as dark as night even in the morning light. From Historic Pittsburgh

blackens every object; even snow can scarcely be called white in Pittsburgh."[2]

An 1868 air pollution ordinance, the city's first, did little to mitigate the problem. The discovery of natural gas as an alternative fuel brought some temporary improvement in the 1880s, which whetted the public's appetite for clean air but did not bring lasting improvement. Andrew Carnegie declared that "the man who abolishes the Smoke Nuisance in Pittsburgh is foremost of us all."[3] Yet additional ordinances in 1892, 1895, 1906, and 1907 were halfheartedly enforced and ineffective.

Still, Pittsburgh's foul air remained on the minds of reform-minded Progressives. It was anathema to both the City Beautiful Movement and social welfare concerns. While the suffrage battle was just getting underway, back in 1911, Eliza had taken great interest in a comprehensive study by the Mellon Institute of Industrial Research that published ten bulletins on the economic, psychological, legal, and technical impact of the smoke. The study argued that the smoke was costing businesses and residents of the city some ten million dollars every year, not to mention a blight on real estate, unfavorable notoriety, and a health menace.[4] The scourge had been tolerated, however, as a by-product of industrial prosperity.[5] Creation of a separate Bureau of Smoke Regulation in 1916 and a new ordinance in 1917 failed to make a difference, and conditions had only worsened in the ensuing years.

Now, in the early days of 1941, as Pittsburgh was busy manufacturing munitions to use against Hitler, the smoke had intensified to a level that fairly demanded some sort of action. Yet the city's Bureau of Smoke Regulation had been eliminated by council as an economy measure just two years earlier. A four-year survey by the Works Progress Administration had gathered sufficient data to justify a new ordinance and to inform combustion engineers who could then determine the best methods to proceed against the pollution. "We have all the information that could possibly be collected," said Dr. I. Hope Alexander, city director of public health. "All I want Mayor Scully to do is to use it."[6] Alexander asked the mayor for an ordinance "with teeth." An editorial in the *Press* declared, "FACTS, FACTS are everywhere—but not a drop of action. That, in brief, explains the smoke situation in Pittsburgh. If every survey on the smoke question were burned in front of City Hall, it would make quite a conflagration! But now the time is at hand for action—time to build a fire under the City Administration. What are we waiting for?"[7]

There emerged a model that provided a modicum of hope. St. Louis had been just as smoky as Pittsburgh but had successfully cleared its skies in the space of just one year. Their arsenal for the fight contained two weapons. The first was a switch to smokeless fuel, either anthracite coal or natural gas. The second was the installation of stokers, devices that automatically fed coal to a furnace, ensuring efficient and complete combustion of coal. Offsetting the added expense of the smokeless fuel and stokers, however, it was estimated that the St. Louis citizenry was saving twenty million dollars in cleaning bills, doctors' fees, and real estate depreciation.[8] The head of the citizens' committee that oversaw the St. Louis transformation advised, "Everybody was behind us—the people, the newspapers, 152 civic clubs, the city administration. That's the only way such a campaign can be successful. It's got to have the support of the people. The city administration can't do it. They're in politics and are licked from the start."[9]

In Pittsburgh, opposition came from industry, from coal owners and miners, and from the politicians who wanted to appease those special interests. Public sentiment, however, seemed to be demanding change. Still, public officials were reluctant to impose meaningful action, and Mayor Scully was dragging his feet on appointing a committee to address the problem. What was needed was an organized civic uprising.

Rallying public support and pressuring government officials for a worthy reform—that was something Eliza knew how to do. With a proven track record of nearly two decades leading the league, she had the power to convene, and she did not cower at the risk of bringing together people on all sides of an issue. At a league-sponsored Smoke Abatement Luncheon on February 27, 1941, more than a thousand people filled the ballroom of the William Penn Hotel and overflowed into the balconies and anterooms. It was described as "one of the largest and most representative gatherings ever assembled in Pittsburgh to boost a civic improvement!"[10] Mayor Scully's new Smoke Committee had just held its first meeting the night before.

At the elongated speakers' table with Eliza were representatives of the coal industry, the railroads, labor unions, the electrical industry, the school board, the medical profession, the judiciary, city government, the major newspapers, and several civic organizations. Women's clubs throughout the county were invited to send representatives, as were the Pittsburgh Housing Association, Civic Club of Allegheny County, the Taxpayers' League, the Federation of Social Agencies, the Legislative Council of Western Pennsylvania, the Allied Boards of Trade, American Association of University Women, Council of Jewish Women, Engineers' Society, the University of Pittsburgh, and many other organizations.[11]

In opening the program, Eliza observed, "Enough organizations are represented here to put this campaign across if we all put our shoulders to the wheel."[12] The invited speaker was Raymond R. Tucker, Commissioner of Smoke Regulation in St. Louis, who affirmed that the enactment of an effective smoke ordinance, and its subsequent enforcement, required the coordinated efforts of all citizens of a community. With so many divergent interests in the room, the open forum discussion after Tucker's talk drew lively debate.

The league wasted no time in broadening the community coalition to support the smoke abatement initiative. They formed a Co-Operating Committee for Smoke Elimination to work in tandem with both the mayor's committee and the Civic Club's Smoke Abatement Committee, later renamed the Smoke *Elimination* Committee. Soon after the luncheon Eliza announced, "Never has a civic campaign met with such enthusiastic response. Names of organizations and individuals are being added almost hourly."[13] This was an issue that everyone could relate to. The "ugly, death-dealing smog"[14] was a pervasive and irrefutable hazard to life in Pittsburgh. Public opinion had at last coalesced.

Just weeks later, league members heard a presentation by technical experts, who made the point that smoke—with its tar vapors and soot particles—was not just an annoyance and a health hazard but also a valuable fuel that should not be wasted. They pointed out that Pittsburghers were spending from nine to fifteen million dollars each year on smoke and its effects.[15] Some contended that processing plants designed to drive off the volatile elements of coal to produce smokeless fuel would also generate a by-product useful in manufacturing explosives, which were needed for the war effort.[16]

There followed a series of public hearings and informational meetings over the course of two-and-a-half months, sponsored by the Pittsburgh Smoke Committee, where doctors, housewives, scientists, and engineers testified to packed houses. One doctor asserted that city residents suffered from more colds and sinus disease as well as an affliction he dubbed a "Pittsburgh Nose," a condition brought on by the irritation of the nasal membranes by soot. Another blamed dirty air for a disproportionate incidence of deafness in Pittsburgh.[17] The health threat even extended to psychological issues, described by one Carnegie Tech professor as false hysterias and imagined illnesses, not to mention depressed moods.[18]

The head of the University of Pittsburgh biology department and curator of botany at the Carnegie Museum outlined the effects of smoke on plant life. Soot coated the leaves and needles of plants and trees, causing them to fall prematurely and robbing the city of normal fall colors.

To showcase the woman's perspective, about two hundred women, some speaking on behalf of organizations that represented tens of thousands more, attended a special council hearing chaired by Eliza. Aside from complaining of the burden of cleaning up all the soot, dozens of these women testified that the "death-dealing smog" drove individuals and sometimes entire families away from the city. One neighbor of the Hazelwood mills declared, "In the past we always said 'Smoke means work,' but since we have studied the subject we have found that smoke means waste, drudgery and sickness."[19] One went so far as to blame the rising divorce rate on the stress of living with smoke.[20] Eliza closed with a statement of full commitment: "We don't want to hurt industry; we don't want to hurt labor; but we want smoke elimination. We are ready to fight for it; even to ringing doorbells if necessary."[21] The mere thought of tens of thousands of women taking to the streets must have evoked daunting flashbacks to the battle for suffrage thirty years earlier.

There were, of course, pollution deniers. One, a Dr. Samuel R. Haythorn, laughed at the characterization of smoke as a health menace, merely calling it, as so many others had, "a nuisance." "Pittsburgh is Pittsburgh," he said. "We will probably have to take some of the smoke if we want to stick around here." He added, "We have statistics that can be interpreted many ways. The health problem shouldn't be made the goat."[22] Another, Dr. Laurence Shaffer of Carnegie Tech's physiology department, maintained that bad air was often used as an excuse for imaginary illness. He insisted, "If we had smoke 365 days a year and 24 hours a day, it wouldn't affect people physiologically."[23]

Nonetheless, in the face of overwhelming public support, the city proceeded. Council passed the new smoke ordinance, 8 to 1, on July 7. The next day, with the Police and Firemen's Band playing just outside his office, the mayor signed the ordinance, which would become effective October 1, 1941. (Some argued that the ordinance was rushed through to ensure that the strong popular opinion in its favor would be satisfied just as Mayor Scully and six Democratic councilmen were about to launch reelection campaigns.)[24] The ordinance laid out two methods for smoke abatement: the use of smokeless fuels such as anthracite, natural gas, or fuel oil, or if bituminous coal were used, the incorporation of mechanically fired stokers that automatically fed the coal into the burner at a prescribed rate that reduced smoke.

The regulations would be applied first to industrial and commercial buildings and were only scheduled to apply to residential properties two years hence, despite that experts estimated that 70 percent of the problem was caused by private dwellings. The new ordinance was to be administered by a city Bureau of Smoke Prevention whose staff of twelve included seven inspectors.[25] Almost immediately, home stokers appeared in county fair exhibits, and ads proliferated for the devices, which could be purchased from local department stores for as little as $160 or as much as $400 and would take five to ten years to pay for themselves.

Touting a smokeless alternative to coal, the *Press* featured an article about how the installation of automatic gas heating might yield sufficient spare basement space to create living areas. Such notions would ultimately lead to the advent of the finished basement.[26]

Then, just as the smoke control effort was gaining significant traction, there came a galvanizing interruption. Two days before the attack on Pearl Harbor, on December 5, 1941, the *Sun-Telegraph* had run a bold headline: "Japs Answer U.S. On Troops, Willing to Continue Talks." Battles on the local front were still garnering attention. Just below the main headline, a photo of Eliza ran with a smaller headline, "Mrs. Smith's Water Bill Ignored: Crusader Hoped City Would End Service After 16 Months." It seems that Eliza had been complaining to city officials for a couple years about water rents not being collected. She was told that the city would not cut off water service to poor people. "So I quit paying my bill," she said. "I'm not poor, and I wanted to see whether they'd shut off my water." She waited to see how long it would take. After a reporter called attention to her stunt, she promptly paid the bill, annoyed that her experiment had been cut short. She thought that, at the very least, they might have heckled her a bit.[27] A *Sun* editorial later commented, "Pittsburgh could use a few more civic leaders with her energy and imagination."[28]

Now, with the country plunged abruptly into war, Eliza and the league pivoted to meet the needs of national defense in a conflict that would com-

As the United States entered World War II, Eliza's sons, Kenny (left) and Temp Jr. (right) interrupted their Harvard educations to serve in the Navy.

mand the attention of all Americans and subsume all other efforts. Eliza cited three ways that the league could assist with the war effort: "guard democratic government by better understanding it and by being ready to resist inroads made by persons and conditions; furnish up-to-the-minute information on non-defense spending so that those government officials trying to eliminate non-essentials from our budgets may have intelligent help; provide a medium, already set up and functioning, through which women can contribute their intelligence and service to the problems to be faced."[29] They immediately turned their programming to prepare the membership. An all-day defense institute sponsored by the state league and the local league's Friday Morning Club brought in speakers to talk about the US Offices of Civilian Defense, the wartime services of the Red Cross, the differences between this conflict and the First World War, the chances of victory, civilian health and morale, physical fitness, and more. Lucy contributed a talk on "Taxation and Defense."[30]

Among the war-related issues that caught Eliza's attention was fair housing. She and the league executive committee condemned a bill passed by the House of Representatives that would radically increase the rents charged in defense housing projects and "harmfully restrict disposition of the defense housing units" after the war.[31] She backed her interest in fair housing through service on the local housing board as it was developing its first public housing, a fourteen-hundred-unit development.

The war in Europe also spawned a new interest in national issues and foreign policy, drawing more and more women into league activities. Lucy and Eliza battled a 1940 proposal that would have permitted the president to seize industries if deemed advisable for national defense, calling it "Hitlerism at its worst."[32]

The league also participated in a scrap drive in 1942 to keep mills supplied with vital metals. Eliza served on the Woman's Committee of the Allegheny County Council of Defense, which spread the word door-to-door among local housewives of the "dire need of salvaging every ounce of tin, fats and metals." It was part of a larger initiative that sought out scrap wherever it could. The buried streetcar rails of the Pittsburgh Railways Company alone were estimated at 370 tons, although some question existed as to whether the yield would justify the cost. Auto graveyards were seen as another promising source of scrap, as were German cannons captured during the First World War and then put on display in the city's parks.[33]

As the war raged on into 1944, Eliza had definite ideas about who should be at the peace table. Certainly women should be present, she maintained, preferably "two-fisted fighters." "What we need are fair-minded women, with wisdom and guts, too at the Peace Table." "But I deplore that such a question must be asked," she added. "We are still living in a man's world and we have got to make it a man-and-woman's world. We don't want a democracy of men; we want a democracy of the human race." In an interview with the *Pittsburgh Post-Gazette*, she noted that women had lost rather than gained in their struggle for equality during the twenty-five years since the Nineteenth Amendment. "One particular reason that we must be represented at an international conference," she said, "is that we must see that our sisters in other countries who have lost their status as free humans are given their rights again. I do not think that women in one country can progress as long as any nation treats its women as slaves." The main reason women should be represented in any peace negotiations, she said, was because "they have the biggest stake" in wars. "As the mother of the race, she spends the best years of her life producing sons that will be sent to fight. Mothers should be represented so that their sons' and daughters' sons will not have to go through the same experience." She went so far as to identify three women who "could fight and not let America be tramped upon" at the peace table: Anne O'Hare McCormick, a foreign news correspondent and the first woman to win a Pulitzer Prize in journalism; Agnes Elizabeth Ernst Meyer, a journalist who lobbied for the creation of the Department of Health, Education and Welfare and whose family purchased *The Washington Post* in 1933; and Clare Boothe Luce, a leading conservative who would ultimately serve as a member of Congress and the US Ambassador to Italy and wife of the publishing magnate.[34]

In May 1945, Eliza announced her retirement after five years as president of the state league so that she could devote her entire time to the county league. She would be laser-focused on the local league for the rest of her life.

V-J Day on September 2, 1945, brought a flood of mixed emotions. Certainly there was relief and joy as servicemen and women headed home. Yet even in victory, there was still a sense of danger over the perceived nuclear threat of Russia. Eliza used it as a clarion call to get out the vote. As the fall Election Day approached, she was quick to point out that millions had given their lives to preserve the principles of self-government, and asked, "Can we in Allegheny County show that we do not intend to waste this highly paid for privilege?"[35]

It was then that David L. Lawrence emerged as a candidate for mayor. Born the same year as Eliza, 1889, Lawrence grew up in modest circumstances that stood in marked contrast to Eliza's privileged childhood. Now, at age fifty-six, he was a beguiling Irishman with a winning smile and laughing eyes behind thick, rimless glasses. He stood five-foot-nine inches, which put him just about eye to eye with Eliza, and his imposing, broad-shouldered frame was always dressed for success in a coat, tie, and white shirt with French cuffs.

Lawrence had made up for his limited formal education by apprenticing himself for twenty years to Attorney William J. Brennan, where he learned the business of politics and the art of compromise. Beginning his political career in 1920 as Democratic chairman, Lawrence built a Democratic machine that was ready to spring into action when the pendulum finally swung the party's way in 1932. He courted ethnic minorities, including Blacks, and won Western Pennsylvania for Roosevelt.[36]

True to its nonpartisan stance, the league welcomed Lawrence to the speaker's platform at a mayoral candidates' luncheon that fall of 1945, along with his opponent, Robert N. Waddell. But Eliza would spar with him relentlessly from that day forward, insisting to those in her inner circle that "one day Davey's foot will slip." Oft indicted but never convicted, Lawrence operated his political machine under Eliza's ever-vigilant watch. She became the constant thorn in his side, he her greatest nemesis.

* * *

Slowed by the war, enforcement of the new smoke ordinance was not fully implemented for five years, with an effective date of October 1, 1946, for industry and commercial establishments and a year later for the residential sector. "Like sin," wrote one journalist as the war came to a close, "smoke is something that practically everyone is against. But some would try to eliminate it gradually, while others favor a bold step."[37] Now, as the postwar economy struggled to find equilibrium, the coal industry and mine labor were, not surprisingly, less than eager to eliminate the source of their livelihoods. Eliza was more assertive, more forward-thinking. "The war has demonstrated that when we need something in this country we get it," she declared.[38]

Working with other partners, the league continued to push the agenda forward, and the Allegheny Conference on Community Development established a United Smoke Council. In November 1946, the league set up seven booths in downtown department stores to collect signatures urging the county commissioners to pass countywide smoke control legislation.

Jumping on the bandwagon, in his first speech as the city's new mayor in 1946, David Lawrence said, "I am convinced that our people want clean air. There is no other single thing which will so dramatically improve the appearance, the health, the pride, the spirit of the city."[39]

So it was that the turnaround finally came to fruition. By 1948, visibility in downtown Pittsburgh had improved by 67 percent. By 1954, the city received 89 percent more sunshine. In 1946, smoke impaired visibility one out of every four daylight hours, but by 1958, that same metric had changed dramatically to one out of every fifty-six daylight hours.[40]

Certainly the league championed other issues during the postwar period, including housing, better garbage disposal and rat control, teachers' salaries, restaurant grading, employment, consumer products, and the standard of living. They advocated for a survey of the city's public school system, whose 1945 budget showed a deficit of nearly a million dollars.[41] The survey was conducted by Columbia Teachers College at a cost of fifty thousand dollars. The city faced a choice of more state aid, higher taxes, or a reduction in services.

Under Eliza's leadership, the league also conducted a spot check of county assessments, with forty league members studying a thousand properties. They cited inefficiency in the management of the records as well as a gross lack of uniformity in assessed values, which ranged from 60.2 to 119 percent of recent sales. Their recommendation was to look more holistically at blocks of properties in order to move toward more consistency in valuations.[42]

Getting out the vote was, as ever, a priority after the war. "Women Hold Balance in Coming Elections" read a headline in October 1946. Eliza was quoted on the possibility of women outnumbering men at the polls, if only they voted. "The total number of women registered in the United States is 46,403,210—a most imposing figure," she said. "Politicians, far and wide, realize the fact that women may decide the battles in almost every state and they are making an all out effort to capture the women's favor." She added, "I hope this election will see the biggest women's vote ever cast." Women had the opportunity, if they voted to support a "strong foreign policy," to keep the nation at peace. "It is a duty and responsibility that transcends personal gain and personal aggrandizement."[43]

Eliza also served on a committee of sixty-nine civic leaders, physicians, ministers, and social workers to review the county's adoption procedures. She joined a committee of the Crusade for Children, chaired by Mrs. David L. Lawrence, to raise part of the sixty million dollars needed to feed hungry children in Europe. But for both Eliza and the league, smoke control remained their most lasting contribution of that wartime era.

* * *

Even as the scourge of smoke was beginning to abate, by 1948, racketeering in Pittsburgh had reached a level that fairly demanded public inquiry. A grand jury of twenty-two men and women was called to hear evidence about fraudulent business dealings, specifically gambling, liquor law violations, extortion, and bribery. Eliza joined local church leaders, concerned with "the decency of the town," in demanding a special prosecutor to aid the grand jury probe. Their contention was that the rackets were rampant in the city under political protection. "This is a very serious situation," Eliza said in a statement sent to the governor urging the appointment of an outside prosecutor. "Most citizens believe the police have been generally lax in law enforcement. They feel sure rackets have flourished openly. Since the Democratic machine is under fire, we should begin an impartial investigation from outside Pittsburgh. Mr. Rahauser, a new Democratic district attorney, would be in a very embarrassing position to have to try members of the machine which put him into office. Even if he honestly prosecutes and gets no convictions the cry will be politics."[44]

Just days after Eliza spoke out in support of the racketeering investigation, while she and Temp were at the farm, burglars entered their Shady Avenue house through a rear window and ransacked the second and third floors. The thieves took a thousand dollars' worth of valuables but also opened drawers, overturned cushions, and searched filing cabinets.[45] One had to wonder if the break-in was an attempt to intimidate. But it didn't stop Eliza.

* * *

Temp and Eliza bought dozens of horses to supply his new pharmaceutical business, Ben Venue Laboratories.

As the war, and then the decade, were coming to a close, Eliza was continuing to build her political capital, while Temp was continuing to build a business, one that drew upon his two great loves—chemistry and horses. Eliza's financial independence made it possible for Temp to follow his entrepreneurial instincts, and he had founded Ben Venue Laboratories in 1938 to produce products for the pharmaceutical industry from the urine and blood of pregnant mares. The company came to be known largely for two of its innovations. The first, artificial estrogen, was marketed by Ayerst Laboratories and is still on the market today under the name of Premarin. Ben Venue also perfected the production of freeze-dried blood plasma and got involved in the business of penicillin. At least as long as the war lasted, the plasma and penicillin ventures were lucrative. By this time, both Eliza and Temp were engaged in demanding and often stressful full-time pursuits. Each was entirely supportive of the other. But neither one answered to anyone.

Meanwhile, the next generation of the Kennedy clan was moving forward with courtships and marriages. Young Julian married, followed by Kenny, Temp, and eventually Barbara. Grandchildren would follow over the course of the next fifteen years, six for Lucy and John, and eight for Eliza and Temp.

It was during that postwar family-building period that Lucy and John decided to retire and to move full time to the farm. She quickly found her niche there as president of the Talbot County School Board. Lucy's decision

Lucy and John (seated) celebrated their fiftieth anniversary at the farm in May 1957 with children Eliza, Barbara, and Julian.

was quite unexpected for one who had steeped herself in Pittsburgh politics for more than three decades. "Won't she miss her friends?" asked one friend upon hearing the news. Her daughter Eliza was quick to reply, "Only her enemies!"

22 POLICING THE POLICE

Two weeks before Christmas 1948, Pittsburgh residents reeled in horror as a twelve-year-old girl was brutally murdered in her kitchen. Carole Lee Kensinger, a pretty seventh grader, had been baking a cake while her parents were out at a neighborhood bowling alley. They returned to find blood splattered over the kitchen walls, refrigerator, table, door, and utility cabinet. Dark, sticky red footprints led out the back door, down the steps, and into the alley. Carole Lee lay in the next room, at the end of a fifteen-foot bloody trail. She had been stabbed thirty-six times, and her hand, clutching the phone receiver, had been nearly hacked off. The crime shocked and confounded even the most hardened detectives and morgue attendants. Bits of skin and hair were found under the victim's fingernails, indicating a struggle, but there was no robbery or sexual assault involved, according to police. Still, they believed the slayer was a "sex fiend," although detectives could only speculate that rape was the motive.

The police assigned fifty-four extra officers to the manhunt. They first investigated three teenage boys who had previously taunted Carole Lee with obscene gestures and language. They ran down hundreds of false leads, grabbing and questioning more than a hundred suspects. The *Sun-Telegraph* inserted itself into the investigation, offering a reward with the caveat that the city editor would receive all tips and then turn them over to police, presumably only after capitalizing on their sensational nature. All three newspapers offered a thousand dollars each for information leading to the arrest of the murderer.

Just two weeks prior to Carole Lee's murder, residents of her small Brushton neighborhood had asked Mayor Lawrence for some police protection and had been assigned two patrolmen to walk beats. But no one had noticed anything out of the ordinary until Carole Lee's parents returned home. One neighbor noticed a man loafing near the Kensinger home, leaning against a pole about 9:40 that evening. Otherwise, all had seemed normal.

The detectives posed for dramatic photos of the crime scene, holding the bloody phone and dusting the blood-stained kitchen utensils for fingerprints. The morgue report described in gruesome detail the nature of the thirty-six wounds, which the newspapers, in turn, published for public consumption. A prominent psychologist warned that the killer, "an aggressive sadist," might strike again.

Carole Lee Hensinger's was not the only grisly murder that year. The city's safety director called the mounting wave of sex crimes a serious problem. He compared the postwar outbreak of sex crimes to the wave of kidnappings after World War I. "During the past year, our police force here has brought in nearly 700 perverts and sex deviates," he explained, "but we must look to our best medical minds and to our courts for the final cure."[1]

Not long after, just steps from the Kensinger residence, another assault targeted two small girls—a toddler and an infant—in their home. While both survived, the attack served to heighten the public anxiety. In the wake of that incident, the city increased the number of uniformed officers in the neighborhood and cracked down on speakeasies.[2] Nonetheless, angry residents threatened to recruit a vigilante force and appealed for power to patrol the district and arrest any suspected perpetrators on sight.[3] More than a hundred of them marched on city hall and demanded more police protection. One resident pointed out that "patrol cars are all right. But you can't peer behind a hedge or between houses from an automobile." Another charged that some of the beat officers deserted their posts for coffee shops and ignored dark alleys. Council's response was disappointing. While one member declared that he would introduce an ordinance to increase the force by a hundred beat patrolmen that year and another hundred the next, there was little support for any meaningful reform.[4]

With no real progress in the hunt for the Kensinger murderer, residents were tensely on alert. A note hurled through the window of a home with an eight-year-old daughter fueled the fear. It simply read, "You are next."[5]

The city was ill-equipped to handle the crisis. The FBI conducted tests of the physical evidence found, since the city had no crime lab. Nor was the police department forthcoming about its homicide statistics. An FBI investigation of the department determined that there was no headquarters control over the police and that crime reporting by the precincts was spotty at best. In one sample precinct, only 60 percent of crimes were reported. The rest, any incidents that did not result in an arrest, were routinely logged into what they called a "butcher book," quietly kept at the precinct level. By 1949, most major American cities had overhauled their crime reporting. Pittsburgh, however, had not.

According to some reports, by August 1949 police in the tri-state area were sitting on sixteen unsolved murders, including the Kensinger case.[6] The *Post-Gazette* introduced a "Somebody Knows" campaign to encourage tips from the public, offering a five-thousand-dollar reward and the guarantee of complete secrecy for the informants. The paper had a pool of fifty thousand dollars reserved for clues leading to conviction in up to ten of the cases.[7]

Then, in late November 1949, nearly a year after the Kensinger slaying, another particularly gruesome murder shook the city. At 11:20 on a Friday night, thirty-eight-year-old Jean Brusco was rounding a corner just steps from her home in Shadyside when she was attacked from the rear by an assailant who cracked her head in half with a "blunt instrument." She was then dragged away into the darkness. Her purse, spilled open, lay in a pool of blood where she had fallen. Next to it was her hat.

The crime did not go unwitnessed. Peering through the venetian blinds from a third-story window across the street, a horrified neighbor saw the attack in the light of a streetlamp, and her husband called the police. He was told he had the wrong station and was directed to call another. The desk sergeant there sent three officers to the wrong address, in a private car and without radios. After forty-five minutes, the victim's family put in another call to the station. The police did not actually arrive on the scene until twelve thirty in the morning, more than an hour after the attack. The precinct did not report to headquarters for more than an hour. No search was made of the neighborhood, and the detective bureau did not send out a message to all stations until 1:55 a.m., two-and-a-half hours after the attack. The police search did not begin until after the victim's three brothers had already searched the area.

The victim's half-naked and battered body was finally found the next morning, sprawled in the snow-covered backyard of a house across the street— not by the police, but by the milkman, who nearly stumbled over it. The FBI was again called in to investigate the physical evidence. In the meantime, the eye witness received an anonymous phone call telling her to keep her mouth shut or she would "get what the other woman got."[8]

After ten days, a thousand phone calls, fifty traceable tips, and a review of more than three thousand known sex offenders, not a single clue to the killer's identity had been uncovered. The superintendent heightened the panic with a public bulletin to women: "Some woman in this city is knowingly, or unknowingly, harboring a murderer.... The man who killed Jean Brusco had blood on his clothes. Check the clothes and shoes in your home. Is there any blood, by now a dark brown stain, on any of them? Has the man in your house attempted to clean or wash any clothes? Are any of his clothes missing? This man is a vicious killer. His pent-up passion may lead to another killing. You, yourself, may be his next victim. This man is living somewhere in this city. Is he in your home?"[9]

As questions arose about the shoddy police work, Mayor Lawrence bristled and became defensive. Reporters remarked that Pittsburgh's murder rate was approaching that of Los Angeles, to which the mayor retorted, "Oh, not that bad. They have one out there every hour." He later announced, "Your information is all wrong. I got in contact with Harvey Scott (superintendent of police) and he told me that plainclothesmen were on the job five minutes after they were called." But the neighbors said they never saw them. Detective Inspector Fred Good said that Miss Brusco's murder proved that the city faced an "emergency situation." "We can't be sure that our wives or daughters are safe on our streets," he said. "No one is safe."[10] Superintendent Scott assigned the entire homicide team of eight to the case, aided by six other detectives and ten patrolmen.

The superintendent laid a share of the blame for the rash of sex crimes on the fashions favored by "modern" women. Citing tight sweaters and plunging necklines, he insisted, "The dress designers seem bent on bringing out every ounce of sex appeal in a woman. Women of a certain type sit in bars unescorted. They walk the streets alone. They entice male drinkers and the obvious result follows." "Our real problem," he added, "is the bobby-soxers. They are the sweater girls—just kids showing off."[11]

The Brusco case took on huge proportions partly because it was symptomatic of the conditions that had long plagued the police department. It was apparently the spectacular event needed to bring things to a head.

Outraged, Eliza and an entourage of two hundred angry women stormed city council on December 13, 1949. Eliza fairly shook with contained fury as she spoke:

> The women of the city are afraid—and mad. They're afraid to be alone at night on the streets of Pittsburgh; they're afraid not only for themselves but for their children . . .

It is empty sounding, indeed, to talk of vast roadways, parks and skyscraper projects while we allow petty little politicians to scuttle our prestige and greatness. Why build a beautiful façade if we permit the foundation and structure to remain rotten and ugly?

The only way that this problem can be solved is for the Mayor and the Council to remove politics from the police force. If you are going to make the streets of Pittsburgh safe for women and children, this is a MUST. It is common gossip that if you want to be on the police force, a ward chairman or someone powerful in politics has to be your sponsor . . . We realize that the largest police force in the world would continue to be inefficient as long as ward chairmen are permitted to exercise any control over the Police Department.

When ward chairmen abuse their political power by bringing pressure to bear on policemen, forcing them to toe the line or be relegated to undesirable beats or shifts, forcing them to pitch in and round up the vote at election time, demanding that they turn a deaf ear to the rackets profitable to political bosses—then only a hard-hitting cleanup campaign, backed by the administration and citizens, determined to strip unscrupulous ward bosses of all control over police, can give us efficient, dependable police protection in Pittsburgh.

Either your Superintendent of Police is so hamstrung by politics or is so inefficient that he does not know how to organize a well-trained, well-disciplined police force.

The Mayor admits laxity, and that is a long step on our road to improvement, because on the Mayor's shoulders rests the entire responsibility for the administration of the police force.[12]

Emboldened by thunderous applause, Eliza urged that a contingent fund be set up in the 1950 budget for a central alarm system and a modern crime laboratory. It could be funded, she said, by collecting twelve million dollars in outstanding delinquent real estate taxes, three hundred thousand dollars in uncollected water bills, and a million dollars in unpaid parking tickets.

She closed with a final warning: "Gentlemen, we lay the problem in your lap. We want no more clutching hands to reach out and grab us when we step out of doors at night."[13] "And," she added, "we may be back again, again, and again."[14]

As was her wont, Eliza had her facts in order before unleashing on council. What she had discovered was a host of embarrassing findings. Civil service exam scores did not figure in police promotions, making it possible for a man with a 75 on a lieutenant's exam to be awarded a job over one who scored 98. Applicants needed only an eighth-grade education. No experience was necessary to become a detective, and twelve out of thirty-five detectives had been hired without experience. There was little or no training. The department had become a political dumping ground. Any police officer could be instantly fired by the ward boss who had secured him the job in the first place. Pittsburgh's budget for its police bureau was substantially below those of other big cities such as San Francisco, Boston, St. Louis, and Washington, DC. And the city lacked two essential tools for modern detective work—a crime laboratory and a ballistics bureau.

What they did have was a hematologist by the name of Dr. John Suess, enlisted specifically for the Brusco case. Suess applied the latest technology of the time, examining a number of iron and lead pipes and articles of clothing, treating specimens with benzidine, a colorless crystalline compound that turned blue or green upon contact with blood. The specimens were also treated with sulphuric acid and placed under an ultraviolet light, where they would glow orange. To double-check the result, ammonia hydroxide was added, and if the color turned red, the specimen could be confirmed as blood. Further testing determined whether the blood was of human origin and the blood type. But it was still not possible to determine whether a blood specimen came from a particular victim or suspect.[15]

Badly shaken by the public outcry, Lawrence demanded an accounting from the superintendent of police. He began with the top brass, but the tongue-lashing was quickly extended as the city's forty-two police lieutenants and, in turn, the sergeants, the detectives, and all other personnel were called on the carpet. Why were there delays? Why did the police fail to find Jean Brusco's body? Why had they never solved the year-old Kensinger case? He excoriated the police leaders for handing out "cream puff penalties" to subordinates who should be suspended or fired for their offenses.[16] "We will not tolerate any further slovenly work anywhere in the department," he told them.[17]

Cartoonist Cy Hungerford captured the moment with the top brass in the *Post-Gazette*. His "Expert Advice," published December 15, depicted the mayor, dressed as Santa Claus, with a child, labeled "police department" over his knee, to whom he was delivering a punishing whack with a large paddle. The mayor was standing on a carpet splattered with muddy footprints labeled "Ward Chairmen," "Rackets," and "Politics." Pointing in from the doorway was an angry woman, labeled "Women Voters," who shouted "Your carpet needs the beating!" Hungerford gave the original drawing to Eliza.

The league kept Lawrence's feet to the fire, and he reportedly had further meetings with his police superintendent and inspectors, ordering them to shut down the racketeering in their districts "at once." "I know you can't drive out every numbers writer," he said angrily. "But I also know that horse rooms, slot machines, dice games and other rackets can't operate without you men knowing it."[18]

Shoddy police work was not a new problem, nor was it unique to Pittsburgh. Since the first publicly funded, organized police force with full-time officers had been created in Boston in 1838, public law enforcement in America was at best inconsistent in its quality. Particular problems existed in the South, where policing was largely centered on preservation of the system of slavery. As immigration swelled the population in industrial cities like Pittsburgh, most major US cities had established police forces by the late 1880s, with officers crafting their own definitions of law and order, controlled by the political machines, who often used police to harass their opponents or to turn a blind eye to illegal drinking, gambling, and prostitution. Recognizing this, in 1929 during Prohibition, President Hoover had appointed the Wickersham Commission to investigate the ineffectiveness of law enforcement nationwide. One solution, they contended, was to make police independent from political party ward leaders by redrawing the maps of police precincts so that they would not correspond with political wards.[19]

In 1949 Pittsburgh, however, the problem still existed. The Fraternal Order of Police had its own proposals for reform. In addition to adding men to the force, to be chosen on the basis of Civil Service exams, they advocated a ninety-day training period, extra pay for night and motorcycle duty, new vacation schedules, and an eight-hour-day and forty-eight-hour week, as well as a public relations office to centralize communications and a central records office.

Shadyside residents, unsatisfied with the city's response, formed their own Citizens Crime Committee, led by the rector of Trinity Cathedral. Eight other

Assisted by Cy Hungerford in a front-page cartoon, the League of Women Voters kept Mayor Lawrence's feet to the fire. From *Pittsburgh Post-Gazette*, December 15, 1949

prominent clergymen, along with Eliza's husband Temp and son Kennedy, served on the committee, whose goal was "to take the police department out of politics and help make it an efficient and effective law enforcement agency."[20] They vowed to coordinate with groups across the city and worked closely with the league. Their first meeting in early December reportedly filled the auditorium of Liberty School in Shadyside with five hundred people, while another five hundred stood in the corridors and yard, listening the proceedings on a loudspeaker. But when the committee leaders confronted the mayor about taking politics out of police appointments, Lawrence replied, "The present system is more in keeping with the Democratic process. The Mayor should have the right to place men in positions that will help him carry out his policies." And he held his ground, reportedly stating later that he believed that ward chairmen should have the right to make police appointments or promotions and that he was unwilling to make the position of police superintendent a non-political job. [21]

By the end of December, after a brief, four-hour trial, six police officers involved in the Brusco case had been fined fifty dollars each for "neglect of duty," and a seventh had been retired. The city added a hundred men to the force, most of them war veterans. The rookies were provided two weeks of training from men trained at the Northwestern University police school and the FBI school in Washington, with edicts that "A uniform doesn't give you the right to lord it over people and to take advantage of them" and "You are neither prosecutor, persecutor or executioner."[22] They were out in the streets by the end of January 1950. A new head of the homicide division was hired, a man who had been trained by the FBI.

The work load was daunting. By year's end, the police reported that the city had seen 108 rape cases, 694 other sex cases, and twenty-seven murders.[23] Pennsylvania's stiffest penalty for rape was seven-and-a-half to fifteen years, and offenders were automatically eligible for parole after serving the minimum sentence. And during the preceding two years, it was reported, an average of thirteen sex offenders were released monthly.[24]

The problem was rampant nationwide, where it was estimated that about sixty-one thousand rapes had occurred in 1948, prompting FBI director John Edgar Hoover to declare that "The sex criminal has replaced the kidnaper as a threat to the peace of mind of the parents of America. The time has come to call a halt." In large cities, rape cases known to police had reached an all-time peak at fifty percent above prewar levels. Pressure was mounting for a federal sexual psychopath law.[25]

At the state level, by the 1950s half of the states had sexual psychopath laws that civilly committed individuals after criminal sentences were served. In Pennsylvania, efforts were forwarded to enact a state law that would (1) segregate sex criminals in special institutions, (2) require psychiatric examination prior to parole, (3) require life terms for habitual sex offenders, and (4) provide proper treatment of sex psychopaths during their incarceration.[26]

Meanwhile, an additional spotlight was turned on the local department by a *Post-Gazette* staff writer, who wrote a series of exposé articles entitled "What's Wrong With Our Police?" The veteran police reporter asked a series of questions, among them, "Why do rackets, most notably the evil, all-pervading, demoralizing numbers racket that debauches city officials and school children alike, flourish brazenly and openly?" and "Why are recurrent police scandals, so plainly and unmistakably involving graft and corruption in the police system, whitewashed and forgotten by city officials and law agencies—the guilty not only unpunished but rewarded with preference and promotion?" "Year by year," he wrote, "I've watched police administration in Pittsburgh become more fumbling and inefficient, more venal, more arrogant." He compared the staffing and budgets of Pittsburgh's force with those in other cities and found the local department sorely wanting, the only one without the proper tools for forensic work, where evidence was frequently lost, compromised, or destroyed. He described the homicide squad of fifteen years earlier, which had nineteen trained men, a ballistics expert, and two big Packards, each with a mounted machine gun, contrasting it with the current squad of eight who frequently chased suspects on foot, on streetcars, or in hastily borrowed cars.[27]

The story of the slipshod Brusco investigation—"They Get Away With Murder in Pittsburgh"—appeared months later in *Collier's Magazine*, which asserted that "Pittsburgh's bumbling, ward-bossed police bureau functions merely as a political auxiliary of the Democratic Party.... A good many honest folk in Pittsburgh . . . are fed up with having murderers and sex criminals roam at large in their town because of the police department's classic ineptitude. They are tired of hearing the taunt, 'Murder is safer in Pittsburgh—safer for the murderer.' They are sick unto death of a bureau of police so hamstrung with politics that an inexperienced hack can be picked off the street today and sworn in as a detective tomorrow—if a ward chairman so decrees." The *Collier's* author quoted Eliza extensively, concluding that she had "put her finger" on the problem. He also recounted a conversation he had on primary day that year in the office of a "combination cop-and-ward-chairman."

"Where is he?" the author asked another officer.

"Out electioneering."

"But I thought cops couldn't hold office anymore."

"Don't worry about that," laughed the officer.

"But the cops are out of politics," insisted the author, quoting a statement from the mayor that morning.

"Yeah, sure," grinned the officer, "if they're out of politics they're out of a job."[28]

Pittsburgh had long been plagued by an unhealthy alliance between the police department and organized crime. Mayor Kline had promised to break up the alliance. After he left office, in 1934, city council had authorized a Police Research Commission to examine the operation and make recommendations for improvement. The Commission had estimated that the yearly amount paid to police by the rackets for protection was five million dollars. In 1937, the Institute of Public Administration of New York City was also invited to study the bureau and make recommendations for improvement. Yet now, more than a decade later, things were still in disarray. This time, fueled by the Jean Brusco murder, the city invited the International Association of Chiefs of Police in 1950 to assess the bureau.[29]

Eliza became known for her surprise visits to the Central Police Bureau and was dubbed the "arch foe of the Pittsburgh Police Department" by the same reporter who described her as "the crusading woman in the gay-flowered hat."[30] As in the days of the Kline investigation, word of her visits would spread quickly, and after one such visit, the *Sun-Telegraph* reported that "traffic was

Women Stir Central Police Station Dust

Dust that has been collecting in abandoned areas of the dingy Central Police Station was given a thorough stirring yesterday morning when two determined women visited the building.

Mrs. R. Templeton Smith, president, and Mrs. Paul F. Eichenlaub, treasurer of the Allegheny County League of Women Voters, explained they had just stepped by to see what progress—if any—had been made in the suggested improvements they were told were in prospect four months ago.

They found no major improvements in evidence. But they were partially satisfied by the information furnished by J. W. Slusser, former head of the city police school and now co-ordinator of police communications and records. He promised that an immediate improvement program, costing approximately $27,000, will be under way within a week.

Mrs. Smith was openly critical however of the police system of placing men of low rank and correspondingly low salaries in important executive positions. She conceded that Mr. Slusser, who took the police training course at Northwestern University, was adequately qualified to begin his

Dubbed "the arch foe of the Pittsburgh Police Department," Eliza became known—and feared—for her surprise visits. From *Pittsburgh Post-Gazette*, May 20, 1950

heavy through doors marked 'Exit.'" As the story unfolded, Eliza acknowledged, "I hear the politicians are laughing at us. I don't doubt it, but we have just begun to scratch the surface."[31] They also deemed the offices "untidy."[32] The league visitors drew attention to the fact that the only four FBI-trained officers in the department were serving not in leadership capacities but as patrolmen. Eliza readily identified two patrolmen, both FBI-trained, whom she declared should be in leadership positions, James Slusser and Joseph Flynn.

By fall 1950 the city had established a Central Communications and Records Room with a three-person switchboard and a recording device. James Slusser was put in charge of the new center and a year later would be promoted to superintendent, the first non-political appointee to the job.[33] Joseph Flynn was put in charge of the Homicide Division. The county also created a crime laboratory in the county courthouse and eventually acquired a new "mechanical sleuth" to the new facility.[34] A photo of the new polygraph being tested ran in the paper next to an article detailing the investigation of the still unsolved Kensinger case being conducted by a private sleuth, working as a volunteer, outside the realm of the police department.[35]

But true reform came slowly. The league had already collected statistics from thirty-two major cities about the qualifications for police service and how that service was delivered. In 1951, a survey of the department by the International Chiefs of Police Association recommended an additional 480 patrolmen. By 1958, only 184 had been hired.[36] Many on the force resented Eliza's scrutiny and censure. When they finally got around to collecting the unpaid parking tickets she had suggested as a revenue source for reforming the department, they served summons to private citizens in their homes—in the wee hours—explaining, "Don't blame us. Mrs. R. Templeton Smith is responsible for this. She's putting on a drive." Her response? "When our political police start to make a reform, they apparently want it to be as unpleasant as possible for the public. Please understand that I am not blaming the beat men for doing as they are told. But, whoever is telling them to serve parking summonses after midnight should explain what he is trying to prove."[37]

By January 1951, Lawrence announced that detectives would be put under Civil Service, appointing them on the basis of merit rather than at the direction of ward bosses. Ultimately, the reorganization would usher in not only a more modern operation but also a new philosophy of police. Educational requirements became more stringent. Testing included both intelligence and aptitude for police work. Training was extended from two weeks to ten. And the function of police expanded from merely fighting crime to a broader caregiving capacity. Mayor Lawrence would take all the credit.

Continuing their vigilance, the league made a study of additional solutions. They invited the directors of the Chicago and St. Louis Crime Commissions to share how their privately funded commissions had helped to curtail organized crime and corruption in their respective cities. In introducing them, Eliza delivered yet another "scorching verbal blast" of the corruption in local government.[38] "The sordid facts of political skulduggery now being uncovered by the special grand jury," she declared, "focuses the need for some means of keeping a vigilant check on City and County officials, our courts and police. It has become increasingly evident that many officials—under the present administration—have been abusing the trust which the public has placed in them."[39] The man from St. Louis referred to the Jean Brusco murder as "an incredible bungle—Keystone cop stuff."[40] As the league was considering the feasibility of such a "watchdog" commission in Pittsburgh to control crime and graft in the city and remove it from politics, the expert advised, "It is an old axiom in police administration that the people get exactly the type of law enforcement they deserve. You get just what you demand and for which you are willing to pay. . . . Instead of merely being shocked by the fact that your police lieutenants 'make a nickel or two off the numbers racket,' go deeper and ask yourself if you are paying your policemen a wage commensurate with their duties. . . . Lip service and window-dressing are not sufficient. Fumigation is what you must have."[41] They also invited Dr. Alan Moritz, a Western Reserve

University professor and national crime expert, to publicly assess the city's plans for a modern crime lab.[42]

The league redoubled its efforts to establish a crime commission in 1952 after the fourteen-month grand jury had completed its work. In a statement to the press, Eliza warned, "The probe has ended but the danger from corrupt politicians, racketeers and unscrupulous policemen is still with us. . . . The future battle against tainted government is up to the citizens."[43]

By 1953, metropolitan Pittsburgh had experienced ten brutal, unsolved murders. "Killers are loose around Pittsburgh," the *Press* reported, "who make the FBI's 10 'most wanted' criminals look like naughty boys."[44] Some of those murders involved racketeers engaged in illegal underworld activity, while others seemed to randomly target ordinary citizens. The new crime lab was handling some eight hundred to a thousand cases a year, brought in by the city's homicide, burglary, robbery, and narcotics squads.

Eliza and the league would still be calling for police reform in 1957 and 1958.[45] Eliza criticized the department, then under control of the same man she had supported for the post, James Slusser, charging that burglars, rapists, murderers, and kidnappers appeared to operate in Pittsburgh "in safety, or if not in safety, at least . . . on relatively good odds."[46] In 1958, Eliza petitioned directly the Allegheny County Court of Common Pleas, in an attempt to circumvent the district attorney, for a new grand jury investigation. The DA's office responded defensively, suggesting that the onus was on private individuals to ferret out the links between police and the rackets. Eliza fired back that if customers could find gambling and vice joints, police should be able to do likewise.[47]

Affirming Eliza's charge, a US Attorney speaking before the league in 1959 said, "Don't let any police official tell you they don't have enough police to close things up. Fifty policemen can close Pittsburgh overnight if they are given the go-ahead. If gambling exists in East Liberty, Downtown or any other district, the police inspector should know about it. If he doesn't he should be fired." He concluded, "All the grand jury probes in the world won't stop organized rackets from operating unless public officials want them stopped. . . . You have the power to vote them out of office if they fail. . . . Tell them you want your city and county cleaned up. . . . But don't forget to vote and not just talk."[48]

Eliza also served on a committee to raise a memorial reward fund for information leading to the arrest and conviction of the slayer(s) of four Pittsburgh

women in the preceding year, including Jean Brusco.[49] Yet in the midst of all
the talk about reform, even with some improvements in the system, the Carole
Lee Kensinger and Jean Brusco cases were never solved. They remained an
indelible stain on the city's law enforcement operation.

23 MORE SCANDAL AND SLEIGHTS OF HAND

No one was safe from scrutiny. Even as Eliza and the league continued to push for police reform, they tackled another scandal plaguing the city. It had begun early on April 26, 1949, a regular workday morning, when a truck owned by Allegheny Asphalt and Paving Company barreled along suburban Route 8, lost a wheel, and crashed into another truck traveling in the opposite direction. The Allegheny Asphalt truck was driven by George Manko, a city employee, who was seriously injured. The other passenger, Salvatore (Sam) DiIelsi, a stone mason employed by the city, was killed. When questioned, Manko said that they had been heading for the summer home of City Council President Thomas E. Kilgallen in neighboring Butler County, where they were to perform repair work. They also planned to work at the home of Howard "Buck" Gross, who headed the city's skilled labor force.[1]

The incident—quickly dubbed the "Free Work" scandal—drew widespread public attention and, although it took a year to gather steam, escalated into an investigation of the use of public labor, equipment, and materials on private jobs. A veteran reporter for the *Pittsburgh Sun-Times* and former state police crime expert, Willard Schauer, was assigned to the story, and according to the paper's editorial staff, worked on it for a year with assistance from Eliza before breaking his account.[2] As the facts slowly came out, the case rocked the town.

In May 1950, just days after DiIelsi's widow filed a worker's compensation suit against the city, Eliza took her accountant from the Kline investigation to pay a visit on the city controller, Edward Frey. They told Frey they were interested in the bookkeeping of traffic court and the City Department of Lands and Buildings and formally asked for the department's audit reports and a description of its accounting controls. Frey was soon engaged in an investigation, parallel to one by City Solicitor Anne X. Alpern, to investigate payroll and other records. He insisted that Eliza "did not prod [them] into anything," that the controller was the "watchdog of the city treasury."[3] But the timing was undeniable. Mayor Lawrence once again had been embarrassed and forced into action.

When Lawrence finally did respond, requesting open hearings by city council, hearings he had previously declared unnecessary, Eliza responded with "Why did he wait so long?" Lawrence insisted that his investigation—a "goldfish bowl" inquiry—would be thorough and transparent, giving every person the chance to confront his accuser. Eliza simply said, "People won't have confidence in a self-investigation."[4]

Within a week, the public hearings were underway. For nine days, Eliza sat in the packed chambers, relishing every word of the stormy proceedings as the men involved squirmed anxiously on the edge of their seats and exchanged nervous glances. Some eighty-two witnesses generated more than two thousand pages of testimony.[5] They heard claims that Council President Thomas E. Kilgallen used a city auto and city gasoline to commute to and from his summerhouse in neighboring Butler County. Frey himself was accused of using city labor to do chores on his farm. And tips continued to come in to City Solicitor Anne X. Alpern by letter and telephone.[6] The testimony filled multiple pages of the three major newspapers.

The grieving widow, Mrs. DiIelsi, testified that Kilgallen, with the mayor's backing, had sought her silence, saying, "I've taken it up with the mayor, and I'll see that you're well taken care of." At the same time, she confessed that city workmen on city time had worked on her home as well. Kilgallen had offered her seven hundred dollars in cash, she testified, and after a call to Joseph Barr at Democratic headquarters, asked her to sign a release. She had refused. The seven hundred dollars, she said, would not even cover half her funeral bills. She added that Kilgallen had offered to "create a job" for her or one of her two daughters.[7] Further investigation revealed that records of hours worked in the books kept by the head of laborers did not match those of the city payroll department. The former appeared to have been altered.

In the end, council "rejected" Mrs. DiIelsi's "sensational" testimony. In the midst of the investigation, a payroll clerk in the Department of Lands and Buildings shot himself two days before he was scheduled to go on the witness stand. His widow testified that Mr. Gross, who had been convicted of attempted jury tampering during the Kline investigation two decades earlier, had ordered the clerk to tamper with his time books and to lie under oath. She claimed he had taken his life rather than commit perjury. Manko and Gross were dismissed from their jobs. Ultimately, the city's investigation was predictably dismissive of the charges. They did, however, recommend some reforms to city procedures to enhance recordkeeping and prohibit moonlighting by city employees for city officials. No action was taken against either Frey or Kilgallen, who nonetheless called the whole affair a "diabolical plot."[8] As the hearings unfolded, Lawrence was en route to Europe on vacation.

Meanwhile, the county was engaged in a grand jury investigation of its own. When the jury of twenty-one was empowered in June, twelve of the jurors were women. Informants wrote letters to the county controller, James W. Knox, and copied Eliza at the league.[9] As one *Press* editorial stated, "The Allegheny County League of Women Voters is going to ask for a look at the books. And that public-spirited organization and its energetic president, Mrs. R. Templeton Smith, can be depended on to make a thorough check. Council should do that job—but if it won't, the women can."[10]

To Eliza and her compatriots, the incident was symptomatic of a wider problem warranting a wider inquiry. The Free Work investigation had been insufficient, Eliza argued. "This investigation was so narrow in scope that—no matter what Council's decisions may be—the public will not know that its City Government as a whole is free from taint. Only one sector of the Department of Lands and Buildings was involved. If inefficiency, laxity, and perhaps corruption can be common in one area, why should the public presume all other areas of City Government economically and efficiently run[?] No real audit of City Records was made. No investigation is complete without it."[11] With that, she distributed a petition requesting the governor to step in, to be circulated to the general population by league members. "Quick action is essential," she insisted.[12]

It was then that the league and the Citizens Crime Committee telegrammed the governor requesting a special prosecutor and grand jury probe into all city departments, backed by state police detectives, to "investigate published charges of corruption against high city officials and to present such charges to the grand jury if well founded." Noting that the three major Pittsburgh newspapers supported the request, the telegram went on to say that city council was implicated and refused to act, that the district attorney refused to act, that the city controller would not investigate himself, and that the city solicitor was powerless. "Action by you is the only hope which the citizens of Pittsburgh have for either prosecution of malfeasance in office or the restoration

The Balking Democratic Donkey   —By Hungerford

In the midst of the Free Work scandal, Cy Hungerford lampooned the Democratic machine. From *Pittsburgh Post-Gazette*, June 9, 1950

of confidence in our government," the telegram concluded.[13] Some of the players, Mr. Frey among them, became defensive. Mayor Lawrence remained curiously silent. Eliza once again had her picture on the front page.

Cartoonist Cy Hungerford again captured the moment in his "The Balking Democratic Donkey," in which two characters representing the Citizen's Crime Committee and the League of Women Voters, the latter bearing a remarkable resemblance to Eliza in her flowered hat, try desperately to drag a donkey labeled "Pittsburgh Politics" in the direction of the Free Work investigation as the governor stands by with a whip.[14]

That summer, the district attorney for the county, William Rahauser, and the Pennsylvania attorney general, Charles Margiotti, battled for control of the investigation. Each accused the other of being biased, and rightly so. Rahauser was beholden to the Lawrence machine, and Margiotti had represented Mrs. DiIelsi in her suit against Kilgallen, Gross, Manko, and Allegheny Asphalt. Some argued that the Free Work probe was a politically motivated stunt designed to embarrass Mayor Lawrence. The dispute rose to the State Supreme Court, which ultimately ruled in Margiotti's favor, assigning the investigation to the state.

The state announced its six deputy prosecutors in early September. They were to focus not only on the misuse of labor and materials by the city and the county but also on the rackets, bribes, police connections with the rackets, irregularities in public works contracts, and "official protection" of illegal liquor-selling practices. Kennedy Smith, Eliza's son, was among the six deputies, only two of whom were Democrats.

By mid-December, more than a hundred witnesses and fifteen hundred pages of testimony later, the grand jury recommended that Kilgallen and Frey be indicted, along with Gross, Manko, the Allegheny Asphalt & Paving Co. and its owners, and Kilgallen's brother-in-law. Kilgallen insisted, "I have done nothing wrong." Lawrence said nothing. The *Sun-Telegraph* called it "an auspicious beginning for a long-needed municipal house cleaning" and credited Eliza with giving "unstintingly" of her time to get it started.[15]

Still not entirely satisfied, Eliza also asked for a broader inquiry by the Senate Crime Investigating Committee into vice and corruption in Pittsburgh and Western Pennsylvania. This time she had the backing of the two US senators from Pennsylvania and a group representing some five hundred clergymen. The conditions in the region, she wrote in a telegram to the committee chair, were "as bad or worse than anything yet encountered by the committee." The pastors added, "We are faced with the difficult task of securing the cooperation of men who have been elected to office for the purpose of enforcing the laws of our state and nation, and then either because of ignorance, incompetence, fear or collusion are playing false to their sacred trust."[16]

Mayor Lawrence dismissed the whole probe as "a side show."[17] The editors of the *Pittsburgh Press* rushed to the city's defense, damning the mayor with faint praise:

> Mayor Lawrence has shown an exceptional leadership in developing the city, in creating the "new" Pittsburgh, in trying to settle labor disputes, in protecting and promoting the city's interests on many fronts. But his police department is an incomprehensible mixture of alertness, indifference and ordinary stupidity. . . . And some of the other departments under his command have been woefully negligent and brazenly adverse [sic] to cleaning up the consequent irregularities—to use a polite term. . . . Then how does it happen he can be a really fine and capable Mayor in some respects, and still manage to be either ignorant or naïve or negligent on these other things which are giving his Administration, and the city, such a scandalous name? . . . It is all a little puzzling. But one thing is sure. City Hall had better get hold of itself. It had better put the brooms and shovels to work. It had better start hitting its betrayers, and hitting them hard.[18]

When the league opposed a state income tax (which was favored by Republicans), it was rumored that a deal was afoot in the GOP that would choke off the grand jury investigation in return for Democratic support of the tax. Eliza "scorchingly" compared the deal to "killing your watchdog in hope of trading his remains for a dead cat."[19]

As it mushroomed, the Free Work probe and its aftermath would cast a shadow over the Lawrence administration for half its length, extending into 1956. By that time, with indictments hanging over the defendants, Gross had died before his trial could begin, Frey was found not guilty, and Kilgallen's trial had been postponed several times until the charges were dropped. In the interim, Kilgallen had left politics when his embarrassed party refused to endorse him for reelection.[20]

Meanwhile, throughout the 1950s, Eliza continued to be the city's most consistent critic. She led the league in a "scrimmage" with city council's finance committee over its $34 million 1951 budget in December 1950, during which she declared, "Unbalanced budgets and profligate expenditures are leading us to the brink of disaster."[21] She railed against the city's failure to collect delinquent taxes, its refinancing of bond obligations rather than paying them off, the lack of metered charges for water service, and the failure to collect delinquent parking tickets, which alone should have produced more than a million dollars in revenue but instead collected only seventy thousand dollars. And she continued to criticize the politics in the police department.

Eliza had her detractors, to be sure, and not only among those who were her direct targets. In a speech on the floor of the state Senate that made front-page news, Senator Elmer Holland called her "a frustrated old lady who would like to be mayor of Pittsburgh and who tries to keep her name in the paper." Rising to the defense of his Democratic friends in city government, Holland declared, "This inquisition should be ended." One had to wonder if, fearing a counterattack, he had intentionally waited until Eliza was on a two-week tour of the Canadian Rockies to make his accusation. Holland's fellow senator, Republican John Walker, spoke on her behalf. "I think she has made a real contribution to civic betterment," he said. "I wish there were thousands of women in my district like Mrs. Smith because she is ever alert, whether you are friend or foe, to see to it that you try to measure up to the responsibilities of public office . . ."[22]

The Post-Gazette editors also rushed to her defense, calling the attack "in extremely poor taste, and adding, "Policemen quail and city officials tremble when she pays them an unexpected visit to see if they are toeing the mark. If she has been indirectly instrumental in besmirching some names around City Hall it is only fair to assume that some of the mud would splatter on her.... The gentleman from the Southside should keep his attacks on a higher plane, restricting himself to the merits of the argument without indulging in personalities...."[23]

A columnist in the *Sun-Telegraph* wrote, "It is not the purpose of this piece to spring to the lady's defense, as she is entirely capable of taking care of herself." Recalling the Kline investigation twenty years before, he added,

What the Republicans of that day had to say about Mrs. Smith and her colleagues when they demanded a hearing on the City Supplies Department would make Sen. Holland's speech sound like a child's recitation at a tea party....

But when the investigation was over, the grand jury had completed its work and the verdicts were rendered, the Republican city administration was discredited and collapsed at the next election.

Mrs. Smith was a Republican, yet she, more than anyone else, was responsible for driving her own party out of power at City Hall, and some Republican officials at that time told her so and reproached her for it in the lean years which followed....

She could have cashed in on it herself in a political way, but to this writer's knowledge she never aspired to any political office aside from Republican district committeewoman in the Fourteenth Ward.

She just went right along with the thankless task of trying to reform government, regardless of party, not caring whom she attacked, making enemies right and left, but armed with that power which is given to anyone who fights for principle.[24]

Another columnist, a woman, wrote, "I'd like to see a lot more frustrated old ladies announce for office, threaten probes and otherwise needle politicians into screams. Their yells prove they're vulnerable."[25]

In 1951, the Pittsburgh Junior Chamber of Commerce honored Eliza and Temp jointly for their community service.

More support came in letters to the editors. "His attack on Mrs. Smith is a personal attack on every steel worker and coal miner that dares complain and protest the outrageous swindle of the taxpayers' hard-earned wage," one wrote. "He seems to show such great concern for the few thousands that the taxpayers must pay for this probe. Of course, the millions, millions, hundreds of millions and, yes, billions, of dollars politicians are swindling the taxpayers must not be mentioned or discussed by the taxpayers. I only wish the Lord would create 100 more Mrs. R. Templeton Smiths in Pittsburgh."[26] One letter to the *Press* said, "... more than once, when men have completely muddled a situation, it has been a woman who stepped in and set things right. ... I haven't voted in recent years because I've been fed up with our political slates, but believe me, if Mrs. Smith wants to run for mayor I'll be at the polls. And so will everyone of the non-voters I can lay my hands on."[27]

It seemed that Senator Holland had hit a public nerve.

At its 1951 banquet, the Pittsburgh Junior Chamber of Commerce awarded its Presidents Award jointly to Eliza and Temp. Temp was cited for his work as chairman of the 1950 Community Chest campaign in Allegheny County and Eliza for her work on police reform and the grand jury Free Work probe.

* * *

The league was the only opponent to the thirty-million-dollar bond issue to fund Pittsburgh's Renaissance—a comprehensive forty-three-million-dollar program of urban redevelopment and renewal of the water system, street upgrades, improvements to city buildings, and expansion of park and recreational facilities—which was put up to a public referendum in September

1956. It was the largest bond issue ever floated by the city. Eliza and the league pointed out that 24 percent of the valuation of the city had gone onto the tax-exempt list.

In 1957 she spoke in favor of a city ban on billboards, a contentious battle that pitted the city and private pro-redevelopment interests against the labor and the outdoor advertising industry. "I don't think our renaissance should be crowned with beer signs," she snapped.[28]

* * *

In the midst of the ongoing investigations that followed the Free Work scandal, Eliza and the league took on yet another crusade. This time it was the city's proposal to turn the water department over to an independent water authority. Proponents of the authority plan said it was the most prudent way to revamp the water system and retire its debt without raising taxes or water rates. Eliza protested the proposal, which she maintained would take the city's water system beyond the control of the people and beyond the purview of the Public Utility Commission. Undemocratic, she called it. It was an attempt to circumvent constitutional debt limitations, she said. "A public corporation that is not directly subject to the control of the electorate can become autocratic and all sufficient. . . . The public has a right to have detailed reports of their activities and intimate knowledge of their programs. Since the service rendered by the authority vitally effect [sic] the welfare of its citizens they should operate under glass and not behind closed doors."[29]

As an alternative, Eliza advocated a pay-as-you-go system under which water revenues alone would be used to maintain and improve the water system. Opponents of the authority plan established The Citizens Committee on Water, with Eliza as head of its executive committee, and they referred to the "mañana city administration." When council president announced that the city would sell the water system regardless of public opinion on the subject, Eliza declared that council's "deliberate policy of neglect" was "deplorable and indefensible."[30] She railed against them for siphoning money from the water system to apply to other purposes and embarrassed the city by quoting administration officials from the mayor on down. And when the *Post-Gazette* sponsored a panel discussion among five experts on the subject, Eliza was the only woman at the table.[31] The committee issued a blistering statement to the public: "City Council had a hearing and passed the proposal for an authority while you, the public, were squatting in front of your televisions watching America elect a new president."[32]

The league accused the mayor of balancing his 1953 budget using financial "sleight of hand magic," in which *both* the water system's revenue and the proceeds of its sale to an authority would be counted as income. In a blistering statement, the league noted that "Sleight of hand artists expect us to fail to see the left hand in the vest pocket because we are fascinated by the right hand gesticulating in the air.... We believe that financial sleight of hand is unseemly when practiced by a high public official and inexcusable when used by one to whom the electorate has been so generous and forgiving in the last 20 years." They asked, "How can the Mayor sell the water bureau, use some of the sale price to 'balance the budget,' and still retain all the revenues from the sale of water by a city owned water system?"[33] "You cannot sell your waterworks and own it, too."[34] Eliza was also quick to point out that the water department had more than a million dollars in uncollected water bills on its books.

*   *   *

And so it continued. Every year, as the city budget came up for public review in December, Eliza was there, armed with the facts, pointing out inconsistencies, railing against inefficiency, and embarrassing the administration. For Lawrence in particular, she was a "perennial foe."[35] She called him "the most wily political boss ever to gain control of our city." Speaking on behalf of John Drew, a Republican who purportedly had been pulled out of retirement as a judge to run for mayor, she had this to say about the "crafty" Lawrence: "Politics make strange bedfellows, particularly when the political boss has undisputed control of the spending of 50 million a year plus an additional ten millions [sic] in bond funds and is willing to hand out political favors in both high and low places."[36] Even when *Fortune Magazine* lauded Lawrence for his accomplishments and called him one of the nation's nine best mayors, Eliza remained unconvinced. "Had the author spent as much time here as I have," she began, "and watched as closely as I have what Mayor Lawrence's unprecedented 12 years as mayor have done to the city, I feel he would have been a little hesitant in lavishing such undeserved praise." She continued, "One thing the article emphasized is that Lawrence has been a political boss. The moral fiber of our city has deteriorated so much under this type of government that what used to be looked upon as a crime now takes on the glow and halo of public virtue in the hands of a deft manipulator like Lawrence. The racketeers, grown arrogant during 12 years of coddling by the Lawrence type of politics, only recently took to tossing bombs all over town while the rank and file of police, ready willing and able to do a good police job, stood by helplessly."[37]

By the end of 1958, it appeared that Eliza might be running out of steam. For the 1959 budget hearings, she did not appear but issued a statement charging that "more than ever" it was useless to appear before council. "Only the most naïve," she said, along with Mrs. Kenneth Fields, "would fail to suspect that councilmanic decisions have jelled before the hearing is held."[38] "At this time council must already have had its hand poised above the public's pocket."[39]

Yet Eliza would continue to rail against the city budget for the rest of her life. In 1960, the "sharp-tongued critic" leveled her usual stinging attack, charging that the fifty-nine-million-dollar budget was presented to the public too late, and was too high, with too many on the payroll, some of them overpaid, along with a particular criticism that the cost of operating city government was going up three times as fast as the cost of living.[40] How was it, she asked, that even though Pittsburgh's population had declined 10.8 percent and its ranking dropped from twelfth to sixteenth, the city budget continued to grow?[41]

Recalling for these retrospectives some of her favorite anecdotes from decades of political watchdogging, Eliza told the story of finding large salary entries for painters but very little money for paint. "When we pressed one official about that," she recounted, "he said: 'Are you so naïve? Painters vote, but paint does not.'"[42] At the hearing over a proposed wage tax for the city, she referenced the paint issue. As usual, she had done her homework and determined that the industry-standard ratio between paint and labor was around one to four. "Does it take $39,000 of labor to spread $1,800 worth of paint?"[43] With "a shy smile like some school girl," she followed with, "Remember, gentlemen, I have only been talking about one tiny bureau with seven employees. You have more than 6800 employees. Are they all necessary? Are they all working hard?"[44]

Through it all, Eliza continued to be a frequent speaker at women's clubs on topics such as "Let's Be Serious, Alert, Alive and Interested," "Your Money is What You Make It," "Good Government Down to the Grass Roots," "Politics Is Every Woman's Business—Especially Yours," and "Don't Underestimate the Power of Women." The league, with the support of twenty-five other women's organizations, also spearheaded the creation of a speaker's bureau on the topic of Civil Defense, training an estimated one hundred women to speak on the topic.

In Eliza's mind, she said, "good government is an expression of Christian citizenship. In our democracy our religious freedom is safeguarded by the Constitution. Our political freedom is safeguarded by our own active participation in government. If we fail to elect courageous and honest men— we stand in grave danger of losing all our liberties."[45] That fall, she became involved with the Crusade for Freedom, a campaign that sought signatures on a "declaration of freedom" to demonstrate "to the enslaved peoples behind the Iron Curtain that we actively believe that there is still a chance for them to be free," according to Eliza. She added that any money collected was to be used to set up radio stations "to beam the truth behind the Iron Curtain."[46] The Crusade provided the funding for Radio Free Europe.

* * *

In the last decade of her life, Eliza's personal politics shifted decidedly—and openly—to the right. As the Cold War waged on and she doubled down in her battles with Lawrence's Democratic machine, she aligned herself with 1950s conservatism even as she insisted that the league remained nonpartisan. She was chosen as a founding trustee of Americans for Constitutional Action (ACA), a nonpartisan, but conservative, organization established as a counter to Americans for Democratic Action (ADA) and to "sustain, strengthen and defend the spirit and principles of the Constitution of the United States, as these were defined by the Foundation Fathers of our Republic." It was led by four-star Admiral Ben Morell, USN (Ret.), the chief of the World War II Seabees and retired chairman of Jones & Laughlin Steel Corporation. Formed in 1958, in anticipation of the 1960 presidential election, the fourteen-member ACA board included Democrats, Republicans, and Independents with shared interests in opposing the socialists and centrists. Eliza joined a board of other luminaries such as Edgar Eisenhower, eldest brother of the president; former President Herbert Hoover; Felix Morley, Pulitzer-Prize-winning author of *Freedom and Federalism*; General Robert Johnson, board chair of Johnson & Johnson; Dr. Walter B. Martin, past president of the American Medical Association; Loyd Wright, former president of the American Bar Association; and General Robert E. Wood, former chairman of Sears Roebuck.[47] When the

board met, Eliza was the only woman in the room. The ACA published a volu-
minous "Index" that rated the voting records of members of Congress in 280
record votes taken in 1957, 1958, and 1959 according to seven criteria: "for
sound money and against inflation, for economy and conservation and against
waste, for a private competitive market and against governmental interference,
for local self-government and against central government intervention, for
private ownership as opposed to governmental ownership, for individual
liberty and against coercion, and for national security."[48] It seemed that the
ADA and the ACA agreed on only one thing: neither approved of Lyndon
Johnson as John F. Kennedy's running mate. The ADA looked upon him as
"a hopeless relic of the Dark Ages dedicated to stamping out progress," while
the ACA saw him as "a wild-eyed radical ready to tear the republic apart."[49]
Of the conservative organization, Eliza said, "We are probably a little 'horse
and buggy' for the liberals, but we still think those are good ideas."[50]

Locally, she also helped to organize The Conservative Association of Western Pennsylvania and was elected to its first board of directors. That group
ultimately merged into the ACA as a branch chapter.

Eliza had now squarely identified herself with conservative political
thought. Nonetheless, in 1955, she was named to a bipartisan committee of
five women organization leaders formed by the Pennsylvania Bar Association
to campaign for the elimination of partisan politics in the election of judges.

The national League of Women Voters did not share Eliza's conservative
bent, nor did they appreciate her independence. As the Kensinger murder
investigation was unfolding in 1948, a "smoldering feud" had erupted between
the Allegheny County League and the national organization, with the local
league refusing to conform to the requirements of the national league. The
national board voted to expel the local league because "it has refused to
amend its bylaws to provide a uniform statement of name, purpose, policy and
membership requirements." The national folks thought that the local name
should be The League of Women Voters of Allegheny County. They objected
to the local league's fundraising approach, which focused on benefit events
rather than solicitation. Eliza, not one to be submissive, pointed out that the
Pittsburgh group had two thousand members and was formed before there
even was a national group. She and the membership refused to be swayed. The
Post-Gazette reported that Eliza blasted a "you-can't-fire-me; I quit" statement
at the nationals and prepared to go solo, rejecting the "package dictation from
Washington." She was particularly miffed that the national league released

their letter to the press before sending it to the local league.[51] The nationals took the locals to federal court, and the dispute continued for more than four years, but to no avail. Unscathed, Eliza's league would carry on.

* * *

Ultimately, Eliza's attention would return to the recurring theme with which the She Devils' half-century saga had begun: the issue of voting. Initially championing voting rights for women, they had gone on to advocate for accurate and defensible voting machines as well as thorough review of the voting rolls to purge unsubstantiated registrations. Now, in the wake of the 1960 general election, Eliza was suspicious of the particularly high voter turnout in the wards where Lawrence's Democratic machine wielded control. She organized a volunteer team, largely composed of older women, to begin reviewing the registration lists and then visit any location that was not an apartment building but listed more than twelve voters in residence.

In a letter to County Commissioners' Chairman William D. McClelland on February 1, 1961, Eliza referenced "ample evidence that registration rolls are not accurate" and "widespread disregard for election laws last November 8."[52] She called for a bipartisan purge from the rolls of deceased persons, what she called "tombstone voters," not to drag the November election into a contentious battle but rather to be prepared for the next Election Day.

The investigation harkened back to an earlier time, in 1933, when "ghost" or "phantom" voters had been an issue and county investigators were charged with the task of ferreting out potential voter fraud as Republicans were accused of adding ten thousand new names to the rolls. In that probe, addresses of many newly registered voters turned out to be vacant lots, garages, billboards, and a statue.[53]

Now, nearly thirty years later, McClelland thanked the league for its "constant vigilance" but insisted that an independent investigation was already underway as a regular annual checkup. "Such has been the policy for many years in our county," he added. McClelland then invited Eliza to personally check the elections department's handling of registration lists. "If, following that," he wrote, "you feel the need of further conferences or hearings before the commissioners, we will be glad to meet with you."[54]

Elections Director Will Alton rushed to his own defense, citing a multiple-check system designed to keep the registry as accurate as possible: (1)

comparing those who voted against absentee voters of all categories, (2) removing voters who didn't go to the polls in November and no longer live at their registered addresses, (3) notifying those who haven't voted for two consecutive years that they must register, and (4) removing deceased voters from the rolls. In addition, he pointed out, "We have about 7,000 watchers of both parties at the polls, and it's their duty to challenge anyone who doesn't live where he says he does."[55]

As evidence of the efficacy of the system, Alton pointed out that with both county and city registrations down, the November 1960 election had the highest percentage of turnout—88 percent—for the biggest election in the history of the county. The lower the registration numbers and the higher the turnout percentage, he maintained, the less dead wood on the rolls.

Nonetheless, Eliza and the league—working with George W. Shankey Jr., president of a local secretarial school and Fourteenth Ward Republican committeeman—spent about three months sleuthing and uncovered a number of irregularities and set forth an eleven-point system for reform. According to the "Shankey-Smith" investigation, the county registration lists contained some seventy thousand ineligible voters and some ten thousand improper or illegal votes in the 1960 election. They cited registration and voting of nonexistent persons and the failure to remove the names of phantom voters from the voting rolls, as well as many persons voting in districts in which they did not reside. Among the latter were forty city employees, including an alderman, the Pittsburgh Housing Authority director, and high-ranking captains of the police and fire departments.[56]

In a series of long and tedious hearings, the County Registration Commission reviewed nearly eight hundred challenges, one by one, based on hard evidence unearthed by league volunteers. The league ladies canvassed individual addresses to see if the number of registered voters listed matched the number of inhabitants. Often they did not match. Some of the addresses listed for voters turned out to be driveways and alleys, parking lots, demolition sites, and garages. A man who "died in May and voted in November" was not an isolated incident. It was also found that five hundred of thirty-five hundred pieces of first-class campaign literature mailed to city payrollers in the previous year were returned for incorrect addresses, indicating that many living and voting addresses did not match.[57] Some might maintain that these inconsistencies represented careless recordkeeping. Shankey, Eliza, and the league called it collusion on the part of party workers and election boards.

Adding to the onus put on private citizens to police the registration lists, state law required that Shankey and the league would have to take the initiative and serve notice on violating registrants twenty-four hours before petitioning the registration commission. In a joint statement, Eliza and Shankey explained that phantom voters would automatically be maintained as long as they remained active. "As long as votes are cast in these names," they said, "no mail checkup will be made and those names will remain on the voter rolls. These are the bad ones, because they represent a deliberate fraud which cannot happen without collusion of party workers and election boards." By April 1961, about two thousand volunteer hours had gone into the research.[58]

Before the month was out, the investigation had prompted a new Post Office Department policy out of Washington that would make available to local election boards all change-of-address cards of individuals who move.[59] In the first twelve months alone, more than eighty-four thousand change-of-address cards were filed by patrons of the Pittsburgh Post Office and its branches. Further investigation revealed that more than twenty-eight thousand were still registered at their old addresses. More than twenty thousand voters who didn't re-register at their new addresses were dropped, with more than four thousand registrants who had died.[60] County officials claimed that three hundred persons were displaced daily through moving or death.[61] Newspaper accounts did not agree as to the effectiveness of the effort, reporting wildly divergent numbers, but the election director dubbed it "a very successful venture."[62]

In a letter to Miss Helen Frick, daughter of Henry Clay Frick and a supporter of the league, Eliza wrote, ". . . one of the county investigators told one of our people that he had never worked so hard in his life. His comment was, "You people were pretty agile—we had a hard time keeping up with you." She went on to detail what she described as "an excellent hearing":

It was a dignified performance with no name-calling, just a firm demand for something to be done. The evidence presented was well documented and irrefutable. The commissioners were surprised by so much definite information. When Mr. Shanky [sic] began to present his material he took street lists and read name after name of illegal registrants, told why the name should not be on the list and then told whether the person had voted. There were large numbers of tombstone votes cast by people who had died several years before but had voted regularly at each election. Warehouses—where no one lived—had numerous registrants, six room houses came up with fourteen to twenty inmates, and one apartment on Shady Avenue had fifty-three residents but seventy people voted. Every name mentioned was carefully documented, coldly and factually presented. We estimated that there were 70,000 illegal registrations and over 10,000 illegal votes cast. Mr. Alton, the head of the Bureau of Elections, said our estimate was low on the first figure, that it should be 85,000. So perhaps we are low on the second figure also.

"We are letting them know we are not through," she added, and "the boys are worried. They knew the conditions existed, of course, but they were surprised at the accurate data we compiled. We intend to keep pressing until the whole mess is cleaned up at least as far as we can accomplish it. . . ." She went on, "The town is wide-open and the underworld is being thoroughly protected by the present administration. Even I, as an old hand in the game, felt my hair rising at the disclosures." Stating that "Honesty at the ballot box is so fundamental in our form of government that tampering with it cannot be tolerated," Eliza concluded, "I believe we are really creating a stir."[63]

* * *

In the midst of the whole voting investigation, the Pittsburgh Press Club held its third annual Gridiron Show, a satirical spoof on local politics that drew an audience of 450 for an evening of "amateur histrionics." The show ribbed prominent figures, among them President Kennedy, complete with a Pittsburgh accent, and Governor David L. Lawrence, singing out of tune, along with Chancellor Edward H. Litchfield of the University of Pittsburgh, County Commissioner William D. McClelland, and Mayor Joseph Barr. Eliza was mocked as well, shown running for mayor and singing "Seventy-six women's clubs are in back of me" to the tune of 76 Trombones and sounding, according to one reporter, "a bit like Ethel Merman, the undisputed First Lady of musical comedy."[64] Eliza, always able to laugh at herself, was unfazed.

V Legacy

24 ACCOLADES AND EULOGIES

Always a bit eccentric, Lucy began in her final years to suffer from debilitating breakdowns that sometimes defied reason and required intervention. In one instance, she was taken to a hospital outside Baltimore after a dramatic episode at home. "Saddest day of my life," John wrote in his diary. "My dearest girl taken away against her will."[1]

After a series of weakening mini-strokes and a prolonged battle with colon cancer, on June 30, 1962, Lucy died peacefully in a Pittsburgh hospital as John entertained their grandchildren at the farm. She was eighty-two. John sobbed freely, while one of the maids in the Emerson Point kitchen callously remarked, "Guess the old bat's gone."[2]

Notices of Lucy's death appeared in newspapers across the nation, from the *Philadelphia Inquirer* and *New York Daily News* to the *Paducah Sun*, *South Bend Tribune, Kansas City Star, Green Bay Press-Gazette,* and *Duncan, Oklahoma, Banner,* all the way to the *San Francisco Examiner.*

Lucy was remembered largely for her role in the suffrage movement.

It was her role as an early leader in the suffrage movement and a founder of the League of Women Voters for which Lucy was most widely recognized. As the former head of both the Allegheny County Equal Franchise Federation and the Pennsylvania suffrage organization from 1915 to 1920 and its successor, the Pennsylvania

327

League of Women Voters, from 1920 to 1928, she had established her reputation as an outspoken leader with the tenacity to stick with a battle until it
was won. She was also remembered as an advocate for education reform, both
in Pennsylvania and as the former chair of the Talbot County School Board
after her retirement to Maryland. Lucy and John's youngest daughter Barbara
had preceded her in death, succumbing to cancer just five years earlier at the
age of thirty-nine. John would follow in 1963.

* * *

Meanwhile, in the last decade or so of her life, Eliza continued to collect accolades for her five decades of tireless civic service, ten years in pursuit of the vote
and forty as head of the league. In 1953, she had been named a Distinguished
Daughter of Pennsylvania, one of three Pittsburgh women named that year
and one of sixty women who had received that honor up to that date.[3]

The adulation also took the form of retrospective articles. In early 1953,
one of Eliza's journalistic fans did a retrospective article on her thirty-two
years of "putting politicians on the spot . . . without regard to parties or personalities." The writer praised Eliza's tenacity, saying, "She has not become
cynical and she has not lost one bit of her enthusiasm. She just keeps asking
questions—where are the records, the vouchers, the supplies accounts, the
break down and the cost sheets."[4] In 1959, a writer for the *Sun-Telegraph* did
a feature on Eliza titled "City Officials' No. One Nemesis—Mrs. Smith." Calling her work "a labor of love," he pointed out that she and David Lawrence,
by then governor of the Commonwealth of Pennsylvania, had "never seen
eye-to-eye, to put it mildly."[5]

While she was still grieving the loss of Lucy, in 1962 Eliza was the guest
of honor at a dinner in Pittsburgh, where she was celebrated as the city's "sting
of conscience" and lauded for her "many years of faithful service in the cause
of good citizenship and good government."[6]

Spring 1964 found Eliza campaigning with her ACA colleague Admiral
Ben Moreell for positions as delegates to the Republican National Convention. The Smith-Moreell team announced that they were in the battle "because
we are fed up with pseudo-statesmen and politicians whose wishbones are
where their backbones ought to be, and who are past masters of surrender,
compromise, appeasement, and accommodation." They added, "We are fed
up with Robin Hood government that promises to rob the rich to pay the

poor, and then ends up robbing both the rich and poor to pay Robin Hood."[7] Eliza and the Admiral were the underdogs, fighting against the GOP-endorsed slate and vowing to support Senator Barry Goldwater unequivocally at the convention, from the first ballot until he was nominated or withdrew. Come Election Day on April 28, the underdogs were trounced, although their hero won the nomination to oppose President Lyndon Johnson in November.

Renowned as a political activist, Eliza Kennedy Smith was also a doting grandmother to eight grandchildren, including her namesake, the author.

Tired, defeated, and feeling poorly, there was nothing for Eliza to do but retreat to the farm for the summer. It was then that her health failed precipitously. Eliza felt miserable, and as the summer dragged on, the stress of losing young Temp's beloved father-in-law, Clifford Fergus, was possibly the last straw. The day after Cliff's funeral, on a hot August afternoon in 1964, Eliza collapsed and was taken to the hospital, where doctors found a "cannonball" in one lung and "several marbles" in the other. Unlike her sister, Eliza had never smoked. Yet years of sitting in smoke-filled council chambers had taken their toll.[8] And Temp had no idea that his years of puffing on a pipe in their second-floor library had likely subjected her to the ill effects of secondhand smoke as well. It was a secret villain whose dangers had yet to be identified. The problem was only exacerbated by the foul air that had hung over the city for decades.

Doctors had tried chemical treatments and nitrogen mustards, the scourge of World War I that would later be found at least somewhat effective in fighting cancer. But Eliza's condition worsened quickly, and it soon became apparent that there was nothing more they could do for her.

Rushing from the Duquesne Club downtown to her hospital bedside in nearby Oakland, Eliza's son Kennedy rattled around in the back of a cab that was dodging potholes, occasionally slamming violently into an unavoidable pit in the paving. As the cab plunged into one particularly deep crater, the driver, unaware of his passenger's identity, cursed and said, "Why doesn't Mrs. R. Templeton Smith do something about that?"

But Eliza had fought her last battle. She was taken home to live out her remaining days in the comfort of her own room at 1336 Shady Avenue. It was there that she died in her sleep on October 23, 1964, just weeks shy of her seventy-fifth birthday. Not until later that year did the US Surgeon General issue the first report linking tobacco, secondhand smoke, and cancer.

The obituaries quoted a range of community leaders and political players. The *League News* lamented the loss:

> We of the Allegheny County League of Women Voters have lost our beloved leader of over forty years. During these years we and the whole community have looked to Eliza Kennedy Smith to take up the cudgel for cleaner, more efficient, more economical government. She has been our voice, often a lone voice speaking in a wilderness of corruption. To the world, we were Mrs. Smith's League. As individuals, we were largely anonymous foot soldiers mustered to battle.

> Now she is gone. There is no magic name, no well-known voice the community accepts, though we must admit that in recent years, some foot soldiers had a way of resting by the roadside, confident that Eliza would do it. . . .

> No one person has the accumulated shrewdness, political know-how, and prestige, of a Mrs. Smith. This means that we must muster from each his best! Together we can advance at a pace that will guarantee our value to the community. . . .[9]

In the *Pittsburgh Post-Gazette*, she was described as "a stout-hearted, determined hard-hitting battler for the right as she saw it in government." Noting her "aggressive, ever-pressing attacks," the obituary went on to say, "Although her statements on public affairs were usually of the barbed variety calculated to make a stung politician jump out of his chair in anger, they were delivered in a calm, soft-spoken manner that salved the wound."[10] The *Pittsburgh Press* called her "a relentless, tenacious watchdog of the City's purse strings" who "hounded the coattails of both Republican and Democratic administrations."[11]

The *North Hills News Record* called her "a woman of courage and conviction" and declared that "good government never had a better friend." Describing Eliza's personal style, the editors wrote, "She did not harangue, scold, threaten or brow-beat. What she had to say she expressed in calm words and in logic. She was sure of the rightness of her cause. She was the bitter foe of injustice, inefficiency, waste and complacency in government. She hounded alike Democratic and Republican officials for what she considered to be mistakes, blunders and plain stupidity. Some of them winced when she spoke but they admired her for her sincerity." They concluded, "There is none to take her place."[12]

US Congressman Jim Fulton eulogized her as "the conscience of Pittsburgh," pointing out that "she devoted her whole life to personifying the contribution of the American Woman to our public good, and integrity in government."[13] Senator Barry Goldwater telegrammed that "her contribution to American civil and political life will endure."[14]

Thirty-six years later, in 2000, her memory was still strong when the Allegheny County League of Women Voters' president wrote, "I will be forever grateful that eighty years ago a spunky, savvy Mrs R. Templeton Smith fought diligently for . . . the right to vote. But she didn't stop there. Mrs. Smith had both insight and foresight. . . . We are the beneficiaries of her legacy."[15]

The half century since Eliza's death has failed to produce the likes of Lucy and Eliza, suspicious and disillusioned enough to take action relentlessly for more than half a century, yet never letting their disenchantment with the system make them so jaded as to give up and declare the mission hopeless. They never abandoned the belief that underrepresented populations should be served and not abused by the system and that government should be administered in a prudent, frugal, and fair manner for the benefit of all, rich and poor, Republican and Democrat, man and woman. They were originals, those She Devils. They left a legacy, of admirers, of family members who are the keepers of their stories, of the stories themselves. Nearly sixty years later, the need for vigilance such as theirs is as great as ever, and the inner sanctum of political corruption still stands waiting for others like Lucy and Eliza to storm the doors.

ACKNOWLEDGMENTS

My name may be on the cover, but this book represents the effort of many. First and foremost, I am indebted to my father, Templeton Smith, who preserved so much of the family archives and chronicled the lives of Julian Kennedy, Eliza Kennedy Smith, and R. Templeton Smith, providing the beginnings of the story's framework. Likewise, my cousins Ted and Sally Smith and second cousin Peter Shefler augmented that collection with additional family archives. And second cousin John Miller shared his collection of family papers as well as his own memoir and personal insights about his grandmother, Lucy Kennedy Miller, which provided a critical window into her delightfully colorful character.

It seemed the more I researched, the more I realized I didn't know. Several people provided essential source material that proved invaluable. Gloria Forouzan in the City of Pittsburgh mayor's office, who championed the Pittsburgh Suffrage Centennial, was a super sleuth at tracking down relevant news articles and images and interpreting them to tell the suffrage story. John Paul Deley, Matthew Strauss, and their colleagues at the Detre Archives of the Senator John Heinz History Center were always hospitable and helpful with research. Kay Fleischner, my research assistant and now a student at Northeastern University, quite capably cataloged and digested twenty oversized scrapbooks and photo albums covering the period of 1920 to 1960, keeping me fueled with her enthusiasm along the way. Jay Devine, a professor of history at Carnegie Mellon University, was helpful in making sense of the Progressive Era in which some of the story unfolded. In more recent years, Lee Gutkind, the "godfather of creative nonfiction," was a helpful critic of my narrative style. Novelist Will Acer has served as a valued reader and accountability partner, sharing his knowledge of the publishing industry and his skill as a storyteller. My brother, Templeton Smith, generously read early drafts with a critical eye.

Sam Christenfeld read the entire manuscript and summarized the story in a series of brilliant haikus. As I approached the finish line, Alexis Obernauer was a constant and enthusiastic cheerleader.

Luck introduced me to my editor at Carnegie Mellon University Press, Cynthia Lamb, and their production coordinator, Connie Amoroso. Without their enthusiasm, support, and diligence, this book would never have seen the light of day.

And to all those who have traveled alongside at various times over the past fifteen years as I intermittently tackled this project, first as a sideline to a busy professional and personal life and ultimately as my primary vocation, I am greatly indebted for their encouragement and gentle nagging, particularly Mackenzie Carpenter, Susan Creighton, Ann Danneberg, Sharon Dilworth, Katie Hamilton Gewirz, Jean Anne Hattler, David Heitzenroder, Daryln Hoffstot, Betsy Hurtt, Nancy Polinsky Johnson, Peter Johnson, Cathy Kelly, Max King, Andy Masich, Betsy McConnell, Mary Lou McLaughlin, Jodie Moore, Frederic Rosiak, Larry Simms, Don Sutton, Caroline Wentling, Barbara Wheeler, and Steven Zelicoff.

Finally, to my family, my late husband Bill, the most meticulous of editors and an ever-present source of reassurance as long as he lived, and our children Will, Brendan, and Regina, who for more than half their lives listened patiently to She Devils stories and supported my dream of sharing them with a broader audience, I am forever grateful.

Notes

Introduction
1 Letter, Eliza Kennedy Smith to Templeton Smith, January 13, 1937.

Chapter 2 | The Kennedy Clan
1 Bailey Kennedy has alternately been identified as Beasley, Bailiff, or Baliff in geneaology records. See myheritage. com, accessed 5/1/2019, and ancestry.com.
2 Templeton Smith, "Engineer Pittsburgh," unpublished manuscript, 1996, 71.
3 Ibid.
4 *A History of the City of Buffalo: Its Men and Institutions* (Buffalo: Buffalo Evening News, 1908), 86–87.
5 Ibid, 61.
6 John W. Jordan, *Encyclopedia of Pennsylvania Biography* (New York: Lewis Historical Publishing Company, 1914), 2254–2256.
7 Kennedy, Address, 1909, 3–5, in the Yale University Archives.
8 Larry Schweikart, "Julian Kennedy," in *The Entrepreneurial Adventure: A History of Business in the United States* (Belmont, CA: Wadsworth Publishing, 1999), 223, as cited by Smith, "Engineer Pittsburgh," 6.
9 Joseph Green Butler, *Fifty Years of Iron and Steel* (Youngstown, OH: Joseph G. Butler, 1923), 93.
10 Letter, Jennie Eliza Brenneman to Taylor Brenneman, May 21, 1876.
11 Letter, Jennie Eliza Brenneman to Taylor Brenneman, May 30, 1876.
12 Letter, Jennie Eliza Brenneman to Taylor Brenneman, June 13, 1876.
13 Letter, Jennie Eliza Brenneman to Julian Kennedy, undated, as quoted in Smith, "Engineer Pittsburgh," 10.
14 James Howard Bridge, *The Carnegie Millions And the Men Who Made Them: Being the Inside History of the Carnegie Steel Company* (London: Limpus Baker & Co., 1903), 88.
15 Larry Schweikart, "Julian Kennedy," in Encyclopedia of American Business History, 224–225, as quoted in Smith, "Engineer Pittsburgh," 55.
16 Smith, "Engineer Pittsburgh," 26.

Chapter 3 | Growing Up Gilded
1 "Again Stricken: Ill-Fated Johnstown Visited By Another Calamity," *Pittsburgh Commercial Gazette*, December 11, 1889 and "A Theater Panic: Another Terrible Disaster at Johnstown," *Pittsburgh Daily Post*, December 12, 1889.
2 Maurine W. Greenwald and Margo Anderson, Eds., *Pittsburgh Surveyed: Social Science and Social Reform in the Early Twentieth Century*, (Pittsburgh: University of Pittsburgh Press, 1996).
3 Letter, Lucy Kennedy to Eliza Kennedy, November 19, 1900.
4 Letter, Lucy Kennedy to Jennie Eliza Kennedy, November 20, 1900.
5 "House of Julian Kennedy, Esq., Pittsburgh, Pa," Plate, *American Architect and Building News* 92:1648, pt. 1 (July 27, 1907).
6 *Collecting in the Gilded Age: Art Patronage in Pittsburgh, 1890–1910*, organized by DeCourcy E. McIntosh (Pittsburgh: The Frick Art & Historical Center, 1997), 63.
7 Dawn Reid Brean, "Dressed to Impress: Mrs. Peacock and the Legacies of Aristocratic Portraiture," illustrated talk presented at the Frick Pittsburgh, January 23, 2019.
8 *The Bulletin*, September 26, 1896.
9 Hax McCullough, *So Much to Remember: The Centennial History of The Pittsburgh Golf Club* (Pittsburgh: The Pittsburgh Golf Club, 1996).
10 Letter, Eliza Kennedy to R. Templeton Smith, July 30, 1915.
11 Letter, Lucy Kennedy Miller to J. O. Miller, September 18, 1909.
12 Letter, Eliza Kennedy to R. Templeton Smith, July 12, 1914.
13 Letter, Lucy Kennedy Miller to J. O. Miller, August 17, 1909.
14 Ibid.
15 Letter, Lucy Kennedy Miller to J. O. Miller, August 26, 1909.
16 Letter, Lucy Kennedy Miller to J. O. Miller, August 27, 1909.
17 Ibid.
18 Letter, Lucy Kennedy Miller to J. O. Miller, August 24, 1909.

Chapter 4 | Vassar College
1 Peter Bronski, "A Woman's Place," *Vassar Alumnae Quarterly* 107, no. 1 (Winter 2011).

2   Ibid.
3   Ibid.
4   All quotations in this chapter were taken from letters written by Lucy to her parents between 1898 and 1902.
5   Letter, Lucy Kennedy to Jennie Kennedy, March 18, 1901.
6   Augusta Prescott, "Shirtwaists Worn by Society Women," *Pittsburg Press*, September 16, 1906.
7   Letter, Lucy Kennedy to Jennie Kennedy, April 8, 1899.
8   Letter, Lucy Kennedy to Jennie Kennedy, April 23, 1901.
9   Letter, Lucy Kennedy to Jennie Kennedy, March 8, 1901.
10 Letter, Lucy Kennedy to Julian Kennedy, March 18, 1901.
11 Letter, Lucy Kennedy to Jennie Kennedy, April 27, 1900.
12 Letter, Lucy Kennedy to Jennie Kennedy, November 6, 1900.
13 Letter, Lucy Kennedy to Jennie Kennedy, May 14, 1899.
14 Letter, Jennie Kennedy to Lucy Kennedy, February 20, 1899.
15 Letter, Lucy Kennedy to Jennie Kennedy, November 15, 1900.
16 "Vassar Girls at Home," *Pittsburg Press*, March 25, 1910 and "Vassar Girls Return for Ten-Day Recess," *Pittsburgh Post-Gazette*, March 25, 1910.
17 "Suffrage Growth Caused Vassar Head to Resign," *Pittsburgh Gazette Times*, February 19, 1913.
18 Vassar College Annual Catalogue, 1909–1913, https://babel.hathitrust.org/cgi/pt?id=mdp.39015066660229&view=1up&seq=125, accessed April 10, 2020.

Chapter 5 | The Ugly Duckling Unbound
1   "On Robinson Cruso," *Pittsburg Press*, August 25, 1902.
2   "Pittsburg Girl Will Christen Boat," *Pittsburg Post*, July 25, 1903 and "Girl from Pittsburg Christens the Mongolia," *Pittsburg Post*, July 26, 1903.
3   "The Munhall Braun Wedding," *Pittsburg Press*, February 2, 1904; "Dinner Dance at Kennedy Home," *Pittsburg Post*, February 10, 1904 and "Dinner Dance for Bridal Party," *Pittsburg Press*, February 10, 1904.
4   "Will Give a Card Party," *Pittsburg Post*, May 24, 1904 and "Card Party and Dance Given," *Pittsburgh Daily Post*, June 4, 1904.
5   "Returned from Lake Trip," *Pittsburgh Gazette*, August 11, 1904.
6   "Vassar Students' Benefit," *Pittsburg Press*, May 19, 1904.
7   Letter, Lucy Kennedy to John Miller, March 15, 1905.
8   "Society," *Pittsburgh Gazette*, August 13, 1905.
9   Letter, Lucy Kennedy to John Miller, September 17, 1909.
10 John Hawkins Miller, "A Bend in the Silver Spoon: Memories of Emerson Point Farm," unpublished manuscript, December 2011.
11 Letter, Lucy Kennedy to John Miller, undated.
12 "Society," *Pittsburgh Post*, April 21, 1907.
13 Letter, John Miller to Lucy Kennedy Miller, January 20, 1909.
14 Letter, John Miller to Lucy Kennedy Miller, February 3, 1909.
15 Letters, Lucy Kennedy Miller to John Miller, February 5, 13, 14, 1909.
16 Letter, Lucy Kennedy Miller to John Miller, February 22, 1909.
17 Letter, John Miller to Lucy Kennedy Miller, February 24, 1909.
18 Letter, Lucy Kennedy Miller to John Miller, September 15, 1909.
19 Letter, Lucy Kennedy Miller to John Miller, February 17, 1909.
20 Letter, Lucy Kennedy Miller to John Miller, February 25, 1909.
21 Letter, Lucy Kennedy Miller to John Miller, August 19, 1911.
22 Letter, Lucy Kennedy Miller to J. O. Miller, from Crusoe Island, September 14, 1909.

Chapter 6 | Rallying the Troops
1   "Renaissance of Suffrage Movement in America," *Pittsburgh Post*, January 3, 1909.
2   Florence Harper, "Suffrage Worker Describes Day of Campaigning," *Pittsburg Press*, August 13, 1915.
3   Erasmus Wilson, "Quiet Observer: To What Are the Women of the Land Drifting in These Later Days?" *Pittsburgh Gazette Times*, January 28, 1909.
4   Lisa Tetrault, *The Myth of Seneca Falls: Memory and the Women's Suffrage Movement, 1848–1898* (Chapel Hill, NC: The University of North Carolina Press, 2014), 121.

5   Christopher Klein, "The State Where Women Voted Long Before the 19th Amendment," www.history.com, April 1, 2019.

6   Some discrepancy exists in accounts of what constituted the first large-scale meeting. The papers described a gathering at the Rittenhouse Hotel in East Liberty. Lucy described a gathering at the First United Presbyterian Church. *See* "Personal Experiences of Mrs. John O. Miller, Pioneer in Women's Suffrage Cause," unpublished manuscript in author's collection. *See also* "Calendar of Club Events for the Week," *Pittsburgh Post*, December 5, 1909.

7   "Personal Experiences."

8   Ibid.

9   Anna Howard Shaw, *The Story of a Pioneer: Autobiography of Anna Howard Shaw* (Eugene, OR: Wipf and Stock Publishers, 1916).

10   "Personal Experiences," 2.

11   "Federation Will Give Its Support to Women," *Pittsburgh Gazette Times*, February 22, 1910.

12   "Afro-American Notes," *Pittsburg Press*, March 6, 1910.

13   For more of the compelling speech by John R. Clifford, editor of the Martinsburg, West Virginia, *Pioneer Press* and president of the National Independent Political League on President Taft's failings with regard to race, see "League Holds Big Meeting," *Pittsburgh Courier*, September 23, 1911.

14   *Pittsburgh Courier*, February 3, 1912.

15   Emma B. Suydam, "Among the Clubs of Greater Pittsburgh," *Pittsburgh Sunday Post*, May 28, 1911.

16   "Equal Franchise Federation of Western Pennsylvania," *Pittsburgh Sunday Post*, May 28, 1911.

17   Jennie Roessing, quoted in George Swetnam, "Pittsburgh's Determined Suffragettes," *Pittsburgh Press*, November 4, 1956.

18   "Suffragists Will Nab the Bachelors in 1912, If They Don't Watch Out! Single Men Warned," *Pittsburg Press*, December 31, 1911.

Chapter 7 | Launching the Campaign

1   "Women to Begin Fight for Votes," *Pittsburgh Sunday Post*, January 7, 1912; "Suffragists are Ready," *Pittsburgh Post*, January 8, 1912 and Florence E. Little, "Campaigning with the Suffragists," *Pittsburgh Sunday Post*, January 14, 1912.

2   Florence E. Little, "Campaigning with the Suffragists," *Pittsburgh Sunday Post*, January 14, 1912.

3   Ibid.

4   Ibid.

5   "Miss Mary Flinn Makes Plea for Votes for Women," *Pittsburgh Post*, January 9, 1912 and "Woman Suffrage Preached in Vaudeville," *Pittsburgh Gazette Times*, January 9, 1912.

6   Florence E. Little, "Campaigning with the Suffragists," *Pittsburgh Sunday Post*, January 14, 1912.

7   "Women Need Vote, Says Suffragist," *Pittsburgh Sunday Post*, January 14, 1912.

8   Florence E. Little, "Campaigning with the Suffragists," *Pittsburgh Sunday Post*, January 14, 1912.

9   Ibid.

10   "Suffragists are Ready," *Pittsburgh Post*, January 8, 1912.

11   "Actress-Suffragist to Speak in Carnegie Hall," *Pittsburgh Post*, January 4, 1912.

12   "Woman Suffrage Cause Advancing," *Pittsburgh Sunday Post*, January 7, 1912 and "Among the Clubs of Greater Pittsburgh," *Pittsburgh Post*, January 10, 1912.

13   Emma B. Suydam, "Among the Clubs," *Pittsburgh Sunday Post*, January 14, 1912.

14   Ibid.

15   The *Sun* and its sister paper, the *Post*, were forerunners of the *Pittsburgh Post-Gazette*.

16   *Pittsburgh Sun*, February 29, 1912.

17   Ibid.

18   Ibid.

19   "Women Get Out First Suffrage Daily Newspaper," *Pittsburgh Post*, March 1, 1912.

20   "Suffrage Edition of Sun an Epoch," *Pittsburgh Post*, March 1, 1912.

21   A Mere Man, "How the Sun Is Issued By Suffragists," *Pittsburgh Sun*, February 29, 1912.

22   "Suffrage Edition of Sun an Epoch," *Pittsburgh Post*, March 1, 1912.

23   Ibid.

24   "Personal Experiences," 8.

25   Ibid.

26   Frances Orr, "Woman Suffrage Movement," *Pittsburgh Sunday Post*, March 17, 1912.

27   "Make Many Arguments at Suffrage Hearing," *Pittsburgh Post*, March 26, 1912.

28 Anne Weiss, "Leaders Who Battled for Women's Vote to Observe Anniversary," *Pittsburgh Press*, March 17, 1940.
29 *Forty-Third Annual Report of the National-American Woman Suffrage Association*, proceedings of the meeting at Louisville, Kentucky, October 19–25, 1911.
30 Templeton Smith, "One Who Made A Difference," unpublished manuscript, 1995.
31 Carrie Chapman Catt, "Address of the President at the Seventh Congress of the International Woman Suffrage Alliance, Budapest, Hungary, June 1913," in author's collection.
32 "Personal Experiences," 10.
33 "Personal Experiences," 5.
34 "Suffragists Are Active," *Pittsburg Press*, May 13, 1914.
35 "Woman's Suffrage Movement," *Pittsburgh Sunday Post*, October 5, 1913.
36 "Autos Galore and Hundreds Inspect Them," *Pittsburgh Sunday Post*, January 18, 1914.
37 "Personal Experiences," 5.
38 "Farmer's Exhibit Proves Success," *Pittsburgh Post*, January 17, 1912.
39 "Woman Suffrage Movement," *Pittsburgh Sunday Post*, January 28, 1912.
40 "Suffragists Brave Rains," *Pittsburgh Sunday Post*, October 13, 1912.
41 "Pittsburgh Suffragists Plan Rousing Meeting," *Pittsburgh Post*, October 17, 1912.
42 "Women Organize Suffrage Party," *Pittsburgh Post*, October 19, 1912.
43 Emma B. Suydam, "Among the Clubs," *Pittsburgh Sunday Post*, October 20, 1912.
44 "Personal Experiences," 3.
45 Johanna Neuman, *Gilded Suffragists: The New York Socialites Who Fought for Women's Right to Vote* (New York: New York University Press, 2017.)
46 "Suffragists Raise $41,000 in 15 Minutes," *Pittsburgh Post*, December 13, 1915.
47 Emma B. Suydam, "Among the Clubs: Warning to the Anti-Suffragists," *Pittsburgh Sunday Post*, January 7, 1912.
48 "Personal Experiences," 3.
49 Anne Myra Benjamin, *Women Against Equality: The Anti-Suffrage Movement in the United States from 1895 to 1920* (Lulu Publishing Services, 2014), 264.
50 Susan E. Marshall, *Splintered Sisterhood: Gender and Class in the Campaign Against Woman Suffrage* (Madison, WI: The University of Wisconsin Press, 1997), 5.
51 "Anti-Suffragists Issue Circulars," *Pittsburgh Gazette Times*, February 11, 1913.
52 Mrs. Simeon H. Guilford, a member of the executive board of the Pennsylvania Association Opposed to Woman Suffrage, quoted in "Leader of Antis Opposes Poll Watching," *Pittsburgh Gazette Times*, May 23, 1915.
53 "Colloquium Club Invites 'Anti' and Suffragist to Expound Political Beliefs," *Pittsburg Press*, January 8, 1914.
54 Eliza D. Armstrong, "Suffrage Plea for Sympathy Vain, 'Anti' Says," *Pittsburg Press*, July 25, 1915.
55 Euphemia Bakewell, "Woman Suffrage Movement," *Pittsburgh Sunday Post*, May 26, 1912.
56 "Mrs. Miller Sees End of Many Evils in Ballot," *Pittsburg Press*, February 25, 1912.
57 Bob Cupp, "Armstrong Massacre," *TribLive*, September 28, 2007, https://archive.triblive.com/news/armstrong-massacre.
58 "Woman Suffrage Cause Advancing," *Pittsburgh Sunday Post*, January 7, 1912.
59 "Pittsburgh Suffragists," *Pittsburgh Post*, December 20, 1912.

Chapter 8 | Taking the Fight to the Halls of Power
1   Sources differ as to which Pittsburgh women attended. All concur that Lucy and Eliza, the Bakewell sisters, and Mary Porter were there. See Roberta V. Bradshaw, "Suffragists' March to Be Spectacular," *Pittsburgh Gazette Times*, February 16, 1913.
2   "Suffragists and 'Antis' Engage Private Guards," *Pittsburgh Post*, February 21, 1913.
3   "Suffragists Sling Mud, Anti-Suffragists Say," *Pittsburgh Sunday Post*, February 23, 1913.
4   "Suffragists Win Point," *Pittsburgh Post*, January 10, 1913.
5   "Suffrage 'Army' Reaches Capital," *Pittsburgh Post*, March 1, 1913 and "House Grows Boisterous During Suffrage Debate," *Pittsburgh Gazette Times*, March 2, 1913.
6   "Suffragist Paraders Buffet Crowd," *Pittsburgh Post*, March 4, 1913.
7   Roberta V. Bradshaw, "Suffragists' March to be Spectacular," *Pittsburgh Gazette Times*, February 16, 1913.
8   "Women's Parade to Startle the Onlookers," *Pittsburgh Gazette Times*, February 23, 1913.
9   "Suffragist Paraders Buffet Crowd," *Pittsburgh Post*, March 4, 1913 and "Suffragists' Parade Helped Through Mob by Cops and Soldiers," *Pittsburgh Gazette Times*, March 4, 1913.
10 "Suffragist Paraders Buffet Crowd," *Pittsburgh Post*, March 4, 1913.
11 "Women Say Police Didn't Curb Roughs," *Pittsburgh Gazette Times*, March 5, 1913.

12 "Women Angrily Score Police for Insults," *Pittsburgh Post*, March 7, 1913.

13 "Suffragist Paraders Buffet Crowd," *Pittsburgh Post*, March 4, 1913.

14 "Impersonates Liberty in Pageant," *Pittsburgh Post*, February 17, 1913.

15 "Suffragist Paraders Buffet Crowd," *Pittsburgh Post*, March 4, 1913.

16 Ibid.

17 Ibid.

18 "Capital Police Investigation Will Be Asked," *Pittsburgh Post*, March 5, 1913.

19 Angered Women Hiss Witnesses Lauding Police," *Pittsburgh Sunday Post*, March 9, 1913.

20 "Resolution Denounces Police of Washington," *Pittsburgh Post*, March 8, 1913.

21 Ibid.

22 "Mrs. Catt Speaks Tomorrow," *Pittsburgh Sunday Post*, March 9, 1913.

23 "Capital Police Praised," *Pittsburgh Post*, May 30, 1913.

24 "Suffragists Invade Capitol, Asking Vote," *Pittsburgh Post*, April 8, 1913 and "500 Women Welcomed in Capitol," *Pittsburgh Gazette Times*, April 8, 1913.

25 "Suffrage Big Guns Bombard Senators," *Pittsburgh Sunday Post*, April 27, 1913.

26 "Suffragists Will Get Hearing in December," *Pittsburgh Gazette Times*, July 11, 1913.

27 "Democrats Against Suffrage Committee," *Pittsburgh Sunday Post*, January 18, 1914.

28 Frederick M. Kerby, "How Suffragets Will Club Ballot from Congress," *Pittsburg Press*, December 13, 1913.

29 "Women Have Day in Capital of State," *Pittsburgh Gazette Times*, March 19, 1913.

30 "Argue Woman's Right to Vote Before Senate," *Pittsburgh Post*, March 19, 1913. Strong arguments were offered by speakers on both sides of the issue.

31 "Suffrage Host Throngs House," *Pittsburgh Post*, March 18, 1913.

32 "War to Finish Being Urged to Gain Suffrage," *Pittsburg Press*, March 18, 1913.

33 "Road Bond Bill May be Recalled for Final Passage," *Pittsburg Press*, April 7, 1913.

34 "Suffrage Fight Tuesday," *Pittsburgh Daily Post*, March 26, 1913 and "Suffrage Bill Is Likely to Be Defeated," *Pittsburgh Gazette Times*, April 1, 1913.

35 "Woman's Suffrage Movement," *Pittsburgh Sunday Post*, April 6, 1913.

36 John R. Ball, "Suffrage Wins Sudden Victory in the Senate," *Pittsburgh Post*, April 23, 1913 and "Votes for Women Wins in State Senate," *Pittsburgh Gazette Times*, April 23, 1913.

37 Emma B. Suydam, "Among the Clubs," *Pittsburgh Daily Post*, April 24, 1913.

38 "New Era Club Holds Suffrage Meeting," *Pittsburgh Gazette Times*, October 23, 1913.

39 "'Voiceless Speeches' Made by Suffragists," *Pittsburg Press*, October 25, 1913; "Suffragists Prepare for Big Convention," *Pittsburgh Sunday Post*, October 26, 1913 and "In 'Voiceless Speech' Feminists Plead Cause," *Pittsburgh Gazette Times*, October 26, 1913.

40 "Votes for Women Cost More Money," *Pittsburgh Gazette Times*, October 30, 1913.

41 Emma B. Suydam, "Among the Clubs," *Pittsburgh Post*, September 30, 1913.

42 "Suffrage Leader is Assured of Re-Election," *Pittsburgh Gazette Times,* October 29, 1913; "Whole State to be Canvassed by Suffragists," *Pittsburg Press*, October 28, 1913 and "Suffragists' Convention is a Live Affair," *Pittsburg Press,* October 27, 1913

43 "Votes for Women Cost More Money," *Pittsburgh Gazette Times*, October 30, 1913.

44 "Women Can See Ballot by 1915 if They Skimp," *Pittsburgh Post*, October 30, 1913 and "Organization Work Discussed by Suffragists," *Pittsburg Press*, October 30, 1913.

45 "Organization Work Discussed by Suffragists," *Pittsburg Press*, October 30, 1913.

46 "Reforms Urged by Suffragists in Convention," *Pittsburgh Post*, October 31, 1913.

47 "Delegates from State to National Convention," *Pittsburgh Gazette Times*, November 1, 1913.

48 "Suffragists Indulge In Humorous Meeting," *Pittsburgh Post*, October 30, 1913.

49 "Suffrage Leader Flays Wilson for Silence," *Pittsburgh Gazette Times*, December 3, 1913.

50 "Suffragists Will Try to Make Wilson Act," *Pittsburgh Gazette Times*, December 4, 1913.

51 "Jericho March Women's Hope," *Pittsburgh Post*, December 3, 1913.

52 "Suffragists Set a Watch on President," *Pittsburgh Post*, December 6, 1913.

53 "Suffragists Fail in Appeal to President, *Pittsburgh Post*, December 9, 1913 and "Wilson's Refusal to Help Vexes Suffragists," *Pittsburgh Gazette Times*, December 9, 1913.

54 "Leader of the Pittsburgh Suffragists Is Conducting an Energetic Campaign," *Pittsburgh Sunday Post*, December 14, 1913.

55 "To Teach Suffragets Handling of Rioters," *Pittsburgh Post*, December 23, 1913; "Equal Franchise Federation,"

Pittsburgh Sunday Post, December 28, 1913; "Women Take Up Study of Citizenship," *Pittsburgh Gazette Times*, January 14, 1914 and "Suffrage School Begins Sessions," *Pittsburgh Post*, January 17, 1914.
56 "Will Teach Women Handling of 'Mob,'" *Pittsburgh Post*, February 20, 1914.

Chapter 9 | Taking It to the Streets of Pittsburgh
1 "Women Brave Sun and Heckling for Cause," *Pittsburgh Gazette Times*, May 3, 1914.
2 "Some of the 'Generals' in Today's Big Suffrage Parade," *Pittsburg Press*, May 2, 1914.
3 "Women Brave Sun and Heckling for Cause," *Pittsburgh Gazette Times*, May 3, 1914.
4 One source reported that it was Mary and others Euphemia, accompanied by Miss Margaret Whitehead, and Miss Charlotte Pendleton.
5 "Women Brave Sun and Heckling for Cause," *Pittsburgh Gazette Times*, May 3, 1914.
6 Ibid.
7 "Mere Men Get Lost in Shuffle at Start of Suffrage Parade," *Pittsburg Press*, May 3, 1914.
8 "Women Brave Sun and Heckling for Cause," *Pittsburgh Gazette Times*, May 3, 1914.
9 Ibid.
10 "Mere Men Get Lost in Shuffle at Start of Suffrage Parade," *Pittsburg Press*, May 3, 1914.
11 http://www.edwardianpromenade.com/fashion/wwi-wednesday-war-crinoline.
12 "Opposed to Suffrage Women Advertising," *Pittsburgh Post*, May 1, 1914.
13 "Antis Issue Statement on Eve of Parade," *Pittsburg Press*, May 2, 1914.
14 "Mere Men Get Lost in Shuffle at Start of Suffrage Parade," *Pittsburg Press*, May 3, 1914.
15 "Suffrage Day Cheers Women Who Ask Vote," *Pittsburgh Sunday Post*, May 3, 1914.
16 "Women Brave Sun and Heckling for Cause," *Pittsburgh Gazette Times*, May 3, 1914.
17 Ibid.
18 Ibid.
19 "Suffragist Paraders Thank City Officials," *Pittsburgh Post*, May 5, 1914.
20 Gertrude Gordon, "Mere Men Get Lost in Shuffle at Start of Suffrage Parade," *Pittsburg Press*, May 3, 1914.
21 "Parade of Suffrage Hosts Big Success," *Pittsburg Press*, May 3, 1914.
22 "Suffragists on Parade," *Pittsburgh Gazette Times*, May 4, 1914.
23 "Suffrage Day Cheers Women Who Ask Vote," *Pittsburgh Sunday Post*, May 3, 1914.
24 "Exclusive Moving Pictures," *Pittsburgh Gazette Times*, May 10, 1914.

Chapter 10 | Sacrifice and New Strategies
1 "Equal Franchise Federation," *Pittsburgh Daily Post*, May 26, 1914.
2 "Woman Suffrage," *Pittsburgh Sunday Post*, July 26, 1914.
3 "Equal Franchise Federation Leader Will Speak This Evening in Homestead," *Pittsburgh Post*, July 11, 1914, with large photo of Lucy.
4 "Orphans' Picnic Establishes New Success Record," *Pittsburg Press*, July 17, 1914.
5 "Democratic Platform Asserts Big Principles," *Pittsburgh Post*, June 4, 1914.
6 John R. Ball, "Bull Moosers Follow Leads on Democrats," *Pittsburgh Post*, June 5, 1914.
7 "Republican Committee Harmonizes," *Pittsburgh Post*, June 4, 1914.
8 "Suffragist Sacrifice to be Silver and Gold," *Pittsburgh Post*, July 26, 1914 and "Suffragists Ask Women to Give Trinkets," *Pittsburg Press*, July 26, 1914.
9 "Suffragists Ask Women to Give Trinkets," *Pittsburg Press*, July 26, 1914.
10 "Suffragists Give Up Personal Belongings," *Pittsburgh Post*, August 14, 1914; "Jewelry Oddities are Dropped into Suffrage Crucible," *Pittsburg Press*, August 14, 1914; "Suffrage Melting Pot Filling Up," *Pittsburg Press*, August 15, 1914 and "Suffragists to Hold 'Melting Pot Day,'" *Pittsburgh Daily Post*, April 2, 1915.
11 "Suffrage Melting Pot," *Pittsburgh Gazette Times*, April 2, 1915.
12 "Suffragists to Make Sacrifice for the Cause," *Pittsburg Press*, August 9, 1914.
13 "First Day of Exposition is Big Success" and "New Expo Feature Draws Big Crowds," *Pittsburgh Post*, September 3, 1914; "Women's Suffrage," *Pittsburgh Sunday Post*, September 6, 1914 and "Suffrage Booth Attracts Attention," *Pittsburgh Post*, September 9, 1914.
14 "Suffragists Will Give Prizes for Pupils' Best Essays," *Pittsburg Press*, September 15, 1914; "Prize Essay Contest on Woman Suffrage," *Pittsburgh Gazette Times*, September 15, 1914 and Sara Morris, "Equal Franchise Federation," letter to the editor, *Pittsburgh Post*, September 20, 1914.
15 "Peace Button Starts Wave of Enthusiasm," *Pittsburgh Gazette Times*, September 15, 1914.
16 "Women Urged Not to Talk Prohibition," *Pittsburgh Gazette Times*, November 22, 1914.

17 "Think Women's Votes Will End Warfare," *Pittsburg Press*, November 25, 1914 and "Suffrage Cause Non-Partisan," *Pittsburgh Gazette Times*, November 29, 1914.

18 "Pittsburghers Address Suffragist Gathering," *Pittsburgh Post*, November 23, 1914.

19 Agnes M. Scandrett, "Woman's Suffrage," *Pittsburgh Sunday Post*, November 29, 1914.

20 Letter from Woodrow Wilson to Mary M. Childs November 28, 1914, quoted in "Annoying the President," *Pittsburgh Post*, May 24, 1915.

21 "Suffrage Amendment Voted Down," *Pittsburgh Post*, January 13, 1915.

22 John R. Ball, "May Pass Bill on Suffrage This Evening," *Pittsburgh Post*, February 8, 1915.

23 "House to Vote Finally Today on Suffrage," *Pittsburgh Gazette Times*, February 8, 1915.

24 "Suffragists Link Valentine and Vote," *Pittsburgh Sunday Post*, February 14, 1915 and "Suffrage Valentines," *Pittsburg Press*, February 14, 1915.

25 "Woman Suffrage Bill Passes State Senate; Now Goes to Voters," *Pittsburgh Post*, March 16, 1915 and "People May Now Vote on Woman's Suffrage Here," *Pittsburg Press*, March 16, 1915.

26 "Worker Among Chinese Talks for Vote Here," *Pittsburgh Gazette Times*, April 7, 1915; "School Teachers to Hear Angel of Chinatown," *Pittsburgh Gazette Times*, April 10, 1915 and "Ballot Needed by Women to Save Sisters," *Pittsburgh Gazette Times*, April 11, 1915.

27 "Varied Reports of Progress Feature Suffrage Meeting," *Pittsburg Press*, May 25, 1915.

28 "Club Women Leave Field to Suffragists and 'Antis,'" *Pittsburgh Gazette Times*, July 25, 1915.

29 "Pittsburgh Girls Meet for Grand Council Fire in Schenley Park: Suffrage Activities," *Pittsburgh Gazette Times*, June 13, 1915 and "Men's Suffrage Party Plans to Back Up Women" and "Suffrage Campaign by Auto in Four States," *Pittsburg Press*, June 13, 1915.

30 Anna R. Stratton, "Senate Gave Signal Last Week for All-Summer Campaign for Suffrage," *Pittsburgh Gazette Times*, March 21, 1915.

31 Gertrude Gordon, "Suffragists Hear Dr. Shaw at Big Rally," *Pittsburg Press*, May 16, 1915.

32 "Vote Woman's Right Even If Unused," *Pittsburgh Gazette Times*, May 14, 1915, with photo of Anna Howard Shaw and Mrs. J. O. Miller; "World Peace is Predicted," *Pittsburgh Post*, May 14, 1915; "For Suffrage Even If Women Abandon Homes, Says Dr. Shaw," *Pittsburg Press*, May 14, 1915; "Suffragists Assemble at Town Meeting," *Pittsburgh Sunday Post*, May 16, 1915; Gertrude Gordon, "Suffragists Hear Dr. Shaw at Big Rally," *Pittsburg Press*, May 16, 1915 and "$2,500 Pledged for Suffrage Campaign," *Pittsburgh Gazette Times*, May 16, 1915.

33 "Suffragist Hosts Hold 'Rally Day,'" *Pittsburg Press*, May 1, 1915; "First Gun Fired in Suffrage Campaign," *Pittsburgh Gazette Times*, May 2, 1915 and "Suffragists Open Fight," *Pittsburgh Sunday Post*, May 2, 1915.

34 "Speakers Plead Woman Suffrage," *Pittsburg Press*, May 3, 1915.

35 "Chinese Girls are Recruits to Suffrage," *Pittsburgh Post*, April 28, 1915.

36 "Suffragists Plan Big Theater Party," *Pittsburgh Post*, May 6, 1915; "Suffragists Will See Nazimova in 'War Brides,'" *Pittsburg Press*, May 6, 1915 and "Suffragists Pay Homage to Nazimova," *Pittsburgh Gazette Times*, May 11, 1915.

37 "Gay Festival is Held for Suffrage," *Pittsburgh Gazette Times*, June 3, 1915 and "Suffrage Fete Draws Crowd," *Pittsburgh Post*, June 3, 1915.

38 "Gay Festival is Held for Suffrage," *Pittsburgh Gazette Times*, June 3, 1915.

39 "Suffrage Activities," *Pittsburgh Gazette Times*, May 23, 1915 and "Arrangements for Fete-Dansante at 'Cairncarque' Completed," *Pittsburgh Gazette Times*, May 30, 1915.

40 "To Show Women How to Cast Vote at 'Suff' Event," *Pittsburg Press*, May 29, 1915.

41 "Gay Festival is Held for Suffrage," *Pittsburgh Gazette Times*, June 3, 1915.

42 "Suffragets Plan Great Activities for 'The Cause,'" *Pittsburg Press*, March 31, 1915.

43 "Good Roads Move Enthuses Autoists; Suffragists to Aid," *Pittsburg Press*, May 21, 1915.

44 "Women are Striving for Farmers' Votes," *Pittsburgh Post*, March 9, 1915.

45 Lucy Kennedy Miller, speaking to the Pittsburg Commercial Club, June 11, 1915, quoted in "Mrs. Miller Urges Suffrage Cause," *Pittsburg Press*, June 11, 1915.

46 "Suffragist Preaches in Northside Pulpit," *Pittsburgh Post*, May 17, 1915.

47 "Senator Clapp Defends Votes for Women," *Pittsburgh Gazette Times*, May 18, 1915.

48 "Clash on Suffrage Enlivens Meeting of Women's Clubs," *Pittsburgh Post*, September 23, 1915.

49 "Nation-Wide Yellow Blooms for Suffrage," *Pittsburgh Gazette Times*, March 13, 1915.

50 "Women Plant Gardens for 'The Cause,'" *Pittsburgh Post*, April 2, 1915.

51 Ibid.

52 Ibid.

53 "Suffragets Plan Great Activities for 'The Cause,'" *Pittsburg Press*, March 31, 1915.

54   "Two Hundred Preachers Approve Women's Vote," *Pittsburgh Gazette Times*, May 10, 1915 and "200 'Votes for Women' Sermons Yesterday, *Pittsburg Press*, May 10, 1915.

55   "Activities of Suffragists," *Pittsburgh Sunday Post*, July 11, 1915.

56   Rev. James R. Cox of Epiphany Church, quoted in "Equal Franchise Not Contrary to Catholic Faith Says Priest," *Pittsburgh Sunday Post*, August 8, 1915. Cox was the first Catholic priest to receive a degree from the University of Pittsburgh, where he earned a master of economics degree in 1923.

57   "To Seek Man's Vote Through His Stomach," *Pittsburgh Post*, March 31, 1915.

58   *The Suffrage Cook Book*, compiled by Mrs. L. O. Kleber (Pittsburgh: The Equal Franchise Federation of Western Pennsylvania, 1915), 147.

59   Nina Martyris, "How Suffragists Used Cookbooks as a Recipe for Subversion," National Public Radio, November 5, 2015.

60   Andre Chevalier, "Trojan horse of the women of suffrage," Rare Books Digest, https://rarebooksdigest. com/2014/04/18/trojan-horse-of-the-women-of-suffrage.

61   *The Suffrage Cook Book*, 94.

62   *The Suffrage Cook Book*, 38.

63   "Suffrage Cook Book Will Boost 'Cause,'" *Pittsburgh Post*, March 13, 1915.

64   "Suffragists to Tour in Prairie Schooner," *Pittsburgh Post*, July 22, 1915.

65   "Woman's Liberty Bell Starts on Record Trip," *Indiana Weekly Messenger*, June 30, 1915.

66   "Movies Will Show the Suffrage Bell," *Altoona Tribune*, April 5, 1915 and Agnes M. Scandrett, "Silent Clapper on Bell Till Women Get Vote," *Pittsburgh Sunday Post*, June 7, 1914.

67   "Woman's Liberty Bell Starts on Record Trip," *Indiana Weekly Messenger*, June 30, 1915.

68   "Suffragists' Bell Starts Trip Muzzled," *Pittsburg Press*, June 23 1915.

69   "Woman's Liberty Bell Tongue-Tied," *Meyersdale Republic*, July 29, 1915.

70   "Bell is Met at Sewickley," *Pittsburgh Sunday Post*, July 4, 1915 and "Women's Liberty Bell is Welcomed to County," *Pittsburg Press*, July 4, 1915.

71   "Fourth is Fervid Rather Than Noisy," *Pittsburgh Gazette Times*, July 6, 1915.

72   "Silent Army of Suffrage Women March," *Pittsburgh Post*, July 6, 1915; "Silent Parade Features in Celebration," *Pittsburgh Gazette Times*, July 6, 1915 and "Pittsburgers Observe Fourth with Much Spirit" *Pittsburg Press*, July 6, 1915.

73   "Pittsburgers Observe Fourth with Much Spirit," *Pittsburg Press* July 6, 1915; "Silent Army of Suffrage Women March," *Pittsburgh Post*, July 6, 1915; "Fourth is Fervid Rather Than Noisy" and "Silent Parade Features in Celebration," *Pittsburgh Gazette Times*, July 6, 1915. Interestingly, the Equal Franchise Federation had applied to the city for a permit to put the pavilion inside the park, and when they were denied, Lucy wrote a letter of protest to the mayor. The approval stalled on its way through city council, and with smiles on their faces, the councilmen passed it . . . the day after the event. "City May Buy Police Auto," *Pittsburgh Post*, July 7, 1915.

74   "Personal Experiences," 6.

75   "Suffragists Ask Statement of Candidates," *Pittsburgh Gazette Times*, July 11, 1915; "Letter Issued to Candidates," *Pittsburgh Sunday Post*, July 11, 1915 and "Demand Views of Candidates on Suffrage," *Pittsburg Press*, July 11, 1915.

76   "Men Are Apportioned Among Suffragists," *Pittsburgh Post*, August 25, 1915; "Suffragists to Take 'Phone Ballot' Today," *Pittsburgh Post*, August 31, 1915; "Suffragists Take Ballot By Phone," *Pittsburgh Gazette Times*, September 1, 1915 and "'Phone Day' is Success," *Pittsburgh Post*, September 1, 1915.

77   Eliza J. Kennedy, "Women's Work Needed, Says Female Writer," *Pittsburg Press*, July 9, 1915.

78   "Junior Anti Suffragists Will Entertain Hundreds," *Pittsburgh Gazette Times*, May 26, 1915.

79   "Child Labor Law Here Best Yet, Antis Say," *Pittsburg Press*, May 9, 1915 and "'Anti' Writer Assails Record Made by Women," *Pittsburg Press*, September 12, 1915.

80   Mrs. Karl Warmcastle, "Anti Says Women Don't Want Vote," *Pittsburg Daily Post*, October 3, 1915 and "Says Suffrage Agitation is a Minority Idea," *Pittsburg Press*, October 3, 1915.

81   "Don't Want to Vote and Are Ready to Tell Why" and "Pittsburgh Women Who Are Opposed to Equal Suffrage," *Pittsburgh Gazette Times*, January 19, 1913.

82   "Anti-Suffrage Speaker Will Not Debate Issue," *Pittsburgh Gazette Times*, October 10, 1915.

83   "Suffragist Speakers at Moose Carnival," *Pittsburgh Post*, June 24, 1915.

Chapter 11 | Eleventh Inning Pitches for Suffrage

1   "Local Suffragists to Welcome Pirates," *Pittsburg Press*, July 13, 1915.

2   "Fred Clarke Champions Woman Suffrage Cause," *Pittsburgh Sunday Post*, July 11, 1915.

3 "Balloons Carry Admittance to Baseball Game," *Pittsburgh Gazette Times*, September 15, 1915.

4 "Suffrage Balloons to Carry Tickets," *Pittsburgh Post*, September 14, 1915.

5 "Prominent Men Buy Boxes for Suffrage Ball Game," *Pittsburgh Gazette Times*, September 16, 1915.

6 "Suffragists Will Call on Corsairs," *Pittsburg Press*, August 11, 1915.

7 "Suffragists See Pirates Lose, 8-4," *Pittsburgh Gazette Times*, September 17, 1915 and "Giants Register Cluster of Runs on Suffrage Day," *Pittsburgh Post*, September 17, 1915.

8 "Personal Experiences." For more on the Antler Hotel, see "Fire Damage is $100,000," *Pittsburgh Gazette Times*, February 21, 1910.

9 "Suffragists Open Arcade in Old Antler," *Pittsburgh Gazette Times*, September 26, 1915; "Artists Compete at Suffrage Headquarters," *Pittsburg Press*, September 25, 1915 and "New Suffrage Headquarters Open," *Pittsburgh Sunday Post*, September 26, 1915.

10 "Suffragists Will Open New Home," *Pittsburgh Post*, September 24, 1915 and "Poster Contest to Be Part of Suffrage Housewarming," *Pittsburgh Gazette Times*, September 24, 1915.

11 "Suffragists Open Arcade in Old Antler," *Pittsburgh Gazette Times*, September 26, 1915.

12 Ibid.

13 The Carnegie Institute, *Annual Report* (Pittsburgh: The Carnegie Institute, 1915).

14 http://artcontrarian.blogspot.com/2017/12/porter-woodruff-neglected-vogue.html, accessed 2/6/2020.

15 "Bishop Says Man Must Share Vote," *Pittsburgh Gazette Times*, October 1, 1915.

16 "Favors Women Voting," *Pittsburg Press*, October 6, 1915 and "Wilson for Suffrage; Elation and Gloom Felt in Pittsburgh," *Pittsburgh Gazette Times*, October 7, 1915.

17 *Digest of the General Ordinances and Laws of the City of Pittsburgh* (Pittsburgh: Authority of the Mayor and the City Council, 1938), 851–852.

18 "Personal Experiences," 7.

19 The speeches in this chapter are excerpted from Alice Stone Blackwell's "Objections Answered," printed by the Pennsylvania Woman Suffrage Association in 1914. The thirty-seven-page booklet was small enough to be carried anywhere, even tucking neatly into a proper lady's diminutive evening bag.

20 Baseball accounts were derived from baseball-almanac.com, golden rankings.com, and sabr.org.

21 The Braves were reportedly returning a favor by offering their big new stadium to the Red Sox. The Red Sox had allowed the Braves to use their new Fenway Park in 1914 while the Braves' new ballpark was being built.

22 "Personal Experiences," 7. The phrase "Roman Holiday" was a metaphor derived from the poet Byron's description in *Childe Harold's Pilgrimage* (1812–1818) of gladiators fighting to the death for the amusement of spectators: "butchered to make a Roman holiday." Other suffragists who made pitches included Lola Walker, Helen Allen, and Myra Johns.

Chapter 12 | A Pivotal Vote

1 Gertrude Gordon, "Real Suffrage Fight Starts Here Tomorrow," *Pittsburg Press*, October 10, 1915; "Women Will Demonstrate Suffrage Cause by Parade," *Pittsburgh Gazette Times*, October 10, 1915 and "Suffragists Will Parade," *Pittsburgh Sunday Post*, October 10, 1915.

2 "Pageant Today to Aid Equal Suffrage," *Pittsburgh Gazette Times*, October 16, 1915; "Equal Suffrage Message Impressed on Pittsburgh by Huge Pageant of Workers," *Pittsburgh Gazette Times*, October 17, 1915; "Suffragists Are Encouraged by Parade," *Pittsburgh Gazette Times*, October 18, 1915; "7,000 Women in Procession for Suffrage," *Pittsburgh Sunday Post*, October 17, 1915 and Gertrude Gordon, "Throngs Witness Fair Sex Pageant," *Pittsburg Press*, October 17, 1915.

3 Gertrude Gordon, "Suffragists and Antis Clash at Club Luncheon," *Pittsburg Press*, October 18, 1915.

4 Gertrude Gordon, "Both Sides Even More Active in Suffrage Fight," *Pittsburg Press*, October 22, 1915.

5 Gertrude Gordon, "Leading Antis of the East to be Heard Here," *Pittsburg Press*, October 25, 1915.

6 "New Jersey Refuses Women Vote," *Pittsburgh Gazette Times*, October 20, 1915.

7 Gertrude Gordon, "Suffragists Undaunted by Jersey's Vote," *Pittsburg Press*, October 20, 1915.

8 "Antis Rejoice; Suffragists Determined," *Pittsburgh Gazette Times*, October 21, 1915.

9 "Trying to Fix Responsibility for Disaster," *Pittsburg Press*, October 26, 1915.

10 Gertrude Gordon, "Tragedy Stirs Suffrage and 'Anti' Workers," *Pittsburg Press*, October 26, 1915.

11 "Suffragist Cites Fire as an Appeal," *Pittsburgh Post*, October 26, 1915.

12 Gertrude Gordon, "Ministers Will Pray for Woman Suffrage Cause," *Pittsburg Press*, October 28, 1915 and "Supplication for Suffrage Will be Heard from Pulpits," *Pittsburgh Post*, October 28, 1915.

13 "Plea at Polls Will Be Made for Suffrage," *Pittsburgh Daily Post*, November 2, 1915.

14 "Women End Fight Today," *Pittsburgh Post*, November 1, 1915.

15 "Active Advocates of Suffrage for Pennsylvania Women—Their Reasons Tersely Told," *Pittsburgh Gazette Times*, October 31, 1915.

16 Gertrude Gordon, "Fight for Suffrage Nears End," *Pittsburg Press*, October 31, 1915; Julia Morgan Harding, "Antis Confident of Victory in Vote Fight," *Pittsburgh Gazette Times*, October 31, 1915 and Julia Morgan Harding, "'Anti' Reviews Votes' Issues," *Pittsburgh Sunday Post*, October 31, 1915.

17 Mary L. Hay, "Tax Figures of Antis Termed Fallacies," *Pittsburgh Gazette Times*, October 31, 1915.

18 "Suffrage Now with the Jury, Says Leader," *Pittsburgh Sunday Post*, October 31, 1915.

19 "A Prize for You in Pickering's Popular Woman's Suffrage Contest!" *Pittsburgh Sunday Post*, October 24, 1915.

20 "Plea at Polls Will be Made for Suffrage," *Pittsburgh Post*, November 2, 1915.

21 "Personal Experiences," 10.

22 Ibid.

23 "Women Attain 'Equality' at the Polls—Eat Lunch with Election Officers" and "Trick Rouses Suffragist Leaders' Ire," *Pittsburgh Daily Post*, November 3, 1915.

24 Gertrude Gordon, "Suffragists Working Hard at the Polls," *Pittsburg Press*, November 2, 1915.

25 The *Bankers' Magazine, The Banker's Magazine and Statistical Register*, Vol. 49: From July to November, 1894, Inclusive (Reproduced by Forgotten Books, 2017).

26 "New Machines Expedite Tabulating Election Returns," *Pittsburgh Gazette Times*, November 3, 1915.

27 "Personal Experiences," 10.

28 "Allegheny County Gives Majority for Suffrage; State Defeat Conceded," *Pittsburgh Gazette Times*, November 4, 1915.

29 "Women are Hopeful as Returns Come In," *Pittsburgh Gazette Times*, November 3, 1915.

30 Exact election results vary considerably by source, but all agree that it was a landslide for the anti-suffragists.

31 "Women Charge Fraud in Many Districts" and "Women Hopeful As Returns Come In," *Pittsburgh Gazette Times*, November 3, 1915.

32 "Suffragists Working Hard at the Polls," *Pittsburg Press*, November 2, 1915.

33 "Women Charge Fraud in Many Districts," *Pittsburgh Gazette Times*, November 3, 1915.

34 "Election Case Acquittals," *Pittsburgh Post*, January 20, 1916.

35 "Praise County for Suffrage Might Shown," *Pittsburgh Gazette Times*, November 14, 1915.

36 legis.state.pa.us.

37 "Woman's Cause is Defeated," *Pittsburg Press*, November 3, 1915.

38 Ibid.

39 "'Suffrage Not Defeated—Only Postponed,' Says Mrs. Roessing," *Pittsburgh Post*, November 4, 1915 and "Suffragists Rejoicing at Showing Made," *Pittsburg Press*, November 4, 1915.

40 "Woman's Suffrage Defeats," *Pittsburgh Gazette Times*, November 4, 1915.

41 "Personal Experiences," 11.

Chapter 13 | Time Out for Love and Marriage

1 Letter, R. Templeton Smith to Eliza Kennedy, June 8, 1914.

2 Letter, Eliza Jane Kennedy to R. Templeton Smith, July 18, 1914.

3 Letter, R. Templeton Smith to Eliza Jane Kennedy, c. July 23, 1914.

4 Letter, Eliza Jane Kennedy to R. Templeton Smith, undated, summer 1914.

5 Letter, Eliza Jane Kennedy to R. Templeton Smith, July 31, 1915.

6 Letter, Eliza Jane Kennedy to R. Templeton Smith, c. October 9, 1915.

7 Letter, Eliza Jane Kennedy to R. Templeton Smith, c. July 2, 1914.

8 Letter, Eliza Jane Kennedy to R. Templeton Smith, c. July 22, 1914.

9 Letter, Eliza Jane Kennedy to R. Templeton Smith, c. January 28, 1915.

10 Letter, Eliza Jane Kennedy to R. Templeton Smith, c. September 1, 1915.

11 Letter, R. Templeton Smith to Eliza Jane Kennedy, c. June 17, 1914.

12 Letter, R. Templeton Smith to Eliza Jane Kennedy, c. June 18, 1914.

13 Letter, R. Templeton Smith to Eliza Jane Kennedy, c. July 23, 1914.

14 Letter, Eliza Jane Kennedy to R. Templeton Smith, c. June 15, 1914.

15 Letter, Eliza Jane Kennedy to R. Templeton Smith, c. July 14, 1914.

16 Letter, Eliza Jane Kennedy to R. Templeton Smith, c. July 13, 1914.

17 Letter, R. Templeton Smith to Eliza Jane Kennedy, c. June 17, 1914.

18 Letter, Eliza Kennedy to R. Templeton Smith, October 6, 1915.

19 Letter, R. Templeton Smith to Eliza Kennedy, 1915.

20   Letter, Eliza Jane Kennedy to R. Templeton Smith, c. January 25, 1915.
21   Letter, Eliza Jane Kennedy to R. Templeton Smith, c. January 27, 1915.
22   Letter, R. Templeton Smith to Eliza Jane Kennedy, c. June 17, 1914.
23   Letter, Eliza Jane Kennedy to R. Templeton Smith, c. July 25, 1914.
24   Letter, Eliza Jane Kennedy to R. Templeton Smith, c. August 11, 1915.
25   Letter, Eliza Jane Kennedy to R. Templeton Smith, c. July 18, 1915.
26   Letter, Eliza Jane Kennedy to R. Templeton Smith, c. July 29, 1915.
27   Ibid.
28   Letter, Eliza Jane Kennedy to R. Templeton Smith, c. August 11, 1915.
29   Letter, Eliza Jane Kennedy to R. Templeton Smith, c. October 6, 1915.
30   Letter, R. Templeton Smith to Eliza Jane Kennedy, c. October 7, 1915.
31   Letter, R. Templeton Smith to Eliza Jane Kennedy, October 13, 1915.
32   Letter, Eliza Jane Kennedy to R. Templeton Smith, c. July 27, 1915.

Chapter 14 | New Game Plans in the Wake of Defeat
1   "Suffragist to Celebrate Victory Here," *Pittsburgh Gazette Times*, November 11, 1915; "Suffrage Party to Hold
     Victory Celebration Tonight," *Pittsburgh Gazette Times*, November 13, 1915; "Local Suffragists to Celebrate
     on Saturday," *Pittsburg Press*, November 11, 1915 and "Elated Suffragists Plan Celebration," *Pittsburgh Post*,
     November 11, 1915.
2   "Post-Election Meeting Held," *Pittsburgh Post*, November 14, 1915.
3   Gertrude Gordon, "Triumph and Hope Feature Suffrage Rally," *Pittsburg Press*, November 14, 1915.
4   "Suffragists Find Way to Press Fight," *Pittsburg Press*, November 5, 1915 and "Suffragists May Make Fight Through
     New Channel," *Pittsburgh Gazette Times*, November 6, 1915.
5   "Dr. Shaw Quits Presidency of Suffragists," *Pittsburgh Gazette Times*, November 22, 1915 and "Dr. Shaw Will Quit
     as Leader," *Pittsburgh Post*, November 22, 1915.
6   Grace Phelps, "Pittsburghers Made Officers by Suffragets," *Pittsburgh Post*, December 18, 1915.
7   "Suffragists Urge Amendment—Mrs. Catt Makes an Appeal—Scores Lukewarm Enthusiasm," *Pittsburgh Post*,
     February 25, 1916.
8   The convention was held December 14–19, 1915. "Suffragists to Plan New Campaign for Amendment," *Pittsburgh
     Gazette Times*, November 29, 1915.
9   "The Row Among the Suffragists," *Pittsburg Press*, December 3, 1915.
10   Grace Phelps, "Pittsburghers Made Officers by Suffragets," *Pittsburgh Post*, December 18, 1915 and "Life Annuity
     May be Given Anna Shaw," *Pittsburgh Gazette Times*, December 18, 1915.
11   "Suffrage Slate Passes Amid Protests," *Pittsburgh Gazette Times*, December 1, 1915 and "Mrs. Orlady Heads State
     Suffragists," *Pittsburgh Post*, December 1, 1915.
12   "Mrs. Miller Denies Break of Suffragists," *Pittsburgh Gazette Times*, December 3, 1915.
13   "Wilson Gives Comfort to Suffragists; Will Consider Their Cause," *Pittsburgh Gazette Times*, December 7, 1915.
14   "Women Suffragists Get Demand Before Congress," *Pittsburgh Post*, December 7, 1915.
15   "Women Ask Democracy to Back Ballot," *Pittsburgh Post*, December 8, 1915.
16   "Anti-Suffrage Women Gather," *Pittsburgh Post*, December 14, 1915.
17   "Civic Club of Wilkinsburg," *Pittsburgh Sunday Post*, March 5, 1916.
18   "Setback for Suffrage and Prohibition," *Pittsburg Press*, March 29, 1916.
19   John A. Matthews and Alice Hill Chittenden, quoted in "'Antis' Prepare for New Fight," *Pittsburgh Sunday Post*,
     January 16, 1916; Gertrude Gordon, "Anti-Suffrage Forces Join in Luncheon Here," *Pittsburg Press*, January 16,
     1916 and "Anti Suffrage Leaders Urge Preparation," *Pittsburgh Gazette Times*, January 16, 1916.
20   "Preparedness and First Aid Win Time of Pittsburgh Women," *Pittsburgh Post*, February 17, 1916.
21   "Suffragist in Discussion of Preparedness," *Pittsburg Press*, February 14, 1916; "Preparedness Passe in Suffrage
     Party," *Pittsburgh Post*, February 15 1916 and "Club Observes Anniversary with Valentine Luncheon," *Pittsburgh
     Gazette Times*, February 15, 1916.
22   "Women Open War Chest for Election of Men Favorable to the Cause," *Pittsburgh Gazette Times*, March 9, 1916.
23   "Suffragists to Keep up Struggle," *Pittsburg Press*, February 22, 1916.
24   "State Appointment Received by Pittsburgh Suffragist," *Pittsburgh Gazette Times*, April 5, 1916.
25   "Great Throngs Crowd the Big Pure Food Show," *Pittsburg Press*, February 21, 1916.
26   Gertrude Gordon, "New Faith in Men, Says Pankhurst," *Pittsburg Press*, April 30, 1916; "Suffrage Dinner to
     Launch Bread-and-Butter Club," *Pittsburgh Post*, April 24, 1916 and "Mrs. Pankhurst Talks to 1,000," *Pittsburgh
     Sunday Post*, April 30, 1916.

27 Gertrude Gordon, "New Faith in Men, Says Pankhurst," *Pittsburg Press*, April 30, 1916; "Suffrage Dinner to Launch Bread-and-Butter Club," *Pittsburgh Post*, April 24,1916 and "Mrs. Pankhurst Talks to 1,000," *Pittsburgh Sunday Post*, April 30, 1916.

28 "The Suffragists' Bon-Bon Campaign," *Pittsburg Press*, May 6, 1916.

29 "Suffragists Urge Amendment Passage," *Pittsburgh Post*, May 17, 1916 and "Suffrage Tour of Nation Ends in Washington," *Pittsburgh Gazette Times*, May 17, 1916.

30 "Suffragist Chief Attacks Congress," *Pittsburgh Post*, May 11, 1916 and "Half Congress 'Owned,' Says Suffrage Chief," *Pittsburgh Gazette Times*, May 11, 1916.

31 "Suffrage Delegates May 'Bunk' on Boats," *Pittsburgh Post*, April 26, 1916 and "Suffragists Hurry Around Looking for 30,000 Good Beds," *Pittsburg Press*, May 10, 1916.

32 "Suffragists to Sell 'Second Best' Shoes," *Pittsburg Press*, May 7, 1916 and "Suffragists to Sell Shoes to Aid Cause," *Pittsburgh Post*, May 6, 1916.

33 "Equal Franchise Federation Elects," *Pittsburgh Post*, May 23, 1916 and "Suffragists Re-elect Head at Annual Business Session," *Pittsburgh Gazette Times*, May 23, 1916.

34 "Local Suffragets Leave Tonight for G.O.P. Convention," *Pittsburg Press*, June 5, 1916; "Suffragists Arrange Farewell to Delegates," *Pittsburg Post*, June 5, 1916 and "Suffragists Go Tonight," *Pittsburgh Gazette Times*, June 5, 1916.

35 "Thousands Will Be in Chicago for Conventions," *Pittsburg Press*, May 15, 1916.

36 Carrie Chapman Catt and Nettie Rogers Shuler, *Woman Suffrage and Politics: The Inner Story of the Suffrage Movement* (New York: Charles Scribner's Sons, 1923; reprinted by Dover, 2020), 240–241; "Woman's Party Makes Threat of Enmity," *Pittsburgh Gazette Times*, June 7, 1916 and "Pennsylvania Suffragists Parading in the Chicago Downpour," *Pittsburgh Gazette Times*, June 9, 1916.

37 "Women Frame Suffrage Plea to Convention," *Pittsburgh Post*, June 7, 1916.

38 "Women Heckle and Ridicule Party Leaders," *Chicago Tribune*, June 7, 1916.

39 Catt and Shuler, 240–241.

40 "Huge Suffragist Parade to Urge Action by G.O.P.," *Pittsburg Press*, June 4, 1916; "Women Arrive in G.O.P. Camp to Push Cause," *Pittsburgh Post*, June 5, 1916; Frederic J. Haskin, "The Woman's Party," *Pittsburgh Gazette Times*, June 5, 1916 and "Two Factions of Suffragists in Battle for Vote," *Pittsburg Press*, June 5 1916.

41 "Personal Experiences," part 2, 1. *See also* "Suffragists Ready for Chicago Meeting," *Pittsburg Press*, June 4, 1916 and "Suffragists Select Traveling Frocks for Chicago Parade," *Pittsburgh Sunday Post*, June 4, 1916.

42 George Morris, "Parade Avenue in Downpour for the Ballot," "Suffrage Army Storms G.O.P. Fort" and "G.O.P. Committee Hears 3 Sides of Suffrage Issue," *Chicago Tribune*, June 8, 1916.

43 "Suffragets a Game Crew—March in Rain and Slop—Storm Coliseum," *Chicago Day Book*, June 8, 1916.

44 "Personal Experiences," part 2, 1.

45 John B. Townley, "Suffragists from Keystone State Are Doing Share," *Pittsburg Press*, June 7, 1916 and "Suffragists Ready for Chicago Meeting," *Pittsburg Press*, June 4, 1916.

46 "Local Suffragets Leave Tonight for G.O.P. Convention," *Pittsburg Press*, June 5, 1916.

47 "Elephants Are Rehearsed to March for Suffragists," *Pittsburgh Post*, May 12, 1916 and George Morris, "Parade Avenue in Downpour for the Ballot," *Chicago Daily Tribune*, June 8, 1916.

48 "Suffragists to Have Animals as Mascots," *Pittsburgh Sunday Post*, May 21, 1916 and "Animal Mascot for Each State in Vote Parade," *Chicago Tribune*, May 20, 1916.

49 "Parrot Won't Say 'Votes for Women,' So It Loses Its Job," *Pittsburgh Sunday Post*, May 28, 1916 and "This Parrot is One Anti-Feminist Bird," *Pittsburg Press*, June 7, 1916, with photo.

50 "Convention Side Lights," *Pittsburg Press*, June 8, 1916.

51 Catt and Shuler, 243 and Walter J. Christy, "Parley May Turn to Knox to Lead Party," *Pittsburgh Gazette Times*, June 9, 1916.

52 "Suffrage Plank Displeases New Party," *Pittsburgh Gazette Times*, June 9, 1916.

53 Catt and Shuler, 243 and "Text of Progressive Party Platform," *Pittsburgh Gazette Times*, June 9, 1916.

54 "Democrats Seek to Swing Moose Over to Wilson," *Pittsburgh Post*, June 13, 1916.

55 Catt and Shuler, 243 and "Prospects for Plank Elate Suffragists," *Pittsburgh Post*, June 15, 1916.

56 "Warm Fight Over Suffrage is Expected," *Pittsburgh Gazette Times*, June 12, 1916; George Martin, "Suffragists' Uniforms Make Fearful Noise" and John B. Townley, "G.O.P. Ticket Disappoints Democrats," *Pittsburg Press*, June 12, 1916; "Local Woman Leads Fight for Suffrage," *Pittsburgh Gazette Times*, June 13, 1916 and "Women's Mute Plea for Vote Effective," *Pittsburgh Gazette Times*, June 15, 1916.

57 "Suffragists Declare Plank Is Inadequate" and "Convention Ends Adopting Suffrage Plank After Fight," *Pittsburgh*

Post, June 17, 1916. For the entire platform, see "Suffrage Plank Is Inserted in Wilson Platform," *Pittsburgh Gazette Times*, June 17, 1916.

58   "Women Suffragists to Wage Vigorous War on Wilson and Democracy," *Pittsburgh Gazette Times*, June 17, 1916.

59   "Suffragists Will Heckle Candidates for Congress," *Pittsburgh Gazette Times*, August 7, 1916.

60   "70 Congress Candidates Claimed by Suffragists," *Pittsburgh Gazette Times*, October 21, 1916.

61   Iva I. Rowley, "600 Suffragists Gather Near Somerset," *Pittsburgh Gazette Times*, July 8, 1916; "Suffrage Meeting," *Pittsburgh Sunday Post*, July 2, 1916 and "Suffragists Receive New Emblem," *Pittsburgh Post*, July 7, 1916.

62   "Busy Schedule for Suffragists," *Pittsburgh Sunday Post*, September 3, 1916.

63   "Women Enter Paralysis Fight," *Pittsburgh Sunday Post*, July 16, 1916.

64   "Local Suffragists Will Help in Fight Against Scourge," *Pittsburg Press*, July 16, 1916; "Suffragists to Aid Babies," *Pittsburgh Gazette Times*, July 16, 1916; "Women Enter Paralysis Fight," *Pittsburgh Sunday Post*, July 16, 1916; "Suffragists to Help in Fight Against Plague," *Pittsburg Press*, August 1, 1916; "Mothers Reached in Plague Fight," *Pittsburg Press*, August 16, 1916; "Suffragists Wage Fight on Paralysis," *Pittsburgh Gazette Times*, August 2, 1916; "Women to Wage War on Refuse," *Pittsburgh Post*, August 8, 1916; "Child Travel Expected to Cease Today," *Pittsburgh Gazette Times*, August 20, 1916 and "Many Paralysis Cases in State," *Pittsburgh Post*, August 20, 1916.

65   "Council is Told of City's Filth," *Pittsburgh Post*, September 30, 1916.

66   "Suffragists Offer Tobacco to Soldiers," *Pittsburgh Gazette Times*, July 18, 1916; "Suffragists Send Tobacco to Soldiers Off for Front," *Pittsburgh Gazette Times*, July 19, 1916 and "Suffragists Pack Tobacco for Soldiers on Border," *Pittsburgh Post*, July 18, 1916.

67   "Suffragists to Open Voting Booth at Expo," *Pittsburg Press*, September 24, 1916 and "Iva I. Rowley, "Philadelphia, Pa., to Have Federation's Annual Meeting," *Pittsburgh Gazette Times*, September 24, 1916.

68   "Straw Vote Taken by Suffragists," *Pittsburg Press*, October 6, 1916; "Hughes Leads in Voting; Big Majority for Suffrage," *Pittsburgh Gazette Times*, October 31, 1916 and "Guffey Leaves for Conference," *Pittsburgh Post*, October 31, 1916.

69   "Hughes Opens Republican Campaign Here," *Pittsburgh Post*, September 28, 1916.

70   "Suffragists Will Attend Auto Show," *Pittsburg Press*, October 17, 1916.

71   "Suffragists Call Special Convention for September," *Pittsburg Press*, July 2, 1916; "Suffrage Crisis Cause of Meet," *Pittsburgh Sunday Post*, July 2, 1916 and "Women Are Doing Their Part to Aid Troop Mobilization," *Pittsburgh Gazette Times*, July 2, 1916.

72   "Busy Schedule for Suffragists," *Pittsburgh Sunday Post*, September 3, 1916 and "Local Suffragists to Attend National Convention Sept. 6," *Pittsburg Press*, September 3, 1916.

73   Jacqueline Van Voris, *Carrie Chapman Catt: A Public Life* (New York: The Feminist Press at The City University of New York, 1987), 142–152; "Suffragists Won't Indorse Any Party, Women Have Decided," *Pittsburg Press*, September 6, 1916; "Suffragists to Continue Dual Fight," *Pittsburgh Gazette Times*, September 7, 1916; "Plan to Hedge Suffrage Fight Is Voted Down," *Pittsburgh Post*, September 7, 1916; "New Campaign Plans Adopted by Suffragists," *Pittsburgh Post*, September 8, 1916; "Suffragists Adopt Plan of Campaign," *Pittsburgh Gazette Times*, September 8, 1916; "Suffragists to Avoid Party Alliances," *Pittsburgh Gazette Times*, September 10, 1916; "Suffragists Ready for Final Victory," *Pittsburg Press*, September 17, 1916; Iva I. Rowley, "Mrs. J. O. Miller Gives Resume of National Suffrage Meeting," *Pittsburgh Gazette Times*, September 17, 1916 and "Suffragists Paint Victory on Expo Map," *Pittsburg Press*, September 18, 1916.

74   "Suffrage Will Come After War, Mrs. Catt Says," *Pittsburg Press*, September 7, 1916; "New Campaign Plans Adopted by Suffragists," *Pittsburgh Post*, September 8, 1916 and "Suffragists Adopt Plan of Campaign," *Pittsburgh Gazette Times*, September 8, 1916. Catt's full speech in the *Gazette Times* is worthy of a closer look.

75   "Suffragists Called to State Gathering," *Pittsburgh Post*, November 3, 1916 and Gertrude Gordon, "Suffragists Work at Polls; Feel Sure Cause Will Win Out," *Pittsburg Press*, November 7, 1916.

76   Gertrude Gordon, "Suffragists Work at Polls; Feel Sure Cause Will Win Out," *Pittsburg Press*, November 7, 1916.

77   Advertising Notice, Winifred Meek Morris Papers and Photographs, Detre Library & Archives, Senator John Heinz History Center, Pittsburgh, PA.

78   List compiled from handwritten notes and *Pittsburgh Gazette Times* report, November 11, 1916. Winifred Barron Meek Morris Papers and Photographs, Detre Library and Archives Division, Senator John Heinz History Center, Pittsburgh, PA.

79   "3,000 Attend Suffrage Shirt Waist Ball," *Pittsburgh Gazette Times*, November 11, 1916; "Suffragists Hold Shirtwaist Ball; 3,000 Persons Attend," *Pittsburg Press*, November 11, 1916 and "Suffragists Revel at Shirtwaist Ball," *Pittsburgh Post*, November 11, 1916.

80   "3,000 Attend Suffrage Shirt Waist Ball," *Pittsburgh Gazette Times*, November 11, 1916.

81   Ibid.

82 "Suffragists Revel at Shirtwaist Ball," *Pittsburgh Post*, November 11, 1916.

83 "'Ballots for Both,' Suffrage Slogan Now," *Pittsburg Press*, November 13, 1916; "'Ballots for Both' New Suffrage Slogan," *Pittsburgh Post*, November 14, 1916 and "'Ballots for Both' New Slogan for Suffragists," *Pittsburgh Gazette Times*, November 14, 1916.

84 "Suffragets [sic] Condemn Heckling of Wilson," *Pittsburgh Post*, December 14, 1916.

Chapter 15 | Warriors on the Home Front

1 "Women Greet Congress with Suffrage Plea," *Pittsburgh Gazette Times*, January 2, 1917.

2 Robert P. J. Cooney Jr., *Winning the Vote: The Triumph of the American Woman Suffrage Movement* (Santa Cruz, CA: American Graphic Press, 2005), 320.

3 "Suffragists Disown White House Pickets," *Pittsburgh Post*, January 17, 1917 and "Says Suffragists Oppose Militancy," *Pittsburg Press*, January 17, 1917.

4 "Penna. Suffragists Are Not Sympathetic Toward Picketers," *Pittsburg Press*, January 26, 1917.

5 "Suffragists Are Confident Present Lawmakers Will Act," *Pittsburg Press*, January 26, 1917.

6 "Personal Experiences," 13.

7 "Suffragists Are Ready to Give Aid in Event of War," *Pittsburg Press*, February 5, 1917.

8 "State Suffragists Offer Wilson Aid," *Pittsburgh Sunday Post*, February 18, 1917.

9 "Suffragists Will Organize for War Duty," *Pittsburgh Post*, February 26, 1917.

10 "Women Organize to Aid in Successful War," *Pittsburgh Gazette Times*, March 25, 1917.

11 "Demonstration by Suffragists Out [?] Under Ban," *Pittsburgh Gazette Times*, January 1, 1917.

12 "Our First Congresswoman," *Pittsburg Press*, December 10, 1916.

13 "First Congresswoman Good Cook; Trims Her Own Hats," *Pittsburgh Gazette Times*, November 11, 1916.

14 "Woman Wins Election to Congress, First to Gain This Honor," *Pittsburg Press*, November 11, 1916. *See also* Cooney, *Winning the Vote*, 327–328.

15 "Miss Rankin's Installation in Congress Made Ceremony," *Pittsburgh Daily Post*, April 3, 1917.

16 "Miss Jeannette Rankin Praised and Censured for Voting 'No,'" *Pittsburgh Post*, April 7, 1917.

17 "Suffragists Say President is Big Obstacle," *Pittsburg Press*, February 26, 1917.

18 "Banners Carried by Suffragists Ruined by Mob," *Pittsburg Press*, June 20, 1917 and "Crowd Resents Suffrage Slurs at White House," *Pittsburgh Post*, June 21, 1917.

19 "Suffrage Disposed Of, Antis Take to Knitting," *Pittsburg Press*, July 14, 1917.

20 "Suffragists Resume Duty on Picket Line," *Pittsburgh Gazette Times*, July 22, 1917.

21 "Militants Are Egged and Banners Wrecked by Crowds in Capital," *Pittsburgh Post*, August 15, 1917; "Mob Pelts William Bayard Hale for Defending Suffrage Pickets," *Pittsburgh Post*, August 16, 1917; "Capital Police Tear Banners from Hands of Suffragists," *Pittsburgh Post*, August 17, 1917; "Six More Suffragists Arrested After Ignoring Police Order," *Pittsburgh Post*, August 18, 1917; "Senate Bill Aims to Keep Militants from White House," *Pittsburg Press*, August 19, 1917; "Suffragist Prisoners to Do 'Bit' Today in Garden of Workhouse," *Pittsburgh Post*, August 20, 1917; "Suffragist Pickets Are Granted Appeals," *Pittsburgh Post*, August 28, 1917; "Suffragists Facing One Year in Jail," *Pittsburgh Post*, October 22, 1917; "50 Suffrage Flags Destroyed by Crowds at White House," *Pittsburgh Gazette Times*, August 16, 1917; "Capital Police Destroy 'Kaiser Wilson' Banners," *Pittsburgh Gazette Times*, August 17, 1917; "Hopkins Pleads for Suffragists," *Pittsburgh Gazette Times*, August 22, 1917; "Ten Suffragists Fined, *Pittsburgh Gazette Times*, August 30, 1917; "41 Suffragists Under Arrest for Picketing," *Pittsburgh Gazette Times*, November 11, 1917; "Suffragists Rearrested in Second Raid," *Pittsburgh Gazette Times*, November 13, 1917 and "22 Suffragists Ejected from District Jail," *Pittsburgh Post*, November 28, 1917.

22 "Suffrage Leader Forcibly Fed by Washington Prison Doctor," *Pittsburgh Gazette Times*, November 9, 1917 and "Wilson Holds Old Opinion of Suffrage," *Pittsburgh Gazette Times*, November 10, 1917.

23 "Discrediting a Worthy Cause," *Pittsburgh Post*, June 23, 1917; "The War and the Suffragists," *Pittsburg Press*, June 23, 1917 and Cooney, *Winning the Vote*, 345–363.

24 "House Votes Today on Suffrage Bill," *Pittsburgh Post*, April 17, 1917.

25 "House Defeats Suffrage Bill; Vote 101 to 94," *Pittsburgh Post*, April 18, 1917.

26 "Suffragists to Seek Vote on President," *Pittsburgh Post*, April 19, 1917.

27 "Suffragists Routed in Their Last Stand," *Pittsburg Press*, May 29, 1917 and "Legislators to Quit Today Until June 6," *Pittsburgh Post*, May 29, 1917.

28 "Suffragists to Seek Vote on President," *Pittsburgh Post*, April 19, 1917.

29 "Suffragists for Gardening and Canning and Cooking," *Pittsburgh Sunday Post*, June 3, 1917; "Schools to Teach Cooking Economy," *Pittsburgh Post*, June 11, 1917 and "War Cry of Feed 'Em Song for Gardeners, *Pittsburgh Press*, June 17, 1917.

30   "Personal Experiences," 15.

31   "Suffragists for Gardening and Canning and Cooking," *Pittsburgh Sunday Post*, June 3, 1917.

32   Emma B. Suydam, "Man Behind Every Bond; Woman in Public Service," *Pittsburgh Sunday Post*, September 30, 1917.

33   "Suffragists Plan Red Cross Auxiliary," *Pittsburgh Post*, January 10, 1918; "Suffrage Red Cross Auxiliary to Open, *Pittsburgh Sunday Post*, January 20, 1918 and "Franchise Federation to Aid Red Cross Work," *Pittsburgh Gazette Times*, January 10, 1918.

34   "Club News: Suffragists Plan Meeting," *Pittsburgh Gazette Times*, May 19, 1918. *See also* photo of women, including Jennie Kennedy dressed in nursing uniforms, in Winifred Meek Morris Papers and Photographs, Detre Library & Archives, Senator John Heinz History Center.

35   "Dry Platform Hurt Suffragists—Griggs," *Pittsburgh Post*, January 1, 1919.

36   "'Gloomless Sunday' for Soldiers, Plan," *Pittsburgh Sunday Post*, February 3, 1918 and "Transport Troopers as Dinner Guests," *Pittsburg Press*, February 3, 1918.

37   "Soldiers Given Dinner Here by Women," *Pittsburgh Gazette Times*, February 4, 1918.

38   "First Report on Red Cross Drive to be Made Today by Women Team Heads," *Pittsburgh Post*, May 25, 1918; "Street Demonstration Today for Red Cross," *Pittsburgh Gazette Times*, May 25, 1918.

39   *The Christian Register*, Volume 97 (January 10, 1918): 913.

40   Gertrude Gordon, "Warns Against Alien Menace to Our Country," *Pittsburg Press*, November 21, 1917.

41   Ibid.

42   Ibid.

43   "Suffragists to Select War Workers' Board," *Pittsburg Press*, November 20, 1917; "War Service Board Planned by Suffragists," *Pittsburgh Post*, November 20, 1917 and "'Brotherhood' Banquet Theme of Suffragists," *Pittsburgh Post*, November 22, 1917.

44   "Suffragists Will Mix War and Vote Talk," *Pittsburg Press*, November 18, 1917; Emma B. Suydam, "Suffrage and Saving Will Divide Attention," *Pittsburgh Sunday Post*, November 18, 1917 and "Women Attack Pro-Germanism in Legislature," *Pittsburgh Post*, November 22, 1917.

45   Gertrude Gordon, "Twelfth Star Pinned on Flag by Suffragists," *Pittsburg Press*, November 22, 1917; "Suffrage a War Measure," *Pittsburgh Sunday Post*, November 25, 1917. For Anna Howard Shaw's remarks about the militant pickets and Carrie Chapman Catt's remarks about democracy, see "Strong Plea for Suffrage by Mrs. Catt," *Pittsburgh Gazette Times*, November 23, 1917 and "Picketers Flayed by Dr. Shaw in Speech," *Pittsburgh Post*, November 23, 1917.

46   "Suffragists Try to Win Support of Amendment," *Pittsburgh Gazette Times*, December 13, 1917; "Suffrage Vote is Postponed Till January," *Pittsburgh Gazette Times,* December 15, 1917; "Suffragists Gain Allies in Congress," *Pittsburgh Post*, December 13, 1917 and "Congress Delays Vote on Suffrage Until January," *Pittsburg Press*, December 15, 1917.

47   "House Body Planning Rule for Vote Jan. 10 on Suffrage Question," *Pittsburgh Post*, December 19, 1917 and "Suffragists Hope to Win Congressmen," *Pittsburg Press*, December 31, 1917.

Chapter 16 | The Bishop and Mr. Babcock

1   Walter Liggett, *Pittsburgh: Metropolis of Corruption* (Washington, DC: Plain Talk, 1930), in Richard Gazarik, *Wicked Pittsburgh* (Charleston, SC: The History Press, 2018), 11.

2   "Lest We Forget," *Pittsburgh Post*, October 22, 1917.

3   Liggett, in Gazarik, 12.

4   "Lest We Forget," *Pittsburgh Post*, October 22, 1917.

5   Mayor W. A. Magee, "The Answer," *Pittsburg Press*, March 29, 1911.

6   "Personal Experiences of Mrs. John O. Miller," part 2, dictated April 3, 1940, 2. All dialogue in this chapter was recounted by Lucy.

7   According to *The Survey: A Journal of Social Exploration*, which chronicled much of the Progressive Movement nationwide, *Publicity* was launched "primarily for the purpose of illuminating with current news the political situation in Pennsylvania. Its principal program is the promotion of legislation for the suppression of vice, the elimination of liquor from politics, woman suffrage, protection of childhood, and restriction of child and women's labor." *The Survey: A Journal of Social Exploration* 38, no. 21 (August 25, 1917).

8   "Ministers Quiz Candidates at Union Meeting," *Pittsburgh Post*, October 16, 1917.

9   "Common Sense on the Vice Question," *Pittsburgh Post*, September 6, 1917.

10   "Personal Experiences," part 2, 1940, 3.

11   "Babcock Held in High Esteem by Churchmen," *Pittsburgh Sunday Post*, September 16, 1917 and "Babcock

is Best Fitted for Mayor," *Pittsburgh Gazette Times*, September 16, 1917. Rev. Robert Miller, pastor of Third United Presbyterian Church, also endorsed Babcock, according to "Minister Indorses [sic] Babcock for Mayor," *Pittsburgh Post*, October 31, 1917.

12   "Personal Experiences," part 2, 4.
13   "Personal Experiences," part 2, 5.
14   There was no love lost between Julian and Babcock. They had gone at each other over the issue of labor exploitation, Julian citing Babcock's use of prison labor and Babcock accusing Julian of employing unskilled native laborers for construction of the Tata Iron and Steel Company in India. As the election drama was unfolding, Julian penned a scathing defense and doubled down on his criticism of Babcock. *See* "Kennedy Strikes Back at Babcock," *Pittsburg Press*, October 30, 1917.

Chapter 17 | Victory at Last!
1   "State Suffragists to Witness Voting," *Pittsburgh Post*, January 3, 1918.
2   "Wilson Favors Women's Vote Amendment," *Pittsburgh Gazette Times*, January 10, 1918.
3   "Suffrage Victory in House Predicted," *Pittsburgh Press*, January 6, 1918; "Suffragists in Capital," *Pittsburgh Post*, January 9, 1918; "Local Suffragists Ask Congressmen's Support," *Pittsburgh Gazette Times*, January 9, 1917 and "House to Put Measure 'Over' in Landslide," *Pittsburg Press*, January 10, 1918.
4   "Resolution Now Goes to Senate; Passage is Predicted," *Pittsburgh Post*, January 11 1918.
5   "Resolution Now Goes to Senate; Passage is Predicted," *Pittsburgh Post*, January 11 1918; "Suffrage Resolution Passes House; Expect Senate Fight," *Pittsburgh Gazette Times*, January 11, 1918 and L. C. Martin, "Suffrage Fight Swings Today to U.S. Senate," *Pittsburg Press*, January 11, 1918.
6   "Suffrage Only Needs Two Votes in Senate," *Pittsburgh Post*, February 18, 1918 and "Suffragists Feel Sure of Amendment," *Pittsburg Press*, February 18, 1918.
7   Frederic J. Haskin, "On Woman Suffrage . . . ," *Pittsburgh Gazette Times*, January 23, 1918.
8   "National Suffrage Suffers Setback," *Pittsburgh Post*, May 7, 1918.
9   "Wilson Would Offer Women Right to Vote in Recognition of Sacrifices in Great War," *Pittsburgh Post*, June 14, 1918 and "Wilson Urges Senate to Give Vote to Women," *Pittsburgh Gazette Times*, June 14, 1918.
10   "Suffragists Plan Soldiers' Benefit," *Pttsburgh Post*, June 20, 1918 and "Miss Hay Made Acting Head of Suffrage Body," *Pittsburgh Gazette Times*, June 20, 1918.
11   Emma B. Suydam, "Recognition for Women Asked for War Service," *Pittsburgh Sunday Post*, June 2, 1918.
12   "Dr. Shaw Addresses Federation Meeting," *Pittsburgh Post*, May 28, 1918.
13   "Knox is Asked for Expression by Suffragists," *Pittsburgh Post*, June 24, 1918.
14   "Suffragists Lose Round as Senate Defers Vote on Measure," *Pittsburgh Post*, June 28, 1918; "Senate Again Defers Action on Woman Bill," *Pittsburgh Gazette Times*, June 28, 1918 and "War Supply Bills Hold Up Suffrage Amendment," *Pittsburg Press*, June 28, 1918.
15   "Suffragists Lose Round as Senate Defers Vote on Measure," *Pittsburgh Post*, June 28, 1918.
16   "Women Are Hurt in Melee After Arrest of White House Pickets," *Pittsburg Press*, August 13, 1918 and "26 Suffragists Go to Jail in Default," *Pittsburg Press*, August 16, 1918.
17   "Suffrage Carnival Set for June 27," *Pittsburgh Sunday Post*, June 16, 1918; "Suffragists Plan Dance and Midway," *Pittsburgh Post*, June 18, 1918; "Street Dance Planned to Boost Stamp Sale," *Pittsburgh Gazette Times*, June 18, 1918; "Suffragists Ready for Street Dance," *Pittsburgh Sunday Post*, June 23, 1918 and "15,000 at Midway Benefit to Soldiers," *Pittsburgh Post*, June 28, 1918.
18   "Suffragists to Extend Hut Service for Soldiers," *Pittsburgh Gazette Times*, August 18, 1918; Iva I Rowley, "Pittsburgh Making Record for Hospitality to Soldiers," *Pittsburgh Gazette Times*, July 14, 1918; "Plan 'Shell' Booths to Aid Soldiers," *Pittsburgh Sunday Post*, July 14, 1918; "Suffrage Hut for Soldiers Open This Week," *Pittsburgh Sunday Post*, August 4, 1918; Iva I. Rowley, "Soldier Hut at Old City Hall to be Completed This Week," *Pittsburgh Gazette Times*, August 4, 1918; "Soldiers Hut Proves Popular," *Pittsburgh Gazette Times*, August 25, 1918 and "Tank Service Men Want Phonograph," *Pittsburgh Sunday Post*, September 1, 1918.
19   "Senators Demand Action on Suffrage," *Pittsburg Press*, August 25, 1918.
20   "Wilson Aids Suffragists," *Pittsburgh Post*, September 17, 1918 and "Wilson Promises to Help Suffragists," *Pittsburgh Press*, September 17, 1918.
21   "Suffragists Up to Senate," *Pittsburgh Post*, September 18, 1918.
22   L. C. Martin, "Suffrage Vote is Expected in Senate Today; Victory Scented," *Pittsburg Press*, September 26, 1918.
23   L. C. Martin, "Suffragists Pin Hopes to Wilson and Absentees," *Pittsburg Press*, September 27, 1918.
24   "Wilson Please for Women Win No Votes" and "Suffragists in Pittsburgh Disappointed," *Pittsburgh Gazette Times*, October 2, 1918.

25 "111,650 Die From Grip in 46 Big Cities," *Pittsburgh Gazette Times*, January 6, 1919.

26 Sources differ as to the statistical impact of the 1918 flu in Pittsburgh. Some maintain that the death rate—807 per 100,000 residents—exceeded every city in the nation. The Associated Press reported that, among the forty-six largest US cities, Pittsburgh's death rate per thousand of 25.4 was slightly behind Baltimore and Nashville, but had surpassed New York, Boston, Chicago, Washington, and Philadelphia. *See* Influenza Encyclopedia, Pittsburgh, Pennsylvania, produced by the University of Michigan Center for the History of Medicine and Michigan Publishing, influenzaarchive.org/cities/city-pittsburgh.html. *See also* Bill O'Toole, "When the Spanish Flu Swept In, Pittsburgh Failed the Test," *Pittsburgh Quarterly*, April 1, 2020; Brian O'Neill, "Pittsburgh didn't confront the 1918 epidemic in time," *Pittsburgh Post-Gazette*, March 19, 2020 and Pennsylvania Historical and Museum Commission, https://www.phmc.pa.gov/Archives/Research-Online/Pages/1918-Influenza-Epidemic.aspx.

27 "Suffragists Burn Wilson in Effigy," *Pittsburgh Post*, February 10, 1919 and "Wilson Burned in Effigy; 65 Suffragists Locked Up," *Pittsburgh Gazette Times*, February 10, 1919.

28 "Suffrage Beaten for Fourth Time by U.S. Senate; Vote is 55 to 29," *Pittsburgh Press*, February 10, 1919; "Women Lose Long Battle for Suffrage in Senate by Single Vote," *Pittsburgh Post*, February 11, 1919 and "Women Beaten But Start New Ballot Fight," *Pittsburgh Gazette Times*, February 11, 1919. The previous votes had occurred in 1887 (16 to 34), 1914 (35 to 34), and 1918 (54 to 30).

29 "Suffragists Yet Hope; Measure is Reintroduced," *Pittsburg Press*, February 17, 1919.

30 "Suffragists' New Fight is Extended to House; Upper Branch Sure," *Pittsburg Press*, March 2, 1919.

31 T. A. Huntley, "Wilson Waits in Vain for Measures Senate Kills," *Pittsburgh Post*, March 5, 1919.

32 T. A. Huntley, "Suffragists Are Confident of Passage by Required Vote on Amendment," *Pittsburgh Post*, May 5, 1919 and "Penrose Hope of Suffragists," *Pittsburgh Post*, May 5, 1919.

33 "Suffrage Wins in Senate by 56 to 25 Vote," *Pittsburgh Press*, June 5, 1919. Counting paired and absent members, the count was actually 66 to 30 for the measure.

34 John R. Ball, "Pennsylvania Legislature is Seventh to Approve Suffrage Act," *Pittsburgh Post*, June 25, 1919.

35 Robert M. Ginter, "Resolution Adopted by Vote of 56 to 25; Now Goes to States," *Pittsburgh Gazette Times*, June 5, 1919.

36 Robert L. Wallace, quoted in John R. Ball, "Pennsylvania Legislature is Seventh to Approve Suffrage Act," *Pittsburgh Post*, June 25, 1919.

37 John R. Ball, "Pennsylvania Legislature is Seventh to Approve Suffrage Act," *Pittsburgh Post*, June 25, 1919.

38 Ibid.

39 "Beaver Valley," *Pittsburg Press*, December 14, 1919.

40 "Suffragists Elect Mrs. Miller as Head," *Pittsburgh Post*, November 12, 1919.

41 "Lucy Kennedy Miller Fund," *Pittsburgh Post*, December 12, 1919.

42 *Bulletin* of the Pennsylvania League of Women Voters 1, No. 5 (October 1920), in author's collection.

43 Catt and Shuler, 382; "Fight for Suffrage Develops into Hot Debate Over Ruling," *Pittsburgh Post*, March 10, 1920; "Bloch Special Nearing Charleston as Resigned Senator Attempts to Reclaim Seat and Vote Against Suffrage," *Pittsburgh Gazette Times*, March 10, 1920 and "Senator Arrives to Aid Suffrage in West Virginia," *Pittsburg Press*, March 10, 1920.

44 "Suffrage Leaders to Make Fight in Vermont," *Pittsburgh Post*, April 2, 1920; "Delaware Senate Adopts Suffrage House Yet to Act," *Pittsburg Press*, May 6, 1920; "Lower House in Delaware Halts Vote on Suffrage and Adjourns," *Pittsburgh Post*, May 7, 1920 and "Suffrage Finally Loses in Delaware," *Pittsburg Press*, June 3, 1920.

45 "Amendment Adopted by 34th State After Dramatic Campaign," *Pittsburgh Gazette Times*, March 11, 1920.

46 "Suffragists to Take Fight to Vermont and North Carolina," *Pittsburg Press*, April 2, 1920.

47 Linda Rodriguez McRobbie, "The Strange and Mysterious History of the Ouija Board," https://www.smithsonianmag.com/history/the-strange-and-mysterious-history-of-the-ouija-board-5860627.

48 "National Committee Urges G.O.P. States to Ratify Suffrage," *Pittsburgh Gazette Times*, June 2, 1920.

49 "Can't Fool the Suffragists," *Pittsburgh Post*, June 4, 1920.

50 "Seven Women, Penrose and 13 Others to Help Harding with Campaign," *Pittsburgh Post*, June 23, 1920 and "Harding Campaign Committee Named; Senator Promises His Support to Suffrage Cause," *Pittsburgh Gazette Times*, June 23, 1920.

51 Alexander F. Jones, "Women Score Big Victory in Chicago," *Pittsburgh Post*, June 9, 1920.

52 "Two Governors Refuse Plea for Special Legislatures on Suffrage," *Pittsburgh Post*, July 13, 1920.

53 For a detailed look at the six weeks of drama in Tennessee, see Elaine Weiss, *The Woman's Hour: The Great Fight to Win the Vote* (New York: Viking, 2018).

54 "Suffrage to Come Up for Action in Tennessee Monday," *Pittsburgh Sunday Post*, August 8, 1920.

55 "North Carolina Will Defeat Suffrage Is Word Sent to Tennessee," *Pittsburgh Post*, August 12, 1920.

56   "Vote Delayed on Suffrage in Tennessee," *Pittsburgh Gazette Times*, August 13, 1920.

57   "G.O.P. Attitude on Suffrage and League 'Clear as Mud'–Roosevelt," *Pittsburgh Post*, August 14, 1920.

58   "Suffrage Test in Tennessee House Likely to be Ended by Wednesday," *Pittsburgh Post*, August 16, 1920; "Suffrage Vote in Tennessee Lower House Scheduled for This Morning," *Pittsburgh Post*, August 17, 1920 and "House Holds Suffrage Fate in Tennessee," *Pittsburgh Gazette Times*, August 16, 1920.

59   Febb E. Burn, Letter to Harry T. Burn, August 17, 1920, in Harry T. Burn Papers, C. M. McClung Historical Collection, Knox County Public Library, Knoxville, TN.

60   Elaine Weiss, 320 and "Colby Issues Proclamation Announcing Suffrage Act is Basic Law," *Pittsburgh Post*, August 27, 1920.

61   "Mayor Proclaims Saturday Noon for Noisy Celebration on Ratification," *Pittsburgh Post*, August 27, 1920.

62   "Registration Officials Tell Women How to Prepare for Fall Election," *Pittsburgh Post*, August 14, 1920 and "Election Laws Explained for Women of City," *Pittsburgh Gazette Times*, August 14, 1920.

63   "Justice Bell Rings for First Time as New Voters Cheer," *Philadelphia Inquirer*, September 26, 1920.

64   "Votes for Women? Bosh! Here's One at 91 Who Says Suffrage Has Failed," *Pittsburgh Sun Telegraph*, July 29, 1935, 17. For Eliza Armstrong's obituary, see "Anti-Suffrage Leader Dies in East End Home," *Pittsburgh Press*, August 21, 1935.

65   "'Sacred Trust,' Suffrage Chief Says of Victory," *Pittsburgh Daily Post*, August 19, 1920.

66   Weiss, 324.

67   L. C. Martin, "Equality Fight is Only Begun, Says Suffragist," *Pittsburg Press*, August 19, 1920.

Chapter 18 | Life and the Leagues

1   "Join the Allegheny County League of Women Voters," undated pamphlet in scrapbook in author's collection.

2   "Equal Franchise Federation Dies," *Pittsburgh Chronicle Telegraph*, January 14, 1920 and "Suffragists Continue Under Changed Name," *Pittsburgh Sun*, January 14, 1920.

3   "Women's Citizenship Meetings Announced," *Pittsburg Press*, February 29, 1920.

4   "Women Citizens Plan Membership Campaign," *Pittsburg Press*, May 9, 1920.

5   Miscellaneous newspaper clippings in scrapbook in author's collection.

6   "Women to Discuss Celebration Plans," *Pittsburgh Daily Post*, August 20, 1920.

7   Gertrude Gordon, "Women Launch Plans to Vote in November," *Pittsburg Press*, August 19, 1920.

8   "Pennsylvania Stay-at-Homes," *Pittsburgh Sun*, December 18, 1920.

9   Weiss, 325.

10   Lucy Kennedy Miller, undated editorial, in untitled scrapbook, author's collection.

11   "County League of Women to Hear Eastern Organizer; Chairman Assumes Duties; Makes Announcement; Warning for Fall Issued," *Pittsburgh Daily Post*, June 10, 1923.

12   "Women Voters to Question Candidates," *Pittsburgh Daily Post*, August 23, 1923. For photos of one of the League rallies, see "Candidates of Different Parties and Factions Explain Their Platforms," *Pittsburgh Daily Post*, September 13, 1923.

13   "Voters League Annual Session Opens November 12," *Pittsburgh Gazette Times*, October 12, 1924.

14   "League of Women Voters to Enlist County Housewives," *Pittsburgh Gazette Times*, January 6, 1927 and "Club News: League Women Voters," *Pittsburgh Post*, January 6, 1927.

15   Emma B. Suydam, "League of Women Voters' Record It Is Stated, 'Confounds Skeptics,'" *Pittsburgh Post-Gazette*, July 3, 1927.

16   "Women Voters Meet Today in Williamsport," *Pittsburgh Post-Gazette*, November 14, 1927.

17   "Women in Fight to Abolish Fat County Office," *Pittsburgh Press*, January 18, 1925.

18   "Rich Field for Civic Study," *Pittsburgh Post*, January 21, 1925.

19   "'Slush' Fund of Fee-Hungry Collectors is Said $30,000," *Pittsburgh Post*, March 10, 1925. *See also* Mrs. R. Templeton Smith, "Open Letter of Allegheny County League of Women Voters," in scrapbook in author's collection.

20   "Waste by County Hit by Mrs. Miller At Voters' Meeting; Women's League Hears Stories of Wild Expenditure," *Pittsburgh Post*, November 11, 1925 and "Mrs. Miller Again Attacks Office of Commissioners," *Pittsburgh Press*, November 11, 1925.

21   "Spending Orgy Seen in Plan for $750,000 Playgrounds," *Pittsburgh Post*, February 22, 1927.

22   "Women Clubs' Heads Discuss County Bonds," *Pittsburgh Post-Gazette*, June 7, 1928; "Women's Body Asks for Data on Bond Issue," *Pittsburgh Press*, June 11, 1928 and "Opposes Bond Issue: Women's League Head Sends Letter to Members," *Pittsburgh Press*, June 21, 1928.

23   "Hall Attack Called Untrue," *Pittsburgh Sun-Telegraph*, June 21, 1928.

24   "Urges Women Voters Beat County Bonds," *Pittsburgh Post-Gazette*, June 21, 1928.

25   "Association Answers Bond Issue Questions," *Pittsburgh Press*, June 17, 1928; "Bond Issue Association Gives
     Complete Details on Proposal," *Pittsburgh Sun-Telegraph*, June 17, 1928 and "Town Hall Attack Branded
     Untrue," *Pittsburgh Sun-Telegraph*, June 21, 1928.
26   "Women Score Commissioners," *Pittsburgh Press*, September 14, 1929.
27   "League of Women Voters Holds Annual Meeting," *Pittsburgh Post-Gazette*, May 27, 1932.
28   *Bulletin of the Pennsylvania League of Women Voters* 1, No. 5 (October 1920), in author's collection.
29   *Bulletin of the Pennsylvania League of Women Voters* 1, No. 7 (December 1921), in author's collection.
30   The Pennsylvania Papers, *Pittsburgh Sun*, undated pamphlet in author's collection.
31   In seeking the constitutional convention, Lucy came up against her old nemesis from suffrage days, Edward
     Vare, who controlled the Philadelphia machine but who, according to Lucy, did not have "courage enough" to
     vote against the measure. "No bill before the Legislature had a career quite as interesting," she said in her annual
     address to the Pennsylvania League. "While it passed the Senate without serious opposition, certain interests,
     mainly from Philadelphia, began a fight in the House. In this connection, I might say that this city has two votes
     in the lower chamber, one an independent and 40 who vote the mandates of your boss, Mr. Vare." "Women Voters
     Against Changes in Basic Law," Central Press Bureau, November 16, 1923.
32   "Cause and Cure of War Plans Announced," *Pittsburgh Press*, October 21, 1928 and "Club Women Attend War
     Cure Meet," *Pittsburgh Post-Gazette*, November 17, 1928.
33   "'Get Out Vote' Campaign Will Be Begun Here," *Pittsburgh Gazette Times*, June 1, 1924.
34   "Leader of County Women's League Urges Heavy Vote," *Pittsburgh Post*, September 17, 1923.
35   "Erie Acclaims Caravan of Women Voters League," *Pittsburgh Gazette Times*, October 15, 1924.
36   "Woman Scores Minority Rule," *Pittsburgh Gazette Times*, October 8, 1924.
37   "Caravan Women Are Told By Speakers Laws Retard Voting," *Pittsburgh Press*, October 19, 1924.
38   Letter, Eliza Kennedy Smith to R. Templeton Smith, July 26, 1926.
39   Ibid.
40   Letter, Eliza Kennedy Smith to R. Templeton Smith, August 1926.
41   Eliza Kennedy Smith travel journal, June 25–September 25, 1926.
42   Letter, Eliza Kennedy Smith to R. Templeton Smith, August 25, 1926.
43   Letter, Eliza Kennedy Smith to R. Templeton Smith, August 28, 1926.
44   Eliza Kennedy Smith to R. Templeton Smith, date obscured.
45   John Hawkins Miller, "A Bend in the Silver Spoon: Memories of Emerson Point Farm," unpublished manuscript,
     December 2011.

Chapter 19 | She Devils at the Door
1   "No Red Herring," *Pittsburgh Post-Gazette*, February 26, 1931.
2   Smith, "One Who Made A Difference."
3   Resolution of the Allegheny County League of Women Voters, February 25, 1931, in author's collection; also in
     "Women Voters' Demand for Action," *Pittsburgh Press*, February 27, 1931, with photo entitled "Women Voters
     Prepare Petition for Food Probe." *See also* "Food Probe Pressed by Women," *Pittsburgh Sun-Telegraph*, February
     27, 1931; Letter from Mrs. R. Templeton Smith to Mr. John D. Houston, February 27, 1931, in author's collection
     and Letter from John D. Houston to Mrs. R. Templeton Smith, March 2, 1931, in author's collection.
4   Resolution of the Allegheny County League of Women Voters, February 25, 1931, in *Pittsburgh Press*, February
     27, 1931, 2.
5   "Council Bans Open Food Quiz; Kline Forces Flout Demand," *Pittsburgh Press*, March 3 1931 and "Council
     'Buries' Women's Demand for Food Inquiry," *Pittsburgh Post-Gazette*, March 3, 1931.
6   "City Council," *Pittsburgh Press,* March 9, 1931; "Press Presents Summary of City Scandal to Date," *Pittsburgh
     Press*, March 29, 1931 and "Council Gets Last Chance to Act in Succop Probe Today," *Pittsburgh Post-Gazette*,
     March 9, 1931. A political cartoon on March 8, 1931, and a "spicy, inside story" on October 11, 1931, mocked
     the mayor for his extravagances.
7   "An Appeal to the Public," *Pittsburgh Press*, March 8, 1931.
8   William G. Lytle Jr., "Council Gets Final Chance for Inquiry," *Pittsburgh Press*, March 9, 1931.
9   Kenneth M. Gould, "Ways Out of Pittsburgh's Civic Mess?", *Pittsburgh Press*, June 7, 1931.
10   Smith, "One Who Made A Difference," 16.
11   "Yes, It Can be Done," *Pittsburgh Press*, October 11, 1931.
12   "Kline Sends Resignation to City Clerk," *Pittsburgh Post-Gazette*, March 29, 1933.
13   "Power Gone, Kline to Quit Office Today," *Pittsburgh Post-Gazette*, March 28, 1933.
14   Smith, "One Who Made A Difference," 16.

15 "Mayor Kline to Resign Tomorrow," *Pittsburgh Press*, March 27, 1933.

16 Paul Block, "Mayor Kline Should Resign and Prosecution Be Dropped," *Pittsburgh Post-Gazette*, January 27, 1933.

17 "The Doctor's Report," *Pittsburgh Sun-Telegraph*, March 30, 1933.

18 "Threats Sent Three Doctors in Kline Case," *Pittsburgh Press*, March 30, 1933.

19 "No 'New Deal" Yet," *Pittsburgh Press*, March 28, 1933.

20 "Kline Sends Resignation to City Clerk," *Pittsburgh Post-Gazette*, March 29, 1933.

21 "End of the Kline Case," *Pittsburgh Post-Gazette*, March 28, 1933.

22 "Herron Leads City Officials in Paying Tribute to Memory of Kline," *Pittsburgh Sun-Telegraph*, July 23, 1933.

23 "Kline's Rule Over City Politics Under Influence of Evil Star," *Pittsburgh Post-Gazette*, July 24, 1933.

24 "Succop in Jail Praises Kline, Mourns Death," *Pittsburgh Sun-Telegraph*, July 23, 1933.

25 "Life Mistake of Kline Seen in Leaving Bench," *Pittsburgh Sun-Telegraph*, July 23, 1933.

26 "Group of 100 Forms County Hoover Club," *Pittsburgh Press*, October 23, 1932.

27 "League of Women Voters Presents Mrs. Bowman in Political Review," *Pittsburgh Post-Gazette*, March 4, 1933.

28 "Communists Peeved, Heckle Socialist College Debater," *Pittsburgh Press*, November 5, 1932.

29 Lincoln Steffens, "Pittsburg: A City Ashamed: The Story of a Citizens' Party That Broke Through One Ring Into Another," *McClure's Magazine* 21 (May–October 1903), 24-39. The article was later published in Lincoln Steffen, *The Shame of the Cities* (New York: McClure, Phillips & Co., 1904; New York: Sagamore Press, 1957), a book of seven essays written for *McClure's* in 1902 and 1903 about graft in Minneapolis, St. Louis, Pittsburgh, Philadelphia, Chicago, and New York.

30 Rebecca Menes, "Corruption in Cities: Graft and politics in American cities at the turn of the Twentieth Century" (National Bureau of Economic Research, 2001–2003).

31 Steffens, "Pittsburg: A City Ashamed," 24.

32 *See* "Does Big Business Want Things Changed?", *Pittsburgh Press*, June 7, 1931, for a discussion of why big business did not favor a change in the system.

33 *Pittsburgh Press*, March 7–9, 1933.

34 "Vote Machine Contract May Be Let Today," *Pittsburgh Post-Gazette*, February 28, 1931.

35 A taxpayer's lawsuit to withhold payment of the remaining $400,000 balance due ultimately failed. *See* "Women Insist Vote Machines Get New Test," *Pittsburgh Press*, November 30, 1931; "Principals in Probe of County's Vote Machines" and "Vote Machine Probe Breaks Up in Quarrel," *Pittsburgh Press*, May 17, 1932 and "Another Vote Machine Gets a Trial Here," *Pittsburgh Post-Gazette*, March 21, 1933. That summer, the county spent an additional $200,000 remodeling the machines, and in 1933, another $100,000. *See* "Vote Machines Will Be Barred from Election," *Pittsburgh Press*, October 29, 1933.

36 "Women Insist Vote Machines Get New Test," *Pittsburgh Press*, November 30, 1931.

37 "Principals in Probe of County's Vote Machines," *Pittsburgh Press*, May 18, 1932.

38 John K. Morrow, "Vote Machine Alterations are Approved," *Pittsburgh Post-Gazette*, December 15, 1932.

39 "Women to Scan Vote Machines" *Pittsburgh Sun-Telegraph*, March 8, 1933.

40 "Women Start 'Death Watch,'" *Pittsburgh Press*, March 10, 1933.

41 See photo in "Women Examine Vote Machine to See If It Is Foolproof," *Pittsburgh Press*, March 11, 1933.

42 "Women Urge Return to Paper Balloting," *Pittsburgh Press*, April 18, 1933, in scrapbook in author's collection.

43 "It's Easy to Operate a Voting Machine—Just Observe These Simple Instructions," *Pittsburgh Post-Gazette*, September 19, 1933.

44 "Machines Jam, Snarl Voting" ... "Brawls Mark Balloting," *Pittsburgh Sun-Telegraph*, September 19, 1933 and "Voters Jam Polls In Last Minutes of Chaotic Day," newspaper unidentified, September 19, 1933, clipping in scrapbook in author's collection.

45 "Vote Machines Will Be Barred from Election," *Pittsburgh Press*, October 29, 1933.

46 "Two Women to Climax Vote Machine Probe," *Pittsburgh Press*, October 15, 1933.

47 "Voting Machine 'Cheat' Balked," *Pittsburgh Press*, October 17, 1933.

48 "Women Frame Reply to Tax Evasion Charge," *Pittsburgh Press*, March 17, 1933.

49 "Steedle's Tax Charge Denied by Mrs. Miller," *Pittsburgh Press*, March 23, 1933 and "Charge Denied by Mrs. Miller," *Pittsburgh Post-Gazette*, March 24, 1933.

50 "Laughs at Outcome of Steedle-Miller Clash," *Pittsburgh Press*, March 27, 1933.

51 "Tax Mass Meeting Due on Capitol Step," *Pittsburgh Press*, March 24, 1933.

52 "Change Urged in Juvenile Court Method," *Pittsburgh Post-Gazette*, June 15, 1933.

53 "Road Program Urged to Give Jobs to Idle," *Pittsburgh Press*, April 6, 1932 and "'Family-Help-Family' Executive Committee," *Pittsburgh Post-Gazette*, April 9, 1932.

54 "150 Prominent Citizens Mobilize to Fight Coyne, Herron," *Pittsburgh Press*, May 25, 1933.

55 "League Opens Offensive on Herron, Slate," *Pittsburgh Post-Gazette*, June 3, 1933.
56 Ha[r]vey J. Boyle, "Heavyweights Swing Gloves In Political Ring as Play 'Meet the Mayor' Scores With Some," *Pittsburgh Post-Gazette*, September 9, 1933.
57 Ibid.
58 Ibid.
59 "All Mayoralty Aspirants Talk at One Meeting," *Pittsburgh Press*, September 9, 1933.
60 Clipping in author's collection, undated.

Chapter 20 | Vigilance in the Halls of Power
1 Weber, 61.
2 "M'Nair Names Woman As His Budget Aide," *Pittsburgh Press*, November 20, 1933 and "Mrs. Smith Picked On Budget," *Pittsburgh Sun-Telegraph*, November 20, 1933.
3 Vin Sweeney, "Woman Becomes Financial Power Behind New Mayor; Budget Aide Hunts for Political Drones," *Pittsburgh Press*, November 21, 1933.
4 Mrs. R. Templeton Smith, "The League of Women Voters: Its Aim and Policy," *The New American* (1935), 17, in scrapbook in author's collection.
5 Smith, "One Who Made A Difference," 100.
6 Hungerford's cartoons may be found in the presidential libraries of all nine US leaders who served during his years in Pittsburgh.
7 Quin Hall, "Room for Complaint," *Pittsburgh Sun-Telegraph*, March 30, 1934.
8 "McNair Drops Budget Advice. It's No Use!" *Pittsburgh Sun-Telegraph*, May 19, 1935.
9 "Highlights in Colorful Public Career of Former Mayor McNair," *Pittsburgh Post-Gazette*, September 10, 1948.
10 "McNair Rule Lasted Nearly Three Years," *Pittsburgh Post-Gazette*, September 10, 1948.
11 "Vote League Denounces Council," *Pittsburgh Sun-Telegraph*, March 29, 1934.
12 "Scully Offers Plan to Avert Tax Rate Boost," *Pittsburgh Press*, December 13, 1938.
13 "Incinerator Bungle Laid to Politics," *Pittsburgh Post-Gazette*, May 8, 1940 and "Incinerator Treated Like Toy, Women Voters' Leader Says," *Pittsburgh Sun-Telegraph*, May 8, 1940.
14 "Women Open War on Rats," *Pittsburgh Sun-Telegraph*, April 11, 1946.
15 "Women Voters Rap City on Garbage," *Pittsburgh Sun-Telegraph*, May 31, 1946.
16 "Women Voters' President Sees City Manager Need," *Pittsburgh Press*, January 28, 1940 and "Manager Urged for Pittsburgh," *Pittsburgh Post-Gazette*, January 29, 1940.
17 Milton V. Burgess, "Defeat of Home Rule Bill Seen as Assembly Hears District Leaders," *Pittsburgh Sun-Telegraph*, March 19, 1941.
18 Ibid.
19 "Official to Tell of Finance in Cincinnati: Ohio Councilman to Relate Story of $922,000 Surplus," *Pittsburgh Sun-Telegraph*, January 21, 1940.
20 "Party Strife Left Out in Cincinnati," *Pittsburgh Post-Gazette*, January 26, 1940.
21 "Women Hear Plea for City Manager," *Pittsburgh Post-Gazette*, May 16, 1940.
22 "Instruction Offered in Jury Procedure," *Pittsburgh Post-Gazette*, October 7, 1940; "Women Voters Open 'Jury School Oct. 22,'" *Pittsburgh Press*, October 13, 1940 and "Women Voters to Open Jury School Today," *Pittsburgh Press*, October 20, 1940.
23 "C. of C. Assails City Budget 'Juggling,'" *Pittsburgh Sun-Telegraph*, December 2, 1940.
24 "Probe of Scully Vote Supported," *Pittsburgh Sun-Telegraph*, December 1, 1941.

Chapter 21 | Dirty Air and Dirty Dealings
1 Cliff I. Davidson, "Air Pollution In Pittsburgh: A Historical Perspective," *Journal of the Air Pollution Control Association* (1979), 29:10, 1035-1041.
2 Zadock Cramer, *The Navigator*, 1814, quoted in Davidson, "Air Pollution In Pittsburgh: A Historical Perspective," 1035-1041.
3 Davidson, "Air Pollution In Pittsburgh: A Historical Perspective," 1035–1041.
4 John O'Connor Jr., "The History of the Nuisance and of Smoke Abatement in Pittsburgh," *Industrial World* (March 24, 1913): 352-355. Chief Fellow and Associate Director of the Mellon Institute (as well as public relations director for the Smoke Investigation and executive secretary of the Smoke and Dust Abatement League) John J. O'Connor Jr. discussed the issue at length and indicated that Pittsburgh had been trying to find solutions to the problem as early as 1807.
5 One *Press* editorial suggested that "if citizens must have something to indicate prosperity, it would be better for the

community, and cheaper for the industries, to have the plants send up rockets or ring bells when they are working steadily." "Holy Smoke," *Pittsburgh Press*, May 1, 1941.

6   "Anti-Smoke Ordinance Requested," *Pittsburgh Post-Gazette*, January 16, 1941.

7   "Smoking It Out," *Pittsburgh Press*, January 17, 1941.

8   "Heavy Smoke Costs At St. Louis Cited," *Pittsburgh Post-Gazette*, January 25, 1941.

9   "Odds Were Hard to Beat, But So Were Aroused Citizens When St. Louis Waged Battle to End Smoke Pall," *Pittsburgh Press*, January 21, 1941.

10 Gilbert Love, "Big Crowd Representing Civic Groups Backs Anti-Smoke Drive at Luncheon," *Pittsburgh Press*, February 28, 1941.

11 "Club Guests Hear Smoke Discussion," *Pittsburgh Post-Gazette*, February 22, 1941 and Gilbert Love, "Big Crowd Representing Civic Groups Backs Anti-Smoke Drive at Luncheon," *Pittsburgh Press*, February 28, 1941.

12 Gilbert Love, "Big Crowd Representing Civic Groups Backs Anti-Smoke Drive at Luncheon," *Pittsburgh Press*, February 28, 1941.

13 "Civic Clubs Join Committee to Aid Smoke Abatement Drive," *Pittsburgh Sun-Telegraph*, March 13, 1941 and "Civic Groups Unite to Fight Smoke," *Pittsburgh Press*, March 13, 1941.

14 "Housewives Map Smoke Drive Plans," *Pittsburgh Post-Gazette*, March 22, 1941.

15 Ibid.

16 "Smoke Called 'Disruptor' of City's Homes," *Pittsburgh Press*, March 25, 1941. *See also* Martin A. Mayers, "Burning Your Own Smoke," manuscript to be presented before the Smoke Committee of the League of Women Voters, Pittsburgh, March 20, 1941, in author's collection.

17 "Anti-Smoke Plan, Defense Linked," *Pittsburgh Press*, March 25, 1941.

18 "False Hysteria Seen in Smoke Menace Here," *Pittsburgh Sun-Telegraph*, May 23, 1941.

19 Gilbert Love, "Smoke Called 'Disruptor' of City's Homes," *Pittsburgh Press*, March 25, 1941 and "Housewives Map Smoke Drive Plans," *Pittsburgh Post-Gazette*, March 22, 1941.

20 "Smog Scored as 'Nuisance' by Women," *Pittsburgh Sun-Telegraph*, March 25, 1941.

21 Gilbert Love, "Smoke Called 'Disruptor' of City's Homes," *Pittsburgh Press*, March 25, 1941.

22 "'Just a Nuisance' Crusaders Told by Haythorn," *Pittsburgh Sun-Telegraph*, March 27, 1941.

23 "False Hysteria Seen in Smoke Menace Here," *Pittsburgh Sun-Telegraph*, May 23, 1941.

24 "Puzzling Features Of Anti-Smoke Law," *Pittsburgh Sun-Telegraph*, July 11, 1941.

25 For a full description of the ordinance, see "Strict Law Given Council With Full Approval Of Mayor's Commission," *Pittsburgh Press*, June 16, 1941 and related articles.

26 "'S. S. Carefree' Comes Into Being—In a Basement," *Pittsburgh Press*, September 7, 1941.

27 "Mrs. Smith's Water Bill Ignored," *Pittsburgh Sun-Telegraph*, December 5, 1941.

28 "Those Water Rents," *Pittsburgh Sun-Telegraph*, December 24, 1941.

29 Mrs. Charles M. Bregg, "Voters Aid With Defense," *Pittsburgh Sun-Telegraph*, January 16, 1942.

30 "Institute on Defense Is Being Planned By State Voters' League," *Pittsburgh Post-Gazette*, February 24, 1942 and "Civil Health Drive Urged as War Aid," *Pittsburgh Post-Gazette*, February 25, 1942.

31 "Women Assail Shakeup Plan For Housing," *Pittsburgh Post-Gazette*, January 15, 1942.

32 "Industrial Draft Called Hitlerism," *Pittsburgh Sun-Telegraph*, August 31, 1940 and "Draft of Industry Hit by Women," *Pittsburgh Sun-Telegraph*, September 2, 1940.

33 Douglas Naylor, "Revamped Scrap Set-up Ready for All-Out Drive," *Pittsburgh Press*, September 15, 1942, including photo of the Women's Committee of the Allegheny County Council of Defense. *See also* "Women Start Own Campaign to Get Scrap," *Pittsburgh Post-Gazette*, September 15, 1942.

34 Frances Walker, "Strong Women Must Uphold 'Our Way' At Peace Conference," *Pittsburgh Post-Gazette*, January 26, 1944.

35 "Women Voters Urge Big Turnout," *Pittsburgh Sun-Telegraph*, November 2, 1945.

36 Weber, *Don't Call Me Boss*. For a good summary of David L. Lawrence's career, see William S. Dietrich II, "The Business of Politics: The Story of David L. Lawrence," *Pittsburgh Quarterly*, (Fall 2010).

37 "Caution Urged on County Smoke Law," *Pittsburgh Press*, December 21, 1945 and Smith, "One Who Made A Difference," 37-45.

38 "Caution Urged on County Smoke Law," *Pittsburgh Press*, December 21, 1945.

39 https://popularpittsburgh.com/darkhistory.

40 Cliff I. Davidson, "Air Pollution In Pittsburgh: A Historical Perspective," *Journal of the Air Pollution Control Association* (1979), 29:10, 1035-1041.

41 "Pittsburgh's Schools Face Million Deficit," *Pittsburgh Press*, November 17, 1944.

42 "Voters City Variation in Tax Setup," *Pittsburgh Sun-Telegraph*, June 22, 1946.

43 "Women Hold Balance in Coming Elections," *Pittsburgh Post-Gazette*, October 28, 1946.
44 "Church Leaders Join Racket Fight," *Pittsburgh Sun-Telegraph*, July 28, 1948.
45 "Civic Leader's Home Robbed," *Pittsburgh Press*, August 9, 1948 and "Jewel Theft Reported," *Pittsburgh Post-Gazette*, August 8, 1948.

Chapter 22 | Policing the Police
1 "Killer May Strike Again," *Pittsburgh Post-Gazette*, December 20, 1948.
2 "Kensinger Killer Believed Stalking Scene of Crime," *Pittsburgh Post-Gazette*, January 18, 1949.
3 "Vigilantes to Patrol Crime Area Proposed," *Pittsburgh Post-Gazette*, January 18, 1949.
4 John T. Mauro, "More Police Demanded for Brushton," *Pittsburgh Post-Gazette*, January 27, 1949.
5 "Threat Terrifies Brushton Family," *Pittsburgh Press*, March 14, 1949.
6 "Unsolved Murders Previously Listed," *Pittsburgh Post-Gazette*, August 21, 1949.
7 "Somebody Knows! P-G Offers $50,000 for Solving Murders," *Pittsburgh Post-Gazette*, July 11, 1949; "Rules in Solution of Unsolved Cases," *Pittsburgh Post-Gazette*, August 21, 1949 and "Unsolved Murders Previously Listed," *Pittsburgh Post-Gazette*, August 21, 1949.
8 "Jean Brusco Slaying Jolts City," *Pittsburgh Sun-Telegraph*, January 18, 1960.
9 "Crime Cut as Extra Police Go on Night Patrol Duty," *Pittsburgh Sun-Telegraph*, December 8, 1949.
10 "Slip-Shod Police Work Charged in Shadyside Crime," *Pittsburgh Sun-Telegraph*, November 27, 1949.
11 Normal A. Cafarell, "Sweater Girls, Plunging Necklines Blamed for Share in Sex Crimes," *Pittsburgh Press*, December 16, 1949.
12 Smith, "One Who Made A Difference"; "Woman Civic Leader Blasts Police Link to Politics," *Pittsburgh Post-Gazette*, December 14, 1949 and Howard Whitman, "They Get Away with Murder in Pittsburgh," *Collier's Magazine*, September 2, 1950.
13 "Brusco Murder Laxity Charged by Civic Leader," *Pittsburgh Sun-Telegraph*, December 13, 1949.
14 Eliza Kennedy Smith, Speech to City Council, December 13, 1949, in author's collection. In a subsequent undated speech, she cited St. Louis as a model for dealing with sex crimes.
15 Joe Browne, "Blood Expert Aids Brusco Clue Hunters," *Pittsburgh Sun-Telegraph*, December 18, 1949.
16 Smith, "One Who Made A Difference" and "Voters League Blasts Ward Boss Influence, Demands More Cops," *Pittsburgh Press*, December 13, 1949.
17 "39 Police Lieutenants to be Called on Carpet," *Pittsburgh Post-Gazette*, December 14, 1949. *See also* Weber, 302-303.
18 "Close Down Rackets, Mayor Orders Police," *Pittsburgh Press*, May 11, 1950.
19 Olivia B. Waxman, "How the U.S. Got Its Police Force," *Time Magazine*, May 18, 2017, https://time.com/4779112/police-history-origins. Additional resources on the history of police in America are available at https://lawenforcementmuseum.org.
20 "City Group to Demand Police Purge," *Pittsburgh Post-Gazette*, March 9, 1950.
21 "City's Police Bureau Rapped," *Pittsburgh Post-Gazette*, August 25, 1950.
22 "'Don't Be Trigger Happy,' New Cops Advised," *Pittsburgh Press*, February 4, 1950.
23 "City's Box Score on Crime," *Pittsburgh Sun-Telegraph*, December 29, 1949.
24 Thomas P. Snyder, "Sex Law With Teeth Proposed, *Pittsburgh Sun-Telegraph*, December 18, 1949.
25 R. K. McNickle, "Control of Sex Offenses," *Pittsburgh Press*, December 17, 1949.
26 "Judges Renew Plea for State Laws Curbing Sex Crime," *Pittsburgh Post-Gazette*, November 21, 1950.
27 Ray Sprigle, "Politics Blamed for Lax Police System Here," *Pittsburgh Post-Gazette*, February 20, 1950; "Modern Scientific Crime Laboratory Is Lacking Here," *Pittsburgh Post-Gazette*, February 21, 1950 and "Police Here Assigned to Shifts the Way Ward Bosses Want It," *Pittsburgh Post-Gazette*, March 1, 1950.
28 "Clue Hunted in Slaying of Woman in Shadyside," *Pittsburgh Press*, November 27, 1949; "Explain Delay in Death Case, Mayor Demands of Police," *Pittsburgh Press*, November 27, 1949; "City's Police Bureau Rapped," *Pittsburgh Post-Gazette*, August 25, 1950 and Whitman, "They Get Away with Murder in Pittsburgh."
29 Christine Altenburger, "The Pittsburgh Bureau of Police," *Western Pennsylvania History* (January 1966).
30 "Mrs. Smith Raids Police, Demands Sweeping Changes," *Pittsburgh Press*, May 19, 1950 and "Women Stir Central Police Station Dust," *Pittsburgh Post-Gazette*, May 20, 1950.
31 "Women Fight Police Politics," *Pittsburgh Sun-Telegraph*, May 26, 1950.
32 "Women 'Raid' Police Station: Mrs. R. Templeton Smith Hits Use of 4 FBI-Trained Men in Ordinary Police Posts," *Pittsburgh Sun-Telegraph*, May 19, 1950.
33 James Helbert, "Non-Political 35-Year-Old To Head Police," *Pittsburgh Press*, August 12, 1952.
34 "County Gets Lie Detector," *Pittsburgh Post-Gazette*, June 21, 1951.

35   "Investigator Sues Kensingers for $25,000," *Pittsburgh Post-Gazette*, June 21, 1951. The investigator contended that Carol Lee's older brother, Joseph, was the murderer and cited twenty-two separate items of evidence that characterized the nineteen-year-old as a sexual deviant. Joseph identified a blood-stained shirt, found in a garbage can a month after the murder, as his, and he admitted that he had maintained sexual relations with his sister prior to the murder but had a "mental blackout" the evening she died. The brother was arrested four times by off-duty officers or private detectives but was released each time.

36   Dave Welty, "Crime Soars But Public is Not Aroused," *Pittsburgh Sun-Telegraph*, June 24, 1958.

37   "That Isn't Paul Revere—It's Cop with Summons!" *Pittsburgh Sun-Telegraph*, June 4, 1950, with photos of Eliza and Traffic Magistrate John H. Donahue.

38   "Rally Slated in League Crime Drive," *Pittsburgh Sun-Telegraph*, March 11, 1951.

39   "Women Voters Urge Crime Board Here," *Pittsburgh Press*, March 11, 1951 and "Crime Commission Urged," *Pittsburgh Post-Gazette*, March 12, 1951.

40   "Brusco Sex Murder Investigation Denounced as 'Incredible Bungle,'" *Pittsburgh Press*, March 22, 1951 and "TV Seen Deglamorizing Crook," *Pittsburgh Post-Gazette*, March 23, 1951.

41   "Brusco Sex Murder Investigation Denounced as 'Incredible Bungle,'" *Pittsburgh Press*, March 22, 1951.

42   "Crime Laboratory Outlined," *Pittsburgh Sun-Telegraph*, April 28, 1950.

43   "Women Hear Crime Lab Expert" and "Crime Laboratory Outlined," *Pittsburgh Post-Gazette*, April 28, 1950; "Crime Lab to Cost $25,000 Yearly," *Pittsburgh Press*, April 28, 1950 and "Voters League Seeks Group to Curb Crime," *Pittsburgh Post-Gazette*, January 21, 1952.

44   Guy Wright, "10 Unsolved Murders Here Rival FBI's Dishonor Roll," *Pittsburgh Press*, April 5, 1953.

45   "U.S. Urged to Enter Police Probe," *Pittsburgh Press*, March 10, 1957.

46   Pat O'Neill, "U.S. Probe of Police Here Asked," *Pittsburgh Post-Gazette*, March 11, 1957.

47   "Vice Probe Showdown Tomorrow: Judge to Rule on Petition Filed by Mrs. R. T. Smith," *Pittsburgh Post-Gazette*, November 11, 1958.

48   "U.S. Attorney Blasts Racket 'Green Light,'" *Pittsburgh Press*, January 23, 1959.

49   "Reward Fund Started in Killings," *Pittsburgh Press*, November 20, 1950.

Chapter 23 | More Scandal and Sleights of Hand

1   Weber, 309–314.

2   Chester Harris, "'Free Work' Probe—Its Story From Start," *Pittsburgh Sun-Telegraph*, December 14, 1950.

3   "Frey Gets Files on 'Free Work,'" *Pittsburgh Sun-Telegraph*, May 11, 1950.

4   "Council Told to Probe 'Free Work,'" *Pittsburgh Press*, June 9, 1950 and "Lawrence Asks Council Probe Free Work," *Pittsburgh Post-Gazette*, June 9, 1950.

5   "'Free Work' Report Due in 10 Days," *Pittsburgh Sun-Times*, June 26, 1950.

6   "Job Probers Have Power to Subpoena," *Pittsburgh Press*, May 11, 1950.

7   "'Brass' Sought Silence, Widow Says," *Pittsburgh Sun-Telegraph*, June 13, 1950 and "Council Told of Farm Jobs on City's Time," *Pittsburgh Post-Gazette*, June 14, 1950.

8   "Figures in City 'Free Work' Probe," *Pittsburgh Press*, June 30, 1950.

9   "County Probes Own 'Private Job' Charges," *Pittsburgh Press*, May 12, 1950 and "Tenant Tells of Material," *Pittsburgh Sun-Telegraph*, May 15, 1950.

10 "The City Land Deals," *Pittsburgh Press*, May 29, 1950.

11 Eliza Kennedy Smith, Letter to Allegheny County League of Women Voters, June 27, 1950, in Smith, "One Who Made A Difference," 54.

12 Ibid.

13 "Gov. Duff Asked to Send State Police in Work Quiz, *Pittsburgh Sun-Telegraph*, June 8, 1950 and "State Gets Work Scandal Plea," *Pittsburgh Press*, June 8, 1950.

14 "The Balking Democratic Donkey," *Pittsburgh Post-Gazette*, June 9, 1950.

15 "A Good Start," *Pittsburgh Sun-Telegraph*, December 15, 1950.

16 "Women Voters Urge Crime Probe of Area," *Pittsburgh Post-Gazette*, March 26, 1951 and "Pastors Ask Kefauver To Probe Here," *Pittsburgh Post-Gazette*, March 31, 1951.

17 "Mayor Gives Civil Defense Top Priority," *Pittsburgh Press*, January 7, 1951.

18 "City Hall Ought to Get Hold of Itself," *Pittsburgh Press*, April 6, 1951.

19 "Reported Deal to Halt Probe Hit," *Pittsburgh Post-Gazette*, October 26, 1951.

20 For the Lawrence administration perspective, see Michael P. Weber, *Don't Call Me Boss: David L. Lawrence, Pittsburgh's Renaissance Mayor* (Pittsburgh: University of Pittsburgh Press, 1988), 309–314.

21 "Vote League Sharply Raps City's Budget," *Pittsburgh Post-Gazette*, December 9, 1950.

22 "Mrs. Smith Called Mayor Aspirant," *Pittsburgh Press*, July 11, 1951 and "Holland Hasn't Heard From Mrs. Smith—Yet," *Pittsburgh Post-Gazette*, July 12, 1951.

23 "Keep It Clean, Senator," *Pittsburgh Post-Gazette*, July 13, 1951.

24 Milton V. Burgess, "POLITICS: Sen. Holland's Speech Concerning Mrs. Smith," *Pittsburgh Sun-Telegraph*, July 15, 1951.

25 Mrs. Walter Ferguson, "A Woman's View: Look Here, Senator!" *Pittsburgh Press*, August 16, 1951.

26 Valentine Delle Donne, "Vicious Attack," Letter to the Editor, *Pittsburgh Post-Gazette*, July 16, 1951.

27 Mrs. Randall Hageman, Letter to the Editor, *Pittsburgh Press*, July 14, 1951.

28 "Council Finds It's 'In-the-Middle' Zone Over Proposed Action to Ban Billboards," *Pittsburgh Press*, February 21, 1957.

29 J. James Moore, "Water Battle Near Climax," *Pittsburgh Sun-Telegraph*, January 20, 1952.

30 "Council Spurns Water Protests," *Pittsburgh Press*, October 20, 1952.

31 "Ins and Outs of Water Authority Issue," *Pittsburgh Post-Gazette*, October 30, 1952.

32 "Water Step Still Fought By League," *Pittsburgh Post-Gazette*, November 15, 1952.

33 "Women Blast Lawrence, Charge Budget Magic," *Pittsburgh Sun-Telegraph*, December 1, 1952 and "Women Voters Hit Mayor for Budget 'Magic,'" *Pittsburgh Press*, December 1, 1952.

34 "Mayor's Budget," *Pittsburgh Press*, December 6, 1952 and "Budget Foes, Councilmen Trade Blasts," *Pittsburgh Post-Gazette*, December 2, 1952. *See also* "Remarks of Mrs. R. Templeton Smith Before the YMCA Forum Today at Noon Luncheon," news release dated December 18, 1952, in author's collection.

35 "Council to Hold Hearing on Budget," *Pittsburgh Press*, December 7, 1954.

36 "Mrs. Smith Assails Spending at City Hall," *Pittsburgh Sun-Telegraph*, October 3, 1957.

37 "'Fortune' Article On Mayor Hit," *Pittsburgh Sun-Telegraph*, October 30, 1957.

38 "Big, Little Guys Storm Council On Budget," *Pittsburgh Press*, December 19, 1958.

39 "Tax Hike Brings Charges of Political Trickery," *Kittanning Simpson's Leader-Times*, December 24, 1958.

40 Bryant Artis, "Women Scold City on Cost," *Pittsburgh Press*, December 15, 1960.

41 Joseph P. Browne, "League of Women Voters President Raps City Budget," *Pittsburgh Post-Gazette*, December 16, 1960. Other League investigations included a landside on a road for which the county had just paid $185,000 for construction, In 1954, they opposed a new zoning ordinance, which Eliza testified was being rushed through, could cost the taxpayers tens of millions of dollars, and included sufficient discretionary leeway to allow it to be used as a "political weapon." She charged that the "extreme desire for haste on the part of the City Planning Commission is strongly suggestive of ulterior motives."

42 Milton V. Burgess, "Mrs. R. Templeton Smith Fights On After 32 Years," *Pittsburgh Sun-Telegraph*, January 2, 1953.

43 J. James Moore, "City Officials' No. One Nemesis," *Pittsburgh Sun-Telegraph*, January 25, 1959.

44 "1% Pay Tax Approved By Council, 8 to 1," *Pittsburgh Press*, January 25, 1954.

45 Mrs. R. Templeton Smith, "The Lenten Spirit," part of a series, *Pittsburgh Sun-Telegraph*, February 24, 1950.

46 "Clubs Asked To Help Out In Crusade," *Pittsburgh Sun-Telegraph*, September 25, 1950.

47 "Bracing For The Battle In 1960," *The Monroe News-Star*, November 20, 1959.

48 Americans for Constitutional Action, Index, 1960, in author's collection.

49 James Helbert, "Right-Left Hammers Johnson," *Pittsburgh Press*, August 1, 1960.

50 David D. Lewis, "It's A Conspiracy, JFK 'Neighbor' Says," *Pittsburgh Press*, October 4, 1963.

51 "Packaged Thinking for Women," *League News* (January 1949); "Women Voters Ousts Group Here," *Pittsburgh Press*, December 16, 1948. "Women's League Chapter Ousted," *Pittsburgh Sun-Telegraph*, December 16, 1948 and "County Women Voters Dropped by U.S. Group," *Pittsburgh Post-Gazette*, December 17, 1948.

52 "Mrs. Smith Asks Vote Roll Purge," *Pittsburgh Post-Gazette*, February 2, 1961.

53 See *Pittsburgh Press* cartoon, August 25, 1933, depicting County Commissioners swatting "phantom voters" with a giant swatter labeled "Vote List Probe." *See also* "Getting the Gate," *Pittsburgh Press*, September 1, 1933.

54 Jim Lintz, "Vote List Check Offered," *Pittsburgh Post-Gazette*, February 5, 1961.

55 "Mrs. Smith Asks Vote Roll Purge," *Pittsburgh Post-Gazette*, February 2, 1961.

56 Jim Lintz, "362 Added to List Of Absent Voters," *Pittsburgh Post-Gazette*, May 6, 1961 and "Irregularities Uncovered in Allegheny Co.," *Somerset Daily American*, March 31, 1961.

57 "Jim Lintz, "Illegal Voting Here Charged," *Pittsburgh Post-Gazette*, March 31, 1961.

58 Jim Lintz, "Voters' League Asks Removal of 'Phantoms,'" *Pittsburgh Post-Gazette*, April 14, 1961.

59 Douglas Smith, "Post Office Aid In Voter Check To Cover U.S.," *Pittsburgh Press*, April 23, 1961.

60 Jim Lintz, "44 Voters Challenged In Petition," *Pittsburgh Post-Gazette*, November 1, 1961 and William Pade, "44 'Voters' Challenged by League," *Pittsburgh Press*, November 1, 1961.

61 "Hill, Strip Voter Fraud Charge Filed," *Pittsburgh Post-Gazette*, April 18, 1964.
62 William Pade, "44 'Voters' Challenged by League," *Pittsburgh Press*, November 1, 1961.
63 Letters from Eliza Kennedy Smith to Miss Helen Frick, April 24, 1961, and June 12, 1961, quoted in Smith, "One Who Made A Difference," 80–82.
64 Vince Johnson, "Press Club Griddle Sizzles," *Pittsburgh Post-Gazette*, April 23, 1961 and "Satire Governs Steel 'Parley,'" *Pittsburgh Press*, April 23, 1961.

Chapter 24 | Accolades and Eulogies

1   John O. Miller datebook, entry dated March 31–April 1, 1956, in Lucy Kennedy Miller papers.
2   John Hawkins Miller, "A Bend in the Silver Spoon," 17.
3   While she was known primarily for her political work, Eliza was also recognized for her charitable and community service, having lent her wisdom and influence to a handful of causes, among them the Western Pennsylvania Arthritis and Rheumatism Foundation and the Curtis Home for Girls. She and Temp also supported the Western Pennsylvania Kennel Association dog shows to benefit the Pittsburgh Tuberculosis Hospital.
4   Milton V. Burgess, "Mrs. R. Templeton Smith Fights On After 32 Years," *Pittsburgh Sun-Telegraph*, January 2, 1953.
5   J. James Moore, "City Officials' No. One Nemesis," *Pittsburgh Sun-Telegraph*, January 25, 1959.
6   Mary O'Hara, "Good Government Always Her Goal," *Pittsburgh Press*, October 10, 1962.
7   "Goldwater Backers Open Delegate Bid," *Pittsburgh Press*, March 1, 1964.
8   See photo in "Smoke Cloud Envelops Mayor's Budget Observers at Council Meeting," *Pittsburgh Press*, January 27, 1934.
9   Allegheny County League of Women Voters, *League News*, December 1964.
10 Joseph P. Browne, "Mrs. R. Templeton Smith, Civic Leader, Dead at 74," *Pittsburgh Post-Gazette*, October 24, 1964.
11 "Mrs. R. Templeton Smith Dies in Sleep," *Pittsburgh Press*, October 23, 1964.
12 "Friend of Good Government," *North Hills News Record*, November 11, 1964.
13 *Congressional Record—Appendix*, June 10, 1965, 122.
14 Telegram, in Smith "One Who Made A Difference," 118.
15 Allegheny County League of Women Voters 80th Anniversary Appeal, in author's collection.